Lecture Notes in Computer Science 6065

Commenced Publication in 1973
Founding and Former Series Editors:
Gerhard Goos, Juris Hartmanis, and Jan van Leeuwen

Paul R. Cohen   Niall M. Adams
Michael R. Berthold (Eds.)

Advances in Intelligent Data Analysis IX

9th International Symposium, IDA 2010
Tucson, AZ, USA, May 19-21, 2010
Proceedings

 Springer

Volume Editors

Paul R. Cohen
University of Arizona, Department of Computer Science
1040 East 4th Street, Tucson, AZ 85721, USA
E-mail: cohen@cs.arizona.edu

Niall M. Adams
Imperial College London, Department of Mathematics
South Kensington Campus, London SW7 2AZ, UK
E-mail: n.adams@imperial.ac.uk

Michael R. Berthold
University of Konstanz, Department of Computer and Information Science
Box 712, 78457 Konstanz, Germany
E-mail: michael.berthold@uni-konstanz.de

Library of Congress Control Number: 2010926371

CR Subject Classification (1998): H.3, H.4, I.2, F.1, H.2.8, J.3

LNCS Sublibrary: SL 3 – Information Systems and Application, incl. Internet/Web
and HCI

ISSN	0302-9743
ISBN-10	3-642-13061-5 Springer Berlin Heidelberg New York
ISBN-13	978-3-642-13061-8 Springer Berlin Heidelberg New York

springer.com

© Springer-Verlag Berlin Heidelberg 2010
Printed in Germany

Typesetting: Camera-ready by author, data conversion by Scientific Publishing Services, Chennai, India
Printed on acid-free paper   06/3180

Preface

The background to IDA 2010, the 9th International Symposium on Intelligent Data Analysis (IDA), is rather unusual. Previously, the symposia were held biennially at European venues. Over this time, the IDA Symposium had established an identity, a dedicated group of Program Committee members, and a regular audience. However, this success had come at a cost to the original ambitions for the symposium – concerned with interfacing AI, statistics and computer science for important and difficult real-world data analysis problems – being compromised in favor of more standard data mining content. IDA 2010 was organized explicitly to re-align the IDA Symposia series with a set of objectives evolved from the original ambitions. This should be construed *not* as a criticism of routine data mining research but rather as an admission that the IDA symposium had taken the path of least resistance with respect to the call for papers and the reviewing process.

This is the proceedings volume of IDA 2010, a special event held only a year after the eighth symposium in an attempt to revitalize the area of IDA. There were two major changes compared to previous symposia. First, the Call for Papers (CfP) was completely rewritten, placing great emphasis on algorithms and systems that support modelling and analysis of complex real-world systems. Moreover, the CfP explicitly discouraged submissions that might be characterized as "incremental advances in data mining algorithms." Second, the reviewing mechanism was extended to include a "senior Programme Committee," in response to perceived shortcomings in the existing reviewing process. In part, this was an experiment in reviewing which is discussed in our contribution in the present volume.

IDA 2010 took place at the wonderful Biosphere-2 in Arizona, USA, May 19-21, 2010. The invited speakers were Lise Getoor (University of Maryland, USA) and David Krakauer (Santa Fe Institute). The meeting received more than 40 submissions. While this may seem a low number, it should be interpreted in the context of both a new CfP and a novel point in the annual conference calendar. The Program Committee selected 21 submissions for publication. This included five papers which were focussed on important and challenging applications, but were perhaps preliminary – the precise type of submission we were keen to encourage.

It is a pleasure to express our gratitude to the many people involved in the organization of the symposium and the reviewing of submissions. Some specific thanks are in order. These proceedings would not exist without the efforts of Richard Van Stadt. We are indebted to Lupe Jacobo for local organization.

Finally, we are very grateful for the generous support of a number of sponsors: School of Information: Science, Technology and Arts, University of Arizona; Sante Fe Institute; University of Konstanz, Germany, and the ALADDIN project.

May 2010

Paul Cohen
Niall Adams
Michael Berthold

Conference Organization

General Chair

Paul R. Cohen   University of Arizona, USA

Program Chairs

Niall M. Adams   Imperial College, UK
Michael R. Berthold   University of Konstanz, Germany

Publicity Chairs

Elizabeth Bradley   University of Colorado, USA
Jaakko Hollmén   Helsinki University of Technology, Finland

Senior Program Committee Members

Niall M. Adams	Imperial College, UK
Rob St. Amant	North Carolina State University, USA
Tucker Balch	Georgia Institute of Technology, USA
Michael Berthold	University of Konstanz, Germany
Jean-Frannçois Bolicaut	Université Lyon, France
Elizabeth Bradley	University of Colorado, USA
Paul Cohen	University of Arizona, USA
Werner Dubitzky	University of Ulster, UK
João Gama	University of Porto, Portugal
Lawrence Hall	University of South Florida, USA
Howard Hamilton	University of Regina, Canada
Jaakko Hollmén	Helsinki University of Technology, Finland
Adele Howe	Colorado State University, USA
Eammon Keogh	University of California, Riverside, USA
Frank Klawonn	University of Applied Sciences Braunschweig, Germany
Joost Kok	Leiden University, The Netherlands
Rudolf Kruse	Otto von Guericke University, Magdeburg, Germany
Xioahui Liu	Brunel University West London, UK
Tim Oates	University of Maryland Baltimore County, USA
Sajit Rao	Massachusetts Institute of Technology, USA
Sunil J. Rao	Case Western Reserve University, USA

David Salmond   DSTL, UK
Roberta Siciliano   University of Naples, Italy
Michael Stumpf   Imperial College, UK

Programme Committee Members

Christoforos Anagnostopoulos   Imperial College, UK
Fabrizio Angiulli   University of Calabria, Italy
Alexandre Aussem   University of Lyon, France
Tony Bagnall   University of East Anglia Norwich, UK
Bettina Berendt   K.U. Leuven, Belgium
Daniel Berrar   Systems Biology Institute, Tokyo, Japan
Klemens Boehm   University of Karlsruhe, Germany
Christian Borgelt   European Center for Soft Computing, Spain
Bruno Crémilleux   University of Caen, France
Saso Dzeroski   Jozef Stefan Institute, Slovenia
Fazel Famili   IIT - National Research Council Canada,
                                   Canada
Ad Feelders   University of Utrecht, The Netherlands
Ingrid Fischer   University of Konstanz, Germany
Adrian Flanagan   Ofvigo, Finland
Elisa Fromont   University of Saint-Etienne, France
Alex Gammerman   University of London, UK
Gemma Garriga   Université de Paris VI, France
Gerard Govaert   UTC, France
Pilar Herrero   Polytechnic University of Madrid, Spain
Eyke Huellermeier   University of Marburg, Germany
Jiri Klema   Czech Technical University, Czech Republic
Peter Kokol   University of Maribor, Slovenia
Walter Kosters   Leiden University, The Netherlands
Paul Krause   University of Surrey, UK
Pedro Larranaga   Technical University of Madrid, Spain
Nada Lavrac   Jozef Stefan Institute, Slovenia
Hans-J. Lenz   Free University of Berlin, Germany
Trevor Martin   University of Bristol, UK
Dunja Mladenic   Jozef Stefan Institute, Slovenia
Maria-Carolina Monard   University of Sao Paulo, Brazil
Clayton Morrison   University of Arizona, USA
Alberto Munoz Garcia   Carlos III University, Spain
Mohamed Nadif   Paris Descartes University, France
Detlef Nauck   BT, UK
Andreas Nürnberger   University of Magdeburg, Germany
Nicos Pavlidis   Imperial College, UK
Mykola Pechenizkiy   Eindhoven University of Technology,
                                   The Netherlands
José-Maria Peña   Technical University of Madrid, Spain

Ruggero Pensa	University of Turin, Italy
Adriana Prado	University of Antwerp, Belgium
Bhanu Prasad	Florida A&M University, Tallahassee, Florida, USA
Ronaldo Prati	Universidade Federal do ABC, Brazil
Fabrizio Riguzzi	University of Ferrara, Italy
Gordon Ross	Imperial College, UK
Céline Rouveirol	University of Paris-Nord, France
Stefan Rueping	Fraunhofer IAIS, Germany
Antonio Salmeron	University of Almeria, Spain
Maarten van Someren	University of Amsterdam, The Netherlands
Myra Spiliopoulou	Otto von Guericke University Magdeburg, Germany
Martin Spott	British Telecom, UK
Stephen Swift	Brunel University, UK
Dimitris Tasoulis	Imperial College, UK
Maguelonne Teisseire	University of Montpellier, France
Hannu Toivonen	University of Helsinki, Finland
Vincent S. Tseng	National Cheng Kung University, Taiwan
Allan Tucker	Brunel University, UK
Antti Ukkonen	Universitat Pompeu Fabra / Yahoo! Research, Spain
Antony Unwin	University of Augsburg, Germany
Dirk Van den Poel	Universiteit Ghent, Belgium
Zidong Wang	Brunel University, UK

Additional Referees

Jorn Bakker	Natalja Friesen
Albert Bifet	Aneta Ivanovska
Peggy Cellier	Axel Poigne
Marcos Cintra	Georg Ruß
Ivica Dimitrovski	Pancho Tolchinsky
Fabio Fassetti	Katerina Taškova

Table of Contents

Changing the Focus of the IDA Symposium 1
   Niall M. Adams, Paul R. Cohen, and Michael R. Berthold

Invited Papers

Graph Identification (Extended Abstract) 6
   Lise Getoor

Intelligent Data Analysis of Intelligent Systems 8
   David C. Krakauer, Jessica C. Flack, Simon Dedeo,
   Doyne Farmer, and Daniel Rockmore

Selected Contributions

Measurement and Dynamical Analysis of Computer Performance
Data 18
   Zachary Alexander, Todd Mytkowicz, Amer Diwan, and
   Elizabeth Bradley

Recursive Sequence Mining to Discover Named Entity Relations 30
   Peggy Cellier, Thierry Charnois, Marc Plantevit, and
   Bruno Crémilleux

Integration and Dissemination of Citizen Reported and Seismically
Derived Earthquake Information via Social Network Technologies 42
   Michelle Guy, Paul Earle, Chris Ostrum, Kenny Gruchalla, and
   Scott Horvath

Detecting Leukaemia (AML) Blood Cells Using Cellular Automata and
Heuristic Search 54
   Waidah Ismail, Rosline Hassan, and Stephen Swift

Oracle Coached Decision Trees and Lists 67
   Ulf Johansson, Cecilia Sönströd, and Tuve Löfström

Statistical Modelling for Data from Experiments with Short Hairpin
RNAs 79
   Frank Klawonn, Torsten Wüstefeld, and Lars Zender

InfraWatch: Data Management of Large Systems for Monitoring
Infrastructural Performance 91
    Arno Knobbe, Hendrik Blockeel, Arne Koopman, Toon Calders,
    Bas Obladen, Carlos Bosma, Hessel Galenkamp,
    Eddy Koenders, and Joost Kok

Deterministic Finite Automata in the Detection of EEG Spikes and
Seizures 103
    Rory A. Lewis, Doron Shmueli, and Andrew M. White

Bipartite Graphs for Monitoring Clusters Transitions 114
    Márcia Oliveira and João Gama

Data Mining for Modeling Chiller Systems in Data Centers 125
    Debprakash Patnaik, Manish Marwah, Ratnesh K. Sharma, and
    Naren Ramakrishnan

The Applications of Artificial Neural Networks in the Identification of
Quantitative Structure-Activity Relationships for Chemotherapeutic
Drug Carcinogenicity 137
    Alexander C. Priest, Alexander J. Williamson, and
    Hugh M. Cartwright

Image Approach towards Document Mining in Neuroscientific
Publications 147
    Jayaprakash Rajasekharan, Ulrike Scharfenberger,
    Nicolau Gonçalves, and Ricardo Vigário

Similarity Kernels for Nearest Neighbor-Based Outlier Detection 159
    Ruben Ramirez-Padron, David Foregger, Julie Manuel,
    Michael Georgiopoulos, and Boris Mederos

End-to-End Support for Dating Paleolandforms 171
    Laura Rassbach, Ken Anderson, Liz Bradley, Chris Zweck, and
    Marek Zreda

Spatial Variable Importance Assessment for Yield Prediction in
Precision Agriculture 184
    Georg Ruß and Alexander Brenning

Selecting the Links in BisoNets Generated from Document
Collections 196
    Marc Segond and Christian Borgelt

Novelty Detection in Projected Spaces for Structural Health
Monitoring 208
    Janne Toivola, Miguel A. Prada, and Jaakko Hollmén

A Framework for Path-Oriented Network Simplification 220
    Hannu Toivonen, Sébastien Mahler, and Fang Zhou

A Data-Driven Paradigm to Understand Multimodal Communication
in Human-Human and Human-Robot Interaction 232
  *Chen Yu, Thomas G. Smith, Shohei Hidaka, Matthias Scheutz, and
  Linda B. Smith*

Using CAPTCHAs to Index Cultural Artifacts...................... 245
  Qiang Zhu and Eamonn Keogh

Author Index 259

Changing the Focus of the IDA Symposium

Niall M. Adams[1], Paul R. Cohen[2], and Michael R. Berthold[3]

[1] Department of Mathematics, Imperial College London, UK
[2] Department of Computer Science, University of Arizona, USA
[3] Dept. of Computer and Information Science, University of Konstanz, Germany

Abstract. The IDA Symposium series had evolved into a meeting apparently concerned with routine data mining. This report describes our attempts to re-focus the ninth IDA symposium on objectives derived from the genesis of the series. These attempts included a dramatically modified call for papers, and a drastically changed reviewing procedure.

1 Background

Since 1995, The Intelligent Data Analysis (IDA) Symposium series has been a biennial event at locations around Europe. The series has produced a selection of high quality proceedings ([1,2,3,4,5,6,7,8]).

Originally conceived with the objective of promoting work at the intersection of data analytic disciplines (including statistics, machine learning, and artificial intelligence) for dealing with challenging real world problems, the Symposium has lost some of this ambition and focus. Instead of encouraging papers on complex, real-world problems, there was a tendency to favour papers looking much like mainstream data mining or machine learning. A rather unkind characterisation of such material is that it often appears to represent incremental advances on existing methodology and algorithms for *well defined* learning tasks: classification, regression, clustering, etc. While there is absolutely nothing wrong with such fare, there are already ample outlets for it, and there are not enough outlets for research that engages statistics, machine learning and artificial intelligence for modeling complex, real-world systems.

For some time, the IDA council had been keen to orient the IDA series in the direction of the original ambitions, updated according to the tremendous advances in data collection, data storage and analysis methodology that have occurred in the interim. [9] gives some ideas about the modern ambitions for IDA, including the importance of data challenges and the complexity of data analysis *processes* in modern real world problems. In order to address these new ambitions, we convened this extra Symposium (the ninth, in 2010), which broke the biennial cycle and was held for the first time in the USA.

There seem to be a number of possible reasons why the focus of IDA had slipped. First, many authors around the world are keen to submit work about vanilla data mining – a very rich and important subject. Second, aspects of the standard reviewing process may have acted to favour such material. Based on these conjectures, we decided to revise the call for papers and reviewing process.

P.R. Cohen, N.M. Adams, and M.R. Berthold (Eds.): IDA 2010, LNCS 6065, pp. 1–5, 2010.

These revisions are discussed in the following sections, followed by a discussion of what happened, and some recommendations for the future.

We note that the reinvigoration of both conferences and journals seems to be part of the zeitgeist. Many recent conferences are including breaking news sections, or otherwise encouraging different types of submission.

2   Call for Papers

It is interesting to speculate about the the role and importance of the Call for Papers (CfP). Notably, the CfP had perhaps not changed sufficiently between IDA Symposia over recent years. IDA has become a regular part of the conference calendar and developed a specific identify associated with this CfP.

We produced a *completely* rewritten CfP for this symposium. This CfP included the following

> "IDA 2010 . . . particularly encourages papers about
> 1. end-to-end software systems that incorporate several of these [*data processing and analysis*] technologies;
> 2. applications of these technologies to modeling complex systems such as gene regulatory networks, economic systems, ecological systems, resources such as water, and dynamical social systems such as online communities; and
> 3. robustness, scaling properties, and other usability issues that arise when these technologies are put into in practice."

Note the special emphasis on applications, processes, and practicality. The particular tastes and interests of the conveners placed great stress on modeling complex and dynamic systems.

In addition, and notably, the CfP explicitly *discouraged* certain types of submission, with

> "Papers about established technology will only be accepted if the technology is embedded in intelligent data analysis systems, or is applied to analysing and/or modeling complex systems. IDA 2010 does not encourage papers about isolated algorithms that refine, polish, extend slightly, or offer minor variants of established ideas; and it will not publish papers about classification, clustering, dimension reduction, and other conventional data mining topics unless they clearly contribute to problems of modeling complex systems."

Of course, a modified CfP is insufficient: the submitting population may not respond, or the programme committee may not take the details of the CfP into account. This, and other aspects of reviewing, are discussed in the next section.

3   Reviewing

There was a perception that the reviewing of the IDA Symposia (and perhaps many other meetings) had adopted a specific character, perhaps in response to the deluge of data mining papers. Essentially, this reviewing appeared to look for easy rejects, by emphasizing what was wrong with a submission, rather than what was right. This approach often manifested as a narrow criticism of empirical experiments or the presence of free parameters. While these criticisms occasionally cut at the heart of a research effort, they more frequently cite technical infractions. They are the standard criticisms of unengaged reviewers who approach papers looking for reasons to reject them. Narrow, incremental algorithmic papers can be protected from these criticisms, but these are not the kinds of papers we wanted to publish in IDA.

There are two interesting aspects to the IDA view. First, very complicated problems are not going to be handled by single algorithms, but by cleverly constructed processes using a set of carefully designed algorithms. In this context, it is difficult to analyse performance over a collection of public domain data sets. Arguing about empirical performance of algorithms necessarily reduces the problem to pre-processed data sets, with algorithms as filters. This in turn leads to incremental refinements to existing algorithms and increasing abstraction from real problems. Again, we would like to stress that *there is nothing wrong with this approach*, it is simply not what IDA was intended to address. We thus modified the reviewing process for this IDA symposium to prevent easy rejects based on the standard criticisms of narrow, incremental work, and to encourage reviewers to focus on the new CfP.

Our proposed solution was rather ambitious. On the premise that it is easier to reject a paper than accept – which often leads to a specific sort of accepted paper – we felt that the relative anonymity of reviewing was not helping. While not wanting to disregard rigourous technical reviewing, we did want to emphasise the CfP. To this end, we introduced a *senior* PC, in addition to the *regular* PC, whose role was to *overrule* the regular PC if it was felt that a paper had merit with respect to the CfP despite technical shortcomings. However, to make such a judgment, members of the senior PC *had* to be willing (in principle) to publish a short summary in support of the paper *with their name on it*. This is a realisation of the idea that it is easier to trust a reviewer willing to publicly support a paper, than an anonymous reviewer who might be taking the path of least resistance. The senior PC was composed of members of the IDA council, and senior colleagues elected by recommendation.

The reviewing process worked as follows. Each member of the regular PC delivered a report with a recommendation, as in previous years. The regular PC were requested to pay attention to the new CfP, but to provide rigourous review. The *only* thing the senior PC was able to do was overrule a reject decision from the regular PC, at the risk of possibly publishing a short document in support. In this way, either regular or senior PC could recommend acceptance, but only the regular PC could reject. The senior PC were not asked to make reject decisions - they either accepted, or made no comment. This mechanism was simply an attempt to support interesting papers that did not meet the technical standards of narrow, incremental work.

4   What Happened

There were only 40 submissions to the Symposium. This may seem few, but a number of things need to be taken into account, including the new CfP, and a new slot in the calendar that overlapped with big meetings.

The submissions were a mixture of standard material and papers aligned with the new CfP. Each submission was reviewed by members of the regular PC, and at least one member of the senior PC, in the manner described above.

The senior PC recommendations were broadly in line with those of the regular PC. Very few rejects were overruled by the senior PC. We do not have a complete explanation for this – perhaps publicly supporting a paper is too intimidating, or perhaps the papers were not sufficiently exciting to energise the senior PC. On the other hand, many of the regular PC engaged fully with the revised call for papers, and toned down negative reviews, and specifically cited the new CfP in their reviews. When it came to the final decisions, such remarks were valuable and carried significant weight.

In the end, 21 papers were accepted. Five of these were identified as *application* papers, which were accepted because they tackled interesting and challenging application domains, even if their analysis was in some cases preliminary.

5   Where Next?

We were somewhat successful in attracting submissions matching the new CfP. The effectiveness of the revised reviewing process is more equivocal. Requiring the senior PC to "put their money where there mouth is" might have discouraged aggressively supportive reviewing (although this remark lives in the context of the submitted papers). However, the regular PC was sympathetic to the new CfP and reviewed accordingly, for the most part, so there were few opportunities for the senior PC to overrule the regular PC.

What have we learned? The CfP is important, and we think it should change frequently. Reviewing is important, but the two-tier system proved unnecessary because the regular PC generally did what we hoped the senior PC would do, leaving few opportunities for the senior PC to accept papers that it felt were wrongly rejected. It is possible that this role of the senior PC will become more important in future symposia, where we receive more papers. However, encouraging all reviewers to be guided by the CfP is crucial. In future, we might suggest a modified reviewer form, where reviewers are asked explicitly to comment (and score) the extent to which a submission has matched the CfP.

References

1. Liu, X., Lasker, G.E. (eds.): Advances in Intelligent Data Analysis, IIAS, Canada (1995)
2. Liu, X., Cohen, P.R., Berhold, M.R. (eds.): IDA 1997. LNCS, vol. 1280. Springer, Berlin (1997)

3. Hand, D.J., Kok, J.N., Berthold, M.R. (eds.): IDA 1999. LNCS, vol. 1642. Springer, Berlin (1999)
4. Hoffmann, F., Hand, D.J., Adams, N.M., Fisher, D.H., Guimar aes, G. (eds.): IDA 2001. LNCS, vol. 2189. Springer, Berlin (2001)
5. Berthold, M.R., Lenz, H.-J., Bradley, E., Kruse, R., Borgelt, C. (eds.): IDA 2003. LNCS, vol. 2810. Springer, Berlin (2003)
6. Famili, A.F., Kok, J.N., Peña, J.M., Siebes, A., Feelders, A.J. (eds.): IDA 2005. LNCS, vol. 3646. Springer, Berlin (2005)
7. Berthold, M.R., Shawe-Taylor, J., Lavrac, N. (eds.): IDA 2007. LNCS, vol. 4723. Springer, Berlin (2007)
8. Adams, N.M., Robardet, C., Boulicault, J.-F., Siebes, A. (eds.): IDA 2009. LNCS, vol. 5772. Springer, Berlin (2009)
9. Cohen, P.R., Adams, N.M.: Intelligent Data Analysis in the 21st Century. In: [7]

Graph Identification

(Extended Abstract)

Lise Getoor*

University of Maryland
College Park, MD, USA
getoor@cs.umd.edu
http://www.cs.umd.edu/~getoor

There is a growing amount of observational data describing networks— examples include social networks, communication networks, and biological networks. As the amount of available data increases, so has our interest in analyzing these networks in order to uncover (1) general laws that govern their structure and evolution, and (2) patterns and predictive models to develop better policies and practices. However, a fundamental challenge in dealing with this newly available observational data describing networks is that the data is often of dubious quality—it is noisy and incomplete—and before any analysis method can be applied, the data must be cleaned, missing information inferred and mistakes corrected. Skipping this cleaning step can lead to flawed conclusions for things as simple as degree distribution and centrality measures; for more complex analytic queries, the results are even more likely to be inaccurate and misleading.

In this work, we introduce the notion of *graph identification*, which explicitly models the inference of a "cleaned" output graph from a noisy input graph. We show how graph identification can be thought of as a series of probabilistic graph transformations. This is done via a combination of component models, in which the component models construct the output graph by merging nodes in the input graph (entity resolution), adding and deleting edges (link prediction), and labeling nodes (collective classification). We then present a simple, general approach to constructing local classifiers for predicting when to make these graph modifications, and combining the inferences into an overall graph identification framework. The problem is extremely challenging because there are dependencies among the transformation; ignoring the dependencies leads to sub-optimal results and modeling the dependencies correctly is also non-trivial.

Graph identification is closely related to work in *information extraction* [12]; information extraction, however, traditionally infers structured output from unstructured data (e.g., newspaper articles, emails), while graph identification is specifically focused on inferring structured data (i.e., the cleaned graph) from other structured data (i.e., the noisy graph, perhaps produced from an information extraction process). There is significant prior work exploring the components of graph identification individually; representatives include work on collective classification [7,5,6,13], link prediction [4,10,8], and entity resolution [1,2,14]. More recently, there is work that looks at various ways these tasks are interdependent and can be modeled jointly [15,11,16,9,3]. To our knowledge, however,

---

* Joint work with Galileo Namata.

P.R. Cohen, N.M. Adams, and M.R. Berthold (Eds.): IDA 2010, LNCS 6065, pp. 6–7, 2010.
© Springer-Verlag Berlin Heidelberg 2010

previous work has not formulated the complex structured prediction problem as interacting components which collectively infer the graph via a collection of probabilistic graph transformations.

In addition to defining the problem and describing a component solution approach, we present a complete system for graph identification. We show how the performance of graph identification is sensitive to the intra- and inter-dependencies among inferences. We evaluate on two real-world citation networks, with varying degrees of noise, and present a summary of our results showing (1) the overall utility of combining all of the components and (2) some of subtleties involved.

References

1. Benjelloun, O., Garcia-Molina, H., Su, Q., Widom, J.: Swoosh: A generic approach to entity resolution. Technical report, Stanford University (2005)
2. Bhattacharya, I., Getoor, L.: Collective entity resolution in relational data. ACM Transactions on Knowledge Discovery from Data 1(1) (2007)
3. Bhattacharya, I., Godbole, S., Joshi, S.: Structured entity identification and document categorization: two tasks with one joint model. In: KDD (2008)
4. Liben-Nowell, D., Kleinberg, J.: The link prediction problem for social networks. In: CIKM (2003)
5. Lu, Q., Getoor, L.: Link-based classification. In: ICML (2003)
6. McDowell, L., Gupta, K.M., Aha, D.W.: Cautious inference in collective classification. In: AAAI (2007)
7. Neville, J., Jensen, D.: Iterative classification in relational data. In: AAAI Workshop on Learning Statistical Models from Relational Data (2000)
8. O'Madadhain, J., Hutchins, J., Smyth, P.: Prediction and ranking algorithms for event-based network data. SIGKDD Explorations Newsletter 7(2), 23–30 (2005)
9. Poon, H., Domingos, P.: Joint unsupervised coreference resolution with Markov logic. In: EMNLP (2008)
10. Popescul, A., Ungar, L.H.: Statistical relational learning for link prediction. In: IJCAI 2003 Workshop on Learning Statistical Models from Relational Data (2003)
11. Roth, D., Yih, W.-T.: A linear programming formulation for global inference in natural language tasks. In: CoNLL (2004)
12. Sarawagi, S.: Information extraction. Foundations and Trends in Databases 1(3) (2008)
13. Sen, P., Namata, G.M., Bilgic, M., Getoor, L., Gallagher, B., Eliassi-Rad, T.: Collective classification in network data. AI Magazine 29(3), 93–106 (2008)
14. Singla, P., Domingos, P.: Entity resolution with Markov logic. In: ICDM (2006)
15. Taskar, B., Wong, M.-F., Abbeel, P., Koller, D.: Link prediction in relational data. In: NIPS (December 2003)
16. Wick, M.L., Rohanimanesh, K., Schultz, K., McCallum, A.: A unified approach for schema matching, coreference and canonicalization. In: KDD (2008)

Intelligent Data Analysis of Intelligent Systems

David C. Krakauer, Jessica C. Flack, Simon Dedeo,
Doyne Farmer, and Daniel Rockmore

Santa Fe Institute, Santa Fe, New Mexico, 87501, USA

Abstract. We consider the value of structured priors in the analysis of
data sampled from complex adaptive systems. We propose that adaptive dynamics entails basic constraints (memory, information processing) and features (optimization and evolutionary history) that serve to
significantly narrow search spaces and candidate parameter values. We
suggest that the property of "adaptive self-awareness", when applicable,
further constrains model selection, such that predictive *statistical models*
converge on a systems own *internal representation* of regularities. Prin-
cipled model building should therefore begin by identifying a hierarchy
of increasingly constrained models based on the adaptive properties of
the study system.

1 Introduction

The explosion of large, well curated data sets in the biological and social sciences,
coupled to an exponential increase in computing power, has generated a rather
novel predicament for quantitative science. This is the prospect of sophisticated
analysis coupled to remedial comprehension. The traditional bias towards compact descriptions of data, ideally founded on an understanding of microscopic
dynamics and interactions, has until recently, served as the Gold standard for
scientific insight. Maxwell's equations, Newton's theory of color, Einsteins theory
of gravitation, Mendel's "laws" of chromosomal segregation, Boltzman's contributions to statistical mechanics, and Turing's theory of computation, are all
representative of this traditional construction. They all share the very desirable
property of being graspable by a single mind as a coherent unity, and provide
both predictive, and in some cases, engineering insights. We might call this intelligent approach to empirical phenomena - intelligible data analysis. In contrast,
the proliferation of visually stunning illustrations of high dimensional data sets,
that often serve as the conclusion of quantitative analyses, represent intelligently
analyzed, unintelligible data analysis.

So what are we to do? The luxury of assuming simple, typically linear, relationships between elements of a small set of observables, is no longer something
we can afford. Much of the adaptive world does not present itself in this form.
This should not justify ceding prediction to powerful computers, except in those
cases where scientific explanation is not the priority - for example, medical diagnosis or industrial design. In this contribution, we argue for intelligible data
analysis realized through the appreciation of key properties of intelligent, or

P.R. Cohen, N.M. Adams, and M.R. Berthold (Eds.): IDA 2010, LNCS 6065, pp. 8–17, 2010.

perhaps more accurately, adaptive systems. We suggest that adaptive dynamics implies a set of constraints, on both function and mechanism, that can profitably be used to constrain prior beliefs. With these constraints we explore a far smaller number of dimensions than is possible under effectively unlimited processing power with a reduced sensitivity to noise. We can make this claim stronger by recognizing that for many adaptive systems, intelligible data analysis of their own states is at a premium, and so an elementary form of "adaptive self-awareness" or self-observation imposes further limitations on the complexity of a model. Stated differently, if our statistical model for behavior is accurate, we might expect it to converge on the system's own model for behavior.

In summary our principles are as follows:

1. The results of data analysis should be intelligible and not merely predictive.
2. Properties of adaptive dynamics impose cognitive constraints - structured priors - on the space of degenerate explanations.
3. Elementary "adaptive self-awareness" or self-observation imposes further constraints on these solutions.

2   From Kepler's Curves to the Machine-Read Mind

In the following two examples we illustrate on the one hand issues of comprehensibility, and on the other hand, issues relating to the value of a priori system knowledge. In the first example from the 16th century, we discuss how limited computing power can lead to more parsimonious representations of data - celestial orbits. In the second example from our own century, we discuss how classification using machine learning techniques often tells us little about how a cognitive system performs discrimination, when it ignores system mechanics.

2.1   Sensible Bounds on Computability

The contributions of Copernicus and Kepler to our understanding of celestial motion are well known. These are worth summarizing, as they epitomize a canonical mode of intelligent data analysis based on compressed descriptions of carefully curated regularities. From his observatory, Copernicus (1473-1543) made a number of important observations and reached several important insights: (1) The retrograde motion of the planets is a result of the relative motions of the earth, (2) the rotation of the earth is responsible for the apparent rotation of the stars, (3) the annual cycle of the sun is caused by the earth rotation around the sun, and (4) all celestial motion is circular and hence the apparent motion of the planets is based on epicycles moving along larger circles – deferents - neither of which need be orbiting a larger mass.

Kepler (1571-1630) worked on the Mars orbital data provided by Tycho Brahe. After consistently failing to fit Martian motion using circular orbits and ovoids, Kepler determined the path compatible with a simple ellipse. This idea was generalized to all planetary orbits with the sun occupying in each case one focus.

Subject to the limitations of measurement, the Copernican circle was not in all cases demonstrably worse than the Keplerian ellipse. Moreover, Kepler had no mechanical model from which the ellipse could be derived, and hence the criterion for its acceptance was simply parsimony.

In more modern terms, assuming the data to be elliptical, we need a rather unintelligible, infinite Fourier sum (epicycles) to provide a perfect fit. Hence the key to an efficient representation of the data was a rational choice of basis function. Kepler had intuited an appropriate function space in order to derive a compact representation of the data. If Kepler had had access to super computers, and subject to the limits of resolution of the data, there would have been little need to forego the epicycles. It is only later, with Newton and the inverse square law, that the ellipse is provided with foundational support.

The conclusion of this case study is that finite computational power, when coupled to accurate data, can be a powerful selection pressure on model development, selecting against unintelligible, high-dimensional representation. If Copernicus had a sufficiently powerful computer, Kepler and his parsimonious ellipses might have been out of a job.

2.2   Sensible Bounds on Information

Recently some progress has been made in the once questionable pursuit of mind reading. In particular, the extent to which functional magnetic imaging can be used to infer subjective states of mind. The approach is to use appropriate statistical algorithms - support vector machines - to classify brain states upon varied but systematic stimulation.

Kamitani and Tong [17] introduced the idea of "ensemble feature selectivity" - whereby very large populations of cells (V1-V4) in the visual cortex represent each of eight possible stimulus orientations using linear combinations of activity patterns. In a subsequent study, Hanson and Halchenko [18] used activity data from the full brain of ten subjects on two data sets - houses and faces - and using statistical classifiers observed disjoint networks of brain areas diagnostic for either face or house stimuli.

In both studies, the classification did not rely on unique activity at the microscopic level, but statistical averages at the population level. The value of these studies is to illustrate the nature of large-scale statistical localization involved in perception. These projects do not make use of a model or theory of neural activity that constrains the choice of statistical model – the goal is observer discrimination.

The conclusion of this case study is that powerful data analysis tools can be used to reveal consistent correlations between physical and subjective experiences, but that without some form of structured prior, these rely heavily on global information unlikely to be available to the system itself: the experimentalist can see the whole brain, but this is not something we should assume that the discriminating machinery of the brain can see. Consideration of connectivity, for example, might allow for clustering using a more confined function space.

3   Properties of Adaptive Systems

The following brief case studies represent instances of data analyses where prior knowledge of adaptive functions modify those structures and models we use in their analysis. It is our contention that knowledge of these structured priors allows us to place sensible bounds on energetic, computational and memory capacities. These restrict the search space of models according to mechanical principles relevant to the system itself, and will tend to increase the predictive power of models out of sample by eliminating sensitive dependence on high dimensional representations. We seek to avoid problems of over-fitting of data, illustrated through epicycles, or allowing access to global information, assumed in the FMRI studies. These examples span biology, social systems and cultural artifacts.

4   Case Studies in Intelligible Analysis of Adaptive Systems

4.1   Conflict in Animal Society

Conflict plays a critical role in the evolution of social systems -both positive and negative - and is typically manifested in the form of fights between individuals over the course of their lifetimes. Much is understood about control mechanisms [19], [6], [7], [22], factors driving escalation of pair-wise contests [8], [9], [10], [11], the influence of third parties on conflict outcome through coalition formation [12], [13], audience [14], [15], reputation effects [16], and redirected aggression [21]. Less is understood about the causes of conflict, and very little understood about the dynamics of multiparty conflict –conflicts that spread to involve more than two individuals and come to encompass a sizable fraction of a group.

The standard methods for analysis of conflict derive from game theory. Game theory seeks to identify normative strategies that maximize some measure of payoff in the face of uncertainty. Games are classified according to payoff structures (constant sum, non-zero sum, symmetric etc), representation (extensive or normal form), information sets (imperfect, perfect) and solution concepts (weak and strong Nash, evolutionary stable strategy etc). The work of Thomas Schelling is perhaps the best known on conflict, and includes the idea of the focal point of a coordination game - a maximum payoff solution that is independently salient to all non-communicating players.

The problem with game theory is that it provides no quantitative framework for the analysis of large bodies of data relating to strategic interactions. To remedy this deficit we sought to invent an inductive game theory [23], or set of inferential models describing individual decision rules capable of explaining features of strategic time series data. In order to make analysis intelligible and respect the principle of "system self-awareness", we considered a cognitively structured strategy space indexed by memory capacity and coordination load.

The data are as follows. A time series of fight bouts of a given duration alternating with peace bouts. The data are derived from large populations of non-human primates in captivity. Fights-bouts have a membership that is a subset of the total population, whereas peace-bouts include the entire population. We seek to predict membership in a given fight-bout by using information present in previous fight bouts. Hence for any pair of individuals in consecutive bouts A and B, we might want to know the probability that B engages in a fight following a fight involving A. The probabilities will vary for different pairs of individuals. In order to remove time-independent effects on individual participation in fights, we compute $\Delta P(A \rightarrow B)$; the difference between the null-expected P and that measured from the data on the number of fights (N) involving B following fights involving A:

$$\Delta P(A \rightarrow B) = \frac{N(B|A) - N_{\text{null}}(B|A)}{N(A)}, \tag{1}$$

where $N_{\text{null}}(B|A)$ is the average from a large Monte Carlo set of null models generated by time-shuffling the series but not shuffling identities within fights. This model can be extended to include high order correlations.

$$\Delta P(AB \rightarrow C) = \frac{N(C|AB) - N_{\text{null}}(C|AB)}{N(AB)}, \tag{2}$$

as can $\Delta P(A \rightarrow BC)$, the extent to which the presence of an individual at the previous step predicts the presence of a pair at the next step:

$$\Delta P(A \rightarrow BC) = \frac{N(BC|A) - N_{\text{null}}(BC|A)}{N(A)}, \tag{3}$$

These probabilities can be reinterpreted as decision rules that live in the space of two-step correlation functions that vary in the demand placed on memory and the computation of coordination. This class is illustrated in Figure 1. Independent psychological testing and behavioral observation restricts the subset of candidate rules to a few tuples towards the apex of the lattice. Using these simple rules, with suitable coarse graining over individual identities (where A might be some class of indistinguishable individuals), we are able to predict - generate a forward model - for collective features of the population dynamics, including the distributions of fight bouts – consecutive fights that are propagated until termination by a given choice of probabilistic rule set. Hence antecedent knowledge of primate cognition restricts the structure of the statistical model. In so doing, we analyze within an intelligible low-dimensional space of solutions, and respect the endogenous computational properties of the sample population.

4.2   Unintelligent Agents in an Intelligent Economy

As originally observed by Adam Smith, the economy is a complex system in which agents interact with one another to produce aggregate behavior whose emergent behaviors are qualitatively different from those of the individual actors. The mainstream approach to economics over the last fifty years has focused on the strategic interaction of rational agents, typically assuming that the behavior of agents can be modeled as the Nash equilibria of an economic game. Many criticisms of this approach have been made [24]. For example, is it plausible to imagine that real

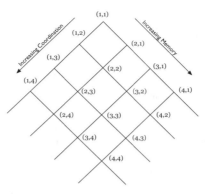

Fig. 1. Structured cognitive prior for strategy space. All strategies live in the space of 1-step Markov transition functions. Starting with the simplest model class $\mathcal{C}(1,1)$, we can add individuals to either the first or second fight, systematically building up strategies of increasing complexity based coordination, and memory constraints.

agents possess the information sources and information processing to do the difficult computations needed to find the equilibria? Perhaps even more detrimental to economics is the fact that for the modeler, since equilibrium models are difficult to formulate and solve, and are generally require analytic solutions, it is necessary to make drastic simplifications. This means neglecting important aspects, such as institutional structure, or dynamic interactions between agents under changing conditions.

At the other side of the spectrum is the subfield of economics called econometrics, which consists of making purely data driven statistical models. This approach fits functions to data, typically without strong priors about the mechanisms generating such data. Many of the best predictive models in economics, such as those that make forecasts of GDP growth or unemployment, are econometric models. This approach suffers, however, from a lack of clear interpretation. It is predictive but not intelligible.

An alternative is to abandon the quest to incorporate the strategic interactions of agents and instead focus on the institutions that structure their behavior. The modern economy has culturally evolved, or engineered, a diversity of instruments to facilitate trading. Hence economic actors and economic markets have co-evolved to solve problems of pressing economic concern, such as the institutions through which goods are bought and sold. The auctions used in the nineteenth century, such as those modeled by Walras, were cumbersome and slow. Modern markets, in contrast, typically employ the continuous double auction, which has the advantage of being fast and convenient to use. Transactions can be made instantaneously and the user need only place trading orders for a given price and volume, rather than needing to compute an entire demand schedule, as was done in the 19th century Paris Bourse.

In zero-intelligence models, agents are assumed to make their decisions more or less at random [25]. They must nonetheless respect the structure of the auction. This means that if the bid placed by a buyer is at a price equal to or greater than the best offer by a seller, there will be an immediate transaction; if not, the bid will sit in an order book, waiting for a seller to make an offer at a lower price. Buyers and sellers can cancel their standing orders at any time. Zero intelligence models have shown that this imposes strong constraints on possible outcomes. Thus, knowing the rates at which orders flow in and out of the market, it is possible to predict properties of prices, such as the volatility (the rate of which prices vary), as well as the average spread (the typical difference between the lowest selling price offered and the highest buying price bid) [26,27].

In this case the prior is incorporated by explicitly addressing how the structure of the market mechanism for making trades shapes outcomes, as reflected in the price. Zero intelligence models can be improved by taking some of the strategic properties of the agents into account, either by empirically characterizing the behavior of real agents, or by imposing the principle of market efficiency, which states that no agent can make riskless profits [28]. It is thus possible to build up from simple models to more sophisticated models , which can make rather striking predictions about the relationship between one set of state variables and another.

4.3   Authenticating Art with Visual Priors

The art object is a product of cultural coevolution – material culture evolving upon the constraints of an evolved perceptual system. The content of figurative or landscape paintings are identifiable by virtue of key shared features with natural scenes and objects. Above and beyond matters of accurate representation, there is individual variation in style. How is recognition of subject maintained alongside a signature of the author.

The process of art authentication – the determination of the creator of a work of art – is a complicated one, accomplished primarily through connoisseurship (the opinion of an expert on the artist in question), often supplemented by various kinds of physical evidence derived from the analysis of the materials used to create the work in question. The connoisseur brings a deep familiarity with the artist, an encyclopedic knowledge of the corpus of work, and experience and information that helps him or her rule on the consistency of the work in question within the body of work. Phrased in this way, the problem of authentication takes on a statistical cast and recently, with the advent of easily obtained high fidelity digital representations of visual art, progress has been made on making sense of a quantitative and statistical approach to authentication (see e.g., [3,2]). This line of work is known as *visual stylometry.*

The methods that have been developed for visual stylometry are varied, but of particular relevance for this paper is recent work that uses the biologically-inspired method of sparse coding [1]. Sparse coding is an idea first developed by Olshausen and Field to understand visual coding [4,5]. The idea is based on the fact that "natural scenes," i.e., those scenes that our visual system encounters every day, have a certain (non-random) statistical structure. Given that, Olshausen and Field hypothesize that the visual system would have evolved to take advantage of that structure in the sense that the structure of the receptive field characteristics in the visual cortex would optimally encode a randomly sampled natural scene. The visual system has evolved a strong prior expectation of the structure of the natural world.

Translated to the domain of visual stylometry, the sparse coding approach takes the form of basis construction for patches of a given size (say $n \times n$) so that a random patch of a (digitized) work of art by a given artist can be reconstructed by using only relatively few basis functions. As applied to the problem of authentication, we start with a corpus of digital representations of secure works by the artist in question. Having fixed the patch size at $n \times n$ we start with the standard basis of n^2 single pixel filters. A training epoch consists of choosing from the secure corpus a random image and then from this, a random collection of $n \times n$ patches. Weights for any given image are chosen by minimizing a natural cost function that trades off between information preservation and sparsity, and having done this. These weights then provide the information from which the basis is updated. Details of this can be found in [1]. Therein, the landscape drawings by Pieter Bruegel the Elder (1525–1569) were analyzed. The secure corpus consisted of eight drawings and, 2048 patches were chosen and 1000 epochs were run in order to find the sparse coding basis. In this framework, authentication is transformed into a question of is a random patch of a questioned work, on average as sparsely represented as a secure work? It turns out that with respect to a set of secure Bruegel drawings and other drawings once attributed to Bruegel, but now no longer believed (by the connoisseurs) to be authentic, this kind of classification framework works well, generally finding practically infinitesimal p-values to support the expert opinions.

Hence rather than apply ad hoc methods of spectral analysis to a field of heterogeneous pixel intensities, a result that tends to exaggerate the dimensionality of the incoming data, one employs insights form the fact that art works both mimic the statistics of natural scenes and have culturally evolved to stimulate organically evolved visual systems. This form of intelligent data analysis renders intelligible results in a form congruent with those natural to evolved mechanisms of perception.

5   Conclusions

In this short paper, we proposed the use of the adaptive property of many complex systems, to short circuit the apparent high dimensionality of data sampled from complex system data sets. We suggest that memory and computing limitations, as well as evolutionary trajectories, can be useful sources of information for structuring a priori constraints on statistical models. In a subset of complex systems, "adaptive self awareness" implies that experimental priors can be informed by the system's own priors. This is because adaptive systems need low-dimensional information about their own states in order to predict and control variables of selective consequence.

We introduced three case studies where these considerations have proved to be of value. The first involved the analysis of conflict time series using probabilistic models in the framework of inductive game theory [23]. The cognitive limitations of the agents placed strong restrictions on the space of plausible decision rules for explaining collective dynamics. The second was the analysis of the double auction mechanism for trading. This mechanism includes significant memory and coordination properties – allowing that very simple Markovian agents are sufficient to account for macroscopic variables such as price-impact functions and volatility. Hence assumptions of infinite memory and computing power required under perfect rationality are eliminated. The third is the use of sparse coding algorithms for authenticating artworks [1]. These algorithms make use of evolved properties of visual systems that exploit redundancies in natural scenes. This significantly reduces the dimensionality of the feature vectors required to cluster paintings.

We see the future of computer assisted scientific research as cleaving to some of the early aspirations of artificial intelligence research. Rather than use Moore's law to solve problems by brute force with little comprehension of the target of analysis (chess is of course the iconic example), use knowledge of the mechanics of the system to constrain the choice of learning model. We leave the last word to artificial intelligence pioneer John McCarthy:

> *"Chess is the Drosophila of artificial intelligence. However, computer chess has developed much as genetics might have if the geneticists had concentrated their efforts starting in 1910 on breeding racing Drosophila. We would have some science, but mainly we would have very fast fruit flies."*

References

1. Hughes, J.M., Graham, D.J., Rockmore, D.N.: Quantification of artistic style through sparse coding analysis in the drawings of Pieter Bruegel the Elder. Proceedings of the National Academy of Sciences USA 107, 1279–1283
2. Hughes, J.M., Graham, D.J., Rockmore, D.N.: Stylometrics of artwork: Uses and limitations. In: Proc. SPIE: Computer Vision and Image Analysis of Art 7531 (2010) (in press)
3. Johnson Jr., C.R., Hendriks, E., Berezhnoy, I., Brevdo, E., Hughes, S., Daubechies, I., Li, J., Postma, E., Wang, J.: Image processing for artist identification – computerized analysis of Vincent van Gogh's painting brushstrokes. IEEE Signal Processing Magazine, Special Issue on Visual Cultural Heritage 25(4), 37–48 (2008)
4. Olshausen, B., Field, D.: Emergence of simple-cell receptive field properties by learning a sparse code for natural images. Nature 381, 607–609 (1996)
5. Olshausen, B., Field, D.: Sparse coding with an overcomplete basis set: A strategy employed by v1. Vision Research 37(23), 3311–3325 (1997)
6. Clutton-Brock, T., Parker, G.: Punishment in animal societies. Nature 373, 209–216 (1995)
7. Frank, S.: Repression of competition and the evolution of cooperation. Evolution 57, 693–705 (2003)
8. Clutton-Brock, T., Albon, S.D., Gibson, R.M., Guinness, F.E.: The logical stag: Adaptive aspects of fighting in red deer (cervus elaphus l.). Anim. Behav. 27, 211–225 (1979)

9. Maynard Smith, J.: The theory of games and the evolution of animal conflicts. J. Theor. Biol. 47, 209 (1974)
10. Parker, G., Rubenstein, D.I.: Role of assessment, reserve strategy, and acquisition of information in asymmetric animal conflicts. Anim. Behav. 29, 221–240 (1981)
11. Taylor, P.W., Elwood, R.W.: The mismeasure of animal contests. Anim. Behav. 65, 1195–1202 (2003)
12. Mesterton-Gibbons, M., Sherratt, T.N.: Coalition formation: a game-theoretic analysis. Behav. Ecol. 18, 277–286 (2006)
13. Noe, R., Hammerstein, P.: Biological markets. Trends Ecol. Evol. 10, 336–339 (1995)
14. Johnstone, R.A.: Eavesdropping and animal conflict. P. Natl. Acad. Sci. USA 98, 9177–9180 (2001)
15. Covas, R., McGregor, P.K., Doutrelant, C.: Cooperation and communication networks. Behav. Process. 76, 149–151 (2007)
16. Nowak, M., Sigmund, K.: Evolution of indirect reciprocity by image scoring. Nature 393, 573–577 (1998)
17. Kamitani, Y., Tong, F.: Decoding the visual and subjective contents of the human brain. Nat. Neurosci. 8(5), 679–685 (2005)
18. Hanson, S.J., Halchenko, Y.O.: Brain Reading Using Full Brain Support Vector-Machines for Object Recognition: There Is No ÒFaceÓ Identification Area. Neural Computation 20, 486–503 (2008)
19. Dreber, A., Rand, D.G., Fudenberg, D., Nowak, M.A.: Winners don't punish. Nature 452, 348–351 (2008)
20. Taylor, P.W., Elwood, R.W.: The mismeasure of animal contests. Anim. Behav. 65, 1195–1202 (2003)
21. Kazem, A.J.N., Aureli, F.: Redirection of aggression: Multiparty signaling within a network. In: McGregor, P. (ed.) Animal Communication Networks. Cambridge University Press, Cambridge (2005)
22. Flack, J.C., Girvan, M., de Waal, F.B.M., Krakauer, D.C.: Policing stabilizes construction of social niches in primates. Nature 439, 426–429 (2006)
23. Dedeo, S., Krakauer, D.C., Flack, J.C.: Inductive game theory and the dynamics of animal conflict. Plos. Computational Biol. (2010)
24. Farmer, J.D., Geanakoplos, J.: ÒThe Virtues and Vices of Equilibrium and the Future of Financial Economics. Complexity 14, 11–38 (2009)
25. Gode, D.K., Sunder, S.: Allocative efficiency of markets with zero-intelligence traders: market as a partial substitute for individual rationality. The Journal of Political Economy 101(1), 119–137 (1993)
26. Daniels, M.G., Farmer, J.D., Gillemot, L., Iori, G., Smith, E.: Quantitative model of price diffusion and market friction based on trading as a mechanistic random process. Physical Review Letters Article no. 108102, 90(10) (2003)
27. Farmer, J.D., Patelli, P., Zovko, I.I.: The Predicitive Power of Zero Intelligence in Financial Markets. PNAS USA 102(11), 2254–2259 (2005)
28. Bouchaud, J.-P., Doyne Farmer, J., Lillo, F.: ÒHow Markets Slowly Digest Changes in Supply and Demand.Ó In: Hens, T., Schenk-Hoppe, K. (eds.) Handbook of Financial Markets: Dynamics and Evolution. Elsevier/Academic Press (2008)

Measurement and Dynamical Analysis of Computer Performance Data

Zachary Alexander, Todd Mytkowicz, Amer Diwan, and Elizabeth Bradley

University of Colorado
Boulder, CO
{alexanz,todd.mytkowicz,amer.diwan,lizb}@colorado.edu

Abstract. In this paper we give a detailed description of a new methodology—nonlinear time series analysis—for computer performance data. This methodology has been used successfully in prior work [1,9]. In this paper, we analyze the theoretical underpinnings of this new methodology as it applies to our understanding of computer performance. By doing so, we demonstrate that using nonlinear time series analysis techniques on computer performance data is sound. Futhermore, we examine the results of blindly applying these techniques to computer performance data when we do not validate their assumptions and suggest future work to navigate these obstacles.

1 Introduction

Traditional performance analysis methods used by the computer systems community implicitly assume that the systems under study are linear and time invariant. Most also treat these systems as stochastic. It has recently been established, however, that computers are actually deterministic nonlinear dynamical systems[1,9]. This not only calls into question those prior analyses—whose underlying assumptions are not in accord with these conditions—but also suggests a new dynamics-based methodology for computer performance analysis. In this paper, we outline this methodology, demonstrate its results, and offer a careful assessment of the five critical assumptions on which it rests, which echo common themes in the intelligent data analysis literature.

Prior work in computer performance analysis has considered primarily statistical techniques ranging from the obvious (mean, median, etc.) to the more involved (e.g., correlation [5] or confidence intervals [4]) for understanding and classifying program performance. These techniques rely on a number of assumptions. For instance, that the underlying system is *linear* and that samples are taken randomly; however, computer systems are nonlinear—e.g., the cost of a load may be two cycles if it hits in the L1 cache or hundreds of cycles otherwise—and a recent paper shows that commercial tools for understanding Java performance do not use random sampling and thus produce incorrect results [10]. It follows that statistical techniques are unable to model some aspects of performance. This paper explores the feasibility of using techniques from nonlinear

P.R. Cohen, N.M. Adams, and M.R. Berthold (Eds.): IDA 2010, LNCS 6065, pp. 18–29, 2010.

dynamics as an integrated, effective methodology for analyzing computer systems. Since these techniques expect the underlying system to be nonlinear and to change with time, they can accurately model performance characteristics that linear, time-invariant techniques cannot. Furthermore, nonlinear time series analysis (TSA) techniques come with their own set of assumptions. In this work, we explain the following key assumptions associated with nonlinear TSA, in the context of computer performance analysis, and evaluate the implications of those assumptions in the context of experiments on real hardware and software.

1. **Data length:** Nonlinear systems behave in complicated ways, often on multiple time scales, and nonlinear time-series analysis algorithms are quite sensitive to data length. Thus, it is critical to have a long-enough trace, but one cannot know *a priori* how long is long enough. We address this assumption with experimental evidence in Section 4.
2. **Sampling rate:** Nonlinear time-series analysis techniques are valid only if the measurements of the system are evenly spaced in time. In the experiment demonstrated in Section 3, this assumption is valid to within .05%.
3. **Smoothness of state space:** A computer is typically regarded to have a finite number of discrete states, but many nonlinear time-series analysis techniques require that the states of the system lie on a continuum. This conflict is resolved in Section 4.2.
4. **Observer effects:** When we make a measurement of a physical system, we are recording the image of a map from the internal state of the system to an observable quantity. Dynamical systems theory requires this mapping to be smooth. This topic is examined in more detail in Section 4.2.
5. **Stationarity:** Nonlinear time-series analysis techniques implicitly assume that a time series is from a single behavioral regime. This concept is explored in Section 5.

2   Dynamical Systems Background

In this section, we provide the reader with some necessary background from the theory of dynamical systems and time series analysis. A longer introduction to the topic can be found in [2].

2.1   Nonlinear Dynamical Systems

A dynamical system is a system that can be completely described at any instant by a fixed set of variables, and whose state evolves with time via a given rule. When those state variables evolve deterministically and continuously in time, the system can be modeled by a differential equation and is known as a *flow*. If there are finitely many state variables, then the differential equation is ordinary [7]. That is, trajectories of the system in state space can be modeled by initial value problems of the ordinary differential equation $\dot{x} = f(x)$, where f is a vector field defined on the state space, X. Alternatively, a deterministic dynamical system is called a *map* if the state variables evolve in discrete time increments. In this case, the evolution of the system is determined by iterations of a function, Φ, on X. When the evolution rule (f or Φ) of a dynamical system is nonlinear, the dynamics can be very complicated, as well as radically different in different regions of state space. In this case, traditional linear tools such as statistical or frequency analysis can produce misleading results.

2.2   Nonlinear Time Series Analysis

The goal of dynamical analysis is to extract information about the state-space behavior of a dynamical system. In particular, we would like to know what typical trajectories look like and how nearby trajectories behave relative to one another. Unfortunately, experimental conditions often restrict one to measuring a single state variable which, at the outset, would seem to omit a great deal of information. One of the central tools for nonlinear time series analysis is known as Takens' delay coordinate embedding theorem, which was introduced to the IDA community in [3]. The theorem was proved in [12], and extended in [11], which is the definitive reference. Given a smooth map, $\Phi : X \rightarrow X$, and a smooth function $h : X \rightarrow \mathbb{R}$, a time delay embedding of dimension m and delay τ is a map $\Psi : A \subset X \rightarrow \mathbb{R}^m$ such that $\Psi(x) = (h(x), h(\Phi^\tau(x)), \ldots, h(\Phi^{(m-1)\tau}(x)))$, where A is an invariant set of Φ. The embedding theorem states that for almost every choice of h (all but a set of measure 0), the map Ψ will be a diffeomorphism, i.e., a map that preserves topology, provided $m > 2d$ where d is the box counting dimension of A. In practice, h is the function that maps the position of the system in state space to an experimental observation and the image points of Ψ lie in a set that is topologically equivalent to the invariant set A, called the attractor. (An attractor A lies within some larger set that contracts to A as time approaches infinity.)

Because the embedding procedure preserves the topology—-but not the geometry—of the state space, most of the analyses that dynamicists apply to embedded data involve computing topological invariants. Two of the most useful topological invariants are the correlation dimension—-one member of the broad family of *fractal dimensions*—and the Lyapunov exponent. Correlation dimension is particularly useful when one is working with chaotic systems because the attractors of such systems are generally fractal (self-similar). The Lyapunov exponent is a measurement of the average rate at which neighboring state-space points separate. This represents the fundamental notion of chaos: any two points (initial conditions) that are arbitrarily close in state space can diverge from each other exponentially.

These definitions and conditions place important requirements on data and algorithms for computing topological invariants. The underlying system must exist on a continuous state space; the measured quantity must be a smooth function of the state variables and be sampled evenly in time; the time series must be long enough to reach and cover the attractor; and it cannot include more than one attractor. These requirements are the formal statements of the assumptions listed in Section 1.

3   A Methodology for Computer Performance Analysis

In this section, we show how the mathematics and algorithms of nonlinear dynamics can be used to characterize computer performance, yielding results that are both more useful and more accurate than those produced by traditional computer-systems techniques. We use an example to demonstrate the analysis methodology; we then explore the various assumptions on which this methodology rests both by varying the parameters of the example and via mathematical arguments. A fuller treatment of this and several other examples, as well as broader discussion of the implications, can be found in [9].

3.1   Preconditions: Program Execution as an Iterated Map

One way to think of a computer executing a program is as an iterated map; each of the N transistors in a computer is either on or off, thus giving rise to a finite state space X of 2^N variables and a deterministic update rule that is dependent upon both the computer's implementation and the program. The map, F, describes how to update the system at any given time step. When a computer program is loaded into memory, the system (software and hardware) has an initial configuration $x_0 \in X$; at each time click, the computer updates each of its N transistors based upon the equation: $x_{n+1} = F(x_n)$. In the following sections, we describe the details of a simple program that leads to a map F and use our methodology to show that its dynamics have strong indications of chaotic dynamics.

3.2   A Microkernel Experiment

We study the simple program,

```
for ( i = 0;  i < N;  i++)
    for ( j = i;  j < N;  j++)
        data [ i ][ j ] = 0;
```

which initializes an array in row major order. Microkernels like this, which are often used in the computer systems community to study computer performance, are far simpler than real programs, but they provide a useful starting point for evaluation of methodologies like the one proposed in this paper. We conjecture that the performance dynamics of this code will represent a single attractor with relatively low dimension. Figure 1(a) shows a time series of cache performance measured during the execution of this code on an Intel Core2® processor. The loop was executed repeatedly and measurements were taken every 100K clock cycles; at each sample time, the number of cache misses that occurred over that 100K cycle window was normalized by dividing by 100K cycles and then recorded. Each data point in Figure 1(a) is one of these measurements. In all, we collected 85K data points; only part of this dataset is shown in the figure. Note that the cache behavior is not purely periodic, as one might expect given the simplicity of this loop; rather, there is interesting dynamical structure evident in this time series. Traditional computer performance analysis techniques would need to be augmented (e.g., via additional instrumentation) to understand this dynamical behavior. The nonlinear dynamics methodology proposed here not only brings out this behavior naturally, but offers immediate and useful information about understanding it (viz., the composition of multiple periodicities in a chaotic signal).

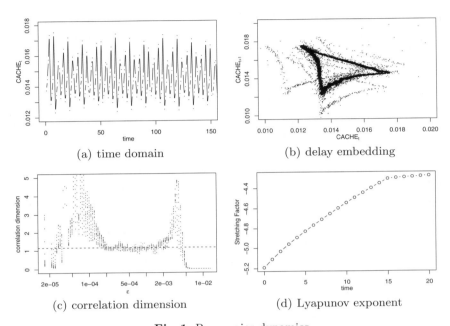

(a) time domain

(b) delay embedding

(c) correlation dimension

(d) Lyapunov exponent

Fig. 1. Row major dynamics

3.3   Reconstructing the Dynamics

The first step in extracting useful information about the dynamics of a time series like Figure 1(a) is to reconstruct the state space using the delay-coordinate embedding process described in Section 2.2. Since neither the dimension nor the time scales are known, this begins with constructing estimates for those values. Using standard nonlinear time-series analysis heuristics—average mutual information to determine the delay τ and false nearest neighbor relationships to estimate the dimension m, both as implemented in the TISEAN toolset [6]—we obtained the embedding parameter values $m = 12$ and $\tau = 1$. Per the embedding theorems, the state-space dynamics can be faithfully reconstructed using these parameter values. A projection of this twelve-dimensional reconstruction is shown in Figure 1(b); this particular projection plots $x(t + \tau)$ versus $x(t)$, where x is the number of cache misses per cycle at time t. This plot clearly brings out the structure that the time series hinted at: the dynamics have a significant periodic component—the dark triangle—but there is evidence of other periodicities at work. This kind of structure is a clear indication of low-dimensional deterministic dynamics.

3.4   Characterizing the Dynamics

To verify the conjecture that the cache behavior of the row-major loop on the Intel Core2® computer has low-dimensional dynamics, we calculated values for various topological invariants of the reconstructed trajectory in Figure 1(b)— the second step in the methodology proposed here. As mentioned in Section 2.2, many such invariants exist. The Lyapunov exponent and the correlation dimension, which we calculate here, are useful in characterizing the dynamics and comparatively easy to extract from experimental data. These quantities not only help us analyze the dynamical system, but they also can be used to strengthen our assumptions that we have *stationarity* and sufficient *data length* as we will see in Section 4.

Correlation dimension. The correlation dimension algorithm effectively measures the fraction of points in state space ($\mathbb{R}^{12}$) that are ϵ-close to each other as ϵ scales from zero. For a self-similar (i.e., fractal) set, this number should grow via a power law, with non-integer power. Self-similarity, as mentioned in Section 2.2, is a strong indication of chaos, but the correlation dimension is more broadly useful as a means for comparing two trajectories—e.g., the cache behavior of the same code on two different computers. To compute it, one plots the logarithm of the correlation sum—a quantity defined in detail in [2]—versus ϵ, as shown in Figure 1(c), and looks for horizontal regions in the curve. (Algorithmic effects, in conjunction with the attractor size, cause the curve to oscillate when ϵ is very large or very small.) The highlighted region in Figure 1(c) suggests a correlation dimension of $1.169 \pm .013$. This is not only a strong validation of the conjecture that the dynamics of the cache behavior of the row-major loop is both deterministic and low dimensional, but also a first indication that they may be chaotic: i.e., that the memory use of this code varies from run to run in a manner that depends strongly on small perturbations.

Lyapunov exponent. The standard algorithms for computing Lyapunov exponents pick pairs of state-space points that are close to each other and then iterate forward in time to track how quickly they spread apart. In Figure 1(d), we have plotted the logarithm of the value of this "stretching factor," averaged over many pairs of points, versus the spreading time. This graph shows textbook form: a straight line up to 15 iterations, followed by saturation when the spread between points reaches the diameter of the attractor in Figure 1(b). The slope of this line is the Lyapunov exponent of the attractor; here, its value is $.057 \pm .0013$ cache misses per cycle. This affirms the conjecture that the cache behavior is chaotic—a result that traditional techniques cannot handle and do not consider.

3.5   Implications for Analysis

Taken together, the non-integer correlation dimension and positive Lyapunov exponent are strong indicators of low-dimensional chaos in the performance of a simple microkernel on a popular microprocessor. This has severe consequences for computer systems performance analysis. For example:

- Computer architects validate architectural simulators by comparing end-to-end metrics (e.g., execution time) on a simulator to end-to-end metrics on a machine that the simulator is supposed to model. Given the chaotic nature of computer systems, such a validation is likely to fail: even a tiny difference in the initial conditions on the simulator and real hardware can cause the simulator and the hardware to produce vastly different end-to-end metrics. Thus, validation may conclude that a simulator does not accurately model the hardware even when it does; and vice versa.
- It significantly complicates the task of understanding the performance of a computer system: we may think we understand how a system performs, but that performance may have more to do with a small, seemingly insignificant, artifact of the initial conditions than with the system itself. For example, prior work [8] shows that small changes to the environment results in dramatically different results from a performance comparison.
- It significantly complicates the task of improving the performance of a computer system: we may think that our new idea improves performance but it may be that the performance improvement is an artifact of something completely irrelevant (e.g., if the particular environment that we used for our experiments is biased towards our new idea [8]).

4   Validation

In this section, we address the five assumptions upon which this methodology rests, using a combination of theory and experiment to establish their validity in the context of computer performance analysis.

4.1   Assumptions Verified by Experiment

Data length. One can test whether or not a time series from a computer performance experiment is long enough to be a representative sample of the dynamics simply by repeating the dynamical analysis on different-size subsets of that series. In the case of Figure 1, for example, the correlation dimension and Lyapunov exponent computed from the first 40K points of the trajectory are identical, up to a standard error interval, to those computed from the full trajectory. This indicates that all of the dynamics that are present in the larger data set are also present in the smaller data set. A related concern is whether the *larger* data set is truly large enough; the fact that its topological invariants do not change if one shortens it somewhat, suggest that it is. Using the first 20K points of the trajectory, however, we found that the correlation dimension was uncomputable, suggesting that this snippet of the time series was an inadequate sample of the dynamics. Establishing these boundaries via this kind of subset testing—and, if needed, longer experiments—is critical to the success of this methodology.

Stationarity. A similar experiment shows that the dynamics are equivalent for disjoint subsets of 40K points (i.e. the first half of the trace vs. the second half). This indicates that the system is in a single regime for the duration of the experiment—i.e., that the time series is measured from a single attractor. Our original intent in starting with a microkernel experiment was to explore whether this was the case, and our conjecture was that the uniform, repetitive dynamics of this microkernel would lead to a single attractor. Real programs, of course, are far more complicated, which can challenge the methodology proposed here. These issues are discussed further in Section 5.

4.2 Assumptions Verified by Theory

Smoothness of state space. Consider the map Φ from the summary of the embedding theorem in Section 2.2. The smoothness of Φ, required by the theorem, is equivalent to the existence of a continuous state space of the computer system. Initially, this appears to be contrary to our description of the computer as having 2^N states for some finite N. The resolution of this issue is a matter of perspective. If we consider the computer system to be an electronic circuit, then its state is determined by the voltage drops across the various components. Most importantly, the behavior of the circuit is described completely by a finite system of ordinary differential equations, $\dot{x} = f(x)$—in other words, the trajectory of the system can be modeled as a flow in a continuous state space.

Furthermore, suppose that $\Phi_t : X \to X$ represents the flow of the vector field f. Since this flow is continuous, it follows that for a fixed t, Φ_t represents a smooth map on a continuous space. In particular, if we let t be the period of a single clock cycle, then $\Phi_t \equiv F$ as defined in Section 3.

Observer effects. The measurement function h is the function that maps the current state of the system to the normalized number of cache misses that occurred over the previous 100K clock cycles. To justify that a dynamical systems-based methodology is the right way to analyze computer performance data like this, we must answer the question: is h a smooth function?

In an experimental setting, one deals with error by expressing the range of the measurement function h in the form of intervals of a fixed (possibly undetermined) length, centered at the experimental observations. Then the smoothness condition will be satisfied up to experimental error if h has a smooth continuous selector—that is, if there is a smooth function $\gamma : X \to \mathbb{R}$, such that $\gamma(x) \in h(x)$ for each $x \in X$.

In the case of the methodology proposed here, we can construct γ explicitly. The dynamical system being studied is a coupling of the computer system and the hardware performance monitor (HPM) on the microprocessor chip that is being used to gather the data. When we read the number of cache misses from the internal register in the HPM, we are making an observation about the voltages across each of the transistors in the register. For simplicity, we imagine that the register contains a number in fixed-point format, though the following analysis is valid for floating-point numbers as well.

Let u_j, v_j be the average values of the voltage across a transistor that is read as a 0 or a 1, respectively, and define the function, $a_j(x) = 2^j \frac{x - u_j}{v_j - u_j}$. We can then define

$\gamma(x) = \sum_{-m}^{m} a_j(x_j)$, where x_j is the voltage across the transistor that represents the bit j units to the left of the decimal place. It is clear that each of the x_j is a state variable of the system and furthermore, that the number of cache misses reported by the HPM is the expected value of γ. It follows that γ is a smooth continuous selector for h and the embedding theorems hold, up to experimental error.

This argument depends on the workings of the hardware performance monitors. Specifically, we are making the assumption that the reading taken from the HPM (the number of cache misses) depends entirely on the state of the computer system and *does not* depend on the state of the HPM. We can easily construct an example where this assumption is violated. If the number of cache misses exceeds the capacity of the HPM register then the register will overflow and produce a discontinuity. In this situation, most of the measurements will be dependent only on the state of the computer system, but isolated measurements (after a rollover) will have *strong* dependence on the state of the HPM, thus producing the discontinuity. We can explore this situation by reading only the k least significant bits from the HPM register and repeating the dynamical-systems analysis. The resulting attractor, as shown in Figure 2 for $k = 10$, clearly differs both geometrically and topologically from those in Figure 1(b). Luckily, the HPM registers on modern microprocessors are typically 64 bits wide and are typically reset at the start of an experiment, so the overflow is extremely unlikely to happen.

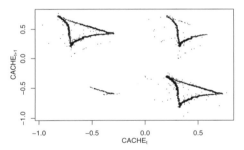

Fig. 2. Embedding obtained from the measurement function corresponding to ten significant bits in the register

Sampling rate. The final requirement for a dynamical-systems based methodology to be effective in a computer performance analysis problem, per the embedding theorems, is that the data are measured at even sampling intervals. Operating systems effects, among other things, can alter measurement timing in a running computer; in order to establish that these variations are within acceptable bounds, we can appeal to the underlying mathematics. In particular, the sampling interval can be assumed to be constant by the continuity of the flow Φ_t. Since the error in the sampling interval is small, this corresponds to a small change in the state of the system under the action of Φ_t. Therefore, the small perturbations in sampling rate can be regarded as small perturbations in state space that are absorbed up to the experimental error represented by the intervals in the range of h.

5   Dynamical Analysis of Complex Programs

In view of the vast differences between microkernels like the one in Section 3 and real programs, the requirement that the data come from a single attractor is a serious potential limitation of the dynamical systems methodology for computer performance analysis. In this section, we explore the results of relaxing that assumption: first by adding various percentages of transient noise to the time series and then by using a program trace that alternates between two different microkernels.

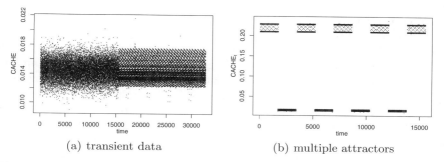

(a) transient data   (b) multiple attractors

Fig. 3. Two relaxations of the single-attractor assumption. Average number of cache misses per cycle over the previous 100K cycles are plotted on the y-axis; the x-axis is time in cycles $\times$ 10^5.

5.1   Transient Data

We first explore how well our methodology works on a data set where various percentages of the row-major program have been replaced with surrogate data (i.e., random data generated to have similar mean and variance as the row-major trace). An example is shown in Figure 3(a). To establish the limits of the techniques on which our methodology is based, we varied the percentage of the trace consisting of surrogate, then embedded the resulting data and computed the correlation dimension and Lyapunov exponent of the reconstructed trajectory. Unsurprisingly, we found that as the noise percentage increases, the calculations diverge from the true values (from Section 3.4) and the error bars grow. The effects play out differently in the two calculations, of course; added noise tends to increase any kind of fractal dimension. As a result, our computation of correlation dimension was inaccurate with any level of surrogate added. On the other hand, the Lyapunov exponent calculations are actually statistically accurate (though with a greater amount of uncertainty). This reflects the greater noise immunity of the associated algorithms, which average over both time and space.

5.2   Multiple Attractors

The experiment in the previous section explores a situation like the one that arises in a program that has a transient phase (e.g., initialization) and then a long, stationary phase. Another common situation in the dynamics of real programs is two or more alternating phases. To evaluate how well our methodology works in that situation, we created a program trace that alternates between the row-major microkernel of Section 3 and a column-major version of the same loop. An example time series from one of these experiments is shown in Figure 3(b). Because of the different ways in which these microkernels touch memory, the time series has two clear regimes: the cache miss rate is high when initializing the array in column-major order and low in row-major order. This translates to two different attractors in drastically different regions of the reconstructed state space—a situation that the dynamical systems methods in the previous sections cannot handle without some preprocessing of the data. One way to do so is to use a 'cut and paste' approach to concatenate the data points from each attractor into a single time series, then analyze the results separately. If we know the attractor boundaries (as in our synthetic example), the cutting-and-pasting is easy. However, in real programs we do not know the attractor boundaries; in future work we will consider using techniques from phase detection and signal processing to identify them.

Using the cut-and-paste approach for our synthetic program, we found that the topological invariant results were statistically identical to the results that we obtained by running each microkernel in isolation. This verifies our hypothesis that the seperate chunks come from the same attractor. The results on the two time series derived by concatenating the chunks are interesting: the correlation dimension is statistically accurate while the Lyapunov exponent is markedly different. This, too, derives from the underlying algorithms: correlation dimension is a static property that does not care about the ordering of the points. The Lyapunov exponent, on the other hand, is dynamic, and the 'paste' operation disturbs the state-space flow at the chunk boundaries.

6   Conclusions

We have shown that computer systems are deterministic nonlinear dynamical systems and that standard nonlinear time series analysis tools provide an effective and theoretically grounded methodology for the study of such systems. We conclude that the computer systems community can benefit greatly from active research in the application of these methods to computer performance analysis. Future contributions to this field are likely to come from multiple academic disciplines as there is a need for the design of novel experiments to provide meaningful time series data; as well as a need for improved time series analysis techniques, tailored specifically for the computer systems community.

References

1. Berry, H., Perez, D.G., Temam, O.: Chaos in computer performance. In: CHAOS (2005)
2. Bradley, E.: Time-series analysis. In: Intelligent Data Analysis: An Introduction. Springer, Heidelberg (1999)

3. Easley, M., Bradley, E.: Reasoning about input-output modeling of dynamical systems. In: Hand, D.J., Kok, J.N., Berthold, M.R. (eds.) IDA 1999. LNCS, vol. 1642, pp. 343–355. Springer, Heidelberg (1999)
4. Georges, A., Buytaert, D., Eeckhout, L.: Statistically rigorous Java performance evaluation. In: Proc. of ACM SIGPLAN Conf. on Object-oriented Programming, Systems, Languages and Applications, October 2007, pp. 57–76. ACM, Montreal (2007), http://buytaert.net/files/oopsla07-georges.pdf
5. Hauswirth, M., Diwan, A., Sweeney, P.F., Mozer, M.C.: Automating vertical profiling. In: Proceedings of the conference on Object oriented programming, systems, languages, and applications (2005)
6. Hegger, R., Kantz, H., Schreiber, T.: Practical implementation of nonlinear time series methods: The [small-caps TISEAN] package. Chaos: An Interdisciplinary Journal of Nonlinear Science 9, 413 (1999)
7. Meiss, J.: Dynamical systems. Scholarpedia 2(2), 1629 (2007)
8. Mytkowicz, T., Diwan, A., Hauswirth, M., Sweeney, P.: Producing wrong data without doing anything obviously wrong! In: Proc. of Int'l Conf. on Architectural Support for Programming Languages and Operating Systems, March 2009, pp. 265–276. ACM, Washington (2009)
9. Mytkowicz, T., Diwan, A., Bradley, E.: Computer systems are dynamical systems. In: CHAOS (2009)
10. Mytkowicz, T., Diwan, A., Hauswirth, M., Sweeney, P.: Evaluating the accuracy of java profilers. In: ACM conference on Programming Language Design and Implmentation, June 2010. ACM, Toronto (2010)
11. Sauer, T., Yorke, J., Casdagli, M.: Embedology. Journal of Statistical Physics 65(3), 579–616 (1991)
12. Takens, F., et al.: Detecting strange attractors in turbulence. Lecture notes in mathematics 898(1), 366–381 (1981)

Recursive Sequence Mining
to Discover Named Entity Relations

Peggy Cellier[1], Thierry Charnois[1], Marc Plantevit[2], and Bruno Crémilleux[1]

[1] Université de Caen, GREYC, CNRS, UMR6072, F-14032, France
`firstname.lastname@info.unicaen.fr`
[2] Université Lyon 1, LIRIS, UMR5205, F-69622, France
`marc.plantevit@liris.cnrs.fr`

Abstract. Extraction of named entity relations in textual data is an important challenge in natural language processing. For that purpose, we propose a new data mining approach based on recursive sequence mining. The contribution of this work is twofold. First, we present a method based on a cross-fertilization of sequence mining under constraints and recursive pattern mining to produce a user-manageable set of linguistic information extraction rules. Moreover, unlike most works from the state-of-the-art in natural language processing, our approach does not need syntactic parsing of the sentences neither resource except the training data. Second, we show in practice how to apply the computed rules to detect new relations between named entities, highlighting the interest of hybridization of data mining and natural language processing techniques in the discovery of knowledge. We illustrate our approach with the detection of gene interactions in biomedical literature.

Keywords: Sequential Data, Recursive Mining, Named Entity Relations, Pattern Discovery, Natural Language Processing.

1 Introduction

Due to the explosion of available textual data, text mining and Information Extraction (IE) from texts have become important topics of study in recent years. In particular, detection of relations between named entities is a challenging task to automatically discover new relationships in texts. The detection of gene interactions in biomedical texts and the discovery of companies relations (sell/buy) in newspapers belong to the scope of that problem. Some previous works use hand-crafted linguistic IE rules for that task which is time consuming [7,5]. Other methods based on Machine Learning (ML) techniques [10] give good results but run as a "black box": their outcomes are not really understandable by a user and Natural Language Processing (NLP) cannot fully take benefit from them.

A key idea of this paper is to propose a cross-fertilization of data mining and NLP techniques to profit from the advantages of the two fields. More precisely, we propose a method based on *recursive sequential pattern mining* with constraints coming from the NLP field to tackle the problem of the discovery of named

P.R. Cohen, N.M. Adams, and M.R. Berthold (Eds.): IDA 2010, LNCS 6065, pp. 30–41, 2010.

entity relations. Sequence mining, in particular sequential pattern mining [1], is a well-known data mining technique that allows to extract regularities in a sequence database. The recursive pattern mining [4] and the constraint-based paradigm [14] enable to give prominence to the most significant patterns. As we will see (Section 2), these techniques have suitable properties for our goal.

The contribution of this work is twofold. First, we propose a recursive pattern mining approach based on constrained sequential patterns to produce a user-manageable set of linguistic IE rules. The recursive sequential pattern mining enables the effective mastering of the number of discovered patterns that are returned. If recursive mining has already been used in the context of itemsets (i.e., data described by items), we show how such a method can deal with sequential data and we prove new properties on recursive pattern mining on sequences. Second, we show how to apply sequential patterns as linguistic IE rules to detect new relations in texts. We illustrate our approach with the detection of gene interactions in biomedical literature. With regards to the issue of the detection of named entity relations, the main advantages of our approach with respect to existing ones are that the results are automatically discovered and easily understandable by a human. To the best of our knowledge, it is the first approach combining sequential pattern mining methods and linguistic information.

The paper is organized as follow. Section 2 presents the background in data mining and existing approaches that tackle the problem of the detection of named entity relations. Section 3 gives the main contributions of this paper. Especially, we describe the discovery of linguistic IE rules to detect relations between entities. Section 4 presents a case study about IE rules for gene interaction detection.

2   Background

This section provides the background on sequential pattern mining and recursive mining. Related work on named entity relation detection is then presented.

2.1   Sequential Pattern Mining under Constraints

Sequential pattern mining [1] is a data mining technique that aims at discovering correlations between events through their order of appearance. Sequential pattern mining is an important field of data mining with broad applications (e.g., biology, marketing, security) and there are many algorithms to extract frequent sequences [19,15,22].

In the context of sequential patterns extraction, a *sequence* is an ordered list of distinct literals called *items*. A sequence S is denoted by $\langle i_1 i_2 \ldots i_n \rangle$ where i_k, $1 \leq k \leq n$, is an item. Let $S_1 = \langle i_1 i_2 \ldots i_n \rangle$ and $S_2 = \langle i'_1 i'_2 \ldots i'_m \rangle$ be two sequences. S_1 is *included* in S_2 if there exist integers $1 \leq j_1 < j_2 < \ldots < j_n \leq m$ such that $i_1 = i'_{j_1}$, $i_2 = i'_{j_2}$, ..., $i_n = i'_{j_n}$. S_1 is called a *subsequence* of S_2. S_2 is called a *super-sequence* of S_1, denoted by $S_1 \preceq S_2$. An extracted sequential pattern, S_1, is *maximal* if there is no other extracted sequential pattern, S_2, such that $S_1 \preceq S_2$. A sequence database SDB is a set of tuples (sid, S) where sid is a sequence ID and S a sequence. A tuple (sid, S) *contains* a sequence T, if T is a subsequence of S. The *support* of a sequence T in a sequence database SDB is the number of tuples in the database containing T: $sup_{SDB}(T) = |\{(sid, S) \in SDB | (T \preceq S)\}|$ where $|A|$ represents the cardinality of set A^1. Note that we do not mention the database when it is clear from the context: $sup(T)$. In this paper, we use sequences of items for sake of simplicity and because it is enough for the case study. However, this approach can be straightforwardly generalized to sequences of itemsets.

The constraint-based pattern mining framework is a powerful paradigm to discover new highly valuable knowledge [13]. Constraints provide a focus on the most promising knowledge by reducing the number of extracted patterns to those of potential interest for the user. More precisely, constraint-based mining task selects all the sequential patterns included in SDB and satisfying a predicate which is called *constraint*. There are a lot of constraints to evaluate the relevance of sequential patterns. The most well-known example is the frequency constraint. Given a minimum support threshold *minsup*, the problem of frequent sequential pattern mining is to find the complete set of sequential patterns whose support is greater than or equal to *minsup*. There are many other constraints highlighting the best sequential patterns with respect to the user objectives [14]. In this work, we will see that we use both syntactic constraints and constraints coming from linguistic information.

2.2 Recursive Pattern Mining

Recursive pattern mining [4] is a process that gives prominence to the most significant patterns and filters the specific ones. The key idea of recursive pattern mining is to repeat the pattern mining process on the output in order to reduce it until few and significant patterns are obtained. That recursive process is ended when the result becomes stable. The final recursive patterns bring forward information coming from each mining step. More precisely, a recursive pattern produces a k-summary (i.e., a set with at most k patterns) summarizing the data according to a measure (e.g., frequency, growth rate) where k is a given number. One of the advantages of recursive pattern mining is that the number of returned frequent patterns is well mastered. If recursive mining is already used with item data [4], to the best of our knowledge, we propose here the first use on sequential data. Such a use requires to demonstrate properties on sequential data and Section 3.5 is devoted to this task.

2.3 Related Work

Several approaches have been widely applied to extract knowledge from texts: NLP, in particular information extraction, and ML.

IE methods need linguistic resources such as grammars. That kind of approaches apply linguistic IE rules to extract information [7,5]. However, the

---

[1] The relative support is also used: $sup_{SDB}(T) = \dfrac{|\{(sid, S) \ s.t. \ (sid, S) \in SDB \land (T \preceq S)\}|}{|SDB|}$.

resources are very often handcrafted. Those methods are thus time consuming and very often devoted to specific corpus. In contrast, ML methods, for example support vector machines or conditional random fields [10], are less time consuming than IE methods. They give good results but they need many features and their outcomes are not really understandable by a user and not usable in NLP systems as linguistic patterns.

A good trade-off is a combination of IE and ML techniques which aims at automatically learning the linguistic IE rules [12,18]. However in most cases the learning process is done with a syntactic parsing of the text (shallow parsing or deep parsing). Therefore, the quality of the learned rules is relied on results of syntactic process which is currently not often a reliable process. Unlike those methods, our proposed approach does not need syntactic parsing of the sentences neither resource except the training data.

Some works [8] do not use syntactic parsing and learn surface patterns using sequence alignment of sentences to derive "motifs". One drawback of that approach is that the sequence alignment implies that patterns are learned with contiguous words. An inexact matching is nevertheless used to apply the patterns on the application corpus. Other works [9] implicitly uses sequence mining in order to compute information extraction rules. However, the number of patterns (i.e., IE rules) is not well mastered and thus they cannot be presented to an expert. Using *n-grams* is another technique very widespread to automatically extract patterns. The drawbacks of n-grams is that the size of the extracted patterns is set for all patterns to n and the elements in patterns must be contiguous. Moreover n-gram can be seen as a specific instance of sequential pattern. Unlike n-grams, in sequential pattern mining, discovered patterns can have different sizes, and items within sequential patterns are not necessarily contiguous.

3   Recursive Sequence Mining to Discover Named Entity Relations

This section presents the discovery of patterns as linguistic IE rules to detect relations between named entities in texts. First, an overview of the approach is given. Second, the use of sequential pattern mining for the detection of named entity relations is explained. Third, linguistic constraints are discussed. Fourth, the algorithm is presented. Finally properties about the recursive pattern mining step are proven.

3.1   Overview

The main idea of our approach is to extract the frequent patterns satisfying user-defined constraints. As the order of words in texts is important, our approach is based on sequential pattern mining which aims at discovering correlations between events through an ordered relation. The order of words within the sentence corresponds to the ordered relation to supply sequential pattern mining. Some linguistic constraints (cf. Section 3.3) are used in order to drive the mining process towards the user objectives. Even if the number of produced patterns is reduced thanks to the constraint, the output still remains too large for individual and global analysis by the end-user. That is why a recursive pattern mining step is performed in order to give prominence to the most significant patterns and to control the output size. That step needs that important properties on recursive pattern mining (cf. Section 3.5) are proven. In addition to usual evaluations by using Precision and Recall measures, Section 4 shows that this small number of computed sequential patterns enables a validation by linguists.

3.2   Sequential Pattern Mining for Named Entity Relations

For the extraction of sequential patterns as linguistic IE rules, the database is built from texts which contain relations and where the named entities are identified and replaced by the specific item *Named_Entity*. In order to avoid problems introduced by the anaphoric structures [23], we consider sequences containing a relation, i.e. a verb or a noun, and at least two named entities.

The choice of the support threshold *minsup* is a well-known issue in data mining. We note in our applications that some interesting words for named entity relation detection are not very frequent so that we set a low value of *minsup*. As a consequence, a huge set of patterns is discovered and it needs to be filtered in order to return only interesting and relevant patterns.

3.3   Linguistic Constraints

In pattern mining, the constraints allow to precisely define the user interest. The most commonly used constraint is the constraint of frequency (*minsup*) because it satisfies suitable mining properties. However, it is possible to use different constraints in conjunction to the frequency [13]. In our work, we use mainly two linguistic constraints on sequential patterns to discover named entity relations.

The first constraint is that the pattern must contain two named entities (C_{2ne}). The set $SAT(C_{2ne})$ represents the set of patterns that satisfy C_{2ne}: $SAT(C_{2ne}) = \{S = \langle i_1 i_2 \ldots i_m \rangle \mid \ |\{j \mid j \in 1 \ldots m \ \wedge \ i_j = Named\_Entity\}| \geq 2\}$. Indeed, the targeted relation is between at least two named entities.

The second constraint is that the pattern must contain a verb or a noun (C_{vn}) in order to express a named entity relation. The set $SAT(C_{vn})$ represents the set of patterns that satisfy C_{vn}: $SAT(C_{vn}) = \{S = \langle i_1 i_2 \ldots i_m \rangle \mid \exists j, verb(i_j) or noun(i_j)\}$ where $verb(i_j)$ (resp. $noun(i_j)$) is a predicate that returns true if i_j is a verb (resp. noun).

Note that other linguistic constraints can be added to give more precision with respect to the kind of searched relations. In the following, for the sake of clarity, all constraints are grouped in only one constraint C_G and $SAT(C_G)$ is the set of patterns satisfying C_G. From the constraint-based paradigm, the C_{2ne} and C_{vn} constraints belong to the category of regular expression constraints introduced by [6].

3.4   Algorithm

Algorithm 1 presents the whole process to discover named entity relations. Firstly, the text is POS tagged (Step 1), i.e., each word is replaced by its lemma and linguistic informations. That step defines the items of the sequence database. The POS tagged text is then sliced in sequences (Step 2). The type of slice size (a sequence) can be for example the phrase, the whole sentence or the paragraph.

Sequential pattern mining is then applied (Step 3) to find the frequent sequential patterns in the database. The patterns are then filtered with respect to user-defined constraints (Step 4). Method *CheckConstrainsts* prunes the sequential patterns that do not satisfy $\mathcal{C}_G$. Therefore, the *constrainedPatterns* set contains all frequent sequential patterns that satisfy $\mathcal{C}_G$. In order to avoid the redundancy between patterns, only maximal patterns (cf. Section 2.1) are kept (Step 5). The computation of the maximality is done in post processing because it is not time consuming. It takes less than 2 minutes. However that phase can be done in the sequential pattern mining step (Step 3).

Even if the new set of sequential patterns, *maximalConstrainedPatterns*, is significantly smaller than the complete set *sequencePatterns*, it can still be too large to be analyzed and validated by a human user. Therefore we use *recursive pattern mining* [4] to filter very specific patterns. As we are interested to keep some patterns for each relation expression, i.e., for each verb or noun, X_i, the set *maximalConstrainedPatterns* is thus divided into several subsets $S(X_i)$ (Step 6)[2]. A subset $S(X_i)$ is the set of all sequential patterns of *maximalConstrainedPatterns* containing the item X_i. More formally, $S(X_i) = \{S \in maximalConstrainedPatterns \mid \langle X_i \rangle \preceq S\}$. Note that X_i are elements labeled as a verb or a noun. The most k $(k > 1)$ representative elements for each $S(X_i)$ are then computed. Each subset $S(X_i)$ is then recursively[3] mined with a support threshold, min_sup_R, equal to $max\{\frac{|S(X_i)|}{k}, 2\}$ in order to extract frequent sequential patterns satisfying $\mathcal{C}_G$ (Steps 7–14). It means that the extracted sequential patterns become the sequences of the new database to mine. That process ends when the number of extracted patterns is less than or equal to k. Some properties about the recursive pattern mining step are given in Section 3.5.

At the end of the process, the number of sequential patterns is well-mastered. Indeed, recursive mining goes on until the number of sequential patterns is less than or equal to k, and as recursive mining always stops (Theorem 1), the number of sequential patterns for each subset is thus less than or equal to k. Therefore the number of returned sequential patterns is less than or equal to $n \times k$ where n is the number of subsets $S(X_i)$ in $SAT(\mathcal{C}_G)$. Note that k is set *a priori* by the user so that sequential patterns can be analyzed by a human. The sequential patterns are then validated by the user and considered as linguistic IE rules for the detection of relations between named entities.

---

[2] The $S(X_i)$ are not necessarily disjoint.

[3] The recursive process is given in iterative writing in Agorithm 1.

Algorithm 1. Discovery of Named Entity Relation Patterns

Input: *text*: text ; *minsup*: support threshold ; *slice_type*: scope of a sequence in text;
   $\mathcal{C}_G$: constraints ; k: recursive mining threshold
Output: *patterns*, set of returned frequent sequential patterns
Method:
 1: *POSTaggedText* := *POS_Tagging*(*text*)
 2: *textSDB* := *Slicing*(*POSTaggedText*, *slice_type*)
 3: *frequentSequentialPatterns* := *SequenceMining*(*textSDB*, *minsup*)
 4: *constrainedPatterns* := *CheckConstraints*(*frequentSequentialPatterns*, $\mathcal{C}_G$)
 5: *maximalConstrainedPatterns* := *Maximal*(*constrainedPatterns*)
 6: *patternSets* := *Split*(*maximalConstrainedPatterns*)
 7: *patterns* := $\emptyset$
 8: **for all** $S(X_i) \in patternSets$ **do**
 9:    **while** $|S(X_i)| > k$ **do**
10:       $min\_sup_R := max\{\frac{|S(X_i)|}{k}, 2\}$
11:       $FP := SequenceMining(S(X_i), min\_sup_R)$
12:       $CP := CheckConstraints(FP)$
13:       $S(X_i) := Maximal(CP)$
14:    **end while**
15:    $patterns := patterns \cup S(X_i)$
16: **end for**

3.5   Properties of Recursive Pattern Mining

In this section, important properties about recursive pattern mining are demonstrated. These properties are new in the context of sequential data.

The first property is about the frequency of the returned patterns. For each subset $S(X_i)$, the k or less extracted sequential patterns returned after recursive pattern mining are frequent in the sequence database *textSDB*. In other words, they belong to the complete set of frequent sequential patterns in *textSDB*, *frequentSequentialPatterns*, with respect to *minsup* (Property 1).

Property 1. Let $S(X)$ be a set of frequent sequential patterns in *textSDB* that contain X. The sequential patterns of $S(X)$ after recursive pattern mining are frequent in *textSDB* with respect to *minsup*.

Proof. The proof is conducted recursively on the number of recursive pattern mining steps.

Base case: No recursive pattern mining. All elements of $S(X)$ are frequent in *textSDB* with respect to *minsup* (Step 3 of Algorithm 1).

Hypothesis: We assume that after j recursive pattern mining steps all elements of $S(X)$ are frequent in *textSDB* with respect to *minsup*. Let $S_j(X)$ be the set of sequential patterns after j recursive pattern mining steps.

Recursive Case: Let $S_{j+1}(X)$ be the set of sequential patterns after $j + 1$ recursive pattern mining steps and $p \in S_{j+1}(X)$. It implies that p is frequent in $S_j(X)$ and thus there exists at least one element in $S_j(X)$, e, such that $p \preceq e$. The pattern e is frequent in *textSDB* (recursive hypothesis). Thanks to the anti-monotonicity of the support, p is thus also frequent in *textSDB*. $\square$

We prove that the recursive pattern mining stops (Theorem 1). Unfortunately, the proof cannot be based on the strictly decreasing of the number of patterns during the recursive pattern mining, because that number may not decrease for some steps. That is why we base the proof according to the size of the largest maximal frequent sequential patterns because it strictly decreases during the recursive pattern mining (Property 2).

Property 2. Let $S_j(X)$ be the result set of sequential patterns recursively mined at step j of the recursive pattern mining (Steps 7-14) and $S_{j+1}(X)$ the result set at step $j + 1$ then: $\forall p \in S_{j+1}(X)$ $|p| < max\{|p_l| \mid p_l \in S_j(X)\}$ where $|p|$ is the size of the pattern, i.e., the number of items in p.

Proof. Let p be an element of $S_{j+1}(X)$: $p \in S_{j+1}(X)$. Let E_p be the set of all elements of $S_j(X)$ such that: $\forall e \in E_p$ $p \preceq e$.

The support threshold for the sequential mining (Step 11) is greater than or equal to 2 (Step 10) and p is frequent in $S_j(X)$. It implies that $|E_p| \geq 2$. However, the elements of $S_j(X)$ are maximal (Step 13), so that the elements of E_p are also maximal (indeed $E_p \subseteq S_j(X)$) and thus p cannot be equal to any element of E_p: $\forall e \in E_p$ $p \not\succeq e$ (i.e., $p \preceq e$ and $p \neq e$) $\Rightarrow \forall e \in E_p$ $|p| < |e|$ and $\forall e \in E_p$ $|e| \leq max\{|p_l| \mid p_l \in S_j(X)\} \Rightarrow |p| < max\{|p_l| \mid p_l \in S_j(X)\}$ □

Theorem 1. *Let k be an integer, $k > 1$. The recursive pattern mining of $S(X)$ stops (cf Algorithm 1).*

Proof. The proof is conducted recursively on the size of patterns of $S(X)$.

Base case: the size of patterns of $S(X)$ is 0. The number of patterns in $S(X)$ is thus 0. In addition, $0 < k$ and thanks to Step 9 of Algorithm 1, the recursive pattern mining stops.

Hypothesis: We assume that the recursive pattern mining stops when the size of patterns of $S(X)$ is lower than or equal to T.

Recursive Case: the size of patterns of $S(X)$ is lower than or equal to $T + 1$. Thanks to Property 2, after one application of the recursive pattern mining on $S(X)$ we know that $S(X)$ contain patterns such that their size is lower than or equal to T. The recursive pattern mining thus stops thanks to the recursive hypothesis.   □

4   Case Study: Discovery of Gene Interaction Patterns

This section presents the discovery of frequent sequential patterns as linguistic information extraction rules for gene interaction detection. The named entities are the genes. Experiments are conducted on texts from biological and medical literature. A linguistic analysis of this case study is given in [3].

4.1   Training Dataset

We merge two different corpora containing genes and proteins to build the training dataset. The first corpus contains sentences from PubMed abstracts, annotated by Christine Brun. It contains 1806 annotated sentences. That corpus is available as a secondary source of learning tasks "Protein-Protein Interaction Task (Interaction Award Sub-task, ISS)" from BioCreAtIvE Challenge II [10]. The second corpus contains sentences of interactions between proteins annotated by an expert. That dataset, containing 2995 sentences with gene interactions, is described in [16]. The training corpus thus contains 4801 sentences.

A POS tagging is then performed on the merged corpus using the *treetagger* tool [17]. The sentences are then split into sequences to build the database. For example, let us consider two sentences that contain gene interactions:

- *"Here we show that <Gene SOX10>, in synergy with <Gene PAX3>, strongly activates <Gene MITF> expression in transfection assays."*
- *"The <Gene Menin>-<Gene JunD> interaction was confirmed in vitro and in vivo."*

Those sentences generate two sequences[4]:

- ⟨ *here@rb we@pp show@vvp that@in/that Named_Entity ,@, in@in synergy@nn with@in Named_Entity ,@, strongly@rb activate@vvz Named_Entity expression@nn in@in transfection@nn assay@nns .@sent* ⟩
- ⟨ *the@dt Named_Entity -@: Named_Entity interaction@nn be@vbd confirm@vvn in@in vitro@nn and@cc in@in vivo@rb .@sent* ⟩

The gene names, i.e., the named entities, are replaced by a specific item, *Named_Entity*, and the other words are replaced by the combinations of their lemma and their POS tag. The order relation between items in a sequence is the order of words within the sentence. For experiments, the sequences of the database are the sentences where each word is replaced by the corresponding item. It means that *slice_type* is the whole sentence.

4.2   Recursive Sequential Pattern Mining

For the sequential pattern mining, we set a support threshold *minsup* equal to 10. With that threshold some irrelevant patterns are not taken into account while many patterns of gene interactions are discovered. We conducted other experiments with greater *minsup* values (15 and 20). With those thresholds some relevant patterns for interaction detection are lost. The number of frequent sequential patterns that are extracted is high. More than 32 million frequent sequential patterns are discovered. Although the number of extracted patterns is high the extraction of all frequent patterns spends only 15 minutes. The extraction tool is *dmt4* [11].

The application of constraints significantly reduces the number of sequential patterns. Indeed, the number of sequential patterns satisfying the constraints is about 65,000. However, that number is still prohibitive for analysis and validation by a human expert. Recall that the application of constraints is not time consuming (couple of minutes).

---

[4] *'rb'*, *'pp'*, ... after *'@'* are tags given by *treetagger*, for example : *'rb'* means *adverb*, *'pp'* means *personal pronoun*.

The sequential patterns, which are computed in the previous step, are divided into several subsets. The recursive pattern mining of each subset exhibits at most k sequential patterns to represent that subset. In this experiment, we set the parameter k to 4. We get 515 subsets (365 for nouns, 150 for verbs). At the end of the recursive pattern mining, there remain 667 candidate sequential patterns that represent interactions. That number, which is significantly smaller than the previous one, guarantees the feasibility of an analysis of those patterns as linguistic IE rules by an expert. The recursive pattern mining of those subsets is not time consuming. It takes about 2 minutes.

The 667 remaining sequential patterns were analyzed by two users. They validated 232 sequential patterns for interaction detection in 90 minutes. It means that 232 sequential patterns represent several forms of interactions between genes. Among those patterns, some explicitly represent interactions. For example, ⟨*Named_Entity deplete@vvn Named_Entity .@sent*⟩, ⟨*activation@nn of@in Named_Entity by@in Named_Entity .@sent*⟩ or ⟨*Named_Entity be@vbd inhibit@vvn by@in AGENE@np .@sent*⟩ describe well-known interactions (inhibition, activation). Other patterns represent more general interactions between genes, meaning that a gene plays a role in the activity of another gene for instance ⟨*Named_Entity involve@vvn in@in Named_Entity .@sent*⟩ or ⟨*that@in/that Named_Entity play@vvz role@nn in@in Named_Entity .@sent*⟩. Most of remaining patterns represent modalities or biological context.

The validated sequential patterns are linguistic IE rules that can be used on biomedical texts to detect interactions between genes. Note that the application of those patterns do not need a syntactic analysis of the sentence.

4.3   Detection of Gene Interactions

Following the case study, we have conducted some experiments in order to evaluate the quality of the sequential patterns found in the previous section from a quantitative point of view. For that purpose, we consider three sets of data well-known in literature: *GeneTag* from the data set *Genia* [20], *BioCreative* from [21] and *AIMed* from [2]. In those datasets, the names of genes or proteins are labeled as named entities. In each corpus, we randomly took 200 sentences and tested whether the linguistic patterns can be applied. For each sentence, we manually measure the performance of linguistic sequential patterns to detect those interactions. Note that we also carried out a POS tagging of those sentences in order to correctly apply the pattern language. Table 1 presents the scores of the application of the patterns as linguistic IE rules: Precision, Recall and *f-score*[5]. The scores are similar in the three corpora. Moreover, the precision is very good and the recall is correct. Further investigations with different values of the parameter k are a promising issue: indeed, higher k is, more specific patterns are.

Note that the scope of the extracted linguistic IE rules in the experiments is the whole sentence. That scope may introduce ambiguities in the detection of interactions and thus false positives when more than two genes appear in

---

[5] The used *f-score* function is : $f\text{-}score = \dfrac{2 \times Precision \times Recall}{Precision + Recall}$.

Table 1. Tests on several corpora

Corpus	Precision	Recall	F-Score
BioCreative [21]	0.92	0.767	0.836
GeneTag [20]	0.909	0.8	0.851
AIMed [2]	0.93	0.84	0.88

the same sentence. Several cases are possible: when several binary interactions are present in the sentence, when the interaction is n-ary ($n \geq 3$) or when an interaction is found with a list of genes. The case of n-ary interactions can be solved with a training dataset containing n-ary interactions. The other two cases can be treated by introducing limitations of pattern scope, for example cue-phrases (e.g., *but, however*). False negatives mainly depend on the absence of some nouns or verbs of interaction in the patterns. For example, the noun "modulation" is not learned in a pattern whereas the verb "modulate" appears. This suggests that the use of linguistic resources (e.g., lexicon or dictionary) can, manually or semi-automatically, improve patterns and thus interaction detection.

5   Conclusion and Future Work

This paper proposes a method based on a cross-fertilization of sequence mining under constraints and recursive pattern mining to produce a user-manageable set of linguistic information extraction rules, such as the discovery relations between named entities. The constraints enable to drive the mining process towards the user objectives by filtering irrelevant patterns. The recursive sequence mining allows the effective mastering of the number of discovered patterns that are returned. In addition, we prove important properties on recursive pattern mining on sequences. To the best of our knowledge, it is the first approach combining sequential pattern mining methods, constraints and linguistic information.

The case study shows the feasibility and the interest of our method to discover the named entity relations. We have conducted experiments on biomedical textual data to detect gene interactions. Our proposed approach does not need syntactic parsing neither resource except the training data. In addition, the patterns as linguistic IE rules are understandable by a user. From a qualitative point of view, it is interesting to note that the subcategorization of the verbs given by the POS tagging indicates the passive or active verbs and identifies the direction of the relation. Prepositions can also convey that kind of information, which is precious when the pattern does not contain a verb. Promising future work consists of designing more complex linguistic constraints and pushing them within the mining process.

References

1. Agrawal, R., Srikant, R.: Mining sequential patterns. In: ICDE. IEEE, Los Alamitos (1995)
2. Bunescu, R.C., Mooney, R.J.: A shortest path dependency kernel for relation extraction. In: HLT/EMNLP, pp. 724–731. ACL (2005)

3. Cellier, P., Charnois, T., Plantevit, M.: Sequential patterns to discover and characterise biological relations. In: Gelbukh, A. (ed.) CICLing 2010. LNCS, vol. 6008, pp. 537–548. Springer, Heidelberg (2010)
4. Crémilleux, B., Soulet, A., Klema, J., Hébert, C., Gandrillon, O.: Discovering knowledge from local patterns in sage data. In: Data Mining and Medical Knowledge Management: Cases and Applications, pp. 251–267. IGI Publishing (2009)
5. Fundel, K., Küffner, R., Zimmer, R.: Relex - Relation extraction using dependency parse trees. Bioinformatics 23(3), 365–371 (2007)
6. Garofalakis, M.N., Rastogi, R., Shim, K.: Spirit: Sequential pattern mining with regular expression constraints. In: Proc. Int. Conf. on Very Large Data Bases, pp. 223–234. Morgan Kaufmann, San Francisco (1999)
7. Giuliano, C., Lavelli, A., Romano, L.: Exploiting shallow linguistic information for relation extraction from biomedical literature. In: EACL, pp. 401–408 (2006)
8. Hakenberg, J., Plake, C., Royer, L., Strobelt, H., Leser, U., Schroeder, M.: Gene mention normalization and interaction extraction with context models and sentence motifs. Genome biology 9(Suppl. 2), S14 (2008)
9. Joshi, S., Ramakrishnan, G., Balakrishnan, S., Srinivasan, A.: Information extraction using non-consecutive word sequences. In: Workshop on Text Mining and Link Analysis IJCAI (2007)
10. Krallinger, M., Leitner, F., Rodriguez-Penagos, C., Valencia, A.: Overview of the protein-protein interaction annotation extraction task of BioCreative II. Genome Biology 9(Suppl. 2), S4 (2008)
11. Nanni, M., Rigotti, C.: Extracting trees of quantitative serial episodes. In: Džeroski, S., Struyf, J. (eds.) KDID 2006. LNCS, vol. 4747, pp. 170–188. Springer, Heidelberg (2007)
12. Nédellec, C.: Machine learning for information extraction in genomics - state of the art and perspectives. In: Studies in Fuzziness and Soft Comp. Sirmakessis (2004)
13. Ng, R.T., Lakshmanan, L.V.S., Han, J., Pang, A.: Exploratory mining and pruning optimizations of constrained association rules. In: ACM SIGMOD (1998)
14. Pei, J., Han, J., Lakshmanan, L.V.S.: Mining frequent itemsets with convertible constraints. In: ICDE, pp. 433–442. IEE Computer Society (2001)
15. Pei, J., Han, J., Mortazavi-Asl, B., Pinto, H., Chen, Q., Dayal, U., Hsu, M.: Prefixspan: Mining sequential patterns by prefix-projected growth. In: ICDE, pp. 215–224. IEEE Computer Society, Los Alamitos (2001)
16. Rosario, B., Hearst, M.A.: Multi-way relation classification: Application to protein-protein interactions. In: HLT/EMNLP, pp. 732–739. ACL (2005)
17. Schmid, H.: Probabilistic part-of-speech tagging using decision trees. In: Proc. of Int. Conf. on New Methods in Language Processing (September 1994)
18. Schneider, G., Kaljurand, K., Rinaldi, F.: Detecting protein-protein interactions in biomedical texts using a parser and linguistic resources. In: Gelbukh, A. (ed.) CICLing 2009. LNCS, vol. 5449, pp. 406–417. Springer, Heidelberg (2009)
19. Srikant, R., Agrawal, R.: Mining sequential patterns: Generalizations and performance improvements. In: Apers, P.M.G., Bouzeghoub, M., Gardarin, G. (eds.) EDBT 1996. LNCS, vol. 1057, pp. 3–17. Springer, Heidelberg (1996)
20. Tanabe, L., Xie, N., Thom, L.H., Matten, W., Wilbur, J.: GENETAG: a tagged corpus for gene/protein named entity recognition. BMC Bioinformatics 6, 10 (2005)
21. Yeh, A., Morgan, A., Colosimo, M., Hirschman, L.: BioCreAtIvE Task 1A: Gene mention finding evaluation. BMC Bioinformatics 6(Suppl. 1), S2 (2005)
22. Zaki, M.: Spade: An efficient algorithm for mining frequent sequences. Machine Learning 42(1/2), 31–60 (2001)
23. Zweigenbaum, P., Demner-Fushman, D., Yu, H., Cohen, K.B.: Frontiers of biomedical text mining: current progress. Brief. Bioinform. 8(5), 358–375 (2007)

Integration and Dissemination of Citizen Reported and Seismically Derived Earthquake Information via Social Network Technologies

Michelle Guy[1], Paul Earle[1], Chris Ostrum[1], Kenny Gruchalla[2], and Scott Horvath[3]

[1] U.S. Geological Survey National Earthquake Information Center, Golden, CO, USA
[2] National Renewable Energy Laboratory, Golden, CO, USA
[3] U.S. Geological Survey National Earthquake Information Center, Reston, VA, USA

Abstract. People in the locality of earthquakes are publishing anecdotal information about the shaking within seconds of their occurrences via social network technologies, such as Twitter. In contrast, depending on the size and location of the earthquake, scientific alerts can take between two to twenty minutes to publish. We describe TED (Twitter Earthquake Detector) a system that adopts social network technologies to augment earthquake response products and the delivery of hazard information. The TED system analyzes data from these social networks for multiple purposes: 1) to integrate citizen reports of earthquakes with corresponding scientific reports 2) to infer the public level of interest in an earthquake for tailoring outputs disseminated via social network technologies and 3) to explore the possibility of rapid detection of a probable earthquake, within seconds of its occurrence, helping to fill the gap between the earthquake origin time and the presence of quantitative scientific data.

Keywords: Twitter, micro-blogging, social network, citizen reporting, earthquake, hazard, geospatial-temporal data, time series.

1 Introduction

Social network technologies are providing the general public with anecdotal earthquake hazard information before scientific information has been published from authoritative sources [1]. The United States Geological Survey (USGS) National Earthquake Information Center (NEIC) rapidly determines the location and size of felt earthquakes within the U.S. and most magnitude 5.0 and greater earthquakes worldwide. The USGS rapidly disseminates this information to National and international agencies, scientists and the general public. Due to the propagation time of seismic energy from an earthquake's hypocenter to globally-distributed seismometers and the latencies in the collection, analysis, and validation of these global seismic data, published scientific alerts can take between two and twenty minutes to produce, depending on the size and location of the quake. In contrast, people in the vicinity of earthquakes are publishing information within seconds of their occurrence via social networking and micro-blogging technologies. This paper describes how the analysis of geospatial-temporal data from social networking sites is being adopted by the

P.R. Cohen, N.M. Adams, and M.R. Berthold (Eds.): IDA 2010, LNCS 6065, pp. 42–53, 2010.

USGS in an attempt to augment its earthquake response products and the delivery of hazard information. While the anecdotal and qualitative information from social networking sites is not a replacement for the high quality quantitative earthquake information from the USGS, mining and publishing this rapidly available information can provide 1) integration of first hand hazard accounts with scientific information, 2) a wide spread outreach tool and 3) potentially provide early detections of reported shaking events.

TED (Twitter Earthquake Detector) is a software application developed to mine real-time data from popular social networking and micro-blogging sites (e.g., Twitter, Jaiku), searching for indicators of earthquake (or other hazard) activity directly from the public. In addition, TED integrates traditional scientific earthquake information, location and magnitude, from the USGS internal global earthquake data stream with geospatial-temporal corresponding citizen reports from popular social networking and micro-blogging sites. One indication of the level of public interest can be inferred when the density of hazard-related chatter in time and a geographic locality corresponds to that of an actual hazard event. When an earthquake is picked up from the USGS internal global earthquake data stream, the system immediately integrates citizen reported firsthand accounts of experienced shaking with the corresponding scientific information. TED then uses these same social networking and micro-blogging technologies to rapidly disseminate the combined scientific and citizen information to a large number of people potentially already "listening". Additionally, analysts working on earthquake response products currently have only scientifically derived location, corresponding population and magnitude information available in the minutes following an earthquake. The rapid integration of firsthand hazard accounts can potentially help guide the initial response actions taken to meet NEIC's mission.

This same detected increase in earthquake related chatter used to infer public interest in an earthquake is being investigated for use as a real-time preliminary indicator of a potential earthquake. Early work has indicated that such detections are possible within seconds of an earthquake and could potentially be used to create preliminary alerts (e.g., emails, pages, and micro-blog updates) for USGS operations staff as an early hazard warning, thus filling the gap from when an earthquake occurs until the time scientific data become available to then confirm or refute the reported shaking event.

We describe the collection, filtering, archiving, and analysis of Twitter data and show how these data can be effectively correlated against the USGS internal earthquake stream as one indication of public interest in an earthquake. Integration of these data successfully augments current earthquake response products produced by the USGS. We also evaluate the usage of these Twitter data as a real-time hazard detection tool. Preliminary results suggest that these data, if handled carefully, can be useful as an early detection indicator.

2   Related Work

Twitter [2] is one of the more widely used micro-blogging platforms, with a global outreach spreading from developed, urban nations to developing countries [3]. It enables a form of blogging that allows users to send short status update messages (maximum of a 140 characters) called *tweets*. Twitter provides access to thoughts, activities, and experiences of millions of users in real-time, with the option of sharing the user's location. This rich source of data is motivating a growing body of scientific literature about micro-blogging. Most of the work has focused on social aspects such as studying user motivations [4,5] and user collaboration [6,7,8]. Some micro-blogging collaboration research has focused specifically on crisis management and collective problem solving in mass emergency events [9,10,11].

Our interest in the use of Twitter data is not for the crisis management that follows a hazard event, rather it is in the rapid assessment, reporting, and potentially the near real-time detection of a hazard event. De Longueville, et al. [12] performed a post-mortem analysis of tweets related to a wild fire near the French city of Marseille. Their analysis showed that the Twitter traffic was generally well synchronized to the temporal and spatial dynamics of the Marseille fire event, but warns that tweets from media sources and aggregators (users that compile and republish existing sources) will complicate automatic event detection. Intelligent blog-based event detection has not been limited to hazard events. Online chatter has been used to predict the rank of book sales [13] and recommend topical news items [14]. Cheong & Lee [3] describe a general collective intelligence retrieval methodology that can be used to mine micro-blogs to identify trends for decision-making.

The USGS has an established history of Internet-based citizen reporting using the "Did You Feel It?" system ("DYFI?") [15], which generates ground shaking intensity maps based on volunteered Internet questionnaires. The DYFI questionnaires allow a calibrated assignment of *Modified Mercalli Intensity* to each submission, producing quantitative map of intensity. The Modified Mercalli Intensity scale [16] is based on postal questionnaires where respondents summarize shaking effects, damage maps produced by emergency response agencies, and reports produced by the earthquake engineering community. The "DYFI?" system provides a calibrated quantitative assessment of an earthquake event; however, it depends on users visiting the USGS website and completing a questionnaire. Collecting a sufficient amount of data to generate an intensity map typically takes on the order of minutes. The data mined from Twitter are neither calibrated nor quantitative; however, an earthquake can be detected on the order of seconds and does not require direct interaction with the USGS website.

3   Methodology

3.1   Gathering Data

TED harvests real-time tweets by establishing a continuous *HTTP* connection to Twitter's Streaming API applying a query parameter to reduce the stream to only tweets that contain one or more of the specified keywords: namely *earthquake*, *quake* and *tsunami* in several languages. The stream of tweets returned from Twitter is in *JSON* format which is then parsed locally and inserted into a *MySQL* database. All of this runs 24x7 in multiple separated redundant processes, in order to compensate for network interruptions or other failures.

In addition to the keyword filtering, other data cleaning techniques are applied to the incoming tweets. Tweets from the multiple processes are merged, ordering the tweets, accounting for duplicates, and filling any data gaps. Data from aggregators, users who regularly redistribute second hand earthquake information, are removed from the data set. The number of aggregator users has thus far remained below one half of a percent of all users that have sent earthquake related tweets over the past five months. Additionally, tweets containing strings commonly used to indicate *retweeting*, rebroadcasting a tweet from another user, are removed. All of these removed tweets are archived in a separate table in the database currently preserved for historical analysis, as necessary.

For each keyword filtered tweet TED archives the tweet creation time, text, Twitter user location, Twitter tweet ID, Twitter user ID, and the time the tweet was inserted into the TED database. Additionally, after each tweet is inserted into the database, the latitude and longitude estimate of the sender's location, if provided, is determined via the Google Maps API Geocoding Service [17] and stored with the tweet. Roughly 15% of the earthquake related tweets that we have archived have come from GPS enabled devices, generally providing very accurate locations at the time of each tweet. Another 35% percent of the tweets have generic user locations such as "123 A St. San Francisco, CA, USA", or "San Francisco, CA, USA", or "San Francisco", or "The Bay Area". The remaining 50% of the tweets do not provide a specific location and are not used by the TED system.

The TED system also ingests seismically derived earthquake information from the USGS near real-time internal global earthquake stream 24x7. From these earthquake messages TED archives the earthquake origin time, region name, hypocenter (latitude, longitude, and depth), the magnitude, and the authoritative source of the scientifically derived earthquake information. These scientific earthquake messages arrive anywhere from two minutes up to around twenty minutes after an earthquake's origin time, depending on the size and location of the earthquake.

3.2 Integrating Seismically Derived and Citizen Reported Earthquake Information

TED integrates firsthand public accounts of shaking with the corresponding scientific information for an earthquake. For earthquakes in areas populated with active Twitter users, TED can then gauge a potential level of public interest in that earthquake by detecting a "significant" and rapid increase in the number of related tweets. When an earthquake location, from the USGS near real-time internal global earthquake stream, is inserted into the system, the tweet archive is searched for geo-spatially and temporally correlated tweets. Geo-spatial correlation is determined by computing distance from the hypocenter (latitude, longitude and depth) for which ground shaking may have been felt. We define an earthquake's possible felt area as all points on the Earth's surface whose hypo-central distance is less than an estimated maximum felt distance Rf, in km, which is a function of magnitude M defined as:

$$Rf = 10^{\,0.3204*M+0.602} \tag{0}$$

We derived *Rf* empirically from felt observations submitted to the "Did You Feel It?" system. This relation does not take into account such factors as spatial variation in ground-motion attenuation and rupture finiteness. However, for our current system this simple approximation has proved sufficient over the three months the system has been running.

Temporal correlation is accomplished by collecting the tweets, in the TED archive, from five minutes before the earthquake origin time up to the time when the data sets are being integrated, which may range anywhere from two to sixteen minutes after the origin time. The time frame before the event origin time measures the present noise level. The time frame after the event is limited to a maximum of sixteen minutes to help limit the input to context relative tweets with firsthand accounts of shaking rather than much of the conversational chatter, retweets, media reports and geographically wider spread reactions that occur in longer time frames following an earthquake.

3.3 Significance Detection

TED uses a geospatial-temporal correlated earthquake tweet data set to infer a level of public interest in an earthquake. Since there are dozens of located, unfelt earthquakes on the planet every day, a check for a significant increase in related tweets helps prevent flooding users with information that they may not find useful and cause users to ignore the information all together. We use a significance ratio function, S, to determine if an earthquake has generated a significant increase in tweet traffic to warrant public distribution. A trigger is declared if S exceeds one. The significance ratio function accounts for the possibility of zero pre-event noise and is defined:

$$S = A/(mB+Z) \tag{1}$$

Where A is the tweets-per-minutes after the event, B is the tweets-per-minute before the event, Z is a constant that defines the required value for A when B is zero to cause a trigger, and m is a constant that controls how much A must increase with increasing noise levels to cause a trigger. For earthquakes with S greater than one, the TED system produces 1) an alert tweet with hypocenter, preliminary magnitude, and region, 2) an interactive map of the plotted epicenter and tweets, 3) a histogram of tweets per time unit around the earthquake origin time, 4) a downloadable KML file that plots tweets over time, 5) a list of the top ten cities with the highest number of tweets, and 6) a web page that includes all of the above and the actual text for all correlated tweets. The purpose of these integrated output products is to rapidly provide a summary of personal accounts from the impacted region to earthquake responders and the public. It is anticipated that TED products will be replaced as validated and calibrated information becomes available. TED will also rapidly provide information via Twitter (instead of only the web and email) and hopefully draw users to the USGS website for detailed information. These output products can augment current earthquake response information provided to USGS analysts and to the public.

3.4 Preliminary Hazard Detection

The analysis of the real-time spatio-temporal data being captured by the TED system may also allow for the rapid detection of an earthquake before quantitative scientific information is available. In fact, creating a time series of earthquake-related tweets and monitoring this time series for spatio-temporal spikes is analogous to how ground motion data from a seismometer are evaluated for earthquake activity. As a proof of concept, three months of filtered and archived tweets were discretized per time unit to create a time series of their temporal distribution. This time series was then scanned for spikes, which are temporally correlated indications of a citizen reported earthquake. The times of these spikes were then compared against the USGS scientifically confirmed catalog of earthquake events [18] as confirmation of an actual earthquake. The early results are promising however, more sophisticated heuristics need to be defined from historical data analysis to better characterize these spikes of chatter and further reduce false detections. This has been left for future work.

4 Difficulties and Issues

It is clear that significant limitations exist in a system based on citizen reporting. The issues that tend to plague the system are lack of quantitative information, out of context tweets, incorrect or lack of geo-locations, and the robustness of external data sources such as Twitter and geo-locating services. The main drawback, because the NEIC's mission is scientific information about earthquakes, is the lack of quantitative information such as epicenter and magnitude. Without quantitative verified data, alerts provoking response measures are not possible. The main advantage of Twitter is speed, especially in sparsely instrumented areas.

Not all tweets containing the word *earthquake* or *quake*, in any language, correspond to people feeling shaking caused by an earthquake. Analysis of data for the past few months indicates that the background level of noise (out of context tweets geographically and time clustered) is generally very low, except following major earthquakes. For example, after the magnitude 4.3 Morgan Hill, CA earthquake on March 30, 2009 the number of earthquake tweets sent from the surrounding region increased from roughly one tweet per hour before the event to 150 tweets per minute for a full five minutes after the event [1]. This is a signal to noise ratio of 9000. However, background noise levels are not constant. For example, in the hours and days following the magnitude 7 earthquake in Haiti in mid January 2010, people all over the planet were tweeting about earthquakes. Fortunately, this kind of chatter is generally not geographically centered and dies down a few days after the event. However, there are other types of chatter that could produce geographically and time centered "earthquake" tweets. For example, a geographically concentrated spike of tweets was observed during the Great California Shake Out [19] in October 2009. One can imagine a large enough group of twitter users enjoying a fun game of Quake while eating Dairy Queen's Oreo Brownie Earthquake dessert producing misleading data for an automated system.

Inaccurate tweet geo-locations are a serious issue when using geospatially related tweets for threshold detections and to map indications of the region exposed to the hazard, or shaking in the case of an earthquake. The location of a tweet is only as accurate as the location string the user entered in their Twitter profile, as this is the location provided with tweets. A location is not required to set up a Twitter account and can be as vague or specific as the user wants. Some Twitter applications for GPS enabled devices update the location string on a per tweet basis, this is about 15% of the earthquake tweets we have seen in the past three months. However, most tweets that provide a location use the static location in the user's profile. Given this, a tweet from a New Yorker on vacation in San Francisco will most likely mis-locate to New York. Since these tweets are likely not spatially correlated, requiring a minimum number of earthquake tweets in a region before declaring it a felt region will reduce their contaminating effect. We expect that tweet location accuracy will increase with time due to both the increased use of GPS enabled devices and Twitter's introduction, in November 2009, of its Geolocation API that will allow users to have their tweets tagged with their current location.

Citizen reporting based hazard detection is only as good as the reporting. It is conceivable that a motivated group of citizens could attempt to spoof a hazard. To avoid "attacks" aimed at fooling the system, refined characterization of detection spikes would help to reduce malicious attacks, but unlikely eliminate them.

5   Results and Evaluation

Analyzing the outputs produced from integrating geo-spatially and temporally correlated citizen reports of earthquakes with seismically derived earthquake information, confirms their potential to augment existing earthquake products produced by the USGS. For example, Fig. 1 shows an interactive Google Map with the earthquake epicenter and correlated tweets plotted. It provides an indication of areas with perceived shaking and provides access to the geo-located tweets' text. Comparing the geospatial distribution of the tweets against the scientifically calibrated "DYFI?" intensity map indicates that the early arriving tweets can roughly correspond with perceived shaking as shown in Fig. 2. This correlation is further explored in *Earle et al.* 2010, [1].

Fig. 1. Earthquake epicenter (circled waveform) and geospatially and temporally corresponding earthquake tweets (balloons) plotted on an interactive Google Map for the magnitude 4.3 earthquake in Southern California on January 16, 2010

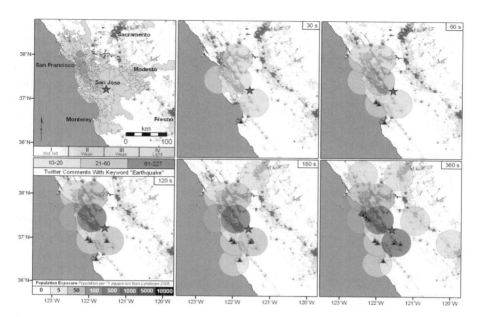

Fig. 2. Comparison of the intensity map (upper left) produced using Internet questionnaires submitted to the USGS "Did You Feel It?" system (DYFI?) [15] to maps produced by counting geospatially and temporally correlated tweets (remaining plots at discrete time intervals after the earthquake) for the magnitude 4.3 earthquake in the San Francisco Bay Area on March 30th, 2009. The colors of the plotted circles indicate the number of tweets in that region. Tweets with precise latitude and longitude geo-locations are plotted as triangles.

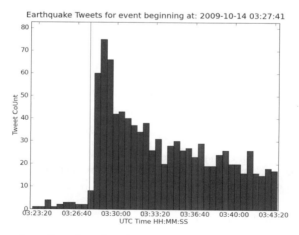

Fig. 3. Histogram of number of earthquake tweets every thirty seconds before and after the magnitude 3.7 earthquake in Pleasanton, CA on October 13, 2009 (local date), with earthquake origin time indicated by the red vertical line at 2009-10-14 03:27:41 UTC

At a glance, the main advantage of mining citizen reports via Twitter is the speed of information availability, especially compared to areas that are sparsely instrumented with seismometers. Even using data from hundreds of globally distributed sensors we cannot detect many earthquakes below magnitude 4.5, due to a lack of available local instrumentation. In limited cases, these earthquakes can be identified. By manually scanning a real-time Twitter search for earthquake tweets, we detected two earthquakes in 2009 that were missed by our real-time seismometer-based earthquake association algorithm. The first was a magnitude 4.7 earthquake near Reykjavik, Iceland. The second was a magnitude 3.1 earthquake near Melbourne, Australia. These earthquakes likely would have been detected in days to weeks using late arriving data and locations from contributing foreign seismic networks, however, Twitter enabled quicker USGS distribution of earthquake magnitude and epicenter.

To further investigate the possibility of detecting earthquakes based on citizen reports, we compared earthquake related tweet activity against the USGS earthquake catalog. To do this comparison we created a time series of tweets-per-minute using a month and a half of archived keyword filtered tweet data as shown in Fig. 4. We then searched the time series for sudden increases in temporally related tweets and then correlated these peaks with earthquakes. All of the major spikes, with the exception of one on October 15th, coincide with earthquakes. The one on October 15th was an emergency preparedness drill conducted by the state of California [19]. It is interesting to note for this spike the onset was much more gradual than the onset for earthquakes. Fig. 3 shows an example of the rapid onset for an actual earthquake. Correct differentiation between rapid and gradual increases in tweet frequency may reduce false detections. It is important to note that earthquakes detected by tweets will only be those felt by human observers. There are dozens of located earthquakes on any given day that are not felt, because they are too deep, and or in sparsely populated areas. A tweet-based system will not detect such earthquakes. This comparison has demonstrated a match of tweet-based detection with actual felt earthquakes.

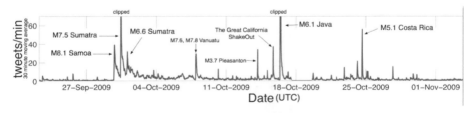

Fig. 4. Plotted time series of earthquake tweets per minute from September 20, 2009 through November 8, 2009 with major spikes identified with corresponding earthquake region and magnitude

For a tweet based detection system to be viable, the number of false detections needs to be low. Background noise from out of context earthquake tweets can increase false detections. An evaluation of the background noise around geospatially and temporally related tweets was performed by comparing the number of tweets before and after a verified earthquake. For every event that TED picks up from the USGS near real-time internal global earthquake stream, it calculates the average number of geospatially and temporally correlated tweets-per-minute for ten minutes prior and post the event origin time. Looking at this noise level for all earthquakes from December 1, 2009 through January 27, 2010 (2291 total) 99% of the earthquakes had 0.1 or less tweets-per-minute in the ten minutes prior to the event. The remaining 1% were typically in the range of 0.1 to 1.8 tweets-per-minute for the ten minutes prior to the earthquake. Figure 3 shows an example of an earthquake with high pre-event noise and still the onset of the earthquake related tweets is clear. The influence of background noise in a geospatially and temporally related tweet data set is small.

In order for tweet based earthquake detection to be useful, it must precede the availability of seismically derived information. From TED outputs we have seen many earthquakes that show an increase in earthquake related tweet frequency that precedes the availability of seismically derived data. For example, the USGS alert for a small, magnitude 3.7, earthquake in a densely instrumented region in central California was available 3.2 minutes after the earthquake's origin time, while a detectable increase in correlated tweet frequency was seen in 20 seconds. In a second case, we examined a large, magnitude 7.6, earthquake in a moderately instrumented region of Indonesia. Initial seismically derived information was available 6.7 minutes after the earthquake's origin time, while a rapid increase in "gempa" (Indonesian for earthquake) tweets was seen in 81 seconds. In both cases, numerous earthquake tweets were available in considerably less time than it took to distribute the initial seismically derived estimates of magnitude and location. This demonstrates that rapid tweet based detection can potentially fill the gap between when an earthquake occurs and when seismically derived information is available.

6 Future Work

Future work includes developing a more sophisticated hazard detection algorithm for the real-time input tweet stream. The current plan is to group keyword filtered tweets into five or ten second time intervals as the tweets are being archived from the Twitter stream in order to produce a continuous real-time tweet time series. A short time interval was chosen to both reduce latency and to help make the time series continuous around clustered earthquake chatter. From this real-time time series both a long term average (LTA) and short term average (STA) will be calculated and used to produce a second time series of STA/LTA ratio, which should further improve the signal to noise ratio (just as it does for automatic seismic phase arrival detection from ground motion time series data from seismometers). This noise reduced time series is what will be monitored for significant increases in the temporal density of hazard related chatter, with the goal of reducing false detections. Current evaluation has shown significant increases in the temporal density of hazard related chatter with a rapid, almost instantaneous, onset within seconds of an earthquake's occurrence. Heuristics need to be further refined from continued historical data analysis to better characterize these spikes of chatter and further reduce false detections. This kind of real-time time series analysis is quite similar to how real-time waveform time series data from seismometers are monitored for seismic activity.

Additionally, further timing analysis is necessary to get a better handle on how long after a hazard event, or categorized types of events (i.e. small earthquake in densely populated area, large earthquake in a sparsely populated area, etc.) tweet based hazard detection can work. We anticipate that relying on external sources for services such as geocoding will be an inherent bottleneck, and may require more robust or internal solutions for such services in order to meet timing requirements in the long term. One step in reducing geocoding time dependencies will be incorporating the use of Twitter's newly added geolocation tags when provided with incoming keyword filtered tweets. This will improve over time as more Twitter client applications incorporate this feature. From a more detailed analysis of our current system we hope to move from a proof of concept to an operational system with defined expectations of reliability and accuracy.

7 Conclusions

While TED's detection and distribution of anecdotal earthquake information cannot replace instrumentally based earthquake monitoring and analysis tools, we have demonstrated that TED can integrate citizen reported and seismically derived earthquake information and then, based on inferred degrees of interest, rapidly disseminate the information to large numbers of people via social networking technologies. Additionally, we have shown that mining and publishing this information can fill the gap between the time an earthquake occurs and the time confirmed scientific information is available. The anticipated impacts of this novel use of social networking sites for the earth sciences include:

- Rapid preliminary indicators of shaking or other hazards in populated areas, potentially before the arrival of seismically validated alerts.
- The ability to pool together and make readily accessible citizen contributed earthquake information (e.g. eye witness reports, shaking felt, photos) from individuals local to a hazard.
- Improved public outreach by providing authoritative earthquake alerts thru social media outlets.
- Provide useful data and products that augment the existing suite of USGS earthquake response products.

There is a high degree of uncertainty and variability in these data derived from anecdotal micro-blogs. Therefore, TED outputs and notifications based on citizen reporting alone cannot definitively state an earthquake occurred but will state that social network chatter about earthquakes, has increased in a specified area at a specified time and seismically derived information will follow. For more information on this project, please e-mail USGSted@usgs.gov or follow @USGSted on Twitter.

Acknowledgments. Funding provided by the American Recovery and Reinvestment Act supported a student, Chris Ostrum, for the development of the TED system. Chris is currently at Sierra Nevada Corp, Englewood, CO, USA. We thank M. Hearne and H. Bolton for internal USGS reviews of this manuscript. Any use of trade, product, or firm names is for descriptive purposes only and does not imply endorsement by the U.S. Government.

References

1. Earle, P., Guy, M., Buckmaster, R., Ostrum, C., Horvath, S., Vaughan, A.: OMG Earthquake! Can Twitter Improve earthquake response? Seismological Research Letters (to appear 2010)
2. O'Reilly, T., Milstein, S.: The Twitter Book. O'Reilly Media, Inc., Sebastopol (2009)
3. Cheong, M., Lee, V.: Integrating web-based intelligence retrieval and decision-making from the twitter trends knowledge base. In: SWSM 2009: Proceeding of the 2nd ACM workshop on Social web search and mining, pp. 1–8 (2009)
4. Zhao, D., Rosson, M.B.: How and why people Twitter: the role that micro-blogging plays in informal communication at work. In: Proceedings of the ACM 2009 international conference on Supporting group work, pp. 243–252 (2009)
5. Java, A., Song, X., Finin, T., Tseng, B.: Why We Twitter: An Analysis of a Microblogging Community. In: Advances in Web Mining and Web Usage Analysis, pp. 118–138 (2009)
6. Honeycutt, C., Herring, S.: Beyond Microblogging: Conversation and Collaboration via Twitter. In: HICSS 2009: Proceedings of the 42nd Hawaii International Conference on System Sciences, pp. 1–10 (2009)
7. Dixon, J., Tucker, C.R.: We use technology, but do we use technology? using existing technologies to communicate, collaborate, and provide support. In: SIGUCCS 2009: Proceedings of the ACM SIGUCCS fall conference on User services conference, pp. 309–312 (2009)
8. McNely, B.: Backchannel persistence and collaborative meaning-making. In: SIGDOC 2009: Proceedings of the 27th ACM international conference on Design of communication, pp. 297–304 (2009)
9. Starbird, K., Palen, L., Hughes, A., Vieweg, S.: Chatter on The Red: What Hazards Threat Reveals about the Social Life of Microblogged Information. In: CSCW 2010: Proceedings of the ACM 2010 Conference on Computer Supported Cooperative Work (2010)
10. Hughes, A., Palen, L.: Twitter Adoption and Use in Mass Convergence and Emergency Events. In: ISCRAM 2009: Proceedings of the 2009 Information Systems for Crisis Response and Management Conference (2009)
11. Vieweg, S., Palen, L., Sophia, L., Hughes, A.: Collective Intelligence in Disaster: An Examination of the Phenomenon in the Aftermath of the 2007 Virginia Tech Shootings. In: ISCRAM 2008: Proceedings of the Information Systems for Crisis Response and Management Conference (2009)
12. De Longueville, B., Smith, R.S., Luraschi, G.: OMG, from here, I can see the flames!: a use case of mining location based social networks to acquire spatio-temporal data on forest fires. In: LBSN 2009: Proceedings of the 2009 International Workshop on Location Based Social Networks, pp. 73–80 (2009)
13. Gruhl, D., Guha, R., Kumar, R., Novak, J., Tomkins, A.: The predictive power of online chatter. In: KDD 2005: Proceedings of the eleventh ACM SIGKDD international conference on Knowledge discovery in data mining, pp. 78–87 (2005)
14. Phelan, O., McCarthy, K., Smyth, B.: Using twitter to recommend real-time topical news. In: RecSys 2009: Proceedings of the third ACM conference on Recommender systems, pp. 385–388 (2009)
15. Wald, D.J., Quitoriano, V., Dengler, L., Dewey, J.W.: Utilization of the Internet for Rapid Community Intensity Maps. Seismological Research Letters 70, 680–697 (1999)
16. Wood, H.O., Neumann, F.: Modified Mercalli Intensity Scale of 1931. Bulletin of the Seismological Society of America 21, 227–283 (1931)
17. http://code.google.com/apis/maps/documentation/geocoding/index.html
18. Earthquakes, http://earthquake.usgs.gov/earthquakes/
19. The Great California Shake Out, http://www.shakeout.org

Detecting Leukaemia (AML) Blood Cells Using Cellular Automata and Heuristic Search

Waidah Ismail[1], Rosline Hassan[2], and Stephen Swift[1]

[1] Brunel University, West London, UB8 3PH, UK
{waidah.ismail,stephen.swift}@brunel.ac.uk
[2] Haematology Department, Universiti Sains Malaysia, Kubang Kerian, Kelantan, Malaysia
roslin@kb.usm.my

Abstract. This paper presents a method for the identification of leukaemia cells within images of blood smear microscope slides, which is currently a time consuming manual process. The work presented is the first stage of a procedure aimed at classifying the sub-types of Acute Myeloid Leukaemia. This paper utilises the techniques of Otsu, Cellular Automata and heuristic search and highlights a comparison between random and seeded searches. We present a novel Cellular Automata based technique that helps to remove noise from the images and additionally locates good starting points for candidate white blood cells. Our results are based on real world image data from a Haematology Department, and our analysis shows promising initial results.

Keywords: Otsu, Cellular Automata, Heuristic search, Hill Climbing, Simulation Annealing.

1 Introduction

Haematologists have concluded that the effectiveness of microscope analysis of human blood smears can be vastly improved by the use of techniques such as image segmentation, classification and white blood cell counts, specifically in the pathology of leukaemia [1, 2]. At the same time, there are difficulties in identifying the various types of blast cells because the diagnosis can be either Acute Lymphoblastic Leukaemia (ALL) or Acute Myeloblastic Leukaemia (AML) which indicates different treatment. With AML, there are 8 subtypes, M0 to M7, which can be differentiated on their morphological features. A counting procedure is needed that should cover over 20% of the immature cells (blast cells) in the marrow for the diagnosis of acute leukaemia.

Recently, computer technology has had a big impact on medical imaging technology. Whole slide digital scanners has made research on pathological image analysis more attractive, by enabling quantitative analysis tools to decrease the evaluation time pathologists spend on each slide. This also reduces the variation in decision making processes among different pathologists or institutions and introduces reproducibility [3].

This paper aims to help the medical doctors in the efficient detection of leukaemia cells. We employ new techniques based on Cellular Automata and heuristic search which can reduce the time taken by a haematologist in detecting leukaemia cells.

P.R. Cohen, N.M. Adams, and M.R. Berthold (Eds.): IDA 2010, LNCS 6065, pp. 54–66, 2010.

This paper is organised as follows: in the rest of this section we detail the motivation behind our paper; in section 2 we describe previous work in the area, section 3 details our proposed methodology for identifying leukaemia cells and section 4 explains in detail our methods. The data sets and experiments are presented in section 5 and are followed by section 6 in which we discuss the results. Lastly, in section 7, we draw conclusions and discuss future research.

1.1 Leukaemia

Blood cancer is a condition known as Leukaemia, and is a disease which has no known cause where the bone marrow produces large numbers of abnormal cells [4]. Diagnosis of blood cancer has been determined by observing the image of a blood sample through a microscope. According to [5] the analysis of white blood cell counts through microscope imagery can provide useful information the about patient's health. When viewing the image of white blood cells, especially for the diagnosis of leukaemia, there are problems in identifying the blast cells if the blasts are minimal in number, the staining of the cells is poor, or if the image is being viewed by an inexperienced morphologist, in these cases the diagnosis might be delayed or incorrect. These problems can also lead to fatigue amongst the medical staff involved with this procedure.

There are many types of leukaemia and each of them is classified according to the specified type of cell which is affected by the disease. The types of leukaemia are:

- Acute Lymphocytic Leukaemia (ALL)
- Acute Myeloid Leukaemia (AML)
- Chronic Lymphocytic Leukaemia (CLL)
- Chronic Myeloid Leukaemia (CML)

This research focuses on the detection of white blood cells within Acute Myeloid Leukaemia (AML) which is a serious illness caused by the abnormal growth and development of early granular white blood cells. AML begins with abnormalities in the bone marrow blast cells, the white blood cells that contain small particles, or granules. The AML blasts do not mature, and they become too numerous in the blood and bone marrow. As the cells build up, they hamper the body's ability to fight infection and cause bleeding. Therefore, it is necessary to treat this disease as soon as possible after diagnosis. The recognition of the blast cells in the bone marrow of the patients suffering from myeloid leukaemia is a very important step, it is followed by categorising it into subtypes which will allow the proper treatment of the patients. The clinicians have to identify these abnormal cells under the microscope in order to detect that a patient is suffering from leukaemia, after which they will need a sample from the patient's bone marrow to count the leukaemia cells (blast cells) to confirm the diagnosis [5].

AML are classified as M0 to M7 according to French-British Group (FAB) classification. The blast cells of these subtypes are different in size, shape, amount of cytoplasm, shape and amount of nucleus and the constituent in the cytoplasm. It is important to identify certain subtypes such as M3 (acute promyelocytic leukaemia) because the treatment is different from other subtypes and it is a good prognosis for the patient. However sometimes morphologists have encountered problems in classifying this subtype and have resulted in misclassification. Inter-observer variation in classification can lead to improper treatment for the patient, which can affect the survival rate of patients.

2   Previous Work

In this paper, we are using four techniques to detect possible leukaemia cells. We use **Otsu's method, Cellular Automata**, and the heuristic search methods of **Hill Climbing** and **Simulated Annealing**. There are a few papers which have attempted to detect white blood cells but not leukaemia cells. Most of the papers are based on morphological techniques. Previous work in [6] has concentrated on using the nucleus for classification through image segmentation. The sample images are extracted from an accredited image repository, the Atlas of Blood Cells Differentiation, which is highlighted in [6]. The datasets consisted of 113 images that contain 134 expert-labelled leukocytes (white blood cells). In [8] a colour gradient method to smooth the image is employed instead of using gray scale before applying a GVF (Gradient Vector Flow) snake based method. Scale-space filtering and the watershed algorithm were applied to colour images for detecting nuclei in [9]. This paper attempted to locate cell membranes, it required a few steps to apply edge detection but the case studies are different from leukaemia cells because leukaemia cells have different features. Another technique using eigen cells for detecting white blood cells was introduced in [10] but this study had limited success in correctly classify all of the white blood cells. Most of these approaches are based on colour images. However, in the case of overlapping cell there can be some problems. In [7] a histogram of pixel counts focusing on the touching cells was created and an edge cutting algorithm was then applied to separate the cells. This technique can be used for touching cells but not for overlapping cells. The technique is not possible to use in this project because cutting the cells will create different morphological features which might lead to incorrect classification.

Cellular Automata have been used in image processing for removing noise in pictures and modelling the development of tumours. This technique is used to transform one image into another. Cellular Automata models have been developed in three-dimensions to show tumour development. A number of studies involving Cellular Automata and cellular image processing have been in the area of tumour growth prediction via 3D simulation. [11, 12]. Cellular Automata can also reduce the noise in cellular images, e.g. in [13] plasma and red blood cells were removed from images.

Heuristic search and optimisation techniques have been previously applied to microscope imagery and the identification of leukaemia cells. Circle detection has been performed using genetic algorithms and sobel's method in [14] which detected circlers but not morphological features. In [15], they apply seed regions by using heuristic search based on the diameter of the cells which are less than 25um. This technique can be performed if the cells do not overlap or have no neighbours. Particle Swarm Optimization combined with Neural Networks was used to escape from local optimum in an application for detecting the colour nucleus in large-scale image data [16]. These ideas can be used as an extension to our research and can help in the clustering of the different types of leukaemia cells.

Our research uses Cellular Automata to remove noise such as plasma and red blood cells. At the same time, it identifies for each point in the image a representation of the shortest distance that point is away from the background. We use Cellular Automata to find the "best" starting point before proceeding to the heuristic search, which is used to search for the best circular regions representing the Leukaemia cells. For the heuristic search based methods we used the two techniques of Hill Climbing and Simulated Annealing.

3   Work Process

In this paper we present two heuristic search based techniques which are aimed at detecting candidate leukaemia cells within an image of a blood smear microscope slide. The difference between the two types of method is that we use a Cellular Automata to locate good starting points in our "seeded" method. Fig. 1 shows the flowchart consisting of the two methods with seeding shown at the top and random at bottom. In the seeded search, the process involves applying Otsu's method, running the Cellular Automata, detecting the starting coordinates, colour image clustering and coordinate overlap checking. With the random method, we use Otsu's method and then start at a randomly generated set of points. Lastly we use Hill Climbing and Simulated Annealing to find the best candidate leukaemia cells.

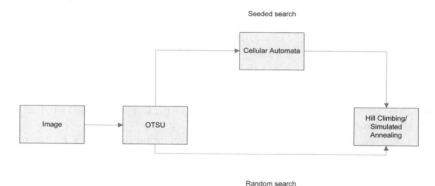

Fig. 1. Research Methodology Flowchart

4   Method

In the following sections we present the methods that we have used in this paper which are Otsu's method, Cellular Automata, coordinate detection, colour image clustering, checking for overlapping coordinates and lastly the heuristic search methods which are Hill Climbing and Simulated Annealing.

4.1   Otsu

We used Otsu's method for extracting objects from their background using the MATLAB image processing toolbox [17]. In applying Otsu's method we use a grey scale threshold for the separation of the two objects between the foreground and background. The results shown in fig. 3(b) and fig. 4(b) are the image with greyscales after applying Otsu's method.

4.2 Cellular Automata

Cellular Automata (CA) are a type of complex system that have very few parameters and are a development of Conway's game of life [19]. In this paper we use a CA to convert a black and white cell image to a matrix (the same size as the input image) where each point in the matrix represents the shortest distance each point in the image is away from the background. We represent the background as white (or "dead") and the cells body (as identified by Otsu) as black (or "alive"). To create the output "distance" matrix, we initially define $C(0)$ as the input image, we then create a series of matrices $C(i)$ where each $C(i)$ is the CA applied to $C(i\text{-}1)$. The CA itself works by looking at each pixel x,y; if the pixel is already "dead" it stays dead, otherwise its immediate adjoining neighbours (City Block distance of one) are examined. If any neighbours are "dead", the point itself becomes "dead" otherwise it remains "alive". We examine only the neighbours of each point, thus a corner point will only have three neighbours to examine. This process is repeated until all of the points within $C(i)$ are "dead" or white.

Throughout the procedure we maintain another matrix CP (the same size as the input matrix), where each x,y element represents the CA iteration that the point "died", i.e. turned from black to white. For example, if after 5 applications of the CA, which has created matrices $C(1)$, $C(2)$, ..., $C(5)$, point 100,200 "dies" (it was "alive" in $C(4)$ but "dead" in $C(5)$, then we set the element 100,200 in matrix CP to 5.

We hypothesise that the values in the CP matrix represent the shortest path between an "alive" point and a "dead" point. Therefore points within the CP matrix with high values represent dense areas of the input image and thus good starting points for locating the largest cells within the input image. An example of the visualisation of matrix CP can be seen in figure 3(c).

Once we have the CA image (the visual representation of matrix CP), we need to identify points of high value which are located next to each other, e.g. dense spots and areas. We first apply a rudimentary filtering based on the expected size (radius) of the five white blood cells (Neutrophil, Eosinophil, Basophil, Monocyte and Lymphocyte). From the literature, and on consulting expert opinion, we have identified that 8 micrometres is a reasonable demarcation between the size of red and white cells. Due to each image possibly being under varying magnification, we assume that the maximum value in the CP matrix corresponds to the size of the largest white cell, and apply a filter accordingly, i.e. we transform the matrix CP to a binary image based on this computed threshold, see fig. 3(d) for an example.

4.3 Detecting Coordinates

Now that we have an indication of where the regions of high density are (as shown in fig. 3(d)) we need to locate the centre of the regions so that they can be used as possible good starting points for locating the white blood cells, i.e. our "seeds". By producing row and column sums over the filtered image, we can define rectangular regions where horizontal and vertical non-zero totals intersect, as seen in fig. 3(e). Using these regions, we can determine the centre of the candidate dense areas, and thus define an x,y starting point. The intensity within the CP matrix at the point will be used as the starting radius r.

4.4 Colour Image Clustering

We now have a candidate list of starting points. We now perform an additional check to identify whether each point is identifying a leukaemia cell. We categorise the cells based on colour, that is how many points are pink i.e. plasma and red blood cells and how many are purple, that is leukaemia cells. Given the colour (three value RGB scale) of a pixel within the circle identified by each potential starting point, we see how close it is (using Euclidean distance) to either a pink or purple vector. Once we have categorised each point, we decide on whether we have a potential leukaemia cell based on whether the pink or purple counts are greater.

4.5 Checking Coordinate Overlap

Once we have detected the starting points, we need to ensure that these starting points do not overlap. Given the centre and radius of two circles, there are three possible states; the circles do not overlap, one circle is contained within another, and the circles overlap. We define a similarity measure which returns a value between 0 (the circles are separate) and 1 (the circles are identical), values in between represent how much of the circles overlap or are contained. We have omitted the derivation of this measure due to space constraints; however we note that it is simple to identify which state (as above) the two circles are in by examining the distance between the centres and comparing this against the two radiuses. The calculation of how much two circles overlap is evaluated by calculating the area of the overlapping segments using Pythagoras's theorem and the circle segment area equation [20]. If two circles overlap then we merge them. We acknowledge that this may not be the correct policy (it is if two circles are contained), but we are leaving this as a task for future work.

4.6 Heuristic Search

We use heuristic search to locate the best position of the required number of circles for each input image. We either have a number of random starting circles, or seeded starting circles depending on if we are using the CA or not. Each circle is represented as an x,y,r triple representing the centre and radius. We use Hill Climbing and Simulated Annealing, which are described in more detail in a later section. We use fitness function number 6 from table 1. The small generator for Hill Climbing and Simulated Annealing are the same, we choose either an x,y or r from one of the circles and randomly add/subtract (equal chance) a value between 1 and 50. Boundary checks are made to ensure that we do not move off the image. The seeded methods can identify the number of circles, however the random methods cannot, hence we set the number of starting circles for the random methods to the same number as the corresponding seeded method.

Table 1. Fitness Function Evaluation

Number	Method	Correlation
1	$F=\sum R(i)((B(i)-W(i))/(B(i)+W(i)))$	0.697
2	$F=\sum (B(i)-W(i))/(B(i)+W(i))$	0.782
3	$F=\sum (R(i)B(i))/(B(i)+W(i))$	0.721
4	$F=\sum (R(i)B(i))/W(i)$	0.879
5	$F=\sum B(i)/(B(i)+W(i))$	0.782
6	$F=\sum R(i)(B(i)+1)/(W(i)+1)$	**0.903**
7	$F=\sum B(i)-W(i)$	0.588
8	$F=\sum B(i)$	0.430

4.6.1 Experiments Finding Fitness Function

We tested a number of potential fitness functions methods before finally choosing the most viable fitness function based on 10 test cases that we ranked from worst to best using a single image. The idea is that we rate how good a potential circle is based on the number of valid points (white points from the black and white image) it covers. We performed a simple correlation analysis based on scale 1 to 10 from best to worst, based on a number of potential circles (we created a number of test cases that were easily ranked). We ranked the images by eye, and correlated the rank against image fitness. The aim was to choose a fitness function whose value agreed most with the ranking. Table 1 details the fitness functions we evaluated, the equations are in abbreviated form, the best performing function, and the one we use in this paper, is described fully in equation 1.

Within equation 1 and table 1, we define C as our list of circles, C_i as the ith circle and $|C|$ as the number of circles within C. $R(i)$ is the radius of circle i, $B(i)$ is the number of black points within circle i for a given image, $W(i)$ is the number of white points for a given image.

$$F(C) = \frac{R(C_i)\left(\sum_{i=1}^{|C|} B(C_i)+1\right)}{\sum_{i=1}^{|C|} W(C_i)+1} \tag{1}$$

4.6.2 Algorithms

The following sections describe the heuristic search methods of Hill Climbing and Simulated Annealing in more detail.

4.6.2.1 Hill Climbing. Hill Climbing is a local search procedure which utilises the concept of searching the neighbourhood of a solution for a better one. This technique iterates a number of times, each time a new point is selected from the neighbourhood of the current point. If that new point provides a better value of the evaluation function, the new point becomes the current point. Otherwise other points in the neighbourhood are selected and tested again. The main disadvantage of using Hill Climbing is that it often gets stuck in a local maxima during the search [21]. Below is the algorithm for Hill Climbing used in this paper.

```
Input: Black and White Image BW
       Number of circles N
       Number of iterations ITER
Create C = N circles (using CA or Random)
Let Fit = F(C) applied to BW (equation 1)
For i = 1 to ITER
    Create Cnew from C using change generator
    Let Fnew = F(Cnew) applied to BW
    If Fnew ≥ Fit
       Fit = Fnew, C = Cnew
    End if
End For
Output: Highest Fitness F and circles C
```

4.6.2.2 *Simulated Annealing.*
Simulated Annealing is a heuristic search technique which aims at improving the problems inherent in Hill Climbing. In Simulated Annealing a temperature is maintained which is used to determine the probability of accepting a worse point [21].

```
Input: Black and White Image BW
       Number of circles N
       Number of iterations ITER
       Start and end temperature TZero, TFinal
Define lamda (equation 2)
Create C = N circles (using CA or Random)
Let t = TZero, Let Fit = F(C)
For i = 1 to ITER
    Create Cnew from C using change generator
    Let Fnew = F(Cnew)
    Diff = fnew - fit, P = exp(Diff/t)
    If Fnew ≥  fit
         Fit = Fnew, C = Cnew
    Else
       If random value (0,1) ≤ P
          Fit = Fnew, C = Cnew
       End If
    End If
    t = lamda × t
End For
Output: Highest Fitness F and circles C
```

The parameter λ is calculated based on [18] shown in eqaution 2:

$$\lambda = \frac{\exp((\log(TFinal)-\log(Tzero))}{j} \qquad (2)$$

5   Data Sets and Experiments

We used ten images of leukaemia cells (AML). An example image is shown in Fig. 3(a) and Fig. 4(a). The images were 1280 by 960 in size. We executed each of the four algorithms 10 times for 10000 iterations; the repeats were so that any sampling bias is removed from the stochastic nature of the algorithms. We used the image data sets from Hospital University Science Malaysia (USM), Kota Bahru, Kelantan.

6   Results

This section shows all the results for the colour image clustering and heuristic search methods.

6.1   Colour Image Clustering

We clustered the pixels using Euclidean distance as described below. By using Euclidean distance we can determine whether a candidate cell is purple (a leukaemia cell (AML)) or pink (either plasma or red blood cells). We acknowledge that basing the clustering on colour alone is not the best method due to variations between image colourings that will change which can change overtime. The result of our methods is shown in table 2 and represents an overall accuracy of 91.5% by using clustering using colour. The outputs are shown in the fig. 3(f).

Table 2. Calculating the clustering for the 10 images

			Actual	
	Image		**Pink**	**Purple**
	1	Pink		
		Purple		3
	2	Pink	3	3
		Purple		
	3	Pink		
		Purple		2
	4	Pink		
		Purple		7
Predicted	5	Pink		
		Purple		5
	6	Pink		
		Purple		3
	7	Pink	11	3
		Purple		
	8	Pink	13	2
		Purple		
	9	Pink		
		Purple		4
	10	Pink		
		Purple		2

6.2   Check Coordinate Overlap

Hill Climbing and Simulated Annealing cannot be performed if the starting circles overlap. This program checks if the circles overlap based on the equation by [20]. A non-overlapping example is shown in fig. 3(f). If the starting circles are shown in fig 2(a) to overlap, then a new random set are generated as shown in fig 2(b).

6.3   Comparison Random/Seeded Hill Climbing and Simulated Annealing

Table 3 compares our four techniques which are Hill Climbing, Hill Climbing seeded, Simulated Annealing, Simulated Annealing seeded on the 7 images which are image 1, 3, 4, 5, 6, 9, 10. As for images 2, 7 and 8 the colour clustering did not target the leukaemia cells as stated in the Table 2. Overall, Simulated Annealing seeded achieves the highest fitness function value in 4 out of 7 cases.

Although Simulated Annealing random gained the highest fitness value in a number of images, it did not target the correct cells. This indicates that our fitness function probably needs improving upon; however, it does indicate that our seeding strategy works effectively. As shown in the final averages in the results table, Hill Climbing seeded has the highest value of all of the methods. This is a surprising result, since one would expect Simulated Annealing to out perform Hill Climbing. However as we are seeding Simulated Annealing, the search may deviate from the seeded point rapidly in the early stages of the algorithm, where Hill Climbing will always improve upon (or maintain) the fitness of the seeded starting points. The table below states the fitness function on which the equation is based (1).

Table 3. Data from Hill Climbing and Simulated Annealing

Image	HC	HCSeed	SA	SASeed	Max.
1	229796.20	2222000.00	94805.21	**2226000.00**	2226000.00
3	141609.90	1051636.00	**1334923.60**	967496.00	1334923.60
4	951630.35	3422380.00	**5260004.69**	3406880.00	5260004.69
5	784762.14	4174590.00	75808.42	**4239900.00**	4239900.00
6	809407.93	2880000.00	**4378871.82**	2884300.00	4378871.82
9	44192.84	3560000.00	189514.99	**3553350.00**	3560000.00
10	515361.48	2062600.00	905159.28	**2062600.00**	2062600.00
Average	496680.12	2767600.86	1748441.14	2762932.29	N/A

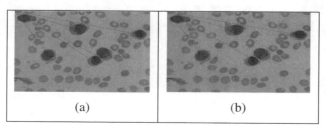

(a)   (b)

Fig. 2. Finding the new coordinate if the starting point circle are overlap

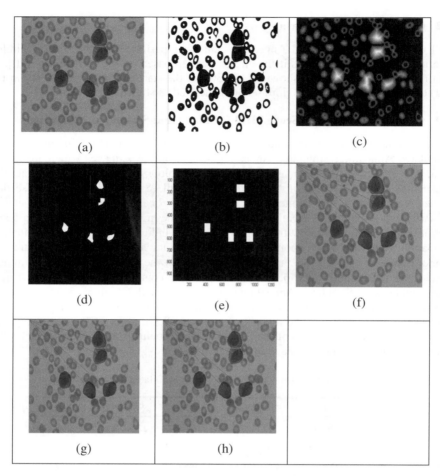

Fig. 3. The seeded search process for Hill Climbing and Simulated Annealing from colour image until detecting the leukaemia cell seeded

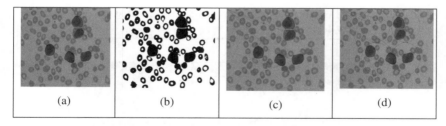

Fig. 4. Example Images from Stages within the Proposed Methodology, (a) Input Image, (b) After the Application of Otsu, (c) After the Application of Random Hill Climbing, (d) After the Application of Random Simulated Annealing

7 Conclusion

In this paper we have presented a comparison between random and seeded search for the location of potential leukaemia cells. With the random search methods, there were only three steps which consist of Otsu's method, random coordinate generation and the application of a heuristic search. The seeded method consists of more steps, which are Otsu's, Cellular Automata seed generation, coordinate location, colour image clustering, and heuristic search.

The Cellular Automata correctly identified good starting points for 7 images after filtering based on the minimum and maximum sizes of white blood cells. These preliminary methods need refining for the other images, and may have failed to work due to the quality of the images. On the 7 images that we applied our work to, an overall accuracy of 91.5% was attained. Our research has identified that the Cellular Automata approach produces excellent starting positions, and that Heuristic search can refine the positions, however, we need to improve our fitness function. Additionally our approach has some limitations when applied to images that contain overlapping cells. These two issues will be the focus of future work. Additionally, we will look into using the circle similarity metric to rate the repeatability of our experiments.

The Heuristic Search method of Simulated Annealing seems to achieve the best overall result but is more variable than Hill Climbing, thus Hill Climbing seeded tends to have a better average.

This research project is still in its infancy, with the overall goal being to identify the individual AML subtypes M0 to M7 using classification techniques such as Neural Networks (as in [6]) applied to the results generated by this paper.

Acknowledgments. We would like to thank the Islamic Science University of Malaysia and the Ministry of Higher Education, Malaysia for supporting this research and providing the scholarship.

References

1. Weinberg, R.: Robert Weinberg. In: One Renegade Cell, The Quest for the Origins of Cancer, London Weidenfeld & Nicolson (1998)
2. Uthman, E.: Blood Cells and the CBC (2000),
   http://web2.airmail.net/uthman/blood_cells.html
3. Hartley, T.D.R., Catalyurek, U., Ruiz, A.: Biomedical Image Analysis on a Cooperative Cluster of GPUs and Multicores. In: 22nd ACM International Conference on Supercomputing, Island of Kos, Aegean Sea, Greece. ACM, New York (2008)
4. Green, R.: Acute leukaemia (2005),
   http://www.netdoctor.co.uk/hearthealth/blood/
   leukaemiaacute.htm
5. Hassan, R.: Diagnosis and outcome of patients with Acute Leukemia. In: Haemotology department. Universiti Sains Malaysia, Malaysia (1996)
6. Puiri, V., Scott, F.: Morphological Classification of Blood Leucocyes by Microscope Image. In: CIMSA 2004 - IEEE International Conference on Computationvl Intelligence far Memrement Systems and Applications, Boston, MA. USA. IEEE, Los Alamitos (2004)

7. Ritter, N., Cooper, J.: Segmentation and Border Identification of Cells in Images of Peripheral Blood Smear Slides. In: The Thirtieth Australasian Computer Science Conference (ACSC), Research and Practice in Information Technology (CRPIT), Victoria, Australia. Australian Computer Society (2007)
8. Zamani, F., Safabakhsh, R.: An unsupervised GVF Snake Approach for White Blood Cell Segmentation based on Nucleus. In: 8th International Conference on Signal Processing, ICSP, Guilin, China (2006)
9. Jiang, K., Liao, Q.G., Dai, S.-Y.: A Novel White Blood Cell Segmentation Scheme Using Scale-Space Filtering And Watershed Clustering. In: Proceedings of the Second International Conference on Machine Learning and Cybernetics, Xi'an (2003)
10. Yampro, P., Pintavirooj, C., Daochai, S., Teartulakarn, S.: White Blood Cell Classification based on the combination of Eigen Cell and Parametric Feature Detection. In: Industrial Electronics and Applications, Singapore. IEEE, Los Alamitos (2006)
11. Moreira, J., Deutsch, A.: Cellular Automaton Models of Tumor Development: A Critical Review. Advances in Complex System 5, 247–267 (2002)
12. Bankhead, A., Heckendorn, R.B.: Using evolvable genetic cellular automata to model breast cancer. In: Genet. Program. Evolvable Mach., pp. 381–393 (2007)
13. Guieb, E.C., Samaneigo, J.M.: Image Noise Reduction Using Cellular Automata. In: CMSC, p. 190 (2007)
14. Ayala-Ramirez, V., Garcia-Capulin, C.H., Perez-Garcia, A., Sanchez-Yanez, R.E.: Circle detection on images using genetic algorithms. Pattern Recognition Letters 27, 652–657 (2006)
15. Nilsson, B., Heyden, A.: Model-based Segmentation of Leukocytes Clusters. IEEE, Los Alamitos (2002)
16. Fang, Y., Pan, C., Liu, L., Fang, L.: Fast Training of SVM via Morphological Clustering for Color Image Segmentation. In: Huang, D.-S., Zhang, X.-P., Huang, G.-B. (eds.) ICIC 2005, Part I, LNCS, vol. 3644, pp. 263–271. Springer, Heidelberg (2005)
17. Otsu, N.: A Threshold Selection Method from Gray-Level Histograms. IEEE Transactions on Systems, Man, and Cybernetics SMC-9, 62–66 (1979)
18. Swift, S., Tucker, A., Vinciotti, V., Martin, N., Orengo, C., Liu, X., Kellam, P.: Consensus clustering and functional interpretation of gene-expression data. In: Genome Biology 2004. BioMed. Central Ltd. (2004)
19. Levy, S.: Artificial Life. Vintage Press, London (1993)
20. Weisstein, E.: Circle-Circle Intersection (2009),
    http://mathworld.wolfram.com/Circle-CircleIntersection.html
21. Michalewicz, Z., Fogel, D.B.: How to Solve It: Modern Heuristics. Springer, Heidelberg (2000/2004)

Oracle Coached Decision Trees and Lists

Ulf Johansson*, Cecilia Sönströd, and Tuve Löfström

CSL@BS Research Group
School of Business and Informatics
University of Borås, Sweden
{ulf.johansson,cecilia.sonstrod,tuve.lofstrom}@hb.se

Abstract. This paper introduces a novel method for obtaining increased predictive performance from transparent models in situations where production input vectors are available when building the model. First, labeled training data is used to build a powerful opaque model, called an *oracle*. Second, the oracle is applied to production instances, generating predicted target values, which are used as labels. Finally, these newly labeled instances are utilized, in different combinations with normal training data, when inducing a transparent model. Experimental results, on 26 UCI data sets, show that the use of oracle coaches significantly improves predictive performance, compared to standard model induction. Most importantly, both accuracy and AUC results are robust over all combinations of opaque and transparent models evaluated. This study thus implies that the straightforward procedure of using a coaching oracle, which can be used with arbitrary classifiers, yields significantly better predictive performance at a low computational cost.

Keywords: Decision trees, Rule learning, Coaching.

1 Introduction

There are situations in predictive classification where interpretable models are required, thus limiting the choice of technique to those producing transparent models. It is, however, generally known that these techniques are weaker in terms of predictive performance than techniques producing opaque models, and yet predictive performance is usually of the utmost importance, both for obtaining accurate predictions from the model and because accurate models have higher explanatory value. In real-life applications, prediction is usually a one-shot event, where a model is painstakingly built using available training data utilized in various ways, and then the model is applied once, and only once, to previously unseen, production, data. Usually, the only important evaluation criterion in this situation is accuracy on the production data. The two main ramifications of the above are that:

---

* This work was supported by the INFUSIS project (www.his.se/infusis) at the University of Skövde, Sweden, in partnership with the Swedish Knowledge Foundation under grant 2008/0502.

P.R. Cohen, N.M. Adams, and M.R. Berthold (Eds.): IDA 2010, LNCS 6065, pp. 67–78, 2010.

a) all work that goes into building the model is really only preparation for the prediction using production data

b) all means of maximizing production accuracy should be employed during model construction.

Few methods are, however, explicitly geared towards this. Various techniques, like cross-validation, hold out available data in order to estimate production accuracy, instead of trying to take advantage of all the available data. The only commonly observed constraint is that *the data on which the model is evaluated must never be used to build the model*. In many cases, however, this constraint is overly restrictive. In some situations, the only unknown data are the *target values* for the production data; all input vectors for the production data are available when building the model, and this data usually consists of a substantial number of instances. A typical example illustrating this is when predictive classification is used to target recipients of a marketing campaign and the training data consists of past response data. Here, the very same customer signatures that will later be used as production data input vectors are available to the data miner and could therefore be used for the model construction.

The purpose of this paper is to suggest a very straightforward, and yet effective, way of increasing production accuracy for transparent models when production data input vectors are available. The proposed method thus requires that bulk predictions are made, and is unsuitable when prediction instances arrive one at a time. The method, drawing inspiration from rule extraction, semi-supervised learning and transductive learning, utilizes a powerful opaque model to label production instances, yielding additional training instances which are then used to build the transparent model. In this context, we name the opaque model the *oracle*, since the target values it produces are treated as ground truth by the training regime of the transparent model.

2   Background

A predictive classification model is a function f mapping each instance $\boldsymbol{x}$ to one label in a predefined set of discrete classes $\{c_1, c_2, \ldots, c_n\}$. Since a predictive classification model should be able to assign every possible input vector to one of the predefined classes, the model must partition the input space; i.e., the classes have to be non-overlapping and exhaustive. Normally, predictive models are obtained by applying some supervised learning technique on historical (training) data. Most supervised learning techniques require that the correct value of the target variable is available for every training instance. A training instance, thus, consists of an input vector $\mathbf{x}(i)$ with a corresponding target value $y(i)$. The predictive model is an estimation of the function $y = f(\mathbf{x}; \theta)$ able to predict a value y, given an input vector of measured values $\mathbf{x}$ and a set of estimated parameters θ for the model f. The process of finding the best θ values is the core of the data mining technique.

For predictive classification, the most important criterion is accuracy, i.e., the number of correct classifications made by the model when applied to novel data should be as high as possible. For situations where a black-box prediction machine is sufficient, most data miners will use techniques like *artificial neural networks* (ANNs), *ensembles* or *support vector machines*, which all have a very good track record of producing accurate models, in a variety of domains. All these techniques produce, however, opaque models, making it impossible to assess the model, or even to understand the reasoning behind individual predictions. When models need to be comprehensible, the most straightforward option is to sacrifice accuracy by using techniques producing less accurate but transparent models, most typically decision trees like C4.5/C5.0 [1] and CART [2], or rule sets like RIPPER [3].

In this paper, we study the situation where transparent models are mandatory and the input vectors in the production set are already determined and available when building the model. In real-world applications, this is actually a very common scenario, meaning that the predictive model is explicitly built for the prediction task at hand. In this exact situation, the unlabeled production instances, i.e., the very same instances that later will be used for the actual prediction, could also be used for building the model.

2.1   Related Work

Semi-supervised learning uses both labeled and unlabeled data when building the models. The main motivation for semi-supervised learning is the fact that labeled data is hard or costly to obtain in many applications, while unlabeled data is often cheap and easily accessible. The overall goal is, of course, to produce better (more accurate) models by using both labeled and unlabeled data, compared to using only labeled data. In most situations, the number of available labeled instances is much smaller than the number of unlabeled instances. It should be noted that semi-supervised classification is still inductive since a model is ultimately built and used for the actual classification.

Naturally, several fundamental approaches to semi-supervised learning, as well as numerous variations, exist; for a good survey see [4]. The simplest approach is *self training*, where a model is first built using the labeled data only, and is then used to label unlabeled instances, thus increasing the size of the labeled data set. This process is normally repeated several iterations, but eventually the final classifier would be trained on a combination of initially labeled instances and instances labeled by the intermediate models. So, simply put, the classifier uses its own predictions to teach itself.

Our approach is somewhat similar to self training, but there are two main differences: First we use one (stronger) classifier to label the instances, and another (weaker but transparent) classifier for the final model. Technically, we refer to this technique as *coaching*. Second, since the purpose is increased accuracy on a specific production set, we explicitly utilize the fact that we have the corresponding production input vectors available.

Transductive learning also utilizes both labeled and unlabeled data, and the overall purpose is similar to our approach; i.e., to obtain high accuracy on specific instances; see e.g. [5]. But the main difference is again that we explicitly focus on situations where the final model must be transparent, leading to a process where a stronger model coaches a weaker.

Rule extraction is the process of generating a transparent model based on a corresponding opaque predictive model. Rule extraction has been heavily investigated in the neural network domain, and the techniques have been applied mainly to ANN models; for an introduction and a good survey of traditional methods, see [6]. There are two fundamentally different extraction strategies, *decompositional* (*open-box* or *white-box*) and *pedagogical* (*black-box*). Decompositional approaches focus on extracting rules at the level of individual units within a trained ANN, while pedagogical approaches treat the opaque model as a black box. The core pedagogical idea is to view rule extraction as a learning task, where the target concept is the function originally learnt by the opaque model. Black-box rule extraction is, consequently, an instance of predictive modeling, where each input-output pattern consists of the original input vector x_i and the corresponding prediction $f(x_i; \theta)$ from the opaque model. Two typical and well-known black-box rule extraction algorithms are TREPAN [7] and VIA [8]. Naturally, extracted models must be as similar as possible to the opaque models. This criterion, called fidelity, is therefore a key part of the optimization function in most rule extraction algorithms. Most, if not all, rule extraction algorithms targeting fidelity use 0/1 fidelity, i.e., maximize the number of identical classifications.

An interesting discussion about the purpose of rule extraction is found in [9], where Zhou argues that rule extraction really should be seen as two very different tasks; rule extraction *for* neural networks and rule extraction *using* neural networks. While the first task is solely aimed at understanding the inner workings of a trained neural network, the second task is explicitly aimed at extracting a comprehensible model with higher accuracy than a comprehensible model created directly from the data set. The motivation for that rule extraction using neural networks may work is that a highly accurate opaque model often is a better representation of the underlying relationships than the set of training instances. One example is that training instances misclassified by the opaque model may very well be atypical, i.e., learning such instances could reduce the generalization capability.

But the opaque model is also a very accurate model of the function between input and output, so it could be used to label novel instances with unknown target values, as they become available. Naturally, the rule extraction algorithm could then use these newly labeled instances as learning examples. Despite this, no rule extraction algorithm that we are aware of use anything but training data (and possibly artificially generated instances) when extracting the transparent model. We have previously showed that the use of *oracle data*, i.e., production input vectors labeled by an opaque oracle model, could be beneficial for rule extraction [10]. In that study, we used our specialized rule extraction algorithm G-REX [11], but in this paper we extend the suggested methodology to general predictive classification. Specifically, only well-known and readily available classifiers are used in this study.

3   Method

As mentioned in the introduction, the purpose of this study was to evaluate whether the use of a high-accuracy opaque model (serving as a coaching oracle) may be beneficial for creating transparent predictive models. More specifically, decision trees and rule sets induced directly from training data only were compared to decision trees and rule sets built using different combinations of training data and oracle data. For simplicity, and to allow easy replication of the experiments, the Weka workbench [12] was used for all experiments[1]. In this study, two kinds of ensemble models were used as oracles, a large Random Forest [13] and a number of RBF neural networks, trained and combined using standard bagging [14]. For the actual classification, J48 and JRip were used since they represent what probably are the most famous tree inducer C4.5 [1] and rule inducer RIPPER [3], respectively. J48 obviously builds decision trees while JRip produces ordered rule sets. In the experimentation, all Weka settings were left at the default values for the different techniques.

For the evaluation, 4-fold cross-validation was used. The reason for not using the more standard value of ten folds was the fact that the use of only four folds results in what we believe to be a more representative proportion between training and production data. On each fold, the ensemble (the Random Forest or the bagged RBFs) was first trained, using training data only. This ensemble (the oracle) was then applied to the production instances, thereby producing production predictions; i.e., labeling the instances. This resulted in three different data sets:

- The *training* data: this is the original training data set, i.e., original input vectors with corresponding correct target values.
- The *ensemble* data: this is the original training instances but with ensemble predictions as target values instead of the always correct target values.
- The *oracle* data: this is the production instances with corresponding ensemble predictions as target values.

In the experimentation, all different combinations of these data sets were evaluated as training data for the techniques producing transparent models; i.e., J48 and JRip. In practice, this setup means that J48 and JRip will optimize different combinations of training accuracy, training fidelity and production fidelity. More specifically, we had the following seven different setups:

- Induction (I): Standard induction using original training data only. This maximizes training accuracy.
- Extraction (E): Standard extraction, i.e., using ensemble data only. Maximizes training fidelity.
- Explanation (X): Uses only oracle data, i.e., maximizes production fidelity.
- Indanation[2] (IX): Uses training data and oracle data, i.e., will maximize training accuracy and production fidelity.

---

[1] Our Weka OracleClassifier will be made available on our webpage.

[2] These describing names, combining the terms induction, extraction and explanation in different ways, are of course made-up.

- Exduction (IE): Uses training data and ensemble data. This means that if a specific training instance is misclassified by the ensemble, there will be two training instances for J48 and JRip, having identical inputs but different target values. So, here training accuracy and training fidelity are simultaneously maximized.
- Extanation (EX): Uses ensemble data and oracle data, i.e., will maximize fidelity towards the ensemble on both training and production data.
- Indextanation (IEX): Uses all three data sets, i.e., will try to maximize training accuracy, training fidelity and production fidelity simultaneously.

Table 1 below summarizes the different setups.

Table 1. Setups

Setup	Data			Maximizes		
	Train	Ensemble	Production	Train Acc	Train Fid.	Prod. Fid.
I	x			x		
E		x			x	
X			x			x
IE	x	x		x	x	
IX	x		x	x		x
EX		x	x		x	x
IEX	x	x	x	x	x	x

3.1 Experiments

This study contains two experiments. In the first experiment, J48 trees and JRip rule sets were built using an oracle ensemble consisting of 30 bagged RBF neural networks. In the second experiment, a Random Forest with 300 trees was used as the oracle. In the experiments, both accuracy and area under the ROC curve (AUC) were used for evaluation. While accuracy is based only on the final classification, AUC measures the ability to rank instances according to how likely they are to belong to a certain class; see e.g. [15]. AUC can be interpreted as the probability of ranking a true positive instance ahead of a false positive. For the evaluation, 10x4-fold cross-validation was used. The reported accuracies and AUCs were therefore averaged over the 4x10 folds. The 26 data sets used are all well-known and publicly available from the UCI Repository [16].

4   Results

Table 2 below shows the accuracy results for J48 in Experiment 1; i.e., when using bagged RBFs as the oracle. Comparing mean accuracies and mean ranks, it is very obvious that the use of production data paid off since IX, EX and IEX (combining production data with training or ensemble data) clearly outperformed the other setups. As a matter of fact, if these setups are explicitly

Table 2. Experiment 1 - Accuracy J48

	I	E	X	IE	IX	EX	IEX
Balance S	.783	.807	.862	.813	.868	.860	.858
Bcancer	.721	.718	.727	.723	.731	.725	.727
Bcancer W	.949	.953	.962	.951	.961	.963	.963
CMC	.508	.514	.515	.521	.528	.520	.526
Colic	.851	.827	.807	.847	.857	.843	.855
Credit-A	.854	.802	.795	.840	.847	.799	.820
Credit-G	.717	.721	.728	.731	.750	.739	.745
Diabetes	.743	.739	.757	.746	.759	.759	.754
Ecoli	.820	.820	.831	.819	.850	.846	.848
Glass	.676	.651	.682	.667	.715	.702	.706
Haberman	.707	.740	.743	.740	.731	.744	.737
Heart-C	.764	.774	.823	.765	.823	.816	.815
Heart-H	.787	.814	.828	.816	.823	.835	.836
Heart-S	.782	.791	.825	.783	.824	.837	.822
Hepatitis	.794	.813	.855	.801	.843	.848	.841
Iono	.894	.881	.911	.888	.924	.914	.918
Iris	.938	.941	.954	.944	.955	.955	.956
Labor	.766	.771	.858	.798	.852	.847	.855
Liver	.632	.621	.638	.631	.659	.646	.641
Lymph	.765	.777	.775	.764	.807	.799	.800
Sonar	.714	.691	.761	.694	.772	.771	.764
Tae	.548	.497	.503	.511	.525	.509	.516
Vehicle	.722	.654	.665	.691	.693	.666	.677
Vote	.963	.946	.946	.955	.960	.950	.956
Wine	.924	.923	.959	.925	.974	.973	.965
Zoo	.933	.933	.911	.942	.949	.949	.959
Mean	**.779**	**.774**	**.793**	**.781**	**.807**	**.800**	**.802**
Avg Rank	**5.37**	**5.92**	**3.94**	**5.00**	**2.02**	**2.98**	**2.77**

compared to standard J48 tree induction (the I setup), the results show that IX and IEX win 22 and lose 4 against standard J48, while EX wins 21 and loses 5.

To determine if there are any statistically significant differences, we use the statistical tests recommended by Demšar [17] for comparing several classifiers over a number of data sets, i.e., the Friedman test [18], followed by the Nemenyi post-hoc test [19]. With seven classifiers and 26 data sets, the critical distance (for $\alpha = 0.05$) is 1.77, so based on these tests, all three approaches utilizing the production data together with training or ensemble data obtained significantly higher accuracies than the three approaches using only training or ensemble data. Furthermore, it is interesting to observe that augmenting the production data with training data only is the best setup overall, clearly outperforming even the other setups also using production data.

Table 3 below shows the AUC results for J48 utilizing bagged RBFs as the oracle.

Table 3. Experiment 1 - AUC J48

	I	E	X	IE	IX	EX	IEX
Balance S	.86	.88	.93	.88	.93	.94	.94
Bcancer	.60	.61	.62	.61	.62	.61	.62
Bcancer W	.96	.95	.97	.96	.97	.96	.97
CMC	.69	.66	.66	.71	.71	.66	.71
Colic	.83	.81	.80	.84	.85	.83	.84
Credit-A	.87	.84	.81	.91	.88	.84	.90
Credit-G	.67	.69	.65	.71	.70	.71	.72
Diabetes	.74	.69	.71	.76	.76	.71	.76
Ecoli	.96	.96	.96	.96	.97	.97	.97
Glass	.81	.76	.80	.81	.81	.78	.84
Haberman	.54	.57	.57	.57	.56	.57	.57
Heart-C	.77	.77	.83	.78	.83	.83	.84
Heart-H	.76	.78	.81	.79	.81	.82	.82
Heart-S	.78	.80	.83	.79	.82	.84	.85
Hepatitis	.66	.71	.76	.69	.76	.77	.76
Iono	.88	.87	.91	.88	.92	.92	.92
Iris	.99	.99	1.00	.99	1.00	1.00	1.00
Labor	.73	.73	.85	.77	.85	.84	.83
Liver	.62	.59	.62	.62	.64	.62	.63
Lymph	.79	.78	.81	.80	.83	.80	.82
Sonar	.72	.69	.77	.71	.77	.77	.77
Tae	.72	.69	.69	.71	.73	.69	.71
Vehicle	.77	.66	.68	.79	.73	.68	.79
Vote	.98	.97	.96	.97	.97	.97	.97
Wine	.96	.95	.98	.96	.99	.99	.98
Zoo	.99	.99	.98	.99	.99	.99	1.00
Mean	**.79**	**.78**	**.81**	**.81**	**.82**	**.81**	**.83**
Avg Rank	**5.13**	**5.90**	**4.35**	**4.19**	**2.65**	**3.62**	**2.15**

Although the mean AUCs over all data sets appear to indicate that all setups performed similarly, the mean ranks give a more detailed and completely different picture. Most importantly, the results clearly show that the use of production data is beneficial also when considering the ranking ability of the models. Looking for statistically significant differences, the differences in mean ranks show that IX and IEX both obtained significantly higher AUCs than standard J48 (I). A closer inspection shows that even if the differences are quite small, the successful approaches have slightly higher AUCs on almost all data sets compared to normal induction. As an example, a pairwise comparison between IX and I shows 23 outright wins for IX and only 2 for I.

Table 4 below shows a summary of accuracy and AUC results for JRip using bagged RBFs as the oracle. Looking at the average ranks on accuracy, IX and IEX are clearly superior to all the other setups. A further analysis shows that IX and IEX obtained significantly higher accuracies than the three setups not utilizing the production data, also when using JRip as classifier. In addition, the two setups combining production data with training data were actually significantly more accurate than setup X, i.e., utilizing only production data. Finally, the difference between EX and I is also statistically significant. The AUC results when using JRip for the classification are quite similar to the J48 results. Here, however, all three setups combining the production data with either training or ensemble data are significantly better than standard JRip (I). In addition, IX, EX and IEX also obtained significantly higher AUCs than both E and X.

Table 4. Experiment 1 - JRip Transparent Model

		I	E	X	IE	IX	EX	IEX
Accuracy	Mean	.775	.772	.780	.785	.800	.796	.802
	Avg Rank	5.12	6.15	4.63	4.35	2.35	3.02	2.38
AUC	Mean	.79	.78	.79	.80	.81	.81	.82
	Avg Rank	4.85	5.73	5.00	4.27	2.62	3.08	2.46

Summarizing Experiment 1, by looking at Table 5 below, where a + indicates a statistically significant difference based on the Nemenyi post-hoc test, the most important result is that the setups combining training data with production data (IX and IEX) obtained significantly higher accuracy and AUC compared to standard model induction (I), both when using J48 and JRip as the actual classifier. In addition, IE and IEX also had significantly better results on a large majority of the data sets compared to X, clearly indicating that building the model using only production data is an inferior choice.

Table 5. Experiment 1 - Significant differences

	I				X			
	J48		Jrip		J48		Jrip	
	Acc	Auc	Acc	Auc	Acc	Auc	Acc	Auc
IX	+	+	+	+	+		+	+
EX	+		+					+
IEX	+	+	+	+		+	+	+

Table 6 below shows a summary of the results from Experiment 2; i.e., when using a 300 tree Random Forest as the oracle. Looking at the J48 mean accuracies and mean ranks, there is a clear ordering showing that IX and EX (using training or ensemble data together with the production data) outperformed X and IEX (using only production data or all three data sets) which in turn outperformed the approaches not utilizing the production data at all, i.e., I, E and IE. Comparing I with E and IX with EX, the obtained accuracies are identical on most data sets. The explanation is that the large Random Forrest managed to obtain perfect training accuracy quite often, thus making the ensemble data identical to the training data. The average ranks for JRip accuracy show that IX and EX are clearly superior to all the other setups. As a matter of fact, the results show that IX and EX obtained significantly higher accuracies than all setups not utilizing the production data. In addition, the two setups utilizing the production data together with either training or ensemble data were significantly more accurate than setup X, i.e., utilizing only production data.

Looking at the AUC results for J48 using the Random Forest as oracle, the picture is familiar. Here, the two best setups are IX and EX, both obtaining significantly higher AUCs than all setups not using the production data, including, of course, normal use of J48 (I). The AUC results when using JRip as classifier, finally, are quite similar to the J48 results. The only difference is that IEX here outperforms both IX and EX. Again, all three setups combining the production data, with either training or ensemble data, are significantly better than setups not using the production data.

Table 6. Experiment 2 - Summary

			I	E	X	IE	IX	EX	IEX
Accuracy	**J48**	**Mean**	.779	.779	.802	.773	.813	.812	.805
		Avg Rank	5.42	5.50	3.38	6.17	1.85	2.12	3.56
	JRip	**Mean**	.775	.774	.787	.778	.804	.804	.807
		Avg Rank	5.35	5.50	4.15	5.81	2.27	2.21	2.71
AUC	**J48**	**Mean**	.79	.79	.81	.77	.82	.82	.81
		Avg Rank	4.83	4.87	4.10	5.98	2.35	2.33	3.56
	JRIP	**Mean**	.79	.79	.79	.78	.81	.81	**.82**
		Avg Rank	4.90	4.79	5.08	5.65	2.73	2.73	2.12

Table 7 below shows the statistically significant differences in Experiment 2. Again, setups using production data, together with training or ensemble data, performed significantly better than standard use of J48 or JRip. A small difference, compared to Experiment 1, is that when using J48 as classifier, building the tree using production data only actually performed relatively well.

Table 7. Experiment 2 - Significant differences

	I				X			
	J48		Jrip		J48		Jrip	
	Acc	Auc	Acc	Auc	Acc	Auc	Acc	Auc
IX	+	+	+	+			+	+
EX	+	+	+	+		+	+	+
IEX	+		+	+				+

The overall result from the two experiments is thus that the setups utilizing production data predictions obtained from the oracle almost always yield significantly better transparent models than normal induction. Furthermore, when using data from the oracle, the best results are obtained when combining production and training data.

5   Conclusions

We have in this paper suggested and evaluated a novel method for increasing predictive performance for transparent models. This method is suitable in the very common situation where the predictive model is built for a specific prediction task, and the input vectors for the actual production data are available already when inducing the model. The procedure consists of building a powerful opaque model, called an oracle, using the available labeled training data and then applying this model on the production instances to obtain predicted values which are used as labels. This oracle data is then combined in different ways with the training data to form a new training set for a classifier producing transparent models. The method is very general in that any opaque model can serve as the oracle and any technique producing transparent models can benefit from using oracle data during training.

The results show that using an oracle coach almost always yields significantly better predictive performance for the transparent model, compared to standard induction using only training data. This result is robust in that it holds for both transparent model representations used, i.e., J48 decision trees and JRip ordered rule sets, for performance measured either as accuracy or AUC and also for both types of opaque oracle models used. Regarding how to use the oracle labeled data, the experiments show that oracle data for production instances should preferably be combined with just the original training instances to obtain the best performance, but that other combinations also utilizing the oracle data were strong alternatives.

The overall conclusion is that the suggested method virtually guarantees increased predictive performance, compared to normal training, at a low computational cost. Oracle coaching is thus recommended if production input vectors are available when building the model, and the situation requires a transparent model.

References

1. Quinlan, J.R.: C4.5: programs for machine learning. Morgan Kaufmann Publishers Inc., San Francisco (1993)
2. Breiman, L., Friedman, J., Stone, C.J., Olshen, R.A.: Classification and Regression Trees. Chapman & Hall/CRC (1984)
3. Cohen, W.W.: Fast effective rule induction. In: Proceedings of the 12th International Conference on Machine Learning, pp. 115–123. Morgan Kaufmann, San Francisco (1995)
4. Zhu, X.: Semi-supervised learning literature survey. Technical Report 1530, Computer Sciences, University of Wisconsin-Madison (2005)
5. Joachims, T.: Transductive inference for text classification using support vector machines, pp. 200–209. Morgan Kaufmann, San Francisco (1999)

6. Andrews, R., Diederich, J., Tickle, A.B.: Survey and critique of techniques for extracting rules from trained artificial neural networks. Knowl.-Based Syst. 8(6), 373–389 (1995)
7. Craven, M.W., Shavlik, J.W.: Extracting tree-structured representations of trained networks. In: Advances in Neural Information Processing Systems, pp. 24–30. MIT Press, Cambridge (1996)
8. Thrun, S., Tesauro, G., Touretzky, D., Leen, T.: Extracting rules from artificial neural networks with distributed representations. In: Advances in Neural Information Processing Systems, vol. 7, pp. 505–512. MIT Press, Cambridge (1995)
9. Zhou, Z.H.: Rule extraction: using neural networks or for neural networks? J. Comput. Sci. Technol. 19(2), 249–253 (2004)
10. Johansson, U., Niklasson, L.: Evolving decision trees using oracle guides. In: CIDM, pp. 238–244. IEEE, Los Alamitos (2009)
11. Johansson, U., König, R., Niklasson, L.: Rule extraction from trained neural networks using genetic programming. In: ICANN, supplementary proceedings, pp. 13–16 (2003)
12. Witten, I.H., Frank, E.: Data Mining: Practical Machine Learning Tools and Techniques, 2nd edn. Morgan Kaufmann, San Francisco (2005)
13. Breiman, L.: Random forests. Machine Learning 45(1), 5–32 (2001)
14. Breiman, L.: Bagging predictors. Machine Learning 24(2), 123–140 (1996)
15. Fawcett, T.: Using rule sets to maximize roc performance. In: IEEE International Conference on Data Mining, ICDM 2001, pp. 131–138. IEEE Computer Society, Los Alamitos (2001)
16. Asuncion, A., Newman, D.J.: UCI machine learning repository (2007)
17. Demšar, J.: Statistical comparisons of classifiers over multiple data sets. J. Mach. Learn. Res. 7, 1–30 (2006)
18. Friedman, M.: The use of ranks to avoid the assumption of normality implicit in the analysis of variance. Journal of American Statistical Association 32, 675–701 (1937)
19. Nemenyi, P.B.: Distribution-free multiple comparisons. PhD-thesis. Princeton University (1963)

Statistical Modelling for Data from Experiments with Short Hairpin RNAs

Frank Klawonn[1,2], Torsten Wüstefeld[3,4], and Lars Zender[3,4]

[1] Department of Computer Science
Ostfalia University of Applied Sciences
Salzdahlumer Str. 46/48, D-38302 Wolfenbuettel, Germany
[2] Bioinformatics and Statistics
Helmholtz Centre for Infection Research
Inhoffenstr. 7, D-38124 Braunschweig, Germany
[3] Chronic Infection and Cancer
Helmholtz Centre for Infection Research
Inhoffenstr. 7, D-38124 Braunschweig, Germany
[4] Gastroenterology, Hepatology and Endocrinology
"Rebirth" Cluster of Excellence
Hannover Medical School
Carl-Neuberg-Str. 1, 30625 Hannover, Germany

Abstract. This paper delivers an example of applying intelligent data analysis to biological data where the success of the project was only possible due to joint efforts of the experts from biology, medicine and data analysis. The initial and seemingly obvious approach for the analysis of the data yielded results that did not look plausible to the biologists and medical doctors. Only a better understanding of the experimental setting and the data generating process enabled us to develop a more suitable model for the underlying experiments and to provide results that are coherent with what could be expected from our knowledge and experience.

The data analysis problem we discuss here is the identification of significant changes in experiments with short hairpin RNA. A simple Monte Carlo test yielded incoherent results and it turned out that the assumptions on the underlying experiments were not justified. With a Bayesian approach incorporating necessary prior knowledge from the biologists, we could finally solve the problem.

1 Introduction

A fundamental part of intelligent data analysis [1] is the combination of expertise in data analysis and in the domain from which the data originate. Both partners, the data analysis expert and the data expert must cooperate and develop a basic understanding of the other's scientific field. This is usually a learning process that takes time and can lead to failures in the initial phase that are seldom reported.

This paper describes an application where biological data from the so called third generation microRNA based shRNA (shRNAmir) technology were analyzed. The data come from mouse experiments and a goal of this project is the characterization of new

P.R. Cohen, N.M. Adams, and M.R. Berthold (Eds.): IDA 2010, LNCS 6065, pp. 79–90, 2010.

cellular signalling networks that are essential for regenerative processes of the liver. The results can lead to new pharmacological strategies for the treatment of patients with chronic liver damages.

The data are similar, but not identical to standard microarray experiments. In microarray experiments, measurements for two or more conditions are taken for the expression of genes and one is interested in identifying those genes with a significant change of expression. In contrast to standard microarray experiments our measurements are based on simple counting procedures requiring a statistical evaluation which is not as obvious as it seems at first sight.

This paper describes the whole process of modelling the problem with failures and success as a case study in intelligent data analysis. Section 2 describes the biological background and Section 3 provides a more abstract and formal definition of the problem. Sections 4 and 5 discuss two approaches that failed to explain the observed data in the end, leading to the finally successful model derived in Section 6. The final conclusions address open problems and future work that will be based on the ideas described in this paper.

2   Biological Background

Our research group is taking advantage of genetic approaches to study the regulation of liver regeneration. The liver has a tremendous potential to regenerate upon tissue damage by toxins or infection. It is unique that, in contrast to many other epithelial organs, differentiated hepatocytes, which normally reside in the G0 phase of the cell cycle, can, upon liver damage, re-enter the cell cycle and give rise to new hepatocytes. However, when chronic liver damage occurs (e.g. chronic viral hepatitis), there is eventually an exhaustion of the regenerative capacity of hepatocytes and only partial compensation by a stem cell compartment (bipotential liver progenitor cells). The consequence is chronic liver failure, which represents a major health problem worldwide. A unique system for conducting multiplex in vivo RNA interference (RNAi) screens for new positive and negative regulators of liver regeneration was developed. Combining a well characterized mouse model of liver repopulation with third generation microRNA based short hairpin RNA (shRNAmir) technology, we show that mouse livers can be stably repopulated with complex shRNAmir libraries [2,3]. RNA interference is a naturally occurring process, where the presence of double stranded RNA leads to a targeted degradation of a cellular messenger RNA which is sequence complementary to one of the two RNA strands. Since its discovery RNA interference is being used routinely to knock down any gene of choice in vitro as well as in vivo. The RNAi pathway can be harnessed in experimental systems by introducing shRNAs into a cell, which after processing by the internal enzymatic machinery releases a double stranded RNA such as an siRNA, which finally releases one strand. This strand can find a sequence complementary messenger RNA and triggers the degradation of the respective messenger RNA, thus reducing or abolishing the amount of corresponding protein.

Using our in vivo RNAi screening platform, we are characterizing new cellular signalling networks which regulate the proliferation of hepatocytes during chronic liver damage. It is the ultimate goal of our work to translate the obtained genetic information into new pharmacological strategies which can increase the liver's regenerative potential during chronic liver damage. Such therapies are holding the great promise to prolong patients' survival until they are eligible for definite treatment by liver- or hepatocyte transplantation.

For our experiments we used the mouse as a model organism. The mouse genome consists of approximately 30000 genes. For this study we used a focused shRNA library with 631 shRNAs targeting 301 genes. Therefore we have in average a coverage of 2 shRNAs per gene. The 301 genes were chosen based on frequent deletions in human HCCs (hepatocellular cancers).

631 shRNAs were introduced into mouse livers. The first half of those livers (n=6) were harvested directly after intrahepatic shRNA delivery. The second half of the population (n=6) underwent a protocol for chronic liver damage (intraperitonal CCl4 treatment) after shRNA delivery into the livers was accomplished. CCl4 induces cell death with subsequent compensatory proliferation of surviving hepatocytes. As mentioned above, in this setting hepatocytes containing an shRNA which confers a proliferative advantage will expand, whereas hepatocyes containing an shRNA whose gene knockdown confers a disadvantage under the conditions of chronic liver damage will be reduced in number over time. To quantify the representation of each shRNA in the whole population, we are using a PCR amplification protocol of all shRNAs in the population. PCR products containing the individual shRNA sequences are then subjected to deep sequencing. In average we are applying 8 - 12 million sequence reads per biological sample. Deep sequencing analysis yields the total number of sequence reads for each hairpin, which together with the total number of applied reads can be used to calculate the percent of representation for each shRNA in the population. If this procedure is done for the starting population (livers directly after shRNA delivery) and for the population after manipulation, both populations can be compared to find out whether a certain shRNA is enriched, stays unchanged or is depleted in the system. However, a straight forward analysis of shifts in shRNA representation is hampered by the fact, that strong changes of single hairpins mask smaller changes or suggest changes in unchanged hairpins. Therefore we needed to establish a specific analysis method for this approach to take the experimental setting into account.

The newly used statistical approach helped us to define bona fide candidates. Already preliminary experiments verified, that one highly enriched hairpin influences the hepatocyte proliferation under chronic liver damage in a positive way, recognized by several biological parameters, like survival.

3   Problem Formalization

In our experiments, short hairpin RNA (shRNA) [4] is attached to genes. Most of the genes will be marked by one specific hairpin, but some of the genes can also be marked by more than one hairpin. This is not just redundancy, but also related to different functions of the gene. We use a few hundred different types of hairpins in our experiments. The number of different types of hairpins will be denoted by h. We deal with a pool of more than 10^{12} genes. Some hairpins can be easier adapted to the corresponding genes, for others it is more difficult. Therefore, when marking the genes with the hairpins, we cannot say in advance, how successful the process is for the different types of genes. Therefore, we draw a sample – the sample size is usually a few million – from the pool of 10^{12} genes and count, how often we find each of the hairpins. Let m_i be the counts for hairpin i ($i \in \{1, \ldots, h\}$). The sample size is therefore

$$m = \sum_{i=1}^{h} m_i.$$

From the theoretical point of view, we draw m balls (genes) from an urn with more than 10^{12} balls of h different colours (types of hairpins) without replacement. Due to the large number of genes in the initial pool compared to the sample we draw, we can neglect the fact that we draw the sample without replacement and consider it as an experiment with replacement. In this way, we can assume that our sample originates from a multinomial distribution with h possible outcomes. We do not know the probabilities for the outcomes, but we draw a sample of size m. Of course, we could estimate these probabilities by $\hat{p}_i = \frac{m_i}{m}$.

After some time, the distribution of the hairpins might have changed and we repeat the experiment again. We do not necessarily draw a sample of exactly the same size. We draw now a sample of size n instead of m from the possibly changed multinomial distribution. We could estimate the probabilities for this multinomial distribution in the same way as before as $\hat{q}_i = \frac{n_i}{n}$ where n_i is now the count for hairpin i for the second sample. This implies $n = \sum_{i=1}^{h} n_i$.

We are now interested in those hairpins i for which the numbers have changed significantly, corresponding to up- or down-regulated genes.

4   The Seemingly Obvious Statistical Model and a Monte Carlo Test

In order to identify those hairpins for which the number has changed significantly from the initial to the final sample, we could apply a statistical test with the null hypothesis that the initial and the final sample originate from multinomial distributions with the same underlying probabilities, i.e. the null hypothesis would be $p_i = q_i$ for all $i \in \{1, \ldots, h\}$.

This test can be easily implemented as a Monte Carlo test [5]. We choose the combination of probabilities for the multinomial distribution that would generate the two samples with highest probability. The maximum likelihood estimator for this problem is obtained by joining the two samples and estimate the probabilities as $\hat{r}_i = \frac{m_i+n_i}{m+n}$. Then we draw two samples from a (pseudo-)random number generator for this multinomial distribution of size m and n. We now obtain simulated estimations $\hat{p}_i^{\text{sim}}$ and $\hat{q}_i^{\text{sim}}$ and can compare these with the estimates $\hat{p}_i$ and $\hat{q}_i$ from the original sample. If

$$\hat{p}_i^{\text{sim}}, \hat{q}_i^{\text{sim}} \in [\hat{p}_i, \hat{q}_i] \quad \text{or} \quad \hat{p}_i^{\text{sim}}, \hat{q}_i^{\text{sim}} \in [\hat{q}_i, \hat{p}_i] \tag{1}$$

holds, then $\hat{p}_i^{\text{sim}}$ and $\hat{q}_i^{\text{sim}}$ variate less than $\hat{p}_i$ and $\hat{q}_i$. In other words, if this is not the case, the difference between $\hat{p}_i$ and $\hat{q}_i$ can be explained by simple random variations in the two samples from the multinomial distribution with the same probabilities.

Of course, we have to repeat this test a large number of times, say 100,000 times. We can then check, how often in these 100,000 simulations condition (1) is satisfied for each hairpin. The proportion of the simulations where this condition is satisfied can be viewed as a (simulated) p-value. We carry out multiple testing here, since we run the test for all h hairpins in parallel. Therefore, a correction for multiple testing must be incorporated into the p-values. We use the simple Bonferroni correction [6] where we have to multiply the obtained p-values with the number of tests we have carried out, i.e. with the number of hairpins h.

Even after Bonferroni correction, more than 90% of the hairpins have a p-value smaller than 0.001. That would mean that more than 90% of the hairpins (or genes) have changed significantly from the initial sample to the final sample. This is in contradiction to all experiences biologists have and does not seem plausible. But what could cause this effect?

To explain this effect, we have to go back to our initial considerations that we do actually draw our samples from very large ($> 10^{12}$), but finite hairpin pools (or poulations). We have made the implicit assumption that the overall size of the pool remains stable which is an incorrect assumption. In order to illustrate the effect of a changing pool size, let us consider a simplified example with much smaller samples and hairpin pools. Assume, our original hairpin pool contains only three different types of hairpins, 1000 of each. So we have diminished the pool size to 3000 instead of the original more than $> 10^{12}$ hairpins in the pool. We draw a sample of size 30 from this pool. In the ideal case, we would obtain 10 representatives from each type of hairpin. Now assume that before we draw the final sample, the first and the second type of hairpin have not changed their quantity and remain at the level of 1000. But the third type of hairpin has increased from 1000 to 4000. So the final sample will be drawn from a pool of hairpins with 1000, 1000 and 4000 replicates from each type. If the final sample has the same size as the initial sample, in our example 30, we would expect in the ideal case to draw 5 hairpins of the first, 5 of the second and 20 of the third type of hairpin. So the counts for the initial sample were (10,10,10) and for the final sample (5,5,20) giving the impression that the quantities of all hairpins have changed (under the wrong assumption that the size of the pool has not changed).

For our real-world data this would mean that if a single hairpin with a high number in the initial sample would change significantly in quantity, the proportions of all other hairpins will be affected, even though they might not have changed in quantity. Therefore, we must take a possible change of the hairpin pool size in our model into account.

5   A Modified Approach

Assume the initial hairpin pool contains k_i^{init} replicates of hairpin i. We do not know these numbers and cannot even estimate them from the sample because we do not know the overall pool size $k^{\text{init}} = \sum_{i=1}^{h} k_i^{\text{init}}$. Since the samples we draw are quite large, we can at least assume that

$$\hat{p}_i \approx \frac{k_i^{\text{init}}}{k^{\text{init}}}$$

holds. The same applies to the final sample that contains the unknown number of k_i^{final} replicates of hairpin i. But we can also assume that

$$\hat{q}_i \approx \frac{k_i^{\text{final}}}{k^{\text{final}}} \qquad (2)$$

holds where $k^{\text{final}} = \sum_{i=1}^{h} k_i^{\text{final}}$

Assume that hairpin i changes from the initial to the final sample by the (unknown) regulation factor c_i, i.e. $k_i^{\text{final}} = c_i k_i^{\text{init}}$. With equation (2), we obtain

$$\hat{q}_i \approx \frac{c_i k_i^{\text{init}}}{\sum_{j=1}^{h} c_j k_j^{\text{init}}}. \qquad (3)$$

When we extend the right hand side of equation (3) by the factor $\frac{\frac{1}{k^{\text{final}}}}{\frac{1}{k^{\text{final}}}}$, we get

$$\hat{q}_i = \frac{c_i \hat{p}_i}{\sum_{i=1}^{h} c_j \hat{p}_j} \qquad (i \in \{1, \ldots, h\}) \qquad (4)$$

where we have replaced approximately in equation (2) by equal. We should choose the regulation factors c_i in such a way that equation (4) is satisfied.

Without any restrictions on the regulation factors c_i, one possible solution would be $c_i = \frac{\hat{q}_i}{\hat{p}_i}$. But this would mean that we explain the changes in the relative frequencies of the hairpins in the two samples by assuming that each hairpin has changed proportionally to the change of the measurements which does not go along with the considerations and the simple example we have provided in the previous section.

From the experience of the biologists we know that most of the regulation factors should be roughly 1. Therefore, we should try to find a solution for the c_i with as little deviations from 1 as possible. This can be formulated as an optimization problem. Minimize the objective function

$$L(c_1, \ldots, c_h) = \sum_{i=1}^{h} (1 - c_i)^2 \qquad (5)$$

under the constraints (4).

To solve this problem, we replace all variable c_i in the objective function (5) by using equation (4) from which we obtain

$$\frac{\hat{q}_i}{\hat{q}_j} = \frac{c_i \hat{p}_i}{c_j \hat{p}_j}.$$

This implies

$$c_i = \frac{\hat{p}_j \hat{q}_i}{\hat{p}_i \hat{q}_j} c_j$$

and for $j = 1$, we finally get

$$c_i = \frac{\hat{p}_1 \hat{q}_i}{\hat{p}_i \hat{q}_1} c_1. \qquad (6)$$

This simplifies the objective function (5) to

$$
L \;=\; (1 - c_1)^2 + \sum_{i=2}^{h} \left(1 - \frac{\hat{p}_1 \hat{q}_i}{\hat{p}_i \hat{q}_1} c_1\right)^2 \;=\; \sum_{i=1}^{h} \left(1 - \frac{\hat{p}_1 \hat{q}_i}{\hat{p}_i \hat{q}_1} c_1\right)^2. \tag{7}
$$

In order to find the minimum of this quadratic function, we compute the root of the derivative.

$$
\frac{dL}{dc_1} \;=\; -2 \sum_{i=1}^{h} \left(1 - \frac{\hat{p}_1 \hat{q}_i}{\hat{p}_i \hat{q}_1} c_1\right) \frac{\hat{p}_1 \hat{q}_i}{\hat{p}_i \hat{q}_1} \;=\; -2 \sum_{i=1}^{h} \left(\frac{\hat{p}_1 \hat{q}_i}{\hat{p}_i \hat{q}_1} - \frac{\hat{p}_1^2 \hat{q}_i^2}{\hat{p}_i^2 \hat{q}_1^2} c_1\right) \;=\; 0 \tag{8}
$$

This leads to

$$
c_1 \;=\; \frac{\hat{q}_1}{\hat{p}_1} \cdot \frac{\sum_{i=1}^{h} \frac{\hat{q}_i}{\hat{p}_i}}{\sum_{i=1}^{h} \frac{\hat{q}_i^2}{\hat{p}_i^2}}. \tag{9}
$$

With equation (6) we obtain the solution

$$
c_i \;=\; \frac{\hat{q}_i}{\hat{p}_i} \cdot \frac{\sum_{j=1}^{h} \frac{\hat{q}_j}{\hat{p}_j}}{\sum_{j=1}^{h} \frac{\hat{q}_j^2}{\hat{p}_j^2}}. \tag{10}
$$

From this equation it is clear that the regulation factors c_i only depend on the ratios of the relative frequencies $\hat{p}_i$ and $\hat{q}_i$, but not on the absolute frequencies. Therefore, a change from an initial count for hairpin i of $m_i = 2$ to a final count of $n_i = 4$ would be treated in the same way as a change from $m_i = 20,000$ to $n_i = 40,000$. But it is obvious that the chance that the change from $m_i = 20,000$ to $n_i = 40,000$ is a pure random effect is much lower than for the change from $m_i = 2$ to $n_i = 4$. Therefore, this simple model is also not suitable for our purposes.

6   A Bayesian Maximum Likelihood Approach

The approach described in the previous section has introduced a penalty for regulation factors deviating from 1, representing the idea that most of the expression values of genes (or hairpins) will not change. This actually represents prior knowledge on the regulation factors. Bayesian methods are designed to take such prior knowledge into account. Therefore we develop a Bayesian approach here with a prior that reflects the knowledge that normally the regulation factors will be close to 1.

   We slightly change the notation in order to handle up- and down-regulations in a symmetric way. If we just use a factor directly, then up-regulation corresponds to values from the infinite interval $(1, \infty)$, whereas down regulations lie in the finite interval $[0, 1)$. Therefore, we use the parametrization e^{c_i} for the regulation factors. In this way, up-regulation is equivalent to $c_i \in (0, \infty)$ and down-regulation to $c_i \in (-\infty, 0)$, so that up- and down-regulation are just a matter of the sign.

   We want to estimate the values for the regulation factors. As mentioned before, we have prior knowledge about the possible values for the regulation factors. This knowledge will be given by a prior distribution $f_{\text{prior}}(x)$. We assume that the priors are independent and that all hairpins have the same type of prior. How we choose the prior, will be discussed later on.

Let us assume that the estimates $\hat{p}_i = \frac{m_i}{m}$ for the probabilities of the multinomial distribution in the first sample are more or less correct. This means we have $\ell \cdot m_i$ hairpins in our original pool of more than 10^{12} hairpins. The constant ℓ is unknown, but independent of the hairpin i. Given the true, but unknown regulation factors e^{c_i}, we find a proportion of

$$q_i = \frac{e^{c_i} \cdot \ell \cdot m_i}{\sum_{j=1}^{h} e^{c_j} \cdot \ell \cdot m_j} = \frac{e^{c_i} \cdot m_i}{\sum_{j=1}^{h} e^{c_j} \cdot m_j}$$

of hairpin i in the final pool. Then the likelihood for drawing n_i replicates of hairpin i ($i \in \{1, \ldots, h\}$) from our final samples is, including the prior,

$$L(c_1, \ldots, c_h) = \prod_{i=1}^{h} f_{\text{prior}}(c_i) \cdot q_i^{n_i}. \tag{11}$$

Note that we have omitted the constant factor

$$\binom{n}{n_1! \cdot \ldots \cdot n_h!}$$

that is independent of the values c_i.

The log-likelihood is then

$$\ln(L(c_1, \ldots, c_h)) = \sum_{i=1}^{h} \left(\ln(f_{\text{prior}}(c_i)) + n_i \cdot \ln(p_i) \right)$$

$$= \sum_{i=1}^{h} \left(\ln(f_{\text{prior}}(c_i)) + n_i \cdot c_i + n_i \cdot \ln(m_i) \right.$$

$$\left. - n_i \cdot \ln \left(\sum_{j=1}^{h} e^{c_j} \cdot m_j \right) \right)$$

$$= -n \cdot \ln \left(\sum_{i=1}^{h} e^{c_i} \cdot m_i \right) + \sum_{i=1}^{h} n_i \cdot c_i + \sum_{i=1}^{h} \ln(f_{\text{prior}}(c_i))$$

$$+ \sum_{i=1}^{h} n_i \cdot \ln(m_i). \tag{12}$$

The prior should definitely be a symmetric distribution with mean zero, preferring no regulation at all and treating up- and down-regulations in the same way. We should choose an uninformative prior. There are various concepts of uninformative priors. Based on the principle of maximum entropy [7], we would have to choose a Gaussian prior for which we still have to fix the variance σ^2. There are, of course, other ways to define uninformative priors that are based on maximizing the entropy or the KullbackLeibler divergence of the posterior distribution or on the Fisher information

(Jeffrey's prior). For an overview on Bayesian inference and priors, we refer to [8]. To keep things simple, we stick to a Gaussian prior with mean $\mu = 0$.

$$f_{\text{prior}}(x) = \frac{1}{\sigma\sqrt{2\pi}} e^{\frac{-x^2}{2\sigma^2}}$$

Inserting this prior into the log-likelihood (12), we obtain

$$
\begin{aligned}
\ln(L(c_1, \ldots, c_h)) = & -n \cdot \ln\left(\sum_{i=1}^{h} e^{c_i} \cdot m_i\right) + \sum_{i=1}^{h} n_i \cdot c_i \\
& - \sum_{i=1}^{h} \left(\ln(\sigma) + \frac{1}{2}\ln(2\pi) + \frac{c_i^2}{2\sigma^2}\right) \\
& + \sum_{i=1}^{h} n_i \cdot \ln(m_i) \\
= & -n \cdot \ln\left(\sum_{i=1}^{h} e^{c_i} \cdot m_i\right) + \sum_{i=1}^{h} n_i \cdot c_i \\
& - \frac{1}{2\sigma^2}\sum_{i=1}^{h} c_i^2 \\
& + \left(\sum_{i=1}^{h} n_i \cdot \ln(m_i)\right) - h \cdot \ln(\sigma) - \frac{h}{2} \cdot \ln(2\pi).
\end{aligned}
$$

(13)

The last line of equation (13) does not depend on the unknown parameters c_i, so that it can be neglected for the maximization of the log-likehood. The log-likelihood (and also the likelihood) is maximized when the function

$$T(c_1, \ldots, c_h) = -n \cdot \ln\left(\sum_{i=1}^{h} e^{c_i} \cdot m_i\right) + \sum_{i=1}^{h} n_i \cdot c_i - \frac{1}{2\sigma^2}\sum_{i=1}^{h} c_i^2 \quad (14)$$

is maximized.

Determining the maximum of this objective function and in this way obtaining the maximum likelihood estimates for the regulation factors c_i is not an easy task. A closed form solution cannot be provided. We apply a gradient method here. We carry out the gradient method twice, using the two obvious and most extreme initializations. The likelihood function consists of two main parts. The priors that are maximized for $c_i = 0$, which is our first initialization, and the factors $q_i^{n_i}$ which are maximized when we choose the raw regulation factors, i.e.

$$e^{c_i} = \frac{n_i/n}{m_i/m} = \frac{\hat{q}_i}{\hat{q}_i} \quad (15)$$

which give our second initialization.

In this way, we obtain two (local) maxima of the likelihood function from the two initializations and in the best case these two local maxima should be more or less identical. This provides also a hint, how much we can trust our result.

We still have to specify the value for σ in our Gaussian prior. We estimate σ based on the raw regulation factors. We compute the values c_i based on equation (15) and estimate the standard deviation from these c_i values. Since we have some very extreme raw regulation factors due to very small counts for some hairpins, we do not estimate the standard deviation by the sample standard deviation, but based on the more robust interquartile range IQR of the values c_i, i.e. $\hat{\sigma} = 1.349 \cdot \text{IQR}$.

7   Results

First of all, it should be mentioned that we carry out Laplace correction [9,10] for the counting. This means that we replace the values m_i and n_i by $(m_i + 1)$ and $(n_i + 1)$, respectively. Of course, this changes the sums m and n to $(m + h)$ and $(n + h)$, respectively. Laplace correction is required, because there are experiments where the initial or the final count for some hairpins is zero. This would require $c_i = \pm\infty$ for our second initialization for the gradient method and would also cause problems in the likelihood function (11) when one of the initial counts m_i is zero. Then the likelihood function would become zero automatically when the corresponding final count n_i is nonzero.

To illustrate how our approach helps to obtain a more realistic picture about the regulation factors, we take a look at results from one of our experiments with $h = 400$ hairpins, an initial sample size of $m = 6,682,558$ and a final sample size of $n = 15,105,284$. Table 1 shows the results for some selected hairpins. The second column shows the initial count of the corresponding hairpin, the third column the final count. The fourth column contains the raw factor according to equation (15). Our maximum likelihood estimates based on the two above mentioned initializations for the gradient method can be seen in the last two columns.

Table 1. Some results from one of our experiments

hairpin no.	initial count	final count	raw factor	estimated factor init. $c_i = 0$	init. c_i = raw factor
1	47	2	−53.12	−18.05	−18.45
2	448	3	−337.55	−108.94	−111.56
3	3940	1534	−5.81	−5.64	−5.79
4	5178	25517	2.18	2.24	2.18
5	18980	43938	1.02	1.05	1.02
6	18385	44546	1.07	1.10	1.07

Negative signs of regulation factors indicate down-regulations. For instance, if equation (15) yields values like 0.5 or 0.25, we would not enter these values in the table, but the values −2.00 and −4.00 instead, respectively.

Most of our data look like the ones in the last two rows where we have more or less no regulation. A certain fraction of the hairpins shows a moderate regulation as for hairpin 3 and 4 in the table. The unregulated and the moderate (raw) regulation factors are confirmed by our approach.

The first two entries are more extreme concerning the regulation factors. Such extreme regulation factors can only occur when at least one of the two counts for the hairpin is comparatively small. Some of these extreme cases are very interesting from the biological and medical point of view. Although our approach still yields very large regulation factors, they are downsized to roughly one third compared to the raw factors.

Comparing the last two columns, the gradient method seems to yield quite similar results for the two extremely different initializations.

As mentioned already in Section 2, the statistical evaluation helped us to define bona fide candidate hairpins that influence the hepatocyte proliferation under chronic liver damage in a positive way.

8 Conclusions

We have a presented a typical experience in intelligent data analysis. In the beginning, the way how to analyze the data seems to be obvious. But it turns out that the initial simplified understanding of the question to be solved by data analysis and the modelling of the process that generates the data were not sufficient to provide suitable answers. Only with the joint expertise, in our case from biology, medicine and data analysis, a solution can be found in the end.

Our project is still in an initial phase. We are now in the process of analyzing data from repeated experiments and need to find out what causes sometimes extreme variations between experiments.

Apart from the estimation of the regulation factors that we have presented in this paper, we are now developing methods to compute confidence intervals for them.

We are also interested in using other priors. But a sensitivity analysis of our Gaussian prior with the respect to the parameter (standard deviation) σ has shown that the results do not change significantly when we vary σ in a reasonable range. Therefore, we would not expect significant changes when we use other priors.

References

1. Hand, D.J., Berthold, M. (eds.): Intelligent Data Analysis: An Introduction, 2nd edn. Springer, Berlin (2009)
2. Dickins, R.A., Hemann, M.T., Zilfou, J.T., Simpson, D.R., Ibarra, I., Hannon, G.J., Lowe, S.W.: Probing tumor phenotypes using stable and regulated synthetic microRNA precursors. Nat. Genet. 37, 1289–1295 (2005)
3. Silva, J.M., Li, M.Z., Chang, K., Ge, W., Golding, M.C., Rickles, R.J., Siolas, D., Hu, G., Paddison, P.J., Schlabach, M.R.: Second-generation shRNA libraries covering the mouse and human genomes. Nat. Genet. 33, 1281–1288 (2005)
4. Paddison, P., Caudy, A., Bernstein, E., Hannon, G., Conklin, D.: Short hairpin rnas (shrnas) induce sequence-specific silencing in mammalian cells. Genes Dev. 16, 948–958 (2002)
5. Zhu, L.: Nonparametric Monte Carlo Tests and Their Applications. Springer, New York (2005)
6. Shaffer, J.P.: Multiple hypothesis testing. Ann. Rev. Psych. 46, 561–584 (1995)

7. Jaynes, E.T.: Probability Theory: The Logic of Science. Cambridge University Press, Cambridge (2003)
8. O'Hagan, A., Forster, J.: Bayesian Inference, 2nd edn. Oxford University Press, Oxford (2003)
9. Cestnik, B.: Estimating probabilities: A crucial task in machine learning. In: Aiello, L.C. (ed.) Proceedings of the ninth European Conference on Artificial Intelligence, pp. 147–149 (1990)
10. Good, I.J.: The Estimation of Probabilities: An Essay on Modern Bayesian Methods. MIT Press, Cambridge (1965)

InfraWatch: Data Management of Large Systems for Monitoring Infrastructural Performance

Arno Knobbe[1], Hendrik Blockeel[1,2], Arne Koopman[1], Toon Calders[3],
Bas Obladen[4], Carlos Bosma[4], Hessel Galenkamp[4],
Eddy Koenders[5], and Joost Kok[1]

[1] LIACS, Leiden University, the Netherlands
knobbe@liacs.nl
[2] Katholieke Universiteit Leuven, Belgium
[3] Eindhoven Technical University, the Netherlands
[4] Strukton, the Netherlands
[5] Delft University of Technology, the Netherlands

Abstract. This paper introduces a new project, InfraWatch, that demonstrates the many challenges that a large complex data analysis application has to offer in terms of data capture, management, analysis and reporting. The project is concerned with the intelligent monitoring and analysis of large infrastructural projects in the public domain, such as public roads, highways, tunnels and bridges. As a demonstrator, the project includes the detailed measurement of traffic and weather load on one of the largest highway bridges in the Netherlands. As part of a recent renovation and re-enforcement effort, the bridge has been equipped with a substantial sensor network, which has been producing large amounts of sensor data for more than a year. The bridge is currently equipped with a multitude of vibration and stress sensors, a video camera and weather station. We propose this bridge as a challenging environment for intelligent data analysis research. In this paper we outline the reasons for monitoring infrastructural assets through sensors, the scientific challenges in for example data management and analysis, and we present a visualization tool for the data coming from the bridge. We think that the bridge can serve as a means to promote research and education in intelligent data analysis.

1 Introduction

In practical projects involving data, one often has to model and analyze complex, dynamic systems. An example of this, which is gaining importance, is the monitoring of infrastructural assets such as bridges, tunnels, etc. [1]. Nowadays, the use of advanced sensing and monitoring systems provides the opportunity to collect real-time information from such structures, in order to monitor their performance and to deduce relevant knowledge for decisions on their maintenance demand. Asset owners can use this information to assess the life time perspective of (crucial) infrastructural links and to plan the window within which maintenance can be conducted. When considering the stock of infrastructural assets in

P.R. Cohen, N.M. Adams, and M.R. Berthold (Eds.): IDA 2010, LNCS 6065, pp. 91–102, 2010.
© Springer-Verlag Berlin Heidelberg 2010

view of service-life assessment, monitoring and sensing systems are very valuable instruments that can be used to extract actual information about its condition and performance.

In terms of condition, sensor systems are mounted in or to structures that monitor the environmental as well as the internal condition. Environmental conditions are related to the climatic changes in which the structure has to be operational, and, in terms of performance, the external and internal actions acting on the structure are recorded. Long and enduring 24/7 monitoring systems are necessary that generate large amounts of data that needs to be evaluated in a smart way such that relevant changes in the data will be noticed and asset management systems will be informed and/or alarmed efficiently.

Managing the huge amounts of data, extracted from the monitoring systems, requires integral knowledge in the field of data management. The best representation for storing the data is not necessarily the best representation for the evaluation of the data. Intelligent Data Analysis is needed for the smart evaluation of data extracted from the degradation mechanisms. The ultimate challenge is to design, develop and optimize a data management system for measuring and reporting the actual performance of large infrastructural projects. Such a system should provide monitoring, notification and reporting services. The goal of such a system is to manage the output of sensors in an optimal way for infrastructure condition assessment.

In this paper we present the InfraWatch project. The goal of this project is to construct a data management system with the above properties for a particular infrastructural asset, the "Hollandse Brug", one of the Netherlands' major highway bridges. All the challenges mentioned above are present in this project. We present some initial experiments on the bridge data, and discuss the concrete challenges of this project and argue that it is interesting for the intelligent data analysis community for a variety of reasons. It contains important challenges, but it also provides an attractive and tangible environment for defining data analysis tasks, demonstrating the value of methods, and promoting research and education in intelligent data analysis.

In the next section we introduce the problem of infrastructural asset monitoring and the entailed requirements for data management and analysis on a general level. After that, we will zoom in on the concrete case of the Hollandse Brug.

2   Monitoring Infrastructure

In view of asset management of large infrastructural projects, monitoring the actual performance in real-time conditions is becoming indispensable. The actual performance of infrastructural assets in relation to their action loads (traffic, climate, etc.), is considered to be the key element for managing the maintenance requests and for the control of the budgets in the long run. Decisions made regarding the maintenance needs can be considered in view of the technical and economical perspective of an infrastructural asset, and even more importantly, in view of its functional perspective. Monitoring the performance of infrastructure requires (1) sensor systems to measure, and (2) data management and intelligent data analysis systems for dealing with the large streams of data coming from the sensors. Both are necessary to come up with an optimized system for condition monitoring. In the design of such a system, choices need to be made for

1. The type of sensors: depending on the used materials and other parameters, different types of sensors can be used to trace a structure's actual condition, i.e. sensors for chloride concentration, moisture content, carbonation, etc.
2. The placement of the sensors: the layout and the grid density for the sensors to be positioned in order to get a reliable response of the condition monitoring.
3. The data management: The data received from the sensors will need to be collected, processed and stored by the system and further processed. Results should be communicated by notification and reporting services.
4. Asset Modelling: In addition to the information coming from the data, for prediction of the condition of the asset in the future, modeling of (parts of) the assets is needed. The combination of the data-driven approach with computational modeling gives predictions about the condition of the asset in the future.

Points 1 and 2 are engineering decisions; from the data management and analysis point of view, we assume the type and configuration of sensors are given and we have no control over them. Point 3, data management, contains a number of challenges that hold for infrastructure monitoring in general, and we will discuss these here. The modeling methods relevant for point 4 will strongly depend on the concrete context. Therefore we will discuss point 4 in the next section, after we have introduced the concrete setting of the Hollandse Brug.

2.1   Data Management

Monitoring systems for infrastructural assets are continuously producing large quantities of data. Clearly, it is infeasible to store on location all sensor output at a high resolution, for example more than once per second. Still, for some applications, such detailed data may be required. At the same time, it is unrealistic to perform all computation required for data analysis on-site. Therefore, a sophisticated data management strategy will have to be developed that brings together computing power and the necessary data. This strategy will have to take into account local data collection at different time-resolutions, periodic replication to an off-line data warehouse, scheduled snapshots of intense measurement, as well as some amount of local data analysis for monitoring recent events.

Data collected in monitoring systems roughly serves two purposes:

1. Large scale data mining for analyzing patterns in the stream of sensor output or between different (types of) sensors, as well as analyzing trends over time, for example for finding so-called concept drift.

2. On-line data analysis of (to a certain degree) real-time data for monitoring
   the integrity of the infrastructure and detecting recent changes.

The first purpose may involve a large range of analysis techniques, and typically requires substantial computational resources. Therefore, this purpose entails the periodic downloading of recent measurement data to a data warehouse, where it can be massaged and analyzed at will. It seems unlikely that all sensor data will be stored at the highest resolution available, at least not for the entire life-span of the infrastructure/monitoring system. The data management system will therefore need to allow for sensor-dependent data storage that may also vary over time. For specific periods of interest, say a notoriously busy day of the year, one may be interested in intense measurement of data, to allow for specific integrated types of data analysis. The effect of varying traffic load on the infrastructure may be assessed by involving video-streams as well as vibration and stress sensors. On the other hand, the influence of weather may be analyzed on a much larger time scale.

The real-time monitoring will clearly have different data management requirements. Such a system component will be using a recent history of sensor output (say one day) to compare these to characteristics of load and infrastructure response over much longer periods, with the intent of detecting recent changes in this relationship. Obviously, this on-line tracking of changes in the infrastructure will have to be done on site, and therefore cannot involve huge amounts of computation. One intended approach is to analyze stress parameters over a longer period off-line, and detect significant patterns and key characteristics that represent nominal behavior of the infrastructure. These patterns may then be uploaded to the monitoring system (with the occasional update), where they can be used to compare to similar results obtained on the recently acquired sensor data. In this way, no large collections of data will need to be stored and processed on-site.

3   The Hollandse Brug

The InfraWatch project is centred around an import highway bridge that is already producing substantial quantities of data: the Hollandse Brug. This is a bridge between the Flevoland and Noord-Holland provinces and is located at the place where the Gooimeer joins the IJmeer (see Figure 1). The bridge was opened in June 1969. National Road A6 uses this bridge. There is also a connection for rail parallel to the highway bridge, as well as a lane for cyclists on the west side of the car bridge. In April 2007 it was announced that measurements would have shown that the bridge did not meet the quality and security requirements. Therefore, the bridge was closed in both directions to freight traffic on April 27, 2007. The repairs were launched in August 2007 and a consortium of companies, Strukton, RWS and Reef has installed a monitoring configuration underneath the first south span of the Hollandse Brug with the main aim to collect data for evaluating how the bridge responds. The sensor network is part of

Fig. 1. Aerial picture of the situation of the Hollandse Brug, which connects the 'island' Flevoland to the province Noord-Holland, and the adjacent railway bridge (top)

the strengthening project which was necessary to upgrade the bridges capacity by overlaying.

The monitoring system comprises 145 sensors that measure different aspects of the condition of the bridge, at several locations along the bridge (see Figure 2 for an illustration). The following types of sensors are employed:

- 34 'geo-phones' (vibration sensors) that measure the vertical movement of the bottom of the road-deck as well as the supporting columns.
- 16 strain-gauges embedded in the concrete, measuring horizontal longitudinal stress, and an additional 34 gauges attached to the outside.
- 28 strain-gauges embedded in the concrete, measuring horizontal stress perpendicular to the first 16 strain-gauges, and an additional 13 gauges attached to the outside.
- 10 thermometers embedded in the concrete, and 10 attached on the outside.

Furthermore, there is a weather station, and a video-camera provides a continuous video stream of the actual traffic on the bridge. Additionally, there are also plans to monitor the adjacent railway bridge.

Clearly, the current monitoring set-up is already providing many challenges for data management. For one, the 145 sensors are producing data at rates of 100 Hz, which can amount to a gigabyte of data per day. Adding to that is the continuous stream of video. Although the InfraWatch projects is in its early stages, data is already being gathered and under provisional monitoring. However, the current data available for analysis consists of short snapshots of stress and video data, that is being manually transported from the site to the monitoring location (typically an office environment or Leiden University). One of the aims of the project is to develop sophisticated methods for data management, as outlined in the previous section.

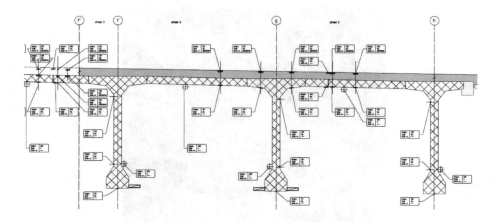

Fig. 2. Detail of the diagram explaining the individual sensor placement

Prior to the start of the InfraWatch project, an initial monitoring application was developed, that allows the visual inspection of both video and sensor information. The application allows the user to navigate through a selected time-frame, and watch the traffic passing over the bridge, while the data over one or more sensors is displayed in synchronised fashion. The user can select the nature of the sensor as well as the location of it, which does not necessarily have to correspond with the location of the camera. Using this application, it is fairly easy to already observe some patterns in the data. For example, the vertical load data nicely corresponds with heavy vehicles passing. However, more sophisticated data analysis should be developed in the course of the project, that also takes into account multivariate behaviour of the data, and spatial relationships between sensors, to name just a few options. In the next sections, we provide some suggestions for the range of analysis approaches this data allows.

4   Data Analysis

We need to distinguish two forms of data analysis: the first form, which we call model construction and which happens offline, consists of analysing data to find patterns in them; the patterns together form a model of the data. The second form, which we call model application, happens online and consists of checking whether the data stream is still consistent with the model. The Hollandse Brug data poses interesting challenges on both sides.

1) Model construction: much data mining research focuses on the model construction task. Many algorithms for detecting patterns in data, and constructing descriptive or predictive models from these patterns, have been described in the literature. The sensor data that we need to deal with here, however, have characteristics that render it impossible to use standard data mining algorithms. First, there is the *temporal* dimension. Each sensor essentially produces a time series of

data. Analysis of time series is a well-investigated problem. However, in this case we cannot analyse each time series on its own: relationships between different time series are relevant. A simple example of this is that a pattern might state that two particular time series normally correlate negatively; but patterns may actually involve much more complicated forms of relationships between (possibly more than two) time series. In addition, these time series may have a different granularity. It is currently not known how such data are best analysed. Second, there is a *spatial* dimension: the sensors are related to each other though their spatial location. The relative position of sensors may be indicated with a graph structure. In that case, patterns may involve combinations of graph structures and time series patterns (for instance, two sensors tend to correlate if they are the same type of sensor and are connected to each other in the spatial graph). It is not obvious how to represent such patterns, and a fortiori no algorithms for discovering them are known. Third, the data are *dynamic*: there may be concept drift, which implies that the patterns relevant at some point in time gradually become less relevant. Models should therefore be adapted regularly. But while a slow shift in the patterns may be normal, a sudden change may indicate a reason for alarm. The question is: how can we distinguish these two different cases?

2) Model application is an equally important task in this context. Model application will happen online, in real-time, with limited computational resources. It is crucial, then, that the developed models can indeed be applied efficiently. This is true for many, but not all models; for instance, for probabilistic graphical models it is known that inference is NP-hard, which makes it non-obvious that they can be applied in this context. The efficient applicability of the learned models is an additional constraint on the data mining task.

Viewed as a whole, we are confronted with data with a complex and evolving relational and spatio-temporal structure. Applying statistical, data mining and pattern recognition techniques to such data is a non-trivial task: there are open questions regarding the optimal representation of the data, how to represent the patterns, what algorithms can be used to detect these patterns in the data (again, existing algorithms will likely not suffice for this task), how to detect significant shifts in the patterns, and how to efficiently detect significant deviations of the data with respect to a given pattern. The development of suitable representations and algorithms to solve these problems is an important research task.

The format of the data and the way it is generated is clearly reminiscent of data streams. The context of this project is somewhat different than what is typically considered in data stream mining: for instance, due to the offline analysis of data, the usual constraints on data stream mining algorithms (namely, that model construction happens online) are less stringent here. This allows us to explore a wider range of algorithms. Nevertheless, it is clear that stream mining is relevant for this project.

In recent years there has been a growing interest in the study and analysis of data streams. Typical examples of such streams include continuous sensor readings. Traditional data mining approaches are not suitable for mining such streams, because they assume static data stored in a database, whereas streams are continuous, high speed, and unbounded. Therefore, streams must be analyzed as they are produced and high quality, online results need to be guaranteed.

Until now, most pattern mining techniques focus either on non-streaming data, or only consider very simple patterns, such as identifying the hot items from one stream, or constantly maintaining the frequencies in a window sliding over the stream. The challenging task is to extend the existing state-of-the-art into two, orthogonal directions: On the one hand, the mining of *more complex patterns* in streams, such as sequential patterns and evolving graph patterns, and on the other hand, more natural *stream support measures* taking into account the temporal nature of most data streams. Clearly, the classical pattern mining algorithms do not fulfil the constraints imposed on stream processing algorithms. Mining data streams, or stream mining, is therefore a challenging task.

The most popular techniques that have been developed so-far are randomization and approximation, sampling, sketches, and summaries. Randomization and approximation techniques render stream mining algorithms sufficiently fast, at the expense of no longer guaranteeing exactness. Sampling implies that a small sample of the data stream is taken, and costly algorithms are run on the sample. Sketches and summaries help dealing with the abundance of data by instead of storing the complete data stream, which is infeasible, a summary of the relevant features is kept that allows for answering queries about the stream approximately.

5   First Experiments

Although the InfraWatch project has only recently started, the sensor network has been up and running for more than a year. During this period, a number of experiments have been performed and specific samples of data have been collected. Some exploratory analysis has been performed to investigate what challenges need to be faced in different aspects of the structural modeling. This section gives some examples.

In theory, one can interpret 'traffic' as a series of discrete events, with events being a vehicle passing a particular point at a certain time. However, each individual event will appear to a vibration or load sensor as a signal over some period of time. This temporal spread of the signal is caused by three factors:

1. The physical size of the vehicle. As a vehicle will have a certain length, it will take some time to pass a particular sensor. One can safely assume that this factor is monotone in the length of the vehicle (in the direction of travel) and its speed.
2. The sensitivity area of the sensor. As the sensor is connected to a rigid part of the structure, any movement of the structure will be conducted along it, causing a change in signal of the sensor, even if the vehicle is not exactly located over the sensor. However the effect of the vehicle on the signal will diminish with the distance from the sensor. In effect, the area of sensitivity will act as a form of smoothing on the signal, producing a bump, rather than

Fig. 3. The 10 axle test truck that was driven across the bridge in the early morning

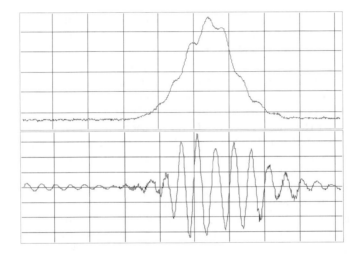

Fig. 4. Measurement of a load (top) and vibration sensor at the moment when the test truck was passing. Individual axles can be observed.

a single peak in the sensor data. The effect of this factor will differ between vibration and load sensors, with the latter being bigger, due to complete bridge sections carrying the load of a vehicle.
3. Specific physical properties of the structure, such as the resonance frequency of the bridge. Sudden events, such as a heavy vehicle entering specific sections of the bridge may cause the bridge to subtly sway at a specific frequency that is a physical property of the bridge, and that depends on structural characteristics, such as the size, weight and rigidity of each section. This resonance will cause a signal that starts at the vehicle passing, but that continues for some duration after the event. A Fourier analysis will reveal such dominant frequencies in the spectrum.

One of the essential tasks of the project is to match the continuous signals caused by these three factors with the discrete events of the actual traffic. One way to approach this, is to consider isolated events, and determine their effect in the sensor-space. Figure 3 shows two pictures of such an isolated test. Trucks were driven with a specific speed (ranging between 50 and 90 km/h) over the sensor network in the early morning, when regular traffic is sparse. Prior to the test, the weight and load distribution over the 10 axles was determined. Different loads were tested, to get a proper variation in examples. Using the resulting data, the sensor-network can effectively used as a Weigh-In-Motion (WIM) system [2].

Figure 4 shows the effect of a test run on both a load and a vibration sensor. The right graph also shows a subtle vibration of the bridge superimposed on the load signal. This vibration was determined to be approx. 2.5 Hz, over a period of one month. Sudden changes, or gradual drift of this resonance frequency can point to structural degradation of the bridge.

An alternative means of matching continuous signals with discrete events is to remove (or at least minimize) the variable of speed. Figure 5 (left) shows a situation of slow-moving traffic on the far lane of the bridge. By careful manual annotation of consecutive individual video-frames, one can determine the individual events, including some estimate of the size of the vehicle. The right graph shows the effect that the five highlighted vehicles have had on one of the strain-gauges. In such slow-moving conditions, the individual bumps can be identified, and matched to the video-stream. However, there will be a certain amount of 'stretch' in the signal, due to the intermittent nature of the passing vehicles. This will make the bumps vary in width in a manner that is somewhat independent of the length of the vehicle.

For the above-mentioned settings, annotation of the video-stream was performed manually, by carefully inspecting individual frames. In order to be able to process large periods of video and sensor-streams, we have been experimenting with automatic detection of vehicles in the images, using a technique for separating the background from the moving traffic (see Figure 6). This technique is flexible and robust, in the sense that it can deal with slight movement of the camera (due to wind and bridge movement), as well as with changing environmental situations (such as weather and lighting). The figure for example shows a rainy day, with a number of large water drops on the lens. Based on the detected location of moving objects, a further aggregation step identifies actual vehicles. The current implementations works fairly consistently, but a clear matching from blobs to events (especially over multiple frames) is still a major challenge.

6   Education Opportunities

Besides being an excellent research challenge and a complex fielded application of Data Mining techniques, the InfraWatch project and its Hollandse Brug are also intended to serve educational purposes [9]. Because of its practical nature, the project will, and has already been an important tool in the teaching of intelligent data analysis techniques to computer science students in the first place. Rather than the traditional focus on basic analysis techniques and algorithms,

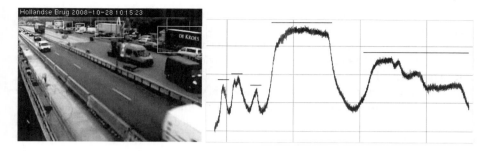

Fig. 5. Slow-moving traffic, and the corresponding output of one of the strain-gauges

Fig. 6. Estimating large blobs of moving objects: (left) the input image, (middle) the expected background over the recent past, (right) the estimated location of moving objects

we now have an opportunity to demonstrate the many complications that tend to arise in actual analysis projects [4,5], and how these should be tackled. These complications include the measuring of data (noise, sensor-failure, ...), the continuous flow of data (data volume, versioning issues, sample rates), the range of analysis paradigms (multivariate analysis, streams, relational aspects), and the inclusion of domain knowledge (spatial aspects, feature extraction). Apart from making the existing data analysis education more attractive and realistic, the project will also serve to attract potential students to analysis-related courses and computer science in general.

7 Conclusion

In this paper we have introduced the InfraWatch project, which has as main goal the setting up of an intelligent infrastructure monitoring system, in particular a data management and analysis system for the Hollandse Brug. It is clear that this system will have online and offline components, and the challenges involved are: determining which functionality is best offered online and offline, determining the optimal representation for online and offline data storage and processing, determining what kind of models are most suitable for this kind of systems, and developing the necessary data analysis techniques for constructing and applying such models.

We believe the project offers a very attractive environment for data analysis for students, scientists and experienced practitioners alike. It provides a tangible and even somewhat spectacular application, with challenges on all levels: students can try to analyse infrastructural data with existing techniques and see what they can find; practitioners can tackle a number of concrete challenges using their expertise on data mining; scientists can study the presented challenges in depth and develop novel techniques and approaches to solve them. Solving the problems defined within the project will require bringing together expertise from very diverse areas in intelligent data analysis, including data and knowledge representation, spatio-temporal data mining, graph mining, sequence mining, data stream mining, computer vision, data visualisation, and more.

Acknowledgements

The InfraWatch project is funded by the Dutch funding agency STW, under project number 10970.

References

1. Dejori, M., Malik, H.H., Moerchen, F., Tas, N.C., Neubauer, C.: Development of Data Infrastructure for the Long Term Bridge Performance Program. In: Proceedings of Structures 2009, Austin, USA (2009)
2. Doupal, E., Calderara, R.: Weigh-In-Motion. In: Proceedings of First International Conference on Virtual and Remote Weigh Stations, Orlando (2004)
3. Džeroski, S., Blockeel, H., Kompare, B., Kramer, S., Pfahringer, B., van Laer, W.: Experiments in Predicting Biodegradability. In: Džeroski, S., Flach, P.A. (eds.) ILP 1999. LNCS (LNAI), vol. 1634, p. 80. Springer, Heidelberg (1999)
4. Knobbe, A.: Data Mining for Adaptive System Management. In: Proceedings of PAKDD 1997, London (1997)
5. Knobbe, A., Marseille, B., Moerbeek, O., van der Wallen, D.M.G.: Results in Adaptive System Management. In: Benelearn 1998 (1998)
6. Meijer, G.: Smart Sensor Systems, Hardcover, 404 p. (2008), ISBN: 978-0-470-86691-7
7. Hastie, T., Tibshirani, R., Friedman, J.: The Elements of Statistical Learning: Data Mining, Inference, and Prediction. Springer, Heidelberg (2001)
8. Bessis, N.: Grid Technology for Maximizing Collaborative Decision Management and Support: Advancing Effective Virtual Organizations. University of Bedfordshire, UK (2009)
9. Gavaldà, R.: Machine Learning in Secondary Education? In: Proceedings TML 2008, Saint Etienne, France (2008),
http://www.lsi.upc.edu/~gavalda/docencia/tml08-revised.pdf

Deterministic Finite Automata in the Detection of EEG Spikes and Seizures

Rory A. Lewis[1,2], Doron Shmueli[1], and Andrew M. White[1]

[1] Departments of Pediatrics & Neurology, University of Colorado Denver,
Anschutz Medical Campus, Denver, CO 80262
[2] Department of Computer Science, University of Colorado at Colorado Springs,
Colorado Springs, CO, 80933

Abstract. This Paper presents a platform to mine epileptiform activity from Electroencephalograms (EEG) by combining the methodologies of Deterministic Finite Automata (DFA) and Knowledge Discovery in Data Mining (KDD) TV-Tree. Mining EEG patterns in human brain dynamics is complex yet necessary for identifying and predicting the transient events that occur before and during epileptic seizures. We believe that an intelligent data analysis of mining EEG Epileptic Spikes can be combined with statistical analysis, signal analysis or KDD to create systems that intelligently choose when to invoke one or more of the aforementioned arts and correctly predict when a person will have a seizure. Herein, we present a correlation platform for using DFA and Action Rules in predicting which interictal spikes within noise are predictors of the clinical onset of a seizure.

1 Introduction

Epilepsy is a neurological disorder that makes people susceptible to recurrent unprovoked seizures due to electrical disturbances in the brain. Unfortunately, 30% of patients that suffer from epilepsy are not well controlled on medication. Only a small fraction of these can be helped by seizure surgery [5]. Therefore, it would be life changing to a large number of individuals if a system could be developed that would predict a seizure hours, minutes, or even seconds before its clinical onset. The challenge in this problem is that the dimensionality is huge; in the human brain there are approximately 100 billion neurons, each with about 1000 connections (synapses)[28]. Even in the rat brain it is estimated that there are approximately 200 million neurons [4], [1]. The connections are wired such that the problem is highly chaotic. In a certain class of seizures it would be helpful if they could be detected even a few seconds prior to the start of a seizure. The dimensionality of the problem can be significantly reduced, with only a small loss of information by recording electrical potentials at multiple points on the surface of the skull or, using depth electrodes, in the hippocampus (EEG). EEGs are accepted as one of the best means of evaluating neurocognitive functions [15]. EEG spike/seizure detection and prediction is made more complicated by the

P.R. Cohen, N.M. Adams, and M.R. Berthold (Eds.): IDA 2010, LNCS 6065, pp. 103–113, 2010.
© Springer-Verlag Berlin Heidelberg 2010

following: (1) For a single individual, no two seizures or even their EEG corre-
lates are exactly alike, (2) seizures from different individuals vary significantly,
(3) there is no single metric that consistently changes during all seizures, (4) correlation among channels can change significantly from one seizure to the next,
and (5) even experts disagree as to what constitutes a seizure [27]. Occasionally,
the reduction in dimensionality does result in an indeterminate mapping from
EEG record to animal state (i.e. it is not surjective or onto). For the reasons
listed above, rigid seizure detection rules do not produce good results [7], [26].
Interictal spikes are brief (20 - 70 ms) sharp spikes of electrical phenomena that
stand out when compared to background EEG rhythms and may be indicative
of an underlying epileptic process. Because they are considered as an indicator
of the presence of epileptic seizures, and may actually precede a seizure (sentinel
spike), the detection of these interictal, transient spikes which may be confused
with artifact or noise is indeed a crucial element in the prediction of epileptic
conditions.

2   Recording Epileptogenesis

Until 1992 most EEG analysis was based on analysis of brain slices [14] or anes-
thetized animals [3]. Kainic acid, a chemoconvulsant extracted from seaweed, was
introduced to induce seizures in animals. This provided a major breakthrough
particularly with the advent of monitoring the animals on video, but the equally
significant subclinical seizures were impossible to detect with video monitoring
alone. The field was further advanced through the development of a tethered
recording system [2] in which multi-channel cortical and sub-cortical recordings
could be obtained. The quality of recordings were further improved by incorporating a small pre-amplifier close to the skull, allowing for a significant increase
in the signal to noise (S/N) ratio. As shown in Figure 1, electrodes were placed
stereotaxically in the hippocampus and secured in the skull [25], [24] Additional
electrodes were placed directly on the dura. Dental cement was applied to hold

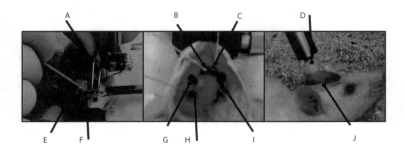

Fig. 1. *Implantable Tethered System Devices*: (A-D) Stereotaxic placement of cortical
electrodes. (E) Dental cement polymer applied to hold the electrodes in place. Note
dental cement on q-tip. (F) The tethered pre-amplifier connects to the implanted electrodes and sends the signals to Epilepsy Monitoring Unit).

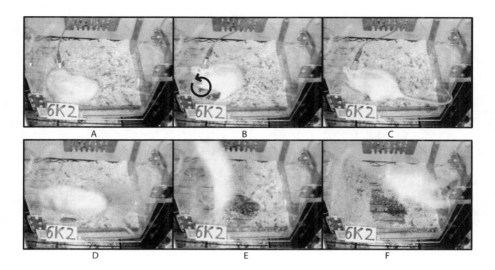

Fig. 2. *Rat 6K2*: Progression of a Clinical convulsive seizure: (A) Video capture shows the Rat to be in a normal sleeping stage. (B-C) Rat exits sleeping stage and starts having a p3 seizure (racine scale). (D-F) The seizure magnitude escalades and leads to a violent uncontrollable seizure - p5 (racine scale).

the electrode pins together in a plastic cap that was later connected to the pre-amplifier. The pre-amplified signal was sent to an amplifier and from there to a computer for storage.

Our facility has the capability of continuously monitoring up to 64 tethered or untethered rats. Untethered rats underwent video monitoring and the tethered rats underwent both video and EEG monitoring. This paper will discuss an algorithm for analyzing the EEG of a rats experiencing an event that evolves into a P5 Seizure [18] This event occurs somewhat infrequently, and we have collected EEG data set with three events that includes both the seizures and several minutes surrounding the events. As seen in Figure 2, a rat experienced a kainite-induced seizure that evolved from stage P3 to P5. In frame A, the rat was sleeping. In Frame B, 58 seconds later, the rat experienced a P3 seizure evidenced by the circular clawing (forelimb clonus). In Frame C, 28 seconds later, convulsive activity stopped and there was no epileptic activity on the EEG. Frame D was taken 1 minute later and at this point the rat began to experience a P5 seizure that lasted several seconds. Frames E and F were taken subsequently and demonstrate the intensity of the seizure. Not seen in this figure is that this rat was eating calmly shortly after the end of the seizure. The availability of EEG data for this seizure and 2 other similar seizures, along with video, allowed us to test the hypothesis that a novel deterministic finite automata (DFA) methodology will be able to differentiate the different aspects (sleeping, P3 seizure, between seizures, and P5 seizure) of the EEG record.

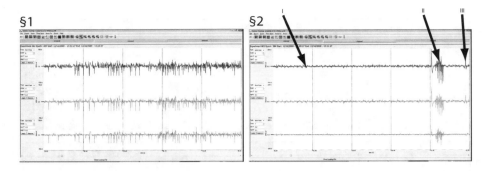

Fig. 3. *Rat p3 seizure (racine scale)*: §1: 6K2's EEG state correlating to Figure 2's Stage B denoted by circular clawing §2: I. Normal EEG wave-form while Rat is a sleep. II. Appearance of Sentinel Spike prior to P3 (Racine Scale) seizure. III. Possible Interictal Spike often misinterpreted as Artifact and vice-versa.

2.1   EEG Analysis

For our analysis EEG potentials were sampled at 800Hz. EEG electrodes were placed bilaterally in the hippocampi (referenced to a common dural screw) and a separate channel recorded from the dura. Each EEG contains a approximately 100,000 time points. As such, its interpretation is non-trivial and attempts at automating the analysis have met with only limited success. In this paper, we seek to demonstrate the efficacy of the DFA algorithm to distinguish all 4 states in each seizure event and distinguish artifact from interictal spikes and other noise. An author (RL) has begun to integrate statistical analysis with Action Rules [9], [19], [21] in Signals with a system influenced Dr. Zdzislaw Pawlak [17], [20], [23]. Fourier Action Rules Trees of signal distortion [10] and 3) Machine

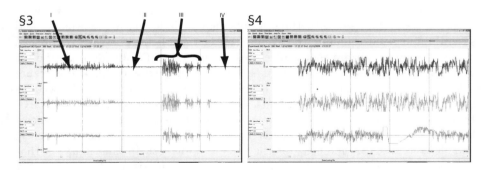

Fig. 4. *Rat P3's Seizure (Racine Scale)*: §3: *I.* A P3 (Racine Scale) seizure in progress. *II.* Period of no Electrographic seizing activity. *III.* Electrographic outburst indicating the violent seizure time. *IV.* End of Electroencephalographic seizure event. §4: Covers periods D, E and F in Figure 2 showing the EEG analysis while 6K2 experiences the P5 (Racine Scale) seizure *Figure 2*.

Learning with Signal Noise, Genetic algorithms [12] and FS-trees, Rough Sets, LERS, PNC2, J45, CART, & Orange. [11]

Figure 3§1 illustrates one rat's normal EEG wave-form while asleep. Point II in Figure 3§1 illustrates a Sentinel Spike, the hallmark indicator that a seizure is imminent. Point III in Figure 3§1 shows a region in which the EEG record deviates from baseline. An important task is to determine whether this deviation is simply artifact or if it represents epileptiform activity (an interictal spike) Figure 3§2 provides details of the P3 seizure. Figure 4§3 provides a zoomed-out overall view of all four stages and Figure 4§4 provides details of the P5 (Racine Scale) stage.

3   Methods

3.1   Deterministic Finite Automata (DFA)

Deterministic finite automata can be used in many applications. We used this methodology to track the current state of a finite-state EEG system. As time moved forward the particular system state would change dependent on such quantities as amplitude, slope, second derivative, Short-Term Fourier Transform STFT (average frequency) as well as other signal features. For the current analysis, programming was done using Visual Basic subroutines and data was stored using the European Data Format (EDF). At time zero we begin at state zero. The state at the next time step is assumed to be dependent only on the current system state and conditions (input state) during the current time step (e.g. slope). A consequence of this is that the current state is independent of the order in which the input states occurred (in this sense it is similar to a Markov chain).

Illustrative Example of our DFA Methodology. To motivate reader understanding we illustrate the concept of our usage of DFA using a simplified transition table given in Figure 5. The table in Figure 5 has a total of ten columns. The first column is the current system state. As one moves from one time point of the EEG to the next, the state of the system changes. The state to which the system changes is based upon the transition matrix; each of the columns in the transition matrix represents a current parametric set (e.g. slope within a particular range). More generally, the columns may represent a condition in which current or past parameters have specified values. It should comprise a collectively exhaustive and mutually exclusive set such that there are no events that either fall into multiple columns or do not fall into any of the columns. One proceeds from one system state at a given time point to the next system state at the next time point until a terminal event occurs. Terminal events can be the identification of spikes, seizures or artifact.

As mentioned previously, the first column of the transition table corresponds to the current system state. The particular input state at the current time (columns 5 - 10) is ascertained by investigating parameters at that time or at prior times. For this example, we have six mutually exclusive, collectively

State	# of 1/4	# of 2/5	# of 3/6	Input 1	Input 2	Input 3	Input 4	Input 5	Input 6
0	0	0	0	0	2	0	0	2	0
1	0	0	1	0	3	0	0	3	0
2	0	1	0	10	4	3	10	4	3
3	0	1	1	11	5	0	11	5	0
4	0	2	0	12	6	5	12	6	5
5	0	2	1	13	7	0	13	7	0
6	0	3	0	14	6	7	14	16	7
7	0	3	1	15	7	0	15	16	0
8	1	0	0	0	10	0	0	10	0
9	1	0	1	0	11	0	0	11	0
10	1	1	0	0	12	11	0	12	11
11	1	1	1	0	13	0	0	13	0
12	1	2	0	0	14	13	0	14	13
13	1	2	1	0	15	0	0	15	0
14	1	3	0	0	14	15	0	16	15
15	1	3	1	0	15	0	0	16	0
16	0	0	0	24	18	17	24	18	17
17	0	0	1	25	19	0	25	19	0
18	0	1	0	26	20	19	26	20	19
19	0	1	1	27	21	0	27	21	0
20	0	2	0	28	22	21	28	22	21
21	0	2	1	29	23	0	29	23	0
22	0	3	0	30	22	23	30	32	23
23	0	3	1	31	23	0	31	32	0
⋮									
n-1	1	3	0	0	30	31	0	32	31
n	1	3	1	0	31	0	0	32	0

Fig. 5. *Sample Transition Table*: where the number of possible states is 31, the number of states with slope too high required for rejection is 2, number of states required for slopes in the range for acceptance is 4, and the number of states with slope too low requiring rejection is 2

exhaustive input states. These are presented in Table 1 where α, β, and γ are limits selected by the authors using expert knowledge of what parameters would be characteristic of spikes. We note that states 4, 5 and 6 are the same as 1, 2,

Table 1. Six mutually exclusive, collectively exhaustive input states. Where α, β, and γ are user selected constants. States 4, 5 and 6 are the same as 1, 2, and 3 except that the second derivative is less then a given value.

	Input State Conditions		
1		$\mid m = \frac{y_2 - y_1}{t_2 - t_1} \mid \; > \alpha \; \wedge \; \mid f"(x) or \frac{d^2 y}{dt^2} \mid \; < \gamma$	
2	$\alpha > \mid m = \frac{y_2 - y_1}{t_2 - t_1} \mid \; > \beta \; \wedge \; \mid f"(x) or \frac{d^2 y}{dt^2} \mid \; < \gamma$		
3		$\mid m = \frac{y_2 - y_1}{t_2 - t_1} \mid \; < \beta \; \wedge \; \mid f"(x) or \frac{d^2 y}{dt^2} \mid \; < \gamma$	
4		$\mid m = \frac{y_2 - y_1}{t_2 - t_1} \mid \; > \alpha \; \wedge \; \mid f"(x) or \frac{d^2 y}{dt^2} \mid \; > \gamma$	
5	$\alpha > \mid m = \frac{y_2 - y_1}{t_2 - t_1} \mid \; > \beta \; \wedge \; \mid f"(x) or \frac{d^2 y}{dt^2} \mid \; > \gamma$		
6		$\mid m = \frac{y_2 - y_1}{t_2 - t_1} \mid \; < \beta \; \wedge \; \mid f"(x) or \frac{d^2 y}{dt^2} \mid \; > \gamma$	

and 3 except that the absolute value of the second derivative $(f''(x) \, or \, \frac{d^2y}{dt^2})$ is less than γ. The purpose of the use of slope $(m = \frac{y_2-y_1}{t_2-t_1})$ is to differentiate between the normal state, the possibility of a spike, and likely artifact (artifact, such as that noted when the animal is chewing, is often distinguished from spike because the slope is much greater).

The purpose of the use of $f''(x)$ is to ensure that there is actually a peak and not just a baseline shift. Columns 2 - 4 indicate the number of times that input states 1 or 4, 2 or 5. or 3 or 6 respectively have occurred. For example, looking at system state 12 one notes that there has been a single event in which the input state 1 or 4 existed, two events in which input state 2 or 5 existed and no events in which the state 3 or 6 existed. To register a spike, there must be two time points in which $(m = \frac{y_2-y_1}{t_2-t_1})$ falls in the range expected for a spike (input states 2 or 5), followed by one time point in which $f''(x)$ is high (input state 5) which corresponds to a peak, followed by two time points in which the slope again falls in the correct range (input states 2 or 5). This sequence must occur before one obtains two slopes greater than the range or two slopes less than the range. In this example a spike is indicated by system state 32. A heuristic definition can then be used to establish the seizure state by requiring a certain number of spikes in a particular time interval (e.g. 20 detected spikes in 10 seconds).

We now consider the sample path through the transition matrix illustrated by the chain of circles noted. For this sample the sequence of input states are assumed to be: $2, 2, 3, 1, 2, 5, 5, 5, 5$ We initially start with state 0, time interval 0.

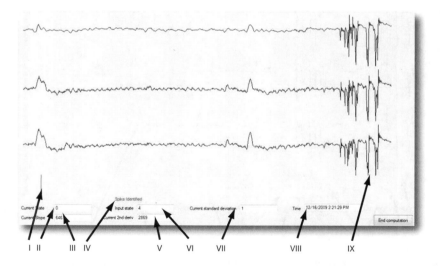

Fig. 6. *Correctly Detecting Spike*: Direct Screen Capture from Visual Studio Platform where *I.* Indicates red line programmed to identify the existence of pre-seizure spike. *II.* Current State. *III.* Current Slope. *IV.* Red "pop-Up" programmed to alert a pre-seizure spike is detected. *V.* Current 2nd Derivative. *VI.* Current Standard Deviation. *VII.* Input State. *VIII.* Time of Day, and *IX.* Beginning of correctly predicted Seizure.

At this time, the slope was calculated to be appropriate for a spike, i.e. $\alpha <|$ $slope \mid < \beta$, with the second derivative γ (input state = 2). As a result the transition matrix indicated a change to system state 2. For the second time interval the input state was calculated to be the same as that in the first time interval (input state = 2), and the transition matrix (row 3, column 6) indicated a change to system state 4. In the next time interval input state 3 was calculated and the system state of 5 ($row5, column7$) was determined. Subsequent input states could then be coupled with the current system states to draw a time path through the transition matrix. In this case, a spike is registered at the end of the path because state 32 is obtained at the end of the chain. Had there been too many slopes that did not meet criteria, the system state would return to zero (see for example system state 9, input state 1).

3.2   Results

For our analysis of the data we used the same six input states given in the example above. These used only the slope and standard deviation to determine the input state. The transition table was significantly bigger, having 336 entries. This required 7 slopes in the correct range, but allowed 4 slopes to be too great and 6 slopes to be too small to terminate a spike search sequence. A screen capture of the code correctly identifying a spike is given in Figure 6. Similarly, a

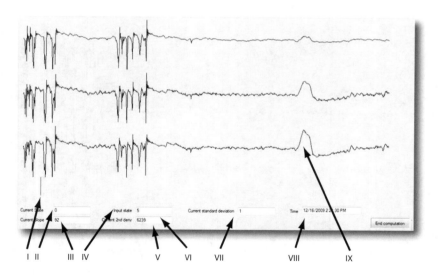

Fig. 7. *Correctly Detecting Artifact*: Direct Screen Capture from Visual Studio Platform where *I.* Indicates red line programmed to identify the existence of Artifact. *II.* Current State. *III.* Current Slope. *IV.* Red "pop-Up" programmed to alert a preseizure spike is detected. *V.* Current 2nd Derivative. *VI.* Current Standard Deviation. *VII.* Input State. *VIII.* Time of Day, and *IX.* Possible spike located visually. Programm soon detects it as a positive.

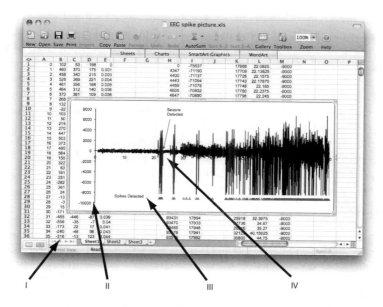

Fig. 8. *Results: Seizure Correctly Predicted*: Code correctly identifies a seizure 6 seconds before its onset. *I.* Excel Spreadsheet with CSV output. *II.* Excel built in graph. *III.* The Spikes Detected references and *IV.* Seizure Detected at location 6 seconds before onset.

screen capture of the code correctly rejecting artifact is given in Figure 7. The algorithm was quite successful at determining the presence of spikes and using the heuristic definitions of seizures ($> 20 spikes$ in $10 seconds$), was able to detect all seizures without difficulty. This determination was made within 6 seconds of the onset of the seizure. Figure 8 gives the EEG recording on which the detected spikes are indicated. Unfortunately, the code was unable, using only slope and standard deviation, to differentiate between either sleep and inter-seizure period or between the P3 and P5 portions of the seizure.

3.3 Conclusions

DFA is an extremely flexible platform that can be used to identify spikes and seizures and to sort various events that occur during seizures. The flexibility allows it to mimic and also use other techniques in its determination. In the present case, we have only scratched the surface of the true capability of the methodology. It is possible to greatly extend our analysis through the use of much more sophisticated input states. These could use algorithms such as Fourier series or wavelet analysis to determine the best path through the transition matrix. It is not restricted to linear analysis such as Neural Networks, Random Forest and Machine Learning's J45 to define strong classifiers for items such as Sentinel Spikes; it is also possible to use sequential non-linear analysis to establish whether or not spikes have occurred. By generalizing the input states to include past parameters, it is even possible to force the current state to be dependent on the path taken to get to the current state. The transition matrix can also be modified in such a way that multiple final deterministic states are possible (i.e. multiple end points could be identified). It is our plan to investigate further methods in which the DFA algorithm can be successfully employed. This includes the process of integrating KDD with the DFA methods and also considering the use of time domain analysis of EEG signal by statistical analysis and characteristics computation [13] with different frequencies [22], non-linear dynamics and chaos theory [8], and intelligent systems such as artificial neural network and other artificial-intelligence structures [6], [16].

References

1. Bandeira, F., Lent, R., Herculano-Houzel, S.: Changing number of neuronal and non-neuronal cells underly post natal brain groiwth in the rat. Proceedings of The National Academy of Sciences of the USA 106(33), 14108–14113 (2009)
2. Bertram, E.H., Wiliamson, J.M., Cornett, J.F., Spradlin, S., Chen, Z.F.: Design and construction of a long-term continuous video-eeg monitoring unit for simultaneous recording of multiple small animals. Brain Res. Brain Res. Protoc. 2, 85–97 (1997)
3. Buckmaster, P.S., Dudek, F.E.: Neuron loss, granule cell axon reorganization, and functional changes in the dentate gyrus of epileptic kainate-treated rats. The Journal of Comparative Neurology 385(3), 385–404 (1998)
4. Korbo, L., et al.: An efficient method for estimating the total number of neurons in rat brain cortex. Journal of Neuroscience Methods 31(2), 93–100 (1990)
5. Firpi, H., Goodman, E., Echauz, J.: Genetic programming artificial features with applications to epileptic seizure prediction. In: IEEE-EMBS 2005, 27th Annual International Conference on Engineering in Medicine and Biology Society, Shanghai, January 17-18, pp. 4510–4513 (2005)
6. Geva, A.B., Kerem, D.H.: Forecasting generalized epileptic seizures from the eeg signal by wavelet analysis and dynamic unsupervised fuzzy clustering. IEEE Transaction of Biomed. Engineering 45, 1205–1216 (1998)
7. Helliera, J.L., White, A.M., Williams, P.A., Dudek, F.E., Staley, K.J.: Nmda receptor-mediated long-term alterations in epileptiform activity in experimental chronic epilepsy. Neuropharmacology 56(2), 414–421 (2009)
8. Lehnertz, K., Elger, C.: Spatio-temporal dynamics of the primary epileptogenic area in temporal lobe epilepsy characterized by neuronal complexity loss. Electroencephalography And Clinical Neurophysiology 95, 108–117 (1995)
9. Lewis, R., Raś, Z.: Rules for processing and manipulating scalar music theory. In: Proceedings of the International Conference on Multimedia and Ubiquitous Engineering, pp. 819–824 (2007)
10. Lewis, R., Wieczorkowska, A.: Categorization of musical instrument sounds based on numerical parameters. June 28-30 in Warsaw Poland 4585/2007, 784–792 (2007)
11. Lewis, R., Zhang, X., Raś, Z.: Mirai: Multi-hierarchical fs-tree based music information retrieval system. June in Warsaw Poland
12. Lewis, R., Cohen, A., Jiang, W., Raś, Z.: Hierarchical tree for dissemination of polyphonic noise. In: Chan, C.-C., Grzymala-Busse, J.W., Ziarko, W.P. (eds.) RSCTC 2008. LNCS (LNAI), vol. 5306, pp. 448–456. Springer, Heidelberg (2008)

13. Litt, B., Esteller, R., Echauz, J., D'Alessandro, M., Shor, R., Henry, T., Pennell, P., Epstein, C., Bakay, R., Dichter, M.: Epileptic seizures may begin hours in advance of clinical onset. a report of five patients. Neuron 30(1), 51–64 (2001)
14. Molnar, P., Nadler, J.V.: Mossy fiber-granule cell synapses in the normal and epileptic rat dentate gyrus studied with minimal laser photostimulation. The Journal of Neurophysiology 82(4), 1883–1894 (1999)
15. Niedermeyer, E., da Silva, F.L.: Electroencephalography – basic principles, clinical applications & related fields. In: Niedermeyer, E., Lopes da Silva, F. (eds.), Williams and Wilkins, Baltimore (1999)
16. Pan, Y., Ge, S.S., Tang, F., Mamun, A.A.: Detection of epileptic spike-wave discharges using svm. In: Proceedings of the 2007 IEEE international conference on control applications. Suntec City, Singapore, pp. 467–472 (2007)
17. Pawlak, Z.: Information systems - theoretical foundations. Information Systems Journal 6, 205–218 (1991)
18. Racine, R.: Modification of seizure activity by electrical stimulation: Ii. motor seizure. Electroencephalogr. Clin. Neurophysiol. 32, 281–294 (1972)
19. Raś, Z., Dardzińska, A.: Intelligent query answering. In: Encyclopedia of Data Warehousing and Mining, pp. 639–643 (2005)
20. Raś, Z., Tzacheva, A., Tsay, L.: Action rules. In: Encyclopedia of Data Warehousing and Mining, pp. 1–5 (2005)
21. Raś, Z., Wieczorkowska, A.: Action rules: how to increase profit of a company. Principles of Data Mining and Knowledge Discovery 1910, 587–592 (2000)
22. Salant, Y., Gath, I., Henriksen, O.: Prediction of epileptic seizures from two-channel eeg. Medical and biolodical Engineering and Computing 36, 549–556 (1998)
23. Tsay, L., Raś, Z.: Action rules discovery system dear method and experiments. Journal of Experimental and Theoretical Artificial Intelligence 17(1-2), 119–128 (2005)
24. White, A.M., Williams, P.A., Ferraro, D.J., Clark, S., Kadam, S.D., Dudek, F.E., Staley, K.J.: Efficient unsupervised algorithms for the detection of seizures in continuous eeg recordings from rats after brain injury. Journal of Neuroscience Methods 152(1-2), 255–266 (2006)
25. Williams, P., White, A., Ferraro, D., Clark, S., Staley, K., Dudek, F.E.: The use of radiotelemetry to evaluate electrographic seizures in rats with kainate-induced epilepsy. Journal of Neuroscience Methods 155(1), 39–48 (2006)
26. Williams, P.A., Hellier, J.L., White, A.M., Clark, S., Ferraro, D.J., Swiercz, W., Staley, K.J., Dudek, F.E.: Development of spontaneous recurrent seizures after kainate-induced status epilepticus. The Journal of Neuroscience 29(7), 2103–2112 (2009)
27. Williams, P.A., Hellier, J.L., White, A.M., Staley, K.J., Dudek, F.E.: Development of spontaneous seizures after experimental status epilepticus: Implications for understanding epileptogenesis. Epilepsia 48 (Series 4), 157–163 (2007)
28. Williams, R.W., Herrup, K.: The control of neuron number. The Annual Review of Neuroscience 11, 423–453 (1988)

Bipartite Graphs for Monitoring Clusters Transitions

Márcia Oliveira and João Gama

LIAAD, FEP, University of Porto,
Rua de Ceuta 118, 4050-190 Porto, Portugal
http://www.liaad.up.pt

Abstract. The study of evolution has become an important research
issue, especially in the last decade, due to a greater awareness of our
world's volatility. As a consequence, a new paradigm has emerged to
respond more effectively to a class of new problems in Data Mining. In
this paper we address the problem of monitoring the evolution of clusters
and propose the MClusT framework, which was developed along the lines
of this new Change Mining paradigm. MClusT includes a taxonomy of
transitions, a tracking method based in Graph Theory, and a transition
detection algorithm. To demonstrate its feasibility and applicability we
present real world case studies, using datasets extracted from Banco de
Portugal and the Portuguese Institute of Statistics. We also test our approach in a benchmark dataset from TSDL. The results are encouraging
and demonstrate the ability of MClusT framework to provide an efficient
diagnosis of clusters transitions.

Keywords: Bipartite Graphs, Change Mining, Clustering, Monitoring,
Transitions.

1 Introduction

The celerity at which the evolution takes place, typically characterized by breaks
and paradigms shifts, has increased exponentially in the last decades. The rapid
progress made in science and technology has contributed to the emergence of a
volatile and fast pace evolving world, which demands new perspectives in knowledge discovery upon data, such as time-oriented perspectives. The paradigm of
Change Mining arises as a consequence of this evolution and encompasses Data
Mining mechanisms that monitor models and patterns over time, compare them,
detect and describe changes, and quantify them on their interestingness [1]. The
Change Mining's underlying challenge lays not only in the adaptation of models
to changes in data distribution but also in the understanding of changes themselves. In this paper we propose the MClusT framework, which is built along
these lines, to tackle the problem of monitoring the transitions experienced by
clusters over time, through the identification of temporal relationships among
them. Our transitions tracking mechanism includes a taxonomy of clusters transitions, a method for tracking clusters obtained at different snapshots, and a
transition detection algorithm.

P.R. Cohen, N.M. Adams, and M.R. Berthold (Eds.): IDA 2010, LNCS 6065, pp. 114–124, 2010.
© Springer-Verlag Berlin Heidelberg 2010

1.1   Applications

The monitoring of the dynamics of cluster structures is very important in many real world applications, since it fosters the creation of sustainable knowledge about the underlying phenomenon and, consequently, the adoption of pro-active attitudes. Besides, it may correlate to some important or critical events in the real applications or unveil the emergence of new ones. For these reasons, this study can benefit several areas, such as Marketing, Fraud Detection, Economy, Sociology and Health. For example, the study of the evolution of customer's segments allow the detection of shifts in preferences and consumer habits, which can sustain the forecast of trends and consequent redefinition of Marketing's strategies and policies. The domain knowledge acquired by these means can act as a powerful differentiating factor in the market and strongly contributes to the creation, or reinforcement, of the company's competitive advantages. Traditional Data Mining is not able to help companies achieve these goals since it relies on static data and does not take into account their evolving nature. Therefore, the study of the dynamics of clusters contributes to the achievement of a greater understanding of cluster's evolutionary processes, broadening horizons and opening new paths in the way of thinking problems.

1.2   Organization of the Paper

This paper is organized as follows. In Section 2 we provide a brief overview of the current state of the art. In Section 3 we formally introduce our MClusT framework. In this section we present our taxonomy for clusters transitions and explain how bipartite graphs can be used to detect and classify external transitions. In Section 4 we show and discuss three experiments, using datasets extracted from Banco de Portugal's Central Balance-Sheet Database (CBSD), datasets from the Portuguese Institute of Statistics (INE) and a benchmark dataset from the Time Series Data Library [23]. Section 5 concludes our study.

2   Related Work

Clustering - the separation and classification of observations - is one of the most basic cultural activities of humankind [2]. For this reason, it has been a recurrent and extremely appealing subject to a wide community of researchers and practitioners from different areas, reflecting the interdisciplinary nature of this technique. Clustering is an unsupervised learning task, since there are no labels assigned to observations. It is also an exploratory Data Analysis technique which aims to find the underlying structure in data, through the discovery of the natural grouping and the hidden relationships in a set of multidimensional observations. The main intention of Clustering techniques is to obtain a set of homogeneous, well-separated, and meaningful clusters. To accomplish this task, a huge variety of algorithms have been developed. These developments are summarized in a few surveys [3][4]. Despite the extensive study of the Clustering problem, there is not much work conducted in the monitoring of cluster transitions. In this context of change, the research endeavor has been mainly directed to the adaptation of clusters to changed populations.

The dynamic nature of most datasets encouraged new directions in research. This effort is clearly present in the areas of Machine Learning and Data Analysis. Currently, there are several algorithms that directly or indirectly aim to capture and, especially, understand the dynamic nature of these datasets, particularly susceptible to the occurrence of changes in the underlying structure. The last decade has been especially profuse in the design of transition detection algorithms. Based on the recent literature, it was possible to deduce a preliminary classification for algorithms built in this context. In general, there are algorithms designed to operate in relatively static (snapshots) or highly dynamic (Data Streams) environments. The first may be focused on the transitions experienced by generic patterns [5,6,7], clusters [8,9,10] or association rules [11,12]. In the context of Data Streams, approaches focusing unclassified data are quite common (here we include clustering algorithms for mobile objects or spatio-temporal objects). Lu & Hang identified the specific requirements for grouping a set of observations in a Data Stream environment [13]. These approaches [14,15,16,17,18,19,20] elect clusters as its main data structure and are concerned with the efficiency and scalability of algorithms.

Based on our knowledge, the only research that addresses a problem closely related to ours is the one presented in [8]. MONIC framework also proposes a cluster transition model to track cluster changes, supporting cluster comparisons across the time axis. However, while it uses the concept of *Cluster Overlap*, MClusT uses a different metric, based on *Conditional Probability*. Moreover, MONIC does not provide an appealing way of visualizing the output. Thus, our approach extends their work, since we resort to Bipartite Graphs to detect and classify cluster transitions, which allows for a visual experience and a better understanding of the monitoring process. The MClusT taxonomy is also distinct.

3   Bipartite Graphs

We developed the MClusT framework in order to model and understand the evolution of clusters structures (also referred to as *Clustering* - Definition 1) obtained at different timepoints. In this context, the concept of evolution refers to transitions experienced by clusters in the time interval under observation $[t_i, t_{i+1}]$.

Definition 1 - CLUSTERING:
A Clustering ξ is a specific partitioning of a dataset D *into* K *partitions, usually denoted as clusters* $\xi = \{C_1, ..., C_i, ..., C_K\}$, *such that:*

1. $C_i \cap C_j = \emptyset$, $\forall_{i \neq j}$ - clusters *are disjoint sets (or mutually exclusive);*
2. $\cup_{i=1}^{K} C_i = D$ - clusters *are collectively exhaustive;*
3. *Observations assigned to a given* cluster *are more similar to each other than to observations assigned to other* clusters *belonging to Clustering ξ.*

In the literature there are, at least, eight taxonomic schemes for the classification of transitions in clusters, patterns or concepts that evolve over time [9,14,16,15,21,20,8,10]. Thus, to capture the changes likely to occur in cluster structures we considered the following taxonomy: **Birth, Death, Split, Merge** and **Survival** of clusters. These transitions are external, as they relate to changes in the whole *Clustering*. The key concept for the detection and evaluation of these transitions is the concept of *mapping*, which can be defined as the process of discovering the exact matches between clusters obtained at timepoint t_i and clusters obtained at a later timepoint t_{i+1}, in case they still exist. In this framework, the *mapping* process explores the concept of conditional probability and is restricted by a pre-defined threshold - Survival Threshold τ -, which assumes the minimum of $\tau = 0.5$. The use of conditional probabilities requires structurally identical datasets, ie, datasets composed by the same observations, in each timepoint under analysis. These conditional probabilities are computed for every pair of possible connections between clusters obtained at different timepoints and they represent the edge's weights in a bipartite graph. The use of bipartite graphs is related to its usefulness in modeling matching problems and the fact that graph based representations are visually appealing, exploiting the power of the eye and human intuition. The foundations of our transitions detection algorithm are based in this idea, which can be defined as follows (Definition 2).

Definition 2 - Weighted Bipartite Graphs:
Given the Clusterings ξ_i, ξ_j ($i < j$), obtained at t_i, t_j, a graph $G = (V, E)$ can be constructed, where V is a set of vertices, or nodes, representing the discovered clusters, and E denotes a set of weighted edges between any pair of clusters belonging to ξ_i and ξ_j. Formally, the weights assigned to the edge connecting clusters $C(t_i)$ and $C(t_j)$ are estimated in accordance with the conditional probability (Equation 1):

$$weight(C_m(t_i), C_u(t_j)) = P(X \in C_u(t_j)|X \in C_m(t_i)) =$$
$$= \frac{\sum P(x \in C_m(t_i) \cap C_u(t_j))}{\sum P(x \in C_m(t_i))}$$

where X is the set of observations assigned to cluster $C_m(t_i)$ ($m = 1, ..., p$) and $P(X \in C_u(t_j)|X \in C_m(t_i))$ represents the probability of X belonging to cluster C_u from t_j knowing that X belongs to cluster C_m obtained at a previous timestamp t_i
$C(t_i) = \{C_1, ..., C_m, ..., C_p\}$
$C(t_j) = \{C_1, ..., C_u, ..., C_r\}$.

In order to detect changes, we formally define the transitions that a cluster $C \in \xi_i$ can experience, with respect to ξ_j, ($i < j$). It was introduced a new threshold to help the definition of these transitions: the Split Threshold ρ (it's assumed, by default, that $\rho = 0.2$). This formal design is based on MONIC framework's external transitions [8] and is depicted in Table 1.

Table 1. Formal definition of clusters transitions, according to the defined taxonomy

Transitions' Taxonomy	Notation	Formal Definition
Cluster's Birth	$\emptyset \to C_u(t_j)$	$0 < weight(C_m(t_i), C_u(t_j)) < \tau \forall m$
Cluster's Death	$C_m(t_i) \to \emptyset$	$weight(C_m(t_i), C_u(t_j)) < \rho \forall u$
Cluster's Split	$C_m(t_i) \overset{\subseteq}{\to} \{C_1(t_j), ..., C_r(t_j)\}$	$(\exists_u : weight(C_m(t_i), C_u(t_j)) \geq \rho) \wedge$ $\sum_{u=1}^{r} weight(C_m(t_i), C_u(t_j)) \geq \tau$
Cluster's Merge	$\{C_1(t_i), ..., C_p(t_i)\} \overset{\subseteq}{\to} C_u(t_j)$	$(weigth(C_m(t_i), C_u(t_j)) \geq \tau) \wedge$ $\exists C_p \in \xi_i \setminus \{C_m\} : weight(C_p(t_i), C_u(t_j)) \geq \tau$
Cluster's Survival	$C_m(t_i) \to C_u(t_j)$	$(weigth(C_m(t_i), C_u(t_j)) \geq \tau) \wedge$ $\nexists C_p \in \xi_i \setminus \{C_m\} : weight(C_p(t_i), C_u(t_j)) \geq \tau$

The implementation of the transition detection algorithm, in software R 2.10.0, was supported by the definitions presented in Table 1. The output data, generated by the algorithm, was then represented through bipartite graphs, which were designed in Microsoft Office Visio 2007.

To better understand our approach, in next section we present our first experiments.

4   Experiments

In order to show the feasibility and application of the proposed framework and glean insights about the evolution of clusters, we experimented MClusT in real datasets extracted from Banco de Portugal's Central Balance-Sheet Database (CBSD) and Portuguese Institute of Statistics (INE). But before the introduction of these case studies, we show an experiment using a benchmark dataset from the Time Series Data Library, available at [23].

4.1   Experiment Using a Benchmark Dataset

We tested the evolution method using a Macro-Economic dataset from the Time Series Data Library. This dataset contains 42 observations representing the quarterly consumer expenditure in U.K. on durable goods, all other goods and services, investment, inventory investment, imports of goods and services, gross domestic product and personal disposable income. We divided this data into two different sets, each corresponding to a period of seven years, since a year has only three observations. We'll refer to the first seven years as t_1 and the latter seven years as t_2. The attributes were normalized using Z-scores, due to significant differences on scale and dispersion. In order to discover the clusters (input of our study) from these datasets, we conducted experiments using two different algorithms for clustering: the Agglomerative Hierarchical Algorithm using Ward's Index, and K-means Partitional Algorithm. Although there were experiments with other algorithms, the mentioned ones have achieved good quality levels. In both algorithms, the determination of the critical clustering structure, through the identification of the best number of clusters (best K), was supported by the analysis of an internal validation measure: the Silhouette Width [22]. Afterwards, we applied our transitions detection algorithm, setting a fixed $\rho = 0.2$ and varying the Survival Threshold ($\tau = 0.5$ and $\tau = 0.8$). However, in this paper we only present results for $\rho = 0.2$ and $\tau = 0.5$. These parameters are more

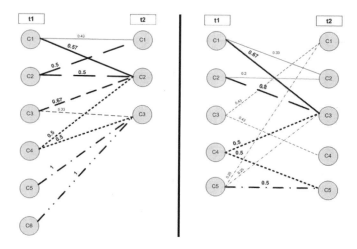

Fig. 1. Bipartite graphs, corresponding to timestamps t_1 and t_2, with the thickness of the edges indicating weights that are equal or greater to Survival Threshold; the edges whose weights are below the Split Threshold were removed from the graphs, due to their insignificance. The right-hand side graph corresponds to the Agglomerative Hierarchical Clustering and the left-hand side to the K-means Clustering.

relaxed and allow the detection of a wider variety of transitions. The resulting graphs, showing the transitions between clusters, are depicted in Figure 1.

Figure 1 is composed by two sub-figures, each corresponding to a different clustering algorithm. The analysis of the bipartite graphs depicted in this figure allows us to know that, using the Hierarchical Algorithm, we obtain a partition in six clusters, at period t_1, and a partition in three clusters in period t_2. On the other hand, using the K-means algorithm, we obtain a partition in five clusters in each period. Regarding cluster transitions we can observe that, using the Hierarchical Algorithm, our approach detects a survival $(C_2(t_1) \rightarrow C_1(t_2))$ and two merges $(\{C_1(t_1), C_2(t_1), C_3(t_1), C_4(t_1)\} \overset{\subseteq}{\rightarrow} C_2(t_2))$ and $\{C_4(t_1), C_5(t_1), C_6(t_1)\} \overset{\subseteq}{\rightarrow} C_3(t_2))$. Alternatively, the results obtained for K-means Algorithm suggest that there were two merges $(\{C_1(t_1), C_2(t_1), C_4(t_1)\} \overset{\subseteq}{\rightarrow} C_3(t_2))$ and $\{C_4(t_1), C_5(t_1)\} \overset{\subseteq}{\rightarrow} C_5(t_2))$, a split $(C_3(t_1) \overset{\subseteq}{\rightarrow} \{C_1(t_2), C_4(t_2)\})$ and three cluster's births $(\emptyset \rightarrow C_1(t_2), \emptyset \rightarrow C_2(t_2)$ and $\emptyset \rightarrow C_4(t_2))$.

4.2 First Case Study - Portuguese Activity Sectors

For the first case study, we extracted three datasets from CBSD. Each dataset corresponds to a year (2005, 2006 and 2007) and consists of 439 observations characterized by 10 continuous attributes. The observations represent activity sectors, according to the higher granularity level of CEA (Portuguese Classification of Economic Activities), and the attributes are financial and economic aggregated indicators (e.g. net income, investment rate and labor productivity). These attributes were also standardized. It should be noted that the activity

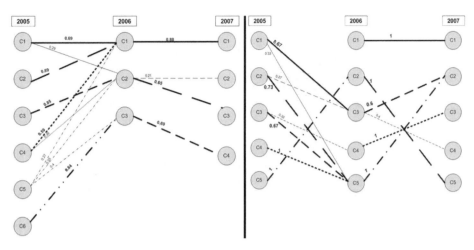

Fig. 2. Bipartite graphs, corresponding to timestamps 2005, 2006 and 2007, with the thickness of the edges indicating weights that are equal or greater to Survival Threshold; the edges whose weights are below the Split Threshold were removed from the graphs, due to their insignificance. The right-hand side graph corresponds to the Agglomerative Hierarchical Clustering and the left-hand side to the K-means Clustering.

sectors and performance indicators are exactly the same, for all periods under analysis (this will generate balanced bipartite graphs, that are graphs with equal cardinality). In order to discover the clusters structure and detect the transitions undergone by clusters, we submitted the datasets to the same experimental conditions as Macro-Economics' datasets. The resulting bipartite graphs are portrayed in Figure 2.

On the right-hand side of Figure 2 we observe two bipartite graphs, one corresponding to transitions experienced during the time interval $[2005, 2006]$ and another one corresponding to transitions occurred during $[2006, 2007]$. In the former, there were two surviving clusters ($C_3(2005) \rightarrow C_2(2006)$ and $C_6(2005) \rightarrow C_3(2006)$), a merge of three clusters ($\{C_1(2005), C_2(2005), C_4(2005)\} \stackrel{\subseteq}{\rightarrow} C_1(2006)$) and a split ($C_5(2005) \stackrel{\subseteq}{\rightarrow} \{C_1(2006), C_2(2006), C_3(2006)\}$). In the latter, all clusters survived ($C_1(2006) \rightarrow C_1(2007)$, $C_2(2006) \rightarrow C_3(2007)$ and $C_3(2006) \rightarrow C_4(2007)$) and a new one has emerged ($\emptyset \rightarrow C_2(2007)$). The left-hand side of Figure 2 corresponds to the K-Means Algorithm' s bipartite graphs. Using the same strategy and the Silhouette Width validation measure, K-means algorithm resulted in a different partition (five clusters to all timepoints under analysis). The detected transitions also differ from the ones obtained for the Agglomerative Hierarchical Algorithm, as expected. Thereby, during $[2005, 2006]$ we detect the survival of two clusters ($C_1(2005) \rightarrow C_3(2006)$ and $C_5(2005) \rightarrow C_2(2006)$), a merge of three clusters ($\{C_2(2005), C_3(2005), C_4(2005)\} \stackrel{\subseteq}{\rightarrow} C_5(2006)$) and two births ($\emptyset \rightarrow C_1(2006)$ and $\emptyset \rightarrow C_4(2006)$). At period $[2006, 2007]$, four clusters survived ($C_1(2006) \rightarrow C_1(2007)$, $C_2(2006) \rightarrow C_5(2007)$ and $C_4(2006) \rightarrow C_3(2007)$), two clusters merged ($\{C_3(2006), C_5(2006)\} \overset{\subseteq}{\to} C_2(2007)$) and a new one has emerged ($\emptyset \to C_4(2007)$).

In this experiment, the differences in terms of transitions between the Hierarchical and the K-means Algorithm are more evident in time interval $[2006, 2007]$. The merge occurred in $[2005, 2006]$ was captured by both Clustering algorithms, so we assumed this was an important transition. The inspection of the dataset suggested that these three clusters were grouped into one because the activity sectors assigned to them experienced a worsening in their economic and financial performance, which was reflected in the mitigation of their initial differences. But why did this happen? To answer this question we searched for relevant information about the topic and we found out that, in 2006, there has been a homogenization of the information process within the SIMPLEX portuguese program, which aimed to incorporate in one document (the Simplified Business Information) and a single delivery operation the information that companies are required to provide to public institutions. Moreover, the reporting of the Business information became mandatory, which contributed to the increase of the coverage degree of CBSD. For this reason, the data became more reliable and complete, reflecting a more realistic image of the country, which may be the cause of the detected cluster's merge.

4.3   Second Case Study - Portuguese Regional Development Index

The second case study was designed using datasets extracted from the Portuguese Institute of Statistics (INE). These datasets focus on the Portuguese Regional Development Index, which are available for year 2004 and year 2006, and can serve as a working basis for multiple stakeholders on issues of territory. Each dataset consists of 30 observations, corresponding to the units of analysis of NUTS III (Nomenclature of territorial units for statistics level III), and 4 continuous attributes, which summarize the regional development in all aspects (Cohesion, Competitiveness and Environmental Quality). Similarly to the first experiment, the observations and attributes are exactly the same for both years. Experimental conditions are also the same. The resulting graphs, that illustrate the transitions, are depicted in Figure 3.

On the right-hand side of Figure 3 is depicted the bipartite graph obtained using the Agglomerative Hierarchical Algorithm. During $[2004, 2006]$ there were three survivals ($C_1(2004) \to C_2(2006)$, $C_2(2004) \to C_3(2006)$ and $C_5(2004) \to C_4(2006)$) and a merge of two clusters ($\{C_3(2004), C_4(2004)\} \overset{\subseteq}{\to} C_1(2006)$). On the left-hand side of the same Figure, corresponding to K-Means Bipartite Graphs, we detect seven survivals ($C_1(2004) \to C_6(2006)$, $C_2(2004) \to C_8(2006)$, $C_3(2004) \to C_2(2006)$, $C_4(2004) \to C_4(2006)$, $C_5(2004) \to C_3(2006)$, $C_6(2004) \to C_7(2006)$ and $C_7(2004) \to C_5(2006)$) and a cluster's birth ($\emptyset \to C_1(2006)$).

To understand the changes suggested by the detected transitions, we inspected the reasons that may be behind these inter-anual differences. Starting with the hierarchical algorithm, we conclude that the cause of cluster's merge is the fact that the sub-regions in the interior of Portugal improved its levels of

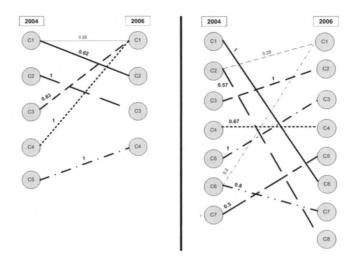

Fig. 3. Bipartite graphs, corresponding to timestamps 2004 and 2006, with the thickness of the edges indicating weights that are equal or greater to Survival Threshold; the edges whose weights are below the Split Threshold were removed from the graphs, due to their insignificance. The right-hand side graph corresponds to the Agglomerative Hierarchical Clustering and the left-hand side to the K-means Clustering.

environmental quality, leading to the convergence of sub-regions in the North and South of the country $(C_3(2004))$ and sub-regions in the interior Center of the country $(C_4(2004))$ into a single group $(C_1(2006))$. Regarding the K-Means Algorithm, the dataset inspection suggested the emergence of a new group of sub-regions $(C_1(2006))$: Minho-Lima, Dao-Lafoes and Cova da Beira, with increasing levels of competitiveness. However, the high number of survivals indicates that, in general, there were no significant differences in the Regional Development Index between 2004 and 2006.

5   Conclusions

In this paper we introduced a framework for addressing the problem of monitoring and detecting changes in cluster structures. The novelty lies in the use of bipartite graphs and conditional probabilities to monitor the transitions defined in the taxonomy. We presented experiments with datasets extracted from Time Series Data Library, Banco de Portugal's Central Balance-Sheet Database and the Portuguese Institute of Statistics to illustrate the applicability and feasibility of MClusT. Despite the fact that results vary according to the selected Clustering Algorithm, in these illustrative examples, the framework proved to be efficient and able to provide an effective diagnosis of the transitions experienced by clusters. As future work we intend to develop a similar method to deal with other representation schemes of clusters, e.g., representations exploring the summary statistics of clusters. It is also our purpose to create a method to assess the quality of transitions suggested by distinct clustering algorithms.

Acknowledgments. Thanks to the support of the project Knowledge Discovery from Ubiquitous Data Streams (PTDC/EIA-EIA/098355/2008).

References

1. Bottcher, M., Hoppner, F., Spiliopoulou, M.: On exploiting the power of time in data mining. SIGKDD Explorations (10), 3–11 (2008)
2. Hampel, F.: Some thoughts about classification. In: 8th Conference of the International Federation of Classification Societies, pp. 1–19. Springer, Poland (2002)
3. Jain, A.K.: Data Clustering: 50 Years Beyond K-means. In: Daelemans, W., Goethals, B., Morik, K. (eds.) ECML PKDD 2008, Part I. LNCS (LNAI), vol. 5211, pp. 3–4. Springer, Heidelberg (2008)
4. Jain, A.K., Murty, M.N., Flynn, P.J.: Data Clustering: A Review. ACM Comput. Surv. (31), 264–323 (1999)
5. Ganti, V., Gehrke, J., Ramakrishnan, R.: A Framework for Measuring Changes in Data Characteristics. In: Proceedings of the 18th ACM SIGACT-SIGMOD-SIGART Symposium on Principles of Database Systems, pp. 126–137. ACM Press, Pennsylvania (1999)
6. Bartolini, I., Ciaccia, P., Ntoutsi, I., Patella, M., Theodoridis, Y.: The Panda framework for Comparing Patterns. Data Knowl. Eng. (68), 244–260 (2009)
7. Chawathe, S.S., Garcia-Molina, H.: Meaningful Change Detection in Structured Data. In: Peckham, J. (ed.) Proceedings ACM SIGMOD International Conference on Management of Data, pp. 26–37. ACM Press, Arizona (1997)
8. Spiliopoulou, M., Ntoutsi, I., Theodoridis, Y., Schult, R.: MONIC: modeling and monitoring cluster transitions. In: Eliassi-Rad, T., Ungar, L.H., Craven, M., Gunopulos, D. (eds.) ACM SIGKDD 2006, pp. 706–711. ACM, Philadelphia (2006)
9. Falkowski, T., Bartelheimer, J., Spiliopoulou, M.: Mining and Visualizing the Evolution of Subgroups in Social Networks. In: IEEE / WIC / ACM International Conference on Web Intelligence, pp. 52–58. IEEE Computer Society, China (2006)
10. Yang, H., Parthasarathy, S., Mehta, S.: A generalized framework for mining spatio-temporal patterns in scientific data. In: Grossman, R., Bayardo, R.J., Bennett, K.P. (eds.) Proceedings of the 11th ACM SIGKDD International Conference on Knowledge Discovery and Data Mining, pp. 716–721. ACM, Illinois (2005)
11. Baron, S., Spiliopoulou, M.: Monitoring Change in Mining Results. In: Kambayashi, Y., Winiwarter, W., Arikawa, M. (eds.) DaWaK 2001. LNCS, vol. 2114, p. 51. Springer, Heidelberg (2001)
12. Baron, S., Spiliopoulou, M.: Monitoring the Evolution of Web Usage Patterns. In: Berendt, B., Hotho, A., Mladenič, D., van Someren, M., Spiliopoulou, M., Stumme, G. (eds.) EWMF 2003. LNCS (LNAI), vol. 3209, pp. 181–200. Springer, Heidelberg (2004)
13. Lu, Y.-H., Huaang, Y.: Mining data streams using clustering. In: Proceedings of the 4th International Conference on Machine Learning and Cybernetics, pp. 2079–2083. IEEE Computer Society, China (2005)
14. Aggarwal, C.C.: On Change Diagnosis in Evolving Data Streams. IEEE Trans. Knowl. Data Eng. (17), 587–600 (2005)

15. Chen, K., Liu, L.: Detecting the Change of Clustering Structure in Categorical Data Streams. In: Ghosh, J., Lambert, D., Skillicorn, D.B., Srivastava, J. (eds.) Proceedings of the 6th SIAM International Conference on Data Mining. SIAM, USA (2006)
16. Aggarwal, C.C., Han, J., Wang, J., Yu, P.S.: A Framework for Change Diagnosis of Data Streams. In: Halevy, A.Y., Ives, Z.G., Doan, A. (eds.) Proceedings of the 2003 ACM SIGMOD International Conference on Management of Data, pp. 575–586. ACM, California (2003)
17. O'Callaghan, L., Meyerson, A., Motwani, R., Mishra, N., Guha, S.: Streaming-Data Algorithms for High-Quality Clustering. In: Proceedings of the 18th International Conference on Data Engineering, p. 685. IEEE Computer Society, California (2002)
18. Elnekave, S., Last, M., Maimon, O.: Incremental Clustering of Mobile Objects. In: ICDE Workshops (2007)
19. Kalnis, P., Mamoulis, N., Bakiras, S.: On Discovering Moving Clusters in Spatio-temporal Data. In: Bauzer Medeiros, C., Egenhofer, M.J., Bertino, E. (eds.) SSTD 2005. LNCS, vol. 3633, pp. 364–381. Springer, Heidelberg (2005)
20. Li, T., Ma, S., Ogihara, M.: Entropy-based criterion in categorical clustering. In: Proceedings of the 21th international conference on Machine learning, p. 65. ACM, New York (2004)
21. Kaur, S., Bhatnagar, V., Mehta, S., Kapoor, S.: Concept Drift in Unlabeled Data Stream. Technical Report, University of Delhi (2009)
22. Rousseeuw, P.J.: Silhouettes: a graphical aid to the interpretation and validation of cluster analysis. Journal of Computational and Applied Mathematics, 53–65 (1987)
23. Time Series Data Library, http://robjhyndman.com/TSDL/

Data Mining for Modeling Chiller Systems in Data Centers

Debprakash Patnaik[1], Manish Marwah[2],
Ratnesh K. Sharma[2], and Naren Ramakrishnan[1]

[1] Virginia Tech, Blacksburg, VA 24061, USA
[2] HP Labs, Palo Alto, CA 94034, USA

Abstract. We present a data mining approach to model the cooling infrastructure in data centers, particularly the chiller ensemble. These infrastructures are poorly understood due to the lack of "first principles" models of chiller systems. At the same time, they abound in data due to instrumentation by modern sensor networks. We present a multi-level framework to transduce sensor streams into an actionable dynamic Bayesian network model of the system. This network is then used to explain observed system transitions and aid in diagnostics and prediction. We showcase experimental results using a HP data center in Bangalore, India.

1 Introduction

Over the last decade, data centers have grown from housing a few hundred multiprocessor systems to tens of thousands of servers in warehouse-sized buildings. However, widespread use of data centers has been accompanied with steep increases in power consumption and high costs, a matter of great concern to both owners and users of data centers. According to the EPA, US data centers have become energy hogs and their continued growth is expected to demand the construction of 10 new power plants by 2011 [1,2]. Globally, datacenters currently consume 1–2% of the world's electricity [3] and are already responsible for more CO_2 emissions than entire countries such as Argentina or The Netherlands.

Data centers constitute a mix of computing elements, networking infrastructure, storage systems along with power management and cooling capabilities (see Figure 1, left), all of which offer opportunities for improving energy efficiency and achieving more sustainable data centers. For instance, huge inefficiencies abound in average server utilization (believed to be at most 10–15%), and thus one approach to achieve greener IT is to use virtualization and migration to automatically provision new systems as demand spikes and consolidate applications when demand falls. Similarly, dynamic management of an ensemble of chiller units in response to varying load characteristics is another strategy to make a data center more energy efficient. There are even end-to-end methodologies proposed [5] that track inefficiencies at all levels of the IT infrastructure "stack" and derive overall measures of the efficiency of energy flow during data center operation.

A key problem is the unavailability, inadequacy, or in-feasibility of theoretical models or "first principles" methodologies to optimize design and usage of data centers.

P.R. Cohen, N.M. Adams, and M.R. Berthold (Eds.): IDA 2010, LNCS 6065, pp. 125–136, 2010.

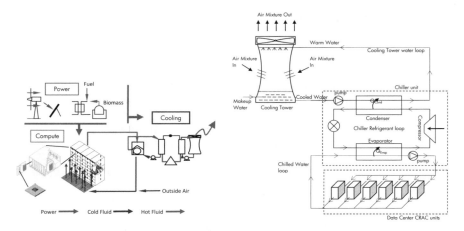

Fig. 1. (left) Elements of a data center [4]. (right) Schematic of a typical cooling infrastructure.

While some components can be modeled, (e.g., an operating curve for an individual chiller unit, a Computational Fluid Dynamics (CFD) based prediction of air flows through rows of racks for static conditions, temperature profiles to reveal hot spots in clusters [6]), these methods are computationally intensive and difficult to deploy in real time. Furthermore, what is missing is the ability to understand complex interactions between the multiple components of data centers. Needless to say, optimizing each component separately does not necessarily lead to a greener installation on the whole. Data-driven approaches to data center management are hence more attractive: by mining sensor streams from an installation, we can obtain a real-time perspective into system behavior and identify strategies to improve efficiency metrics.

2   Data Centers

A typical data center is organized as racks of computing equipment arranged as rows. A large data center could contain thousands of racks occupying several tens of thousands of square feet of space. The cooling infrastructure of a data center typically looks as shown in Figure 1 (right).

The focus of this paper is the chiller ensemble in the data center cooling infrastructure. Each chiller unit is composed of four basic components, namely, evaporator, multistage centrifugal compressor, economizer and water-cooled or air-cooled condenser. Liquid refrigerant is distributed along the length of the evaporator to absorb enough heat from the water returning from the data center and circulated through the evaporator tubes to vaporize. The gaseous refrigerant is then drawn into the compressor. Compressed gas passes from the multi-stage compressor into the condenser. Cooling tower water circulated through the condenser tubes absorbs heat from the refrigerant, causing it to condense. The liquid refrigerant then passes through an orifice plate into the economizer. Flashed gases enter the compressor while the liquid flows into the evaporator to complete the circuit. Some terms used in the context of chillers are given below.

IT cooling load. This is the amount of heat that is generated (and thus needs to be dissipated) at a data center. It is approximately equivalent to the power consumed by the equipment since almost all of it is dissipated as heat. It is commonly specified in kilowatts (KW).

COP. The coefficient of performance (COP) of a chiller unit indicates how efficiently the unit provides cooling, and, it is defined as the ratio between the cooling provided and the power consumed, i.e.,

$$\text{COP}_i = \frac{L_i}{P_i} \tag{1}$$

where L_i is the cooling load on the ith chiller unit and P_i is the power consumed by it.

Chiller utilization. This is the percentage of the total capacity of a chiller unit that is in use. It depends on a variety of factors, mainly, the mass flow rate of water that passes through a chiller and the degree of cooling provided, that is, the difference between the inlet and outlet temperatures ($T_{in} - T_{out}$). For a particular T_{out}, an administrator can control the utilization at a chiller through power capping or by changing the mass flow rate of water.

Ensemble of Chiller Units. The number of chiller units required depends on the size and thermal density of a data center. While one unit may be sufficient for a small data center, several units operating as an ensemble may be required to satisfy the cooling demand of a large data center. Figure 2 shows an ensemble of chiller units that collectively provide cooling for a data center. Out of the five units shown, three are air-cooled while the remaining two are water-cooled.

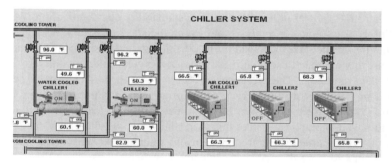

Fig. 2. Five chiller units work in tandem to provide cooling for a large data center

Operational Challenges. Although operating curves for individual chiller units exist, no model is available for operation of an ensemble, especially one consisting of heterogeneous units. Additionally, shift and/or drift of response characteristics with time further complicate their management. The operational goals are to satisfy the cooling requirements while minimizing the total power consumption of the ensemble and maximizing the average lifespan of the units. While multiple factors impact the lifespan of a chiller unit, an important one is: rapid and large oscillations in utilization value. High amplitude and frequent variations in utilization due to varying load or some failure condition result in decreased lifespan, and, thus, need to be minimized.

3   Prior Work

Earlier work in data center management adopt a "first principles" approach by conducting detailed CFD-based modeling of air and temperature flows [7]. The computational infeasibility of such large-scale simulations coupled with the relative ease of gathering real-time data from sensors has led others, most notably within HP labs, to alternatively explore the use of data analysis techniques. For instance, modeling of rack-level temperature data specifically in relation to CRAC layout has been undertaken in [8,9]. Optimization opportunities at multiple levels of smart center architecture have also been studied in [5]. More recent work[10] focuses on sensor data mining to identify anomalous and deviant behavior. Other related work includes the InteMon system from CMU [11,12] that dynamically tracks correlations among multiple time series [13] but only studies a few time series. While all these works constitute important strides in analytics, in order to support high-level knowledge discovery capabilities, we must raise the level of abstraction at which we study and infer patterns from sensor data streams. In particular, we must generalize from correlations and anomalies in time series datasets to being able to model the entire complexity of relationships underlying system variables [14] and, in this manner, promote life-cycle modeling of IT systems. More importantly, sustainability considerations and prior domain knowledge about life-cycle modeling must drive and inform the design of data mining algorithms. Other methods [15] have been proposed to capture the dynamics of time-series by modeling them as Markov chains and then applying clustering to the models to discover different cluster dynamics.

We have recently demonstrated the usefulness of data mining in characterizing utilization of the cooling infrastructure of a data center [16]. In this study, our primary goal was to link the multivariate numeric time series data, e.g., temperatures recorded from chiller units, power utilization etc. to sustainability characterization. We decomposed this goal into cluster analysis and event encoding to obtain abstract symbolic representation of the data, followed by motif mining, and sustainability characterization. Thus, this approach uses motif patterns as a crucial intermediate representation to aid in data reduction. The present work builds upon these successes to develop an actionable model of the data center's cooling infrastructure. Similar motivations can be found in [17] who use a (dynamic) Bayesian network model of a production plant to detect faults and anomalies. Unlike this work, however, we show how such networks can be efficiently learned using frequent episode mining over sensor streams. Furthermore, our networks are defined over clustered representations of the time series data rather than raw sensor signals.

4   Methods

Our proposed framework for analyzing the cooling infrastructure is illustrated in Figure 3. First, data reduction is performed in a few different ways. The raw time series data is compressed using piece-wise aggregate approximation following discretization using equal frequency bins. This helps capture the average dynamics of the variables. A higher-order aspect of the time series involves repeating or oscillatory behavior. This is inferred by mining frequently repeating motifs or patterns in the time series, as described in our earlier work [16]. This information is integrated with the average behavior

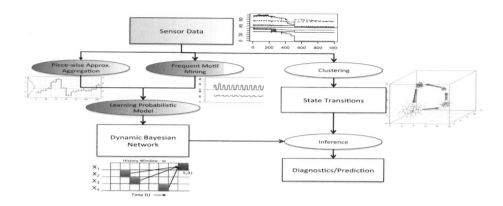

Fig. 3. Framework for modeling data center cooling infrastructure

by recording the windows in which a time series exhibits motif patterns. Finally, it is also pertinent to mine relationships involving "control" actions that were taken during the operation of the chiller units. In this paper, we focus on ON/OFF actions.

A graphical model in the form of a Dynamic Bayesian Network (DBN) is learnt from the above data. This model captures the dependencies between the variables in the system over different time lags. Here, we focus on the target variable of utilization and seek to identify suitable parents for modeling in the DBN. Unlike classical methods to learn BNs [18], we demonstrate a powerful approach to learn DBNs by creating bridges to the frequent episode mining literature [19]. To apply the learned DBN, we define states of the system by clustering together the combined utilization of the chiller units. This allows the operation of the chiller ensemble to be represented as a sequence of state transitions. We now use the dependencies and (conditional) independency relationships found in learning the graphical model to find the most probable explanation behind the state transitions. This framework can then be applied for activities like data center diagnostics, performance improvement, load balancing, and preventive maintenance.

4.1 Motif Discovery

In this work, time series motifs are defined as contiguous sub-sequences that follow the same pattern and repeat several times over the entire time series. Each time series $T = \langle t_1, \ldots, t_m \rangle$ in our data is an ordered collection of real values that a particular variable takes at different sampling times. In order to discover motif in a time series, we first discretize the time-series and use the discretization levels as symbols to encode the time series. This sequence of discrete symbols is then analyzed to detect the change points. We raise the level of abstraction further by doing a run-length encoding of the symbol sequence and noting where transitions from one symbol to another occur. This gives us a sequence of transition events for input to serial episode mining as illustrated below:

Symbol Sequence : d d d d a a a a a c c c c b b b b b b

⇓

Event Sequence : $\langle$(d-a, 5), (a-c, 10), (c-b, 14)

Frequent episode mining is now conducted over this sequence of transitions. We look for serial episodes with inter-event constraints that repeat sufficiently often. The structure of a serial episode is given below.

$$\langle E_1 \overset{(0,d_1]}{\rightarrow} E_2 \dots \overset{(0,d_{n-1}]}{\rightarrow} E_n \rangle \tag{2}$$

Here $E_1, \dots, E_n$ are the event-types in the episode α. Each pair of event-types in α is associated with an inter-event constraint. For example the pair $E_1 \rightarrow E_2$, is associated with $(0, d_1]$ such that in an occurrence of α event E_2 occurs no later than time d_1 of event E_1. The mining process follows the level-wise procedure ala *Apriori*, i.e., candidate generation followed by counting. The candidate generation scheme is based on matching the $n-1$ size suffix of one n-node frequent episode with the $n-1$ size prefix of the another n-node frequent episode at a given level to generate candidates for the next level. The same frequent episode mining algorithm is presented in our earlier work [16]. There it is applied in a slightly different context.

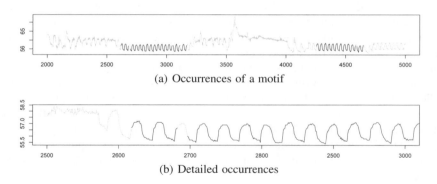

(a) Occurrences of a motif

(b) Detailed occurrences

Fig. 4. Illustration of a repeating motif in the utilization of a water cooled chiller unit

4.2   DBN Structure Learning

In this section we discuss probabilistic graphical models and provide the intuition behind building a graphical model for the variables in the chiller ensemble. We focus on Bayesian networks, specifically dynamic Bayesian networks where the random variables are time-stamped.

A Bayesian network (BN) is a graphical model denoted by $B = (G, P)$ where G is a directed acyclic graph (DAG) and P is a set of conditional probability distributions. The graph $G = (V, E)$ consists of a set of nodes V representing the random variables $\{X_1, \dots, X_N\}$ in the system and a set of directed edges E. Each directed edge in E, denoted by $i \rightarrow j$, indicates that random variable X_i is a parent of random variable X_j.

The conditional probabilities in P are used to capture statistical dependence relationships between child nodes and parent nodes. In particular, given a random variable X_i in the graph, we denote by $\text{par}(X_i)$ the set of random variables that are parents of X_i. The statistical dependence between X_i and its parent nodes $\text{par}(X_i)$ is captured by the conditional probabilities $P(X_i|\text{par}(X_i))$.

To model a discrete-time random process $\mathbf{X}(t), t = 1, \ldots, T; \mathbf{X}(t) = [X_1(t)X_2(t) \cdots X_N(t)]$ as studied here, we use the more expressive formalism of dynamic Bayesian networks. In particular, we focus on time-bounded causal networks, where for a given $w > 0$, the nodes in $\text{par}(X_i(t))$, parents for the node, $X_i(t)$, belong to a w-length history window, $[t - w, t)$. Note that parent nodes cannot belong to the current time slice t for $X_i(t)$.

This assumption limits the range-of-influence of a random variable, $X_k(t)$, to variables within w time-slices of t and also indicates that the random variables $X_i(t)$ and $X_j(t)$ are conditionally independent given their corresponding parent sets in the history window. Further, we also assume that the underlying data generation model is stationary, so that joint-statistics can be estimated using contingency tables.

The learning of network structures involves learning the parent set, $\text{par}(X_i(t))$, for each $X_i(t)$, $i = 1, \ldots, N$. In this work we assume that there are no spurious independencies in the data, i.e., if a random variable $X_j(t - \tau)$ is a parent of $X_i(t)$, then the mutual information $I(X_i(t); X_j(t - \tau)|\mathcal{S})$ conditioned on a subset $\mathcal{S} \subseteq \text{par}(X)$ is always greater than zero. Moreover time-bounded causality enables us to learn the parents of each node $X_i(t)$ independent of any other node in the same time slice. We use a greedy approach to learn the parent set of each node $X_i(t)$. And proceed by adding a node which has the highest conditional mutual information to the parent set of $X_i(t)$ as shown in Eqn 3:

$$\text{par}^{i+1}(X_i(t)) \leftarrow \text{par}^i(X_i(t)) \cup \arg\max I(X_i(t); X_j(t - \tau)|par^i(X_i(t))) \qquad (3)$$

The search is continues until the number of nodes in the parent set is k (where k is an user-defined parameter) or the conditional mutual information drops to zero. The structure learning is then followed by maximum likelihood estimation of the conditional probability tables.

4.3 State Transition Modeling

In analyzing complex systems it is usual to try and summarize the operating characteristics into a finite set of states where the systems spends most of its time. The utilization information of the chiller ensemble is important from both the aspect of efficiency and sustainability. Therefore we define the states of our system in terms of the combined utilization of all the chiller units.

In order to obtain a finite set of states, we fist perform a k-means clustering on the utilization vectors and use the cluster labels as symbols to encode the multi-variate time series of the combined utilization. Thus the multivariate series of utilizations is now encoded as a single long state sequence.

Over the state sequence the points of interest are the times where the system moves from one state to another. The exact transition times can be affected by the clustering scheme used but on the average they capture changes in the operating characteristics.

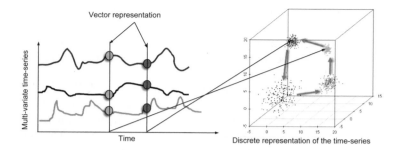

Fig. 5. Illustration of rendering multivariate time series data as a sequence of state-transitions using clustering. The arrows are drawn between corresponding vectors on the time series plot and the 3-d plot.

An interesting question to ask now is: What causes the state transitions to take place. In the context of our modeling, this question translates to: what factors in the system cause the utilization of the chiller to go up or down? This can be answered by observing the changes that take place in the system around the state transitions. The problem with this approach is the lack of availability of sufficient data around the change points. We propose an alternative approach where we decompose the question by asking what causes each of the changes in the chiller units. From the graphical model already learnt we know the set of variables in the system that directly affect the utilization. These variables belong to the parent set of the utilization nodes. The task of finding the most probable causes for a transition amounts to evaluating the following probability distribution:

$$\Pr(\mathcal{S}) = \prod_{i \in \text{Utilization Variables}} \Pr(\mathcal{S}_i | X_i(t) = a_i, X_i(t-1) = b_i) \tag{4}$$

where $\mathcal{S}_i = \text{par}(X_i(t)) \setminus X_i(t-1)$ and $\mathcal{S} = \cup \mathcal{S}_i$. The most likely values that $\mathcal{S}$ takes can be considered the best explanation of the transition. Here t is the time at which a state transition occurs, a_i, b_i are the discrete values the utilization variable takes before and after the state-transitions. These can be approximated by the cluster centers of each cluster used to define a state.

5   Results and Discussion

We applied our methods to chiller data obtained from a large HP production data center covering an area of 70,000 square feet Its cooling demand is met by an ensemble of five chiller units. The ensemble consists of two types of chillers: three are air-cooled and the remaining two are water-cooled. The data is collected from October 21, 2009 to November 13, 2009, totaling over 576 hours of data consisting of over 47 variables.

5.1   Graphical Model

For learning the graphical models, the raw time series data was aggregated over windows of 15 minutes and augmented with results from motif mining conducted over the

Table 1. A few important system variables in the chiller ensemble data

System Variable	Description
AC_CH(i)_EVAP_E_TEMP	Temperature of water entering air-cooled chiller i
MAIN_HEADER_TEMP_1_F	Water temperature at distribution header
WC_CH(i)_IN_TEMP	Temperature of water entering water-cooled chiller i
WC_CH(i)_OUT_TEMP	Temperature of water leaving water-cooled chiller i
AC_CH(i)_RLA	Percentage utilization of air-cooled chiller i
WC_CH(i)_RLA	Percentage utilization of water-cooled chiller i

same data. The motif information is in form of a binary valued sequence for each time series. The binary values indicate whether or not motif occurrences were seen in each 15 minute window. A finer grained representation of the motifs will be explored it the future.

Since utilization of a chiller mostly determines its energy consumption, we have shown that portion of the learned dynamic Bayesian network in Figure 6. Three air-cooled chiller utilization variables: AC_CH1_RLA, AC_CH2_RLA, AC_CH3_RLA; and two water-cooled ones: WC_CH1_RLA and WC_CH2_RLA are shown together with their parents and grandparents. In the DBN, almost every node has itself from the previous time slice as one of its parents, which is expected since the data is continuous valued time series data. In order to assist in creation of a causal Bayesian network, partial domain information was incorporated through constraints such as limiting nodes that could become parents. Three utilization variables show direct dependency on water temperature. This is, again, expected since the aim of the chiller ensemble is to maintain water temperature close to the set point.

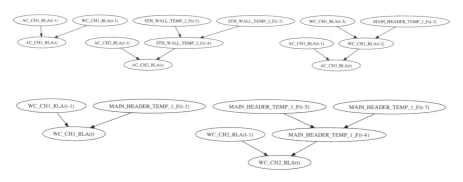

Fig. 6. Graphical Model learned from the discretized time series data. Shown are the parent nodes for only the utilization variables of the five chiller units.

More interesting relationships are revealed by two air-cooled units (1 and 3) that directly depend on the utilization of water cooled chiller. This would indicate that these two chillers ramp up or down based on how the water cooled chiller (which has higher capacity) is operating.

5.2   State Transitions

The operational states of the system, as shown in Figure 7, are obtained by clustering together the combined utilization of all the chillers in the ensemble. Here we use k-means
clustering with $k = 10$ and organize the states in decreasing order of total power consumption. Since the objective of this work is to operate a chiller ensemble more energy
efficiently, we color code the system states to reflect their power consumption. The color
red indicates the maximum power consumption (about 3298 KW) while the color blue
indicates the least consumption (2148 KW). Also shown, for each state, are the average
utilization values of the five chillers as a histogram with first three (starting from the left)
being air-cooled ones and the last two being water-cooled units. The time spent by the
system in each state is also listed (maximum in state 9, while least in state). The arrows
show the transitions between states, with the gray-scale indicating the frequency of the
transition (darkest implying most often).

The system states are mainly characterized by the number and kind of chiller units
operating, their utilization levels and power consumption. Some states are quite similar,
e.g., states 3 and 7, which have the same chiller units operating with not much difference
in their utilization levels. Other states show marked difference, e.g., state 10 has three
chillers operating (one air-cooled and two water-cooled) while state 6 has four working
units (two air-cooled and two water-cooled). Note that consequently state 10 consumes
less power than state 6. A data center chiller operator will be interested in understanding
the variables that influence transitions from state 10 to 6.

Transition: State 10 → State 6. When the chiller ensemble makes a transition from
state 10 to state 6, air cooled chiller-1 turns on. The graphical model can be queried to

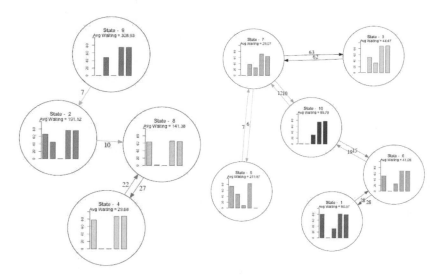

Fig. 7. Transitions in the state-based representation of the combined utilization of the chiller
ensemble. Edges representing 5 or fewer transitions are not shown. And edges representing more
than 5 transitions are labeled by the actual counts.

Table 2. List of most-likely value assignments of the parent-set of node AC_CH1_RLA i.e. utilization of air-cooled chiller 1

$\text{par}(X_i(t))$	Delay	Value	$\Pr(\text{par}(X_i(t))|X_i(t), X_i(t-1))$
WC_CH1_RLA	1	$(75.37, 77.38]$	0.27
WC_CH1_RLA	1	$(72.36, 75.37]$	0.18
WC_CH1_RLA	1	$(77.38, 79.71]$	0.18

provide the most probably explanation for this change. Using the model from Section 5.1, we estimate values of parent of utilization node when these state transitions take place, as listed in Table 2. Note that utilization levels of the parent (WC_CH1_RLA) are high when these transitions take place. These and other similar insights would facilitate more energy efficient management of the chiller resources.

In the future, we also plan to incorporate system alarms as nodes in the graphical model with the objective of discovering the variables that most significantly influence a particular alarm. This causal inference would provide valuable information to a data center chiller operator on corrective steps needed to handle the alarm. Furthermore, operator actions would be added to the model to enable discovery of dependencies between state transitions and such actions. This would allow an operator to query what actions could be taken (if any at all) to move the system from a less energy efficient state to a more efficient one.

6   Conclusions and Future Work

We have presented an expressive framework for reasoning about data center chillers using data mining techniques. Our methods raise the abstraction level from raw sensor streams to networks of relationships between higher order variables. While in this paper we have focused on determining the model structure and dependencies, in the future, we plan to build a diagnostic and advisory system. We will enrich the time series with alarm, sustainability and user action information with the objective of achieving the following goals: (1) inference of the probable cause of a chiller alarm, e.g., an alarm indicating that the water supply temperature has consistently been above the set point; (2) provide best course of action to handle an alarm, with actions learnt from past data; (3) monitor sustainability metrics, such as energy use or carbon footprint, and recommend state changes towards more sustainable operation. Although our current studies have focused on one particular subsystem of a data center, we posit that our methods are general and can be targeted toward other complex system modeling tasks.

Acknowledgements

This work was supported in part by HP Labs, Palo Alto and the Institute for Critical Technology and Applied Science (ICTAS), Virginia Tech.

References

1. Koomey, J.: Power conversion in servers and data centers: A review of recent data and developments. In: Applied Power Electronics Conference, February 25 (2008)
2. Kaplan, J.M., Forrest, W., Kindler, N.: Revolutionizing data center efficiency. Technical report, McKinsey Report (2008)
3. Vanderbilt, T.: Data center overload, June 8. New York Times (2009)
4. Watson, B., et al.: Integrated design and management of a sustainable data center. In: Inter-PACK 2009: Proceedings of ASME InterPACK, New York, NY, USA, July 2009. ASME (2009)
5. Sharma, R., et al.: On building next generation data centers: Energy flow in the information technology stack. In: Compute 2008, Bangalore, India (January 2008)
6. Cameron, K.W., Pyla, H.K., Varadarajan, S.: Tempest: A portable tool to identify hot spots in parallel code. In: ICPP 2007: Proceedings of the 2007 International Conference on Parallel Processing, Washington, DC, USA. IEEE Computer Society, Los Alamitos (2007)
7. Patel, C., et al.: Computational fluid dynamics modeling of high compute density data centers to assure system inlet air specifications. In: ASME IPACK 2001, Kauai, HI (July 2001)
8. Bautista, L., Sharma, R.: Analysis of environmental data in data centers. Technical Report HPL-2007-98, HP Labs (June 2007)
9. Sharma, R., et al.: Application of exploratory data analysis (eda) techniques to temperature data in a conventional data center. In: ASME IPACK 2007, Vancouver, BC (2007)
10. Marwah, M., Sharma, R., Bautista, L., Lugo, W.: Stream mining of sensor data for anomalous behavior detection in data centers. Technical Report HPL-2008-40, HP Labs (May 2008)
11. Hoke, E., Sun, J., Faloutsos, C.: Intemon: Intelligent system monitoring on large clusters. In: 32nd International Conference on Very Large Data Bases, September 2006, pp. 1239–1242 (2006)
12. Hoke, E., et al.: Intemon: Continuous mining of sensor data in large scale self infrastructures. Operating Systems Review 40(3), 38–44 (2006)
13. Papadimitriou, S., Sun, J., Faloutsos, C.: Streaming pattern discovery in multiple time series. In: 31st International Conference on Very Large Data Bases, pp. 697–708 (2005)
14. Morchen, F.: Unsupervised pattern mining from symbolic temporal data. ACM SIGKDD Explorations 9(1), 41–55 (2007)
15. Ramoni, M., et al.: Bayesian clustering by dynamics. Mach. Learn. 47(1), 91–121 (2002)
16. Patnaik, D., et al.: Sustainable operation and management of data center chillers using temporal data mining. In: Proc. 15th ACM SIGKDD Intl. Conf. on Knowledge Discovery and Data Mining, pp. 1305–1314 (2009)
17. Nielsen, T.D., Jensen, F.V.: Alert systems for production plants: A methodology based on conflict analysis. In: Symbolic and Quantitative Approaches to Reasoning with Uncertainty, pp. 76–87 (2005)
18. Friedman, N., Nachman, I., Pe'er, D.: Learning bayesian network structure from massive datasets: The "sparse candidate" algorithm. In: 5th Conf. on Uncertainty in Artificial Intelligence UAI, pp. 206–215 (1999)
19. Patnaik, D., Laxman, S., Ramakrishnan, N.: Discovering excitatory networks from discrete event streams with applications to neuronal spike train analysis. In: IEEE Intl. Conf. on Data Mining, ICDM 2009 (December 2009)

The Applications of Artificial Neural Networks in the Identification of Quantitative Structure-Activity Relationships for Chemotherapeutic Drug Carcinogenicity

Alexander C. Priest, Alexander J. Williamson, and Hugh M. Cartwright

Department of Chemistry, University of Oxford
Physical & Theoretical Chemistry Lab, South Parks Road, Oxford, UK, OX1 3QZ
alexander.priest@chem.ox.ac.uk

Abstract. We investigate which of two Artificial Intelligence techniques is superior at making predictions about complex carcinogen systems. Artificial Neural Networks are shown to provide good predictions of carcinogen toxicology bands for drugs which are themselves used to treat cancerous cells, by using a novel system of molecular descriptors derived from the molecules' mass spectrometry intensities, reduced in dimensionality by Principal Component Analysis, to form a series of orthogonal descriptors which retain 95% of the variance of the original data.

The creation of molecular descriptors from PCA-resolved mass spectrometry data is shown to be superior to the use of Self-Organising Maps, the selection of a series of modal fragments, or the use of every peak (within the confines of the precepts of Artificial Intelligence). A new system of backpropagation which increases network efficacy in this case is also proposed.

Keywords: artificial neural network, ANN, carcinogenicity, QSAR.

1 Introduction

Computer-based drug design is an important area of pharmaceutical chemistry [1,2]. Quantitative Structure-Activity Relationships (QSARs), determined computationally from experimental observations, are widely used to suggest candidate drugs for early screening, reducing both the time and money spent on synthesis and *in vivo* testing [3]. Computational approaches to the design of new drugs have become progressively more significant and sophisticated as computer power has increased, and all major pharmaceutical companies now make extensive use of these methods.

Many properties of a chemical contribute to the decision as to whether it is viable as a drug. Apart from the obvious question of efficacy, the harm that a drug itself presents must be sufficiently low that it not outweigh the drug's therapeutic value. The carcinogenicity and teratogenicity of a drug is an important area in this regard, but modelling these kinds of complex and dynamic systems presents a significant barrier to the advancement of this technology. Chicu, at al. [4] have used statistical methods to predict chemicals' toxicity in crustacea and fish, while Williams [5]

P.R. Cohen, N.M. Adams, and M.R. Berthold (Eds.): IDA 2010, LNCS 6065, pp. 137–146, 2010.
© Springer-Verlag Berlin Heidelberg 2010

predicted the carcinogenic effects of ATPase inhibitors using chemical structure. Conolly et al. [6] modelled respiratory tract carcinogens in a similar way.

Artificial Intelligence techniques have, with great success, provided insight into complex data in other spheres [7,8,9,10,11,12,13,14] suggesting that techniques such as Artificial Neural Networks (ANNs) will provide an accurate link between molecular descriptors and physical data.

However, numerous potential architectures, parameter settings and dimensionality-reduction techniques exist in Artificial Neural Networking and optimising these is an essential step in the use of the method. Furthermore, it is necessary to represent physical phenomena in a theoretical frame and, consequently, discerning a representative series of molecular descriptors is imperative. Matter [15] and Hopfinger et al. [16] proposed that this could be achieved by creating a series of molecular descriptors to represent an energy-minimised three-dimensional drug, and Tanabe et al. [17] subsequently predicted carcinogenicities using three-dimensional geometrical molecular descriptors as a basis for supervised learning. We describe here an extension of their work using mass spectral data, which is surprisingly effective considering its relative simplicity.

2   Molecular Descriptors and Data

A molecular descriptor specifies some feature of a molecule, such as its dipole moment, size, or electron distribution, in an unambiguous way; the complete description of a molecule thus requires many descriptors. Since we can anticipate that the effectiveness of drugs must be related in some way to properties at the molecular level, it is evident that connections exist between a suitably-chosen set of molecular descriptors and the activity of a drug.

Although the most widely used molecular descriptors are a direct expression of properties of the molecule itself, there are many examples where some derivable property of the molecule, such as its infrared spectrum, have been used as descriptors: this is a standard approach in Computational QSAR analysis. We have therefore investigated whether the mass spectra of candidate drugs might constitute suitable proxy molecular descriptors. As mass spectra contain substantial amounts of information about a sample, it is reasonable to suppose that a single mass spectrum might be able to replace a substantial number of more conventional descriptors. Mass Spectrometry data were obtained from the National Institute of Standards and Technology. The data series included a CAS Number, and a list of peaks and their intensities.

The wealth of data in a mass spectrum presents, however, a problem as well as an advantage. When seeking correlations between an experimental spectrum and a drug's properties, unsupportable and unjustified interaction models might emerge through overfitting, so our initial step is to reduce the dimensionality of the data. All mass spectra were treated with Principal Component Analysis, creating a series of quasi-molecular descriptors which contained 95% of the original data variance (Table 1). The number of quasi-molecular descriptors was reduced from several thousand to 146. These new descriptors were preliminarily compared with modal (intensities of popular fragments) and banded (similarly-sized fragments banded together) peaks. These alternative systems were good comparators as they represent other valid

Table 1. 146 Principal Components representing 95% of the variance of the original data

Transformed Data	Cumulative Responsibility
PC 1	0.0709
PC 2	0.1303
PC 3	0.1738
PC 4	0.2076
PC 5	0.2355
PC 6	0.2596
PC 7	0.2823
…	…
PC 140	0.9460
PC 141	0.9468
PC 142	0.9476
PC 143	0.9483
PC 144	0.9491
PC 145	0.9498
PC 146	0.9504

methods of reducing the number of inputs, which is necessary in Artificial Neural Networking to generate realistic, short processing runs. However, these alternative molecular descriptors generated predictions no better than those generated through randomisation (ie if bands had been selected at random). See Section 5.

2.1 Toxicity Data

Training data (oral, rat, TD_{50}) were sourced from the National Toxicology Program (NTP) [18] and The Carcinogenic Potency Project, Berkeley University [19], and carefully concatenated and their units reconciled. These data were logarithmically banded into nine distinct groups (1-9; 1=most carcinogenic, 9=least carcinogenic), and tabulated along with the CAS Number of the chemical which they represented.

3   Self-Organising Maps

The PCA-resolved mass spectra molecular descriptors were used as inputs for 12×12 hexagonal self-organising maps (SOMs) with various interaction settings. No simple relationship between a 2-dimensionally-mapped series of molecular descriptors and the carcinogenicity of a molecule was found (see section 5). Following a series of runs, using a wide range of parameters and architectures this method of dimensionality reduction was discounted. Computational physical and biological scientists should be wary of the use of generic techniques in data mining, except on a case-by-case basis with proper double cross-validation testing. It is the nature of complex systems, such as the activity of carcinogens, that it is hard to understand in advance why one technique succeeds where another fails in discerning patterns and making predictions.

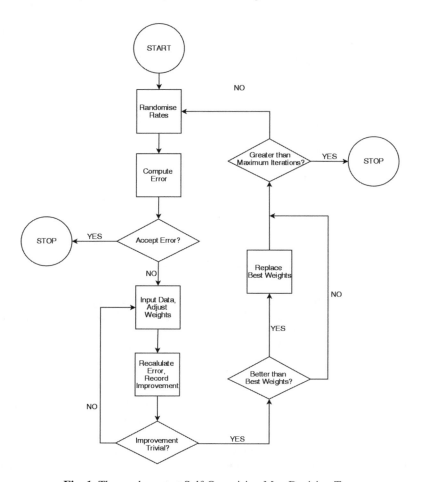

Fig. 1. The random-start Self-Organising Map Decision Tree

4   Artificial Neural Networks

Standard feed-forward Artificial Neural Networks, using a sigmoidal transfer function and a novel backpropagation system (which also guarded against pareto equilibria, when a Neural Network falls into a false minimum, from which it is unable to escape), were then applied to the problem. Where the network was moving away from a real equilibrium a randomisation of the weights occurred, and processing began again. The new system of backpropagation works as follows:

Let w = the weight assigned to the connection between two nodes

   O = output value of a node, following application of the transfer function

   $\varepsilon = T - O$ = the overall error (where T is the target value)

Then the error of the output node,

$$\varepsilon_{kj} = \psi^{-1}(O_{kj}) \times \psi^{-1}(T_{kj}) \tag{1}$$

where $T_{output,j}$ = the ideal output, and the inverse transfer function (reverse of the TF),

$$\psi^{-1}(t) = 100 \times \log\left(\frac{1 + \dfrac{t}{2000}}{1 - \dfrac{t}{2000}}\right) \tag{2}$$

Therefore, the change in connection weight,

$$\Delta w_{kj} = \ell \varepsilon_{kj} \frac{O_{k-1,j} \times w_{k,j}}{\sum_i O_{k-1,i} \times w_{k,i}} \tag{3}$$

where ℓ is the learning parameter. Therefore, let the target output of the hidden layer,

$$T_{kj} = \frac{\displaystyle\sum_i \frac{T_{k+1,i} \times O_{kj} \times w_{k+1,j}}{\displaystyle\sum_h O_{kh} \times w_{k+1,h}}}{N_{k+1}} \tag{4}$$

where N_k=number of nodes in layer k. The system is then processed backwards.

The new system stems from the necessity, with a more complicated data set, to invoke a similar change in error during backpropagation, which will prevent overcorrection. This decreases the time a system takes to arrive at a minimum. This is achieved by calculating the *inverse* error gradient[1] at each node and then using this to calculate the amount by which the weights should be altered in the subsequent iteration. This allows the network to spring out of pareto equilibria when the amount by which each weight changes in each iteration is high, while not adversely affecting the final equilibrium because the change increment is small towards the end. This system was found to reduce typical processing time by 11% as fewer iterations are necessary to achieve the same minimum equilibrium[2].

---

[1] The inverse error gradient is the reciprocal of the error gradient, ie $\left.\dfrac{\partial \varepsilon}{\partial w_i}\right|_{w_{i \neq j}}$.

[2] That is to say that over seven program runs using different carcinogen data sets, the novel system of backpropagation arrived at the minimum error on average 11% faster than an equivalent network using standard backpropagation.

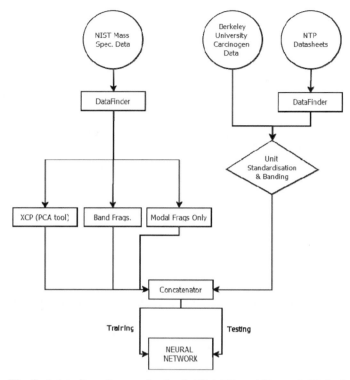

Fig. 2. A data flow diagram for the Artificial Neural Network Method

5   Results

Through the use of ANNs, we were able to accurately identify a QSAR for the prediction of carcinogenicity using PCA-resolved Mass Spectral data to describe the
molecules (Fig 3). This QSAR was tested using a series of molecules not present in the
training set and also by the leave-three-out cross validation method. Leave-three-out
was selected as opposed to leave-one-out to ensure that the system was resolving in
favour of dissimilar molecules. 174 out of 196 test molecules were banded to within the
success criterion (within one band of their actual band as given by Berkeley or the
NTP), representing an accuracy rate of 89%, which we consider viable. This compares
to 53 out of 196 selected accurately following the use of Self-Organising Maps.

Table 2. Average % of correctly-identified carcinogens (one band margin of error)

Processing Architecture	% Accuracy (average)	Weighted-kappa Value
Banded Mass Spec + ANN	20	0.18
Modal Mass Spec + ANN	25	0.21
PCA Mass Spec + SOM	27	0.20
PCA-resolved Mass Spec +ANN	89	0.76

Systems in which the raw data consisted of modal (49/196) or banded (39/196) Mass Spectra failed to identify sufficiently accurate models.

As an additional, if somewhat qualitative, test of reliability, Table 3 shows predicted carcinogenicity band for some drugs compared with their International Agency for Research on Cancer classification. This classification ranks chemicals into 5 groups with the following definitions:

1: *carcinogenic to humans.*
2A: *probably carcinogenic to humans.*
2B: *possibly carcinogenic to humans.*
3: *not classifiable as to its carcinogenicity to humans.*
4: *probably not carcinogenic to humans.*

Table 3. Predicted carcinogenicity band (ANN) for some example drugs compared with their International Agency for Research on Cancer's Classification

Chemotherapeutic Drug	CAS No.	Predicted Carcinogen Band	IARC Group
Chlorambucil	305-03-3	2	1
Cyclophosphamide	50-18-0	2	1
Mechlorethamine	51-75-2	3	2A
Methotrexate	59-05-2	7	3
Fluorouracil	51-21-8	6	3
Uracil	66-22-8	4	2B

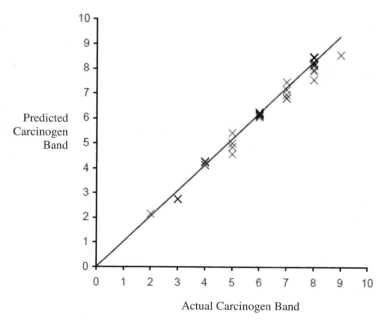

Fig. 3. Carcinogen Band prediction by Artificial Neural Network

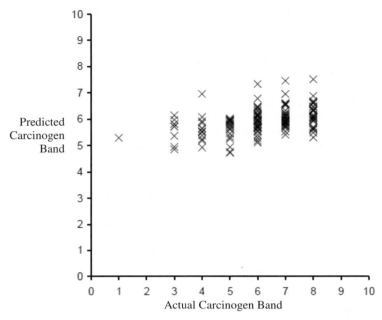

Fig. 4. Carcinogen Band prediction by Self-Organising Map

6 Conclusions

The carcinogenicity of a potential cancer drug is discernible using a series of Artificial Neural Networks and PCA-resolved Mass Spectral data. This clearly implies that mass spectral intensities may be used as reliable molecular descriptors in this, and possibly other cases, through the use of this technique. The selection of a set of the most frequent or banded fragments does not allow accurate prediction.

It has also been shown that reducing the burden of dimensionality does not necessarily compromise the reliability of the process: the selection of a smaller set of orthogonal descriptors is accurately achieved using Principal Component Analysis, but this process is not satisfactory when using Self-Organising Maps, which, with this dataset, destroy the underlying nuances of the data which act as molecular descriptors.

The novel system of backpropagation proposed is both more efficient and reliable in monitoring a series of connection weights within an Artificial Neural Network (11% faster for similar levels of accuracy), and has the potential to be applied more generally in this field.

This application of Artificial Intelligence to a complex pharmaceutical problem has wide-reaching implications for the analysis of complex biological systems by physical and life scientists, as it lays the building blocks for drug design to become even more efficient, and allows doctors prescribing nascent or experimental treatments to understand more fully the drug regime they are recommending.

Further optimisation of the network architecture and the discovery of additional data (both mass spectral and carcinogenicity) would lead to improvements in the accuracy of the network.

Various options are open as to how to proceed. An investigation into the incorporation of Support Vector Machines or Fuzzy processes into the system would be extremely interesting, as would the analysis of a Fuzzy success criterion (currently a prediction is right or wrong, but information on how wrong would be useful).

Acknowledgments

This research has been supported by St John's College, Oxford, the Department of Chemistry at Oxford University and SCAST.

References

1. Walters, W.P., Stahl, M.T., Murcko, M.A.: Virtual screening - an overview. Drug Discovery Today 3(4), 160–178 (1998)
2. Jorgensen, W.L.: The many roles of computation in drug discovery. Science 303(5665), 1813–1818 (2004)
3. Agatonovic-Kustrin, S., Beresford, R.: Basic concepts of artificial neural network (ANN) modeling and its application in pharmaceutical research. Pharm. Biomedical Analysis 22(5), 717–727 (2000)
4. Chicu, S., Hermann, K., Berking, S.: An Approach to Calculate the Toxicity of Simple Organic Molecules on the Basis of QSAR Analysis in Hydraactina echinata Hydrozoa. Cnidaria. Quant. Struct.-Act. Relat. 19 (2000)
5. Williams, W.R.: Relative molecular similarity in selected chemical carcinogens and the nucleoside triphosphate chain. Pharmacology & Toxicology 92(2), 57–63 (2003)
6. Conolly, R.B., et al.: Human respiratory tract cancer risks of inhaled formaldehyde: Dose-response predictions derived from biologically-motivated computational modeling of a combined rodent and human dataset. Toxicological Sciences 82(1), 279–296 (2004)
7. Werbos, P.J.: The Roots of Backpropagation: From Ordered Derivatives to Neural Networks and Political Forecasting. Wiley, Chichester (1994, a reprinting of his Harvard DPhil thesis of 1974)
8. McCulloch, W., Pitts, W.: A logical calculus of the ideas immanent in nervous activity. Bull. Math. Biophys. 5, 115–133 (1943)
9. De Wolf, E., Francl, L.: Neural Networks that distinguish infection periods of wheat tan spot in an outdoor environment. Phytopathology 87, 83 (1997)
10. Rayudu, R., Samarasinge, S.: A network of neural nets to model power system fault diagnosis. In: Proceedings of the Fourth International Conference on Neural Information Processing (1997)
11. Jiang, D., et al.: Progress in developing an ANN model for air pollution index forecasting. Atmospheric Environment 38, 7055 (2004)
12. Rajanayake, C., et al.: Solving the inverse problem in stochastic groundwater modelling with artificial neural networks. In: Proceedings of 1st Biennial Congress of the International Environmental Modelling Society (2002)
13. Chandraratne, M.R., et al.: Prediction of lamb tenderness using image surface texture analysis. Journal of Food Engineering (2005)
14. Limsombunchai, V., Samarasinge, S.: House price prediction: hedonic price model vs artificial neural networks. Kasetsar University Journal of Economics (2005)

15. Matter, H.: Selecting optimally diverse compounds from structure databases: A validation study of two-dimensional and three-dimensional molecular descriptors. Journal of Medicinal Chemistry 40(8), 1219–1229 (1997)
16. Hopfinger, A.J., et al.: Construction of 3D-QSAR models using the 4D-QSAR analysis formalism. Journal of the American Chemical Society 119(43), 10509–10524 (1997)
17. Tanabe, K., Ohmori, N., Ono, S., Suzuki, T.: Neural network based QSARs of chemical carcinogens derived from chemical safety database CAESAR. Pharm. & Phar. 58(Suppl. 1), A32 (2006)
18. National Toxicology Program, http://ntp-server.niehs.nih.gov/
19. Carcinogenic Potency Project, Berkeley University, http://potency.berkeley.edu/

Image Approach towards Document Mining in Neuroscientific Publications

Jayaprakash Rajasekharan[1,*], Ulrike Scharfenberger[2],
Nicolau Gonçalves[3], and Ricardo Vigário[3,**]

[1] Department of Signal Processing and Acoustics, Aalto University School of Science
and Technology, Finland
[2] Department of Computer Engineering, Eberhard-Karls-University Tübingen,
Germany
[3] Adaptive Informatics Research Centre, Aalto University School of Science and
Technology, Finland

Abstract. This paper addresses the issue of a content-based information retrieval system that works on fMRI images from neuroscientific journal publications. We present a general framework for automatic extraction, characterisation and classification of fMRI images, based on their functional properties. The proposed method identifies the section of each of those images, by morphological processing, and estimates the coordinates of the brain activated regions, in relation to a standard reference template using locality preserving projections. Those regions are then segmented, and their physical and geometrical properties evaluated. We formulate a feature vector based on these characteristics, and cluster the images and corresponding journal publications using self organizing maps.

1 Introduction

There is an ever increase in the number of scientific publications in many areas in general, and in neurosciences in particular. Hundreds of articles are published each month, with a considerable amount currently comprising functional magnetic resonance image (fMRI, [1]) experiments.

When comparing the results obtained with a particular experimental setup and existing literature, one may validate, integrate or confront different theories. A proper compilation of all the reported information is therefore crucial, and is currently mostly performed in a rather human-intensive manner. Whether you are a seasoned neuroscientist in search for the explanation for an unexpected activation result, or a machine learning researcher attempting to validate a newly proposed analysis method, it is rather common to spend a considerable amount of time scanning through the vast list of publications, in search for comparable

---

* This paper is based on the M.Sc. theses of Jayaprakash Rajasekharan and Ulrike Scharfenberger, carried out at the Department of Information and Computer Science, Faculty of Information and Natural Sciences, Helsinki university of Technology.
** Corresponding author.

P.R. Cohen, N.M. Adams, and M.R. Berthold (Eds.): IDA 2010, LNCS 6065, pp. 147–158, 2010.

experimental outcomes to yours. The automatic extraction of the relevant information is not always a simple task, and constitutes the subject of information retrieval and data mining [2]. Such meta-research is the topic of the current publication.

The intrinsic multi-modal nature of the publications provides ample scope for mining information at various levels. Such information is encoded both in the image content, as well as in highly structured text structures – title, abstract, captions, and the various sections. Several attempts to build atlases of brain functions often use a considerable amount of curator work, with persons going through the papers, and extracting by hand all the relevant information, e.g., Talairach's coordinates, experimental setups,... In a recent paper, it was estimated that as much as 30 to 60 minutes are required for a research assistant to enter the details of a single publication [3]. Yet, brain atlases comprise information from thousands of such papers. For good reviews of several such atlases, see for example [4,5]. The growing interest in building and exploiting them can be seen, for example, in the lively discussions published in [6].

We believe that it is possible to automize part of the data collecting process, rendering the complete procedure consistent and reproducible for vast amounts of data. The tools presented in this paper can easily be adapted for the analysis and modelling of a complex literature field, in particular when pictorial representations of data or information visualisation is concerned. However, it must be noted that the approach outlined in this paper can only be seen as the first step towards it. With this clear proof-of-concept mindset, we will therefore focus our attention on a rather homogeneous data set, made of activation patterns in fMRI reports.

Consider a typical fMRI image, depicted in Fig. 1. In a cursory glance, it is easy to identify the kind of section of the image (axial, as opposed to sagittal or coronal); the approximate coordinates of that section; the anatomical features of the section; as well as the functionally activated region or "blob" within the section. We do that by relating the image to an internal representation of our

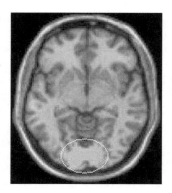

Fig. 1. A prototypical fMRI image. Activity is present in the occipital area, and its intensity is usually reported using a colour code.

anatomical and physiological knowledge of the brain. This relation takes into account physical and geometrical properties of the underlying structural image, as well as of the superimposed blob. In addition to the activation location, typical image analysis features, such as intensity, area, perimeter, shape, compactness, elongation... can be used to fully characterize the activity (c.f. [7]). Such details were collected automatically in our research, and a number of journal publications were clustered accordingly.

In the following sections, we will first describe the extraction and characterization of the brain images and functional activation patters. Classification using the self organizing maps follows. We conclude with some remarks on current limitations of the proposed method, as well as suggestions to overcome them.

2   Image Characterization

We randomly selected 11 articles from various issues of NeuroImage journal by Elsevier publications and extracted about 100 figures using the linux command *pdfimages*. After pre-processing, we identified the fMRI images present in these figures by morphological image processing methods. 144 fMRI images were obtained, each characterized based on its functional properties and physical properties such as volume type, section type and co-ordinates of the section. We incorporated all these characteristics to formulate a feature vector that tries to describe every fMRI image in a 16 dimensional space. The following subsections explain the theory involved at various stages of these processes.

2.1   fMRI Image Extraction

Journal publications have a uniform style of reporting, but the figures in articles have non-homogenous content such as several images, plots, annotations, captions, etc... Hence, it is necessary to morphologically process the figure in order to extract fMRI images of interest. In the first stage of image extraction, figures were pre-processed by means of conventional methods such as histogram equalization, high pass filtering and gray level thresholding. After pre-processing, edge detection using the Sobel method returned edges at those points where the gradient of the figures is maximum, thereby separating the background from the objects in the figures. This was followed by structural operations to distinctly isolate each object in the figure. After filtering out noise and exceedingly small objects, it was possible to segment all the other objects remaining in the figure. After extracting the images corresponding to every object, the next step was to identify and obtain fMRI images based on some simple properties such as colored activation regions, shape metrics and aspect ratio of the sections. The Fig. 2 illustrates the effects of morphological image processing in extracting fMRI images.

2.2   fMRI Image Processing

Once the fMRI images have been extracted, they have to be specifically processed to identify the volume that was used to register and normalize the fMRI

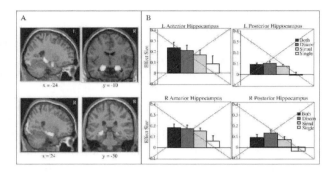

Fig. 2. fMRI image extraction from a figure using morphological image processing methods. The four fMRI images are selected, while the plots on the right side are rejected (note the crossed-out frames).

image. Also, the type of the section needs to be identified in order to estimate the co-ordinates of the section.

Volume Identification

Most articles use either the SPM [8] or Colin [9] volumes to normalize their fMRI images. Colin volumes contain high resolution sections compared to SPM volumes. Regarding the spatial separation between adjacent sections, in SPM volumes is 2mm whereas, in Colin volumes is 1mm. Based on the resolution of the extracted fMRI images, it is possible to differentiate volume types. Simple edge detection using the Canny method finds edges by looking for the local maxima of the gradient of the image. As a result, both strong and weak edges are detected, even in the presence of noise. The fMRI image based on Colin volume has more detailed edges than the SPM volume. Fig. 3 depicts the difference between Colin and SPM volume types.

Section Identification

Since activation regions are three dimensional in nature, views from three different planes are required to represent them in two dimensions. Thus we have axial sections along the transversal plane that travels from the top to bottom, the sagittal section that travels along the median plane from left to right and the coronal section along the frontal plane that travels from front to back. Instead of focusing on the internal features of each section, the shape of the section is used to identify the section type. After appropriate thresholding, the fMRI images are converted to binary images thereby prominently outlining the shape of the section. Simple symmetry serves to distinguish the sections from one another. The axial section is symmetric about both the horizontal and vertical axis. The coronal section is symmetric only with respect to its vertical axis. The sagittal section is asymmetric. Fig. 4 shows how symmetry can be used to distinguish between the different sections of the fMRI image.

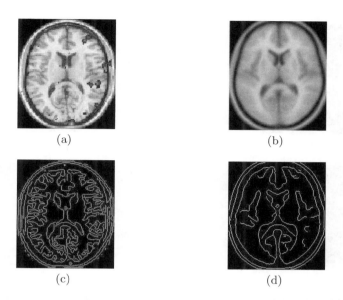

(a)   (b)

(c)   (d)

Fig. 3. Volume identification — (a) image normalized to the Colin reference volume; (b) image normalized to the SPM reference. (c) and (d) are the corresponding images, after edge detection.

2.3 Coordinate Estimation

An extracted fMRI image, with its volume type and section identified, does not completely characterize the image as its relative spatial position is still unknown. However, standard reference templates for every volume type are available. The extracted fMRI image can be compared with the corresponding sections of the standard reference template, and the best matching section will give the relative spatial position or the co-ordinates of the fMRI image. Standard comparison metrics such as mutual information or statistical correlation measures perform poorly. The eigenfaces approach, based on principal component analysis is also not very promising. These failures are due to the fact that images from successive sections of the standard reference templates are almost identical to each other, except for some local features that are subtle in nature. An efficient subspace learning algorithm should be able to discover the nonlinear local manifold structure of the image space which is more important than the global structure in the Euclidean space. A locality preserving projection based method for classification of images [10] is described below.

The image set X is first projected onto the PCA subspace defined by the strongest principal components. Next, a nearest neighbor graph G, with n nodes is constructed, where the ith node corresponds to the image x_i. An edge is placed between nodes i and j if x_j is among the k nearest neighbors of x_i or vice-versa. The constructed nearest neighbor map is an approximation to the local manifold

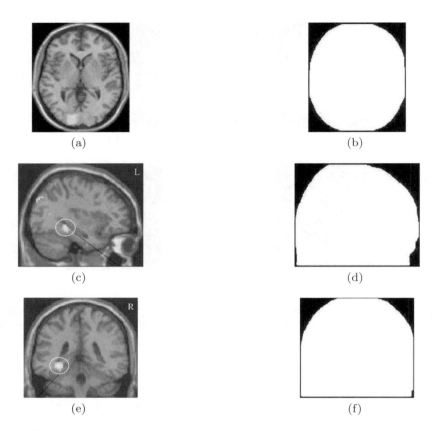

Fig. 4. Section identification — Left column contains the original fMRI images and on the right their corresponding binary masks. From top to bottom, we have axial, sagittal and coronal sections.

structure. A Gaussian kernel can be used as a weight matrix S of the graph G. The eigenvalues and eigenvectors of the generalized eigenvector problem,

$$XLX^T\mathbf{w} = \lambda XDX^T\mathbf{w}, \tag{1}$$

are computed where, D is the diagonal eigenvalue matrix, whose entries are column sums of the matrix S and $L = D - S$ is the Laplacian matrix. The local manifold structure is mapped onto a two dimensional space to select the best matching image.

Fig. 5 shows the results of co-ordinate estimation based on Laplacian-Eigen mapping. For the sample fMRI image (a), the best matching section from the standard reference template is shown in (b). The results of the estimation are compared to sections that are located 4mm away on either side of the best matching section. This gives a good idea of the accuracy of the co-ordinate estimation.

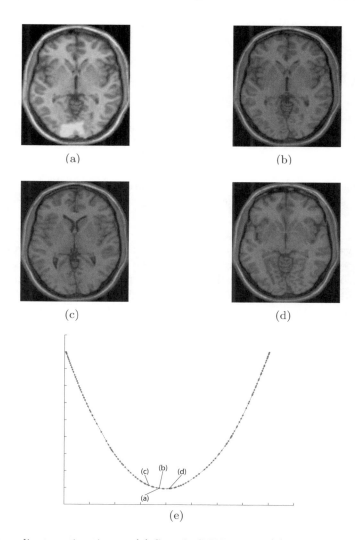

Fig. 5. Co-ordinate estimation — (a) Sample fMRI image; (b) best matching section; (c) and (d) neighboring sections, separated by +/- 4mm from the best matching section. (e) Two dimensional manifold mapping with highlighted sections.

2.4   Activation Region Analysis

Activation regions are generated in response to stimulation. The properties of the activation region largely define the fMRI image and hence it is crucial that a comprehensive analysis of the blobs is carried out in order to classify fMRI images. Activation regions can be easily segmented based on hue information. Fig. 6 illustrates the segmentation of activation regions based on their RGB values.

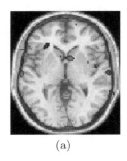
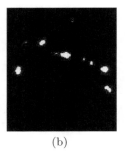

(a)   (b)

Fig. 6. Activation region analysis — (a) sample fMRI image with multiple activation regions; (b) segmented binary image

The physical and geometrical properties characterize the activated region. These properties are obtained by segmenting the activation regions and morphologically processing each region. The location of maximum activation is given by the centroid of mass of the largest activation region. The intensity of the activations is given by its color scale. The size of the activation region is given by its area and perimeter. Even though it not possible to exactly describe an arbitrary shape, various measures are used to try to objectively define the shape. Compactness measures the deviation of the object from a circular shape, whereas the extent of the region is computed as the ratio of the area of the region to the area of the bounding box of the region. Eccentricity specifies the eccentricity of the ellipse that has the same second moments as the region and the Orientation

Table 1. Feature vector for prototype image shown in Fig. 1

#	Property	Value
1	Section of the image	Axial
2	Co-ordinates of the section	68
3	Number of activation regions	1
4	Peak color	Yellow
5	Fringe color	Yellow
6	Area	1535 pixels
7	Perimeter	187 pixels
8	Compactness	0.4532
9	Centroid of mass (x co-ordinate)	97
10	Centroid of mass (y co-ordinate)	198
11	Centroid of color (x co-ordinate)	70
12	Centroid of color (y co-ordinate)	192
13	Eccentricity	0.8012
14	Solidity	0.8148
15	Extent	0.6786
16	Orientation	4.2233

gives the angle between the x-axis and the major axis of the ellipse. Solidity specifies the ratio of the area of the region to that of the area of the smallest possible convex polygon that bounds the region.

In the case of multiple activation regions, each one of them is treated as if it was the only activation region in the fMRI image and a feature vector corresponding to every activation region is formulated. The feature vector for Fig. 1 is shown in Tab. 1.

3   Results

To cluster images with similar activation areas, an algorithm that organizes data according to its similarity was needed. The algorithm should be able to search for similarities between the fMRI images in a higher dimensional space and project them to a lower dimensional space that preserves the input space's distance information [11].

3.1   Self Organization

Self Organizing Map (SOM) [12] is an excellent tool for unsupervised clustering and two dimensional visualization of higher dimensional data spaces and hence, an evident choice for this clustering operation. The SOMs perform a lattice projection that preserves similarity information from the input space, through competitive and Hebbian learning rules.

As an input pattern is fed into the network, the only map unit activated is the winning neuron best representing the input pattern, called best matching unit (BMU). During the learning process, the neighborhood of the winning neuron is also taken into account, by changing the location of the neighbor neurons.

After training, the spatial locations of the neurons in the lattice are indicative of the intrinsic statistical features contained in the input patterns; the continuous input space is mapped on a discrete set of prototype vectors.

A simple explanation of the algorithm follows.

Let $m_j(t)$ denote the weight vector of neuron j at iteration step t, $h_{j,c}$ the neighborhood function centered around the winning neuron c and α the learning parameter. $x(t)$ is the input pattern fed into the network at iteration t.

The winning neuron at time step t is found using the minimum-distance criterion, between the input vector and the weight vectors of the map:

$$c = \arg\min_j \|x(t) - m_j\| \tag{2}$$

Afterwards, the neurons in the neighborhood of the BMU are pulled closer to the input vector, by adjusting the weight vector

$$m_j(t+1) = m_j(t) + \alpha h_{j,c}[x(t) - m_j(t)] \tag{3}$$

Using the feature vectors of the different activation areas, several SOMs with different sizes and initializations were trained. They all exhibited similar results for the different runs, demonstrating the robustness of the method.

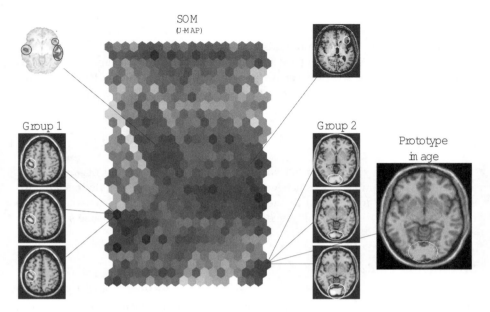

Fig. 7. Self Organizing Map — U-matrix trained with the 16 dimensional feature vectors. Two distinct cluster regions are observed at the lower left and right sides of the map. The prototype image in Fig. 1 joins its natural cluster.

3.2   Image Clustering

144 fMRI images were extracted from 11 articles and clustered using the self organizing maps. The results are shown in Fig. 7. The SOM was trained with a size of 15x10, hexagonal shape and no cylindrical continuity. From the figure, we find that fMRI images with similar activation regions are grouped together. Two clear clusters are expanded in the figure. The one at the lower left side of the map has fMRI images that show activations close to the parietal region, while the images belonging to the cluster at the bottom right show activation in the occipital region. These two clusters exhibit a good degree of separation, typical from the high discriminative ability of the SOMs. Two other, isolated units are also depicted, to illustrate the clear separation attained. One should note that, although the fMRI images that are grouped together exhibited similar functional activation regions, they were extracted from articles that did not follow the same experimental set-up. Furthermore, not all images came from similar reporting formats. In their original publications, the analysed images may appear alone or within a multi-modal image set.

On other hand, the map shows a small number of grouping areas (minima), indicating that, aside from the aforementioned clusters, the data is not rich enough to fully populate other SOM regions. By increasing the number of image sources, the SOM would probably give a better segmentation result.

To evaluate the performance of the clustering, the feature vector of the prototype image shown in Fig. 1 was employed. Naturally, this information was not used during the training phase. As expected, the image fell on group 2, which has a similar functional profile.

The identifications of the relevant figures from articles, and the extraction of the fMRI images therein was somewhat computationally intensive, as it involves scanning through all articles and morphologically processing the figures. However, once in possession of the fMRI images, the construction of the feature vector and the clustering is far less demanding. The clustering process for the 144 fMRI images consumed just about a couple of minutes. When compared to the fully manual mode of compiling information from journal articles [3], our automated approach saves a considerable amount of time and manual labour.

4   Concluding Remarks

Our goal was to develop an automatic content-based information retrieval system for fMRI images, published in neuroscience journals. We presented a framework for clustering these images, based on their anatomical and functional characteristics that involved locality preseving projections over non-linear manifold structures. The clustering was performed over a feature vector comprising physical and geometrical properties, characterizing the activation regions reported in the images. With that in mind, we also proposed a novel method for estimating the coordinates of the activated regions.

As stated earlier, there is a considerable variability in the brain-image-displaying approach. For this reason, our extraction methods could not be applied in a purely automated manner, but a small degree of human intervention was required, to eliminate some non-fMRI images. This intervention may be minimised or even entirely removed by adding prior information on the specific morphological nature of the brain images and by using more complex semantic image processing methods.

With a clear *proof of concept* in mind, we used only a small set of articles and images, yet ensuring the existence of at least two clear groups of activation regions. The results of our clustering are rather encouraging, even when applied to a limited set of fMRI images. The scalability of the feature extraction is clearly linear with the number of images, whereas SOM has been used successfully in very large scale problems. Furthermore, the increase in the number of analysed images should lead to a more representative clustering of neuronal functional activities.

In addition to the extension to larger data sets, future research will focus on the robustness of the method, as well as the integration of these outcomes to a text mining approach. Finally, we hope to test these methods in situations where there is either a clear agreement between different research reports or a challenge between theories. The former is a key aspect to the construction of functional neuro-atlases, whereas the latter may lead to true findings in neuroscience.

Acknowledgments

This study was partially funded by the Academy of Finland through its Centres of Excellence Program 2006-2011.

References

1. Huettel, S.A., Song, A.W., McCarthy, G.: Functional magnetic resonance imaging Sinauer Associates Publishers, Sunderland (2004)
2. Hand, D., Mannila, H., Smyth, P.: Principles of Data Mining. The MIT Press, Cambridge (2001)
3. Laird, A.R., Lancaster, J.L., Fox, P.T.: Lost in localization? the focus is metaanalysis. NeuroImage 48, 18–20 (2009)
4. Van Essen, D.C., Dierker, D.L.: Surface-based and probabilistic atlases of primate cerebral cortex. Neuron 56(2), 209–225 (2007)
5. Laird, A.R., Lancaster, J.L., Fox, P.T.: Brainmap: The social evolution of a human brain mapping database. Neuroinformatics 3(1), 65–78 (2005)
6. NeuroImage 48 (2009)
7. Bankman, I.N. (ed.): Handbook of medical imaging. Academic Press, Inc., Orlando (2000)
8. Friston, K.J.: Statistical Parametric Mapping: The Analysis of Functional Brain Images, December 2006. Academic Press, London (2006)
9. Brett, M., Johnsrude, I.S., Owen, A.M.: The problem of functional localization in the human brain. Nat. Rev. Neurosci. 3(3), 243–249 (2002)
10. He, X., Yan, S., Hu, Y., Niyogi, P., Zhang, H.J.: Face recognition using laplacianfaces. IEEE Transactions on Pattern Analysis and Machine Intelligence 27(3), 328–340 (2005)
11. Laaksonen, J., Koskela, M., Laakso, S., Oja, E.: Picsom—content-based image retrieval with self-organizing maps. Pattern Recogn. Lett. 21(13-14), 1199–1207 (2000)
12. Kohonen, T.: Self-Organizing Maps, 3rd edn., December 2000. Springer, Heidelberg (2000)

Similarity Kernels for Nearest Neighbor-Based Outlier Detection

Ruben Ramirez-Padron[1], David Foregger[2], Julie Manuel[3],
Michael Georgiopoulos[1], and Boris Mederos[4]

[1] School of Electrical Engineering and Computer Science,
University of Central Florida, FL, USA
rramirez@knights.ucf.edu
[2] Wesleyan University, Middletown, CT, USA
[3] University of South Florida, Tampa, FL, USA
[4] Universidad Autónoma de Ciudad Juárez, Ciudad Juárez, Mexico

Abstract. Outlier detection is an important research topic that focuses on detecting abnormal information in data sets and processes. This paper addresses the problem of determining which class of kernels should be used in a geometric framework for nearest neighbor-based outlier detection. It introduces the class of similarity kernels and employs it within that framework. We also propose the use of isotropic stationary kernels for the case of normed input spaces. Two definitions of similarity scores using kernels are given: the k-NN kernel similarity score (kNNSS) and the summation kernel similarity score (SKSS). The paper concludes with preliminary experimental results comparing the performance of kNNSS and SKSS for outlier detection on four data sets. SKSS compared favorably to kNNSS.

Keywords: similarity kernels, similarity scores, outlier detection, nearest neighbors.

1 Introduction

Outlier detection is a growing field within the data mining community. It focuses on detecting abnormal observations in data sets and processes. Detection of credit card fraud, computer networks attacks and suspicious activity in electronic commerce are common applications. Hawkins defined an outlier as "an observation that deviates so much from other observations as to arouse suspicion that it was generated by a different mechanism" [10]. Some of the current definitions of outliers use a global approach, e.g. [12], while others focus on a neighborhood around each data point. The work of Breunig et al. [4] was the first one using scores to describe outliers. Outlier detection methods range from traditional approaches like nearest neighbor-based and statistical methods to more recent approaches such as information theoretic and spectral outlier detection. Our work focuses on the nearest neighbor-based approach, which relies on similarities (or equivalently, on distances) between data points. A recent survey on the different approaches to outlier detection can be found in [5].

P.R. Cohen, N.M. Adams, and M.R. Berthold (Eds.): IDA 2010, LNCS 6065, pp. 159–170, 2010.

The computational complexity of straightforward implementations of nearest neighbor-based outlier detection is $O(n^2)$, where n is the number of data points. Although this is not efficient for large data sets, there are techniques that allow for almost linear complexity without sacrificing much accuracy [3,17,22].

A great number of outlier-detection algorithms are limited to numerical data. They benefit from a variety of statistical techniques and well-established metrics. Currently, there is an increasing interest in working on data sets with non-numerical attributes. Accordingly, several similarity-based outlier detection algorithms have been proposed to deal with non-numerical data. [5].

Kernels methods have given researchers the ability to deal with both numeric and non-numeric data types within a single framework [19]. Several works have proposed the "kernelization" of different outlier detection algorithms [8,19,14,18,15,20]. Kernel functions map input data points to a high dimensional feature space to which simple algorithms are applied implicitly. Of particular interest to our work is the geometric framework proposed in [8]. It applies nearest-neighbor outlier detection techniques to the high dimensional feature space. The distances between two points in the feature space can be easily calculated using the kernel function. However, it is an open problem to determine which classes of kernel functions are well suited to outlier detection problems [21,16].

Our work has three main contributions. First, we introduce the concept of similarity kernels and we argue that similarity kernels should be used for kernel nearest neighbor-based outlier detection. It is noted that our concept of similarity kernel extends the class of isotropic stationary kernels as defined in [9]. For the case of normed input spaces, we propose to restrict kernel nearest neighbor-based outlier detection to the class of isotropic stationary kernels. Those kernels guarantee invariance to translations and rotations in the input space.

Second, two similarity scores using kernels are defined: the k-NN kernel similarity score (kNNSS) and the summation kernel similarity score (SKSS). kNNSS is a characterization in terms of similarity kernels of the well-known k-NN score [5]. Recently, in [1], the outlier score of an observation x was defined as the sum of distances from x to a fixed number of its nearest neighbors. In contrast to that work, SKSS is computed as the sum of the similarities between x and all observations within a ball of a fixed radius centered on x. To our knowledge, SKSS is a new type of density-based score.

Finally, SKSS is compared to kNNSS on two numerical data sets and two categorical data sets. The Gaussian kernel was used in the numerical cases. The Hamming distance kernel [6] and a diffusion kernel [13] were used on the categorical data. It is proved that those categorical kernels are similarity kernels. Preliminary results suggest that SKSS can be a valuable similarity score for nearest neighbor-based outlier detection.

The paper is structured as follows: in Section 2 we provide a brief description of concepts and methods that are relevant to our paper. Our approach is presented in section 3. Our experimental findings are shown in Section 4. Finally, concluding remarks and a few comments regarding future work are provided in Section 5.

2   Related Work

2.1   Kernels

Kernel functions were introduced in machine learning as a way of finding non-linear patterns in data sets through the application of linear methods to a high dimensional representation of the data [7]. Kernels are positive semi-definite functions defined as follows: [19]

Definition 1. *A symmetric function $K : X \times X \to \mathbf{R}$ is called a positive semi-definite kernel function if and only if for any positive integer n, any choice of n objects $x_1, .., x_n \in X$, and any choice of real numbers $c_1, .., c_n$ the following property holds:*

$$\sum_{i=1}^{n} \sum_{j=1}^{n} c_i c_j K(x_i, x_j) \geq 0 \tag{1}$$

Kernel functions are defined on pairs of objects from a variety of data types. For every kernel function $K : X \times X \to \mathbf{R}$ there exists a unique mapping ϕ, $\phi : X \to H$, where H is a high dimensional feature space. Typically, the mapping ϕ is used implicitly through the expression $K(x_i, x_j) = <\phi(x_i), \phi(x_j)>$, where x_i and x_j are data points in X and $<,>$ denotes the inner product on H. Throughout this paper we often refer to a *kernel matrix* K instead of the kernel function K. A kernel matrix is an n x n matrix containing the values of the corresponding kernel function evaluated on all possible pairs of data points from a data set containing n objects. Kernels have been categorized based on whether they are local or not, stationary or non-stationary, separable or non-separable, among other characteristics [9]. Isotropic stationary kernels are of particular interest to our work:

Definition 2. *A kernel function $K : X \times X \to \mathbf{R}$ is isotropic stationary if there is a function $g_K : \mathbf{R} \to \mathbf{R}$ such that:*

$$K(x, z) = g_K(\|x - z\|) \tag{2}$$

It follows from this definition that isotropic stationary kernels are invariant to translations and rotations. The well-known Gaussian RBF kernel is an example of an isotropic stationary kernel. On the other hand, the linear kernel $K(x_i, x_j) = x_i^T x_j$ and the polynomial kernel of degree p, defined as $K(x_i, x_j) = (x_i^T x_j + 1)^p$, are examples of kernels that are not isotropic stationary. [9]

2.2   The Hamming Distance Kernel

The Hamming distance kernel [6] is based on the well-known Hamming distance. To follow the notation given in [6], let us assume a categorical data set consisting of m attributes, where the ith-attribute takes values in a finite categorical domain D_i. The cross product over all domains D_i is denoted by D^m, i.e. $D^m = \prod_{i=1}^{m} D_i$.

Definition 3. *The Hamming distance kernel function $K_H(s,t)$ between two input categorical objects s and t is defined as:*

$$K_H(s,t) = \sum_{u \in D^m} \prod_{i=1}^m \lambda^{\delta(u_i,s_i)} \lambda^{\delta(u_i,t_i)}$$

where $\lambda \in (0,1)$ and $\delta(s_i,t_i)$ is 0 when $s_i = t_i$, and 1 otherwise.

2.3   Diffusion Kernels

Diffusion kernels are a family of kernel functions defined on graphs [13]. Every data point that could possibly appear on the data set is considered a vertex of the graph. Two vertices are linked if and only if they differ on only one attribute. The following expression shows the diffusion kernel we used in our experiments:

$$K_{DK}(\beta)(x,y) = \prod_{i=1}^m \left(\frac{1 - e^{-|D_i|\beta}}{1 + (|D_i| - 1)e^{-|D_i|\beta}} \right)^{\delta(x_i,y_i)} \tag{3}$$

where m is the number of attributes in the data set, $x = (x_1, .., x_m)$ and $y = (y_1, .., y_m)$ are categorical data points, $|D_i|$ is the number of values that the i-th attribute can take, and $\delta(x_i, y_i)$ returns 0 for $x_i = y_i$ and 1 otherwise.

2.4   Geometric Framework for Unsupervised Anomaly Detection

Nearest neighbor-based outlier detection techniques are based on the assumption that outliers appear in low density regions while normal data points are located in highly dense neighborhoods. A distance measure is thus required to be able to define neighborhoods for points in the data set. The geometric framework in [8] is based on the fact that the feature space H is a Hilbert space. Therefore, for every data points y_i, y_j in H the inner product $< y_i, y_j >$ is well defined, and it can be calculated as $K(\phi^{-1}(y_i), \phi^{-1}(y_j))$. Given two data points x_i, x_j from X, the distance $d_\phi(x_i, x_j)$ between x_i and x_j is defined as $d(\phi(x_i), \phi(y_j))$. By using the well-known distance equation $d(y_i, y_j) = \sqrt{< y_i, y_i > + < y_j, y_j > - 2 < y_i, y_j >}$, the following distance equation is obtained:

$$d_\phi(x_i, x_j) = \sqrt{K(x_i, x_i) + K(x_j, x_j) - 2K(x_i, x_j)} \tag{4}$$

Nearest neighbor-based outlier detection methods can be applied to data sets of arbitrary type, provided there is a kernel for that data type.

3   Proposed Approach

This section is divided in three subsections. In the first subsection, we introduce the class of similarity kernels and discuss some basic properties. In the second subsection, a relationship between the class of similarity kernels and the class of isotropic stationary kernels is presented. The advantage of using isotropic stationary kernels for normed input spaces is discussed as well. In the third subsection we offer a definition for two kernel similarity scores on which outlier detection can be based.

3.1   Similarity Kernels for Nearest Neighbor-Based Outlier Detection

To the best of our knowledge, nothing has been published about the classes of kernels that should be used within the geometric framework proposed in [8]. In this paper, we address that question by establishing a relationship between the concept of similarity and a class of kernel functions that we define as similarity kernels. It is required that any similarity function must fulfill the following three properties: First, for any fixed input space X, the similarity of any object to itself is always equal to a constant c. Second, that constant c is an upper bound to the similarity between any two objects in X. Finally, there exists a number d such that d is a lower bound to the similarity of any two objects in X. Based on these properties, we introduce the following definition:

Definition 4. *A positive semi-definite kernel function K defined on some input space X is a similarity kernel if and only if there exist $c \in \mathbf{R}^+$ such that $K(x, x) = c$ for all $x \in X$.*

Note that given a similarity kernel K, equation 4 can be written as:

$$d_\phi(x_i, x_j) = \sqrt{2c - 2K(x_i, x_j)} \qquad (5)$$

Consequently, $K(x_i, x_j)$ can be interpreted as a similarity measure between x_i and x_j. It remains to show that all similarity kernels K satisfy the properties we require from a similarity measure. The first of those properties is fulfilled by definition. To prove that $c = K(x, x)$ is an upper bound for all values of K, let us assume an arbitrary data set D with n objects $\{x_1, x_2, ..., x_n\}$. Let us denote by K the corresponding $n \times n$ kernel matrix. Let x_i and x_j be two arbitrary objects from D, and let z be a vector of length n containing 1 in the position i, -1 in position j and 0 in all remaining positions. Because K is positive semi-definite, we have $z^T K z \geq 0$. Consequently:

$$z^T K z = K(x_i, x_i) + K(x_j, x_j) - 2K(x_i, x_j) = 2c - 2K(x_i, x_j) \geq 0 \qquad (6)$$

$$K(x_i, x_j) \leq c \qquad (7)$$

Following the same approach, but assuming that z is the vector containing 1 in positions i and j and 0 in all remaining positions, it is concluded that -c is a lower bound for all values of the kernel matrix. As a direct consequence of these properties, similarity kernels can be normalized to the interval $[-1, 1]$ simply by dividing the kernel by c.

It is worthy of noting that the closure properties given in section 3.4.1 of [19], which establish how to obtain new kernels from previously defined kernels, are preserved for the class of similarity kernels, i.e.:

1. The sum of two similarity kernels is also a similarity kernel.
2. The product of a similarity kernel and a positive scalar is a similarity kernel.
3. If $K_1(x, y)$ and $K_2(x, y)$ are similarity kernels then $K(x, y) = K_1(x, y) K_2(x, y)$ is also a similarity kernel.

4. If $K(x, y)$ is a similarity kernel, and $\varphi : X \to \mathbf{R}^n$, then $K(\varphi(x), \varphi(y))$ is a similarity kernel.

Other classical operations over similarity kernels produce similarity kernels as well. For instance, a polynomial function with positive coefficients composed with a similarity kernel is a similarity kernel. The composition of an exponential function with a similarity kernel is also a similarity kernel.

3.2   Similarity Kernels and Isotropic Stationary Kernels

From definition 2, it is obvious that all isotropic stationary kernels are within the class of similarity kernels. Isotropic stationary kernels must be defined on normed spaces, while similarity kernels are not constrained to any particular input space. Consequently, the class of isotropic stationary kernels is a proper subset of the class of similarity kernels. For any isotropic stationary kernel, equation 4 can be written as follows:

$$d_\phi(x_i, x_j) = \sqrt{2g_K(0) - 2g_K(\|x_i - x_j\|)} \qquad (8)$$

When X is a normed space, nearest neighbor-based outlier detection methods should be invariant to translations and rotations in X. From definition 2, it is clear that any nearest neighbor-based outlier detection based on an isotropic stationary kernel will remain invariant to translations and rotations in X. On the other hand, given any non-stationary kernel function K, there exists input values x_1, x_2 and $t \in X$ such that $K(x_1, x_2) \neq K(x_1 + t, x_2 + t)$. However, it is not clear whether the non-stationary quality of K could actually influence the accuracy of outlier detection in the presence of arbitrary translations or rotations. The following example provides a positive answer to that question for the case of an arbitrary translation.

We generated a two-dimensional data set containing 4 outliers and 46 non-outliers. A second data set was obtained by adding the vector $(100, 100)$ to all points in the original data set. Figure 1 shows the performance of k-NN outlier detection [8] on both data sets. The polynomial kernel with $p = 2$ was used. The number of neighbors, k, was set equal to 3, and four data points were selected as outliers. The different results obtained show that outlier detection results can become inconsistent under translations in X when a non-stationary kernel is used. We believe that similar examples could be devised for arbitrary rotations when non-isotropic kernels are used. For the sake of invariance, we suggest the use of isotropic stationary kernels whenever possible.

3.3   Kernel Similarity Scores

Our kernel similarity scores make use of the interpretation of each value $K_{i,j}$ of a $n \times n$ similarity kernel matrix K as a similarity measurement. The goal is to calculate a similarity score vector $\mathbf{s}$, where $\mathbf{s}_i$ provides an estimate of how similar x_i is to other objects within a certain neighborhood. Consequently, for

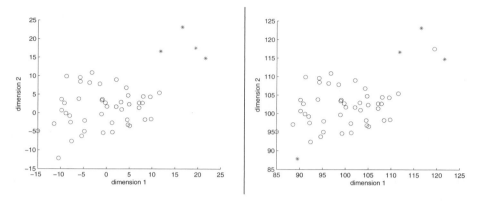

Fig. 1. Outlier detection using k-NN scores with a polynomial kernel of degree 3 and k=3. Detected outliers are denoted by '*'. **Left**: Original data set. **Right**: Original data set translated by (100, 100).

two objects x_i and x_j, if $\mathbf{s}_i < \mathbf{s}_j$ then x_i is more likely to be an outlier than x_j. The vector $\mathbf{s}$ allows ranking objects by their likelihood of being outliers. Those objects having the lowest similarity scores are more likely to be outliers.

In this section we define two specific kernel similarity scores: the k-NN kernel similarity score (kNNSS) and the summation kernel similarity score (SKSS). The k-NN kernel similarity score is a characterization of the well-known k-NN score [5]. It assigns scores to data points based on the sum of their similarities to their k nearest neighbors. To our knowledge, SKSS has not been proposed before in the literature. It uses a density-based approach [12,11], but instead of counting the number of nearest neighbors within a neighborhood of each data point x_i, the SKSS score of x_i is equal to the sum of the similarities between x_i and all data points within a ball of a fixed radius implicitly determined by a parameter p. The definitions for kNNSS and SKSSS follow:

Definition 5. *Let x_i be a point in a data set X with n data points, $K \in \mathbf{R}^{n \times n}$ a similarity kernel matrix defined on X, $K_i \in \mathbf{R}^n$ the i-th row of K, and k a positive integer parameter. The k-NN kernel similarity score of x_i, $kNNSS(x_i, K, k)$, is defined as:*

$$kNNSS(x_i, K, k) = \sum_{j=1}^{k} K_{ij}^s \tag{9}$$

where $K_i^s \in \mathbf{R}^{n-1}$ is the row vector obtained by sorting K_i in descending order without including the diagonal element $K_{i,i}$.

Definition 6. *Let x_i be a point in a data set X with n data points, $K \in \mathbf{R}^{n \times n}$ a similarity kernel matrix defined on X, and $K_i \in \mathbf{R}^n$ the i-th row of K. The summation kernel similarity Score (SKSS) of x_i, $SKSS(x_i, K, p)$, is defined by:*

$$SKSS(x_i, K, p) = \sum_{K_{i,j}^s \geq p} (K_{i,j}^s) \tag{10}$$

where p is a real-valued similarity threshold, and $K_i^s \in \mathbf{R}^{n-1}$ is the row vector obtained from K_i by removing the diagonal element $K_{i,i}$.

Considering that similarity kernels can be normalized in the interval [-1, 1] (or [0,1] when all kernel values are non-negative), it is safe to assume that p lies on that normalized interval.

The computational complexity of calculating both kernel similarity scores for a data set X with n data points is $O(n^2)$, assuming the kernel matrix K is given. Consequently, approximation techniques such as the one mentioned in [8] should be used for applications with large data sets. Because our experiments involved small data sets we did not implement any approximation technique in this work. However, it is worth of noting that kNNSS is slightly more expensive to compute than SKSS when using straightforward implementations. That is because of the sorting step involved in determined the k nearest neighbors for each object.

4   Experimental Comparison of Kernel Similarity Scores

4.1   The Data Sets

We used two numerical data sets and two categorical data sets to compare the performance of kNNSS and SKSS for outlier detection. The data sets were obtained from the UCI Machine Learning Repository [2]. The Gaussian kernel was employed in the numerical cases. The Hamming distance kernel and the diffusion kernel from equation 3 were used in the categorical cases. For some data sets, we randomly removed a substantial amount of samples from one of the classes, in order to comply with the assumption that outliers constitute a small percentage of the data. A brief description of each data set follows.

The yeast data set: A data set consisting of 1484 data points with 8 real-valued attributes. The data points correspond to proteins taken from the SWISS-PROT database. They are classified into ten different classes of localization sites. We chose the 463 proteins with cytosolic or cytoskeletal localization as non-outliers. The 20 proteins corresponding to peroxisomal localization were labeled as outliers.

The breast cancer Winsconsin (diagnostic) data set: It consists of 569 data points with 32 real-valued attributes. It categorizes points as benign or malignant. We used the 357 benign cases from the data set as non-outliers. A random sample of 15 malignant cases were kept as outliers.

The lymphography data set: It contains 148 instances with 18 categorical attributes. Those instances corresponding to the metastases and malign lymph classes form the majority of the data set. The other 6 points, related to the normal and fibrosis categories, were considered outliers.

The post-operative data set: A categorical data set containing 148 instances with 18 attributes. Instances are classified according to where patients should go after surgery: the ICU, home, or the general hospital. The 64 instances where the patients were sent to the general hospital constituted our non-outliers observations. We randomly chose 4 entries from the rest of the data to be outliers.

4.2   The Similarity Kernels

Here we prove that the Hamming distance kernel and the diffusion kernel satisfy our definition of similarity kernels.

From the definition of the diffusion kernel given in section 2.3, it is clear that $K_{KD}(x, x) = 1$ for all $x \in X$. Because all diffusion kernels are positive semi-definite, it is concluded that the diffusion kernel used in this work is a similarity kernel.

The Hamming distance kernel is defined in [6] in the framework of positive semi-definite kernels. It is not immediate from its definition whether it has a constant diagonal. However, the Hamming distance kernel is characterized by the following recursive formulas: [6]

$$K^0(s, t) = 1 \tag{11}$$
$$K^j(s, t) = \left[\lambda^2 (\mid D_j \mid -1 - \delta(s_j, t_j)) + (2\lambda - 1)\delta(s_j, t_j) + 1 \right] K^{j-1}(s, t) \tag{12}$$
$$K_H(s, t) = K^m(s, t) \tag{13}$$

where $1 \leq j \leq m$ and m is the number of attributes in the data set.

Table 1. Experimental results. The columns labeled as 'q' indicate the number of data points to return as outliers. Values in the other columns represent how many of the q tentative outliers were true outliers. The last row of each table shows the sum of true outliers detected through each score.

	Yeast data set		Breast cancer data set	
	Gaussian kernel		Gaussian kernel	
	$\sigma = 3$	$\sigma = 0.5$	$\sigma = 200$	$\sigma = 50$
	kNNSS	SKSS	kNNSS	SKSS
q	k = 16	p = 0.25	k = 10	p = 0.1
5	3	5	5	5
10	8	9	8	9
15	9	9	11	10
20	11	11	12	12
25	11	11	12	12
sum:	42	45	48	48

	Lymphography data set				Post-operative data set			
	Hamming kernel		Diffusion kernel		Hamming kernel		Diffusion kernel	
	$\lambda = 0.2$	$\lambda = 0.4$	$\beta = 0.3$	$\beta = 0.5$	$\lambda = 0.1$	$\lambda = 0.1$	$\beta = 0.9$	$\beta = 0.3$
	kNNSS	SKSS	kNNSS	SKSS	kNNSS	SKSS	kNNSS	SKSS
q	k = 8	p = 0.2	k = 16	p = 0.05	k = 2	p = 0.05	k = 2	p = 0.35
2	2	2	2	2	1	1	1	1
4	4	4	4	4	1	2	1	1
6	5	6	4	4	1	2	1	2
8	5	6	6	5	1	2	2	3
10	6	6	6	6	2	2	2	3
sum:	22	24	22	21	6	9	7	10

It is easy to see that $K_H(s,s)$ is an algebraic expression that depends only on λ and D_j. Consequently, $K_H(s,s)$ is equal to a constant value regardless of the particular data point s. To show that this constant is positive, we set $K^0(s,s) = 1$ as a base step and prove by induction that if $K^j(s,s) > 0$ then $K^{j+1}(s,s) > 0$ for $1 \leq j \leq m$:

$$K^{j+1}(s,s) = \left(\lambda^2(|\, D_{j+1} \,| -1) + 1\right) K^j(s,s) \tag{14}$$

$$= \left(\lambda^2(|\, D_{j+1} \,|) + (1 - \lambda^2)\right) K^j(s,s) > 0 \tag{15}$$

4.3   Experimental Results

A tuning process allowed us to obtain the best values for each kernel and score parameter. The best value of the parameter σ for the Gaussian kernel was obtained from the interval $[0.1, 1000]$ for each similarity score. The best value for the parameters of the categorical kernels were determined, for each similarity score, from the set $\{0.1, 0.2, ..., 0.9\}$. The values for the score parameter k were chosen from the set $\{1, 2, 3, 4, 5, 6, 8, 10, 13, 16\}$. The values of p were restricted to the interval $[0.05, 0.5]$. The experimental results are shown in table 1.

For the breast cancer and the lymphography data sets, both similarity scores performed about equally. For the yeast and post-operative data sets the highest detection rates corresponded to SKSS. Overall, SKSS showed slightly better results than kNNSS.

5   Conclusions

In this paper, the concept "similarity kernel" was introduced by giving a formal definition for it. Similarity kernels should be used for unsupervised nearest neighbor-based outlier detection. For any similarity kernel K, the distance between two points x_i and x_j in the feature space are inversely proportional to $K(x_i, x_j)$. Consequently, the kernel values can be considered as similarity values. Additionally, our definition of similarity kernels satisfy desirable properties of similarity measures. Isotropic stationary kernels should be used for nearest neighbor-based outlier detection whenever possible, in order to maintain invariance to translations and rotations. The class of isotropic stationary kernels is a proper subset of the class of similarity kernels. It would be interesting to determine whether both classes of kernels are the same when constrained to normed spaces.

Two kernel similarity scores were defined in this work: kNNSS and SKSS. The first one is a characterization of the well-known k-NN score in terms of kernels. The second one is a new density-based similarity score. The two scores were compared on four data sets, where SKSS compared favorably to kNNSS. Although these are preliminary results, they suggest that SKSS might be a good alternative to the kNN approach for unsupervised outlier detection. The fact that no sorting procedure is needed to calculate SKSS is another point favoring the use of SKSS.

We believe that the kernel nearest-neighbor approach is an excellent option for domains with a large number of attributes. It could be particularly useful for input spaces with complex data structures for which effective similarity kernels could be defined. However, the values of kernel and score parameters need to be determined in order to obtain good detection accuracy. Consequently, an interesting follow up to this work would be to devise methods for automatic estimation of those parameters. Another interesting path would be to determine which other kernel functions are also similarity kernels.

Acknowledgments. This paper is based upon work/research supported in part by the National Science Foundation under Grant No. 0647120 and Grant No. 0647018. Any opinions, findings, conclusions or recommendations expressed in this material are those of the authors and do not necessarily reflect the views of the National Science Foundation. The lymphography domain was obtained from the University Medical Center, Institute of Oncology, Ljubljana, Yugoslavia. Thanks go to M. Zwitter and M. Soklic for providing the data. The first author gratefully acknowledges the advice of Dr. Avelino Gonzalez from the University of Central Florida, and the support of the College of Engineering and Computer Science and the I2Lab at the University of Central Florida.

References

1. Angiulli, F., Pizzuti, C.: Fast outlier detection in high dimensional spaces. In: Elomaa, T., Mannila, H., Toivonen, H. (eds.) PKDD 2002. LNCS (LNAI), vol. 2431, pp. 43–78. Springer, Heidelberg (2002)
2. Asuncion, A., Newman, D.: UCI Machine Learning Repository, University of California Irvine, School of Information and Computer Science (2007), http://www.ics.uci.edu/~mlearn/MLRepository.html
3. Bay, S., Schwabacher, M.: Mining distance-based outliers in near linear time with randomization and a simple pruning rule. In: Proceedings of the 9th ACM SIGKDD International Conference on Knowledge Discovery and Data Mining, pp. 29–38. ACM Press, New York (2003)
4. Breunig, M., Kriegel, H., Ng, R., Sander, J.: LOF: Identifying density-based local outliers. In: International Conference on Management of Data, pp. 1–12 (2000)
5. Chandola, V., Banerjee, A., Kumar, V.: Anomaly Detection: A Survey. ACM Computing Surveys 41, 15:1–15:58 (2009)
6. Couto, J.: Kernel K-Means for Categorical Data. In: Famili, A.F., Kok, J.N., Peña, J.M., Siebes, A., Feelders, A. (eds.) IDA 2005. LNCS, vol. 3646, pp. 46–56. Springer, Heidelberg (2005)
7. Cristianini, N., Shawe-Taylor, J.: An introduction to support Vector Machines: and other kernel-based learning methods. Cambridge University Press, Cambridge (2000)
8. Eskin, E., Arnold, A., Prerau, M., Portnoy, L., Stolfo, S.: A geometric framework for unsupervised anomaly detection. In: Proceedings of the Conference on Applications of Data Mining in Computer Security, pp. 78–100. Kluwer Academics, Dordrecht (2002)
9. Genton, M.G.: Classes of kernels for machine learning: a statistics perspective. Journal of Machine Learning Research 2, 299–312 (2001)

10. Hawkins, D.: Identification of Outliers. Chapman and Hall, Boca Raton (1980)
11. Knorr, E.M., Ng, R.T., Tucakov, V.: Distance-based outliers: algorithms and applications. The VLDB Journal 8(3), 237–253 (2000)
12. Knorr, E.M., Ng, R.T.: Algorithms for Mining Distance-Based Outliers in Large Datasets. In: Proceedings of the 24rd International Conference on Very Large Data Bases, pp. 392–403 (1998)
13. Kondor, R., Lafferty, J.: Diffusion Kernels on Graphs and Other Discrete Structures. In: Proceedings of the 19th International Conference on Machine Learning, pp. 315–322 (2002)
14. Latecki, L.J., Lazarevic, A., Pokrajac, D.: Outlier Detection with Kernel Density Functions. In: Perner, P. (ed.) MLDM 2007. LNCS (LNAI), vol. 4571, pp. 61–75. Springer, Heidelberg (2007)
15. Oh, J.H., Gao, J.: A kernel-based approach for detecting outliers of high-dimensional biological data. BMC Bioinformatics 10(Suppl. 4), S7 (2009)
16. Petrovskiy, M.I.: Outlier detection algorithms in data mining systems. Programming and Computer Software 29(4), 228–237 (2003)
17. Ramaswamy, S., Rastogi, R., Shim, K.: Efficient algorithms for mining outliers from large data sets. In: Proceedings of the ACM SIGMOD International Conference on Management of Data, pp. 427–438. ACM Press, New York (2000)
18. Roth, V.: Kernel fisher discriminants for outlier detection. Neural computation 18(4), 942–960 (2006)
19. Shawe-Taylor, J., Cristianini, N.: Kernel methods for pattern analysis. Cambridge University Press, Cambridge (2004)
20. Shen, Y.: Outlier Detection Using the Smallest Kernel Principal Components. PhD dissertation, Department of Statistics, Temple University (2007)
21. Schölkopf, B., Smola, A.J.: Learning with kernels. MIT Press, Cambridge (2002)
22. Wu, M., Jermaine, C.: Outlier detection by sampling with accuracy guarantees. In: Proceedings of the 12th ACM SIGKDD International Conference on Knowledge Discovery and Data Mining, pp. 767–772 (2006)

End-to-End Support for Dating Paleolandforms[*]

Laura Rassbach[1], Ken Anderson[1], Liz Bradley[1], Chris Zweck[2], and Marek Zreda[2]

[1] University of Colorado, Department of Computer Science, Boulder, Colorado
[2] University of Arizona, Department of Hydrology, Tucson, Arizona
laura.rassbach@colorado.edu, {kena,lizb}@cs.colorado.edu,
{czweck,marek}@hwr.arizona.edu

Abstract. Experts in scientific fields routinely operate under less-than-ideal conditions. We present a deployed data analysis system for cosmogenic isotope dating, a domain that is fraught with difficult automation issues. First, experts must work with a huge array of possible parameters. Our system ACE handles this issue by pushing the bounds of software flexibility. Furthermore, isotope dating experts reason about groups of samples using a large number of vague and contradictory heuristics. Calvin, an argumentation system, addresses this issue. Our intelligent data analysis tool is in daily use by isotope dating experts.

1 Introduction

Certain kinds of problems are endemic to many scientific fields: the collection and maintenance of vast quantities of data, a need to experiment with various input parameters, and difficulties in interpreting results in a consistent, transparent, and unbiased way. Integrated, usable systems to support experts in these tasks can make an enormous difference to the speed and quality of these experts' work.

One field rife with these problems (and more) is cosmogenic isotope dating. Dating calculations rely on more than a dozen variables, some of which are actually tables of several hundred values. New estimations of these variables are published frequently, sometimes several times a year, making just the task of tracking and understanding background information for dating quite challenging. Using this enormous collection of background data generally involves the scientist experimenting with possible parameter choices to determine which ones make the most sense in context, as well as determine the samples' sensitivity to possible environmental perturbations.

Once a collection of samples has been dated, they need to be interpreted to determine the most likely age of the overall landform. This is a difficult problem: geological processes take place over an extremely long period of time, and evidence remaining today is scarce and noisy. Experts in geological dating, like experts in any field, are only human, and can be biased in favor of one theory over another. In the example in Figure 1, subsurface rocks are exposed over time as the soil around them erodes. A geoscientist would be faced with the situation shown on the right of the figure; his[1] task is to derive the original situation, shown at the left.

---

[*] This material is based upon work supported by the NSF under Grant No. ATM-0325812.
[1] We use the male pronoun purely for linguistic simplicity; obviously some isotope dating experts are female.

P.R. Cohen, N.M. Adams, and M.R. Berthold (Eds.): IDA 2010, LNCS 6065, pp. 171–183, 2010.

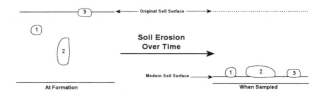

Fig. 1. Deducing past events from the evidence available now

Before our work in this area, many geoscientists kept their background data in Microsoft Excel spreadsheets, and performed dating calculations in custom spreadsheets using the same software. A better solution to this problem would be to store background data in a way that could be identical between different groups, all accessed and used by the same software. Because of the ever-changing nature of this field, software for performing these calculations must be extremely flexible, allowing users to easily write, modify, and share equations and input parameters easily.

Understanding and interpreting ages once they have been calculated was not automated or standardized in any way. Students were expected to pick up analysis techniques by observing experts, and the degree of sophistication in analysis was widely variable. A symbolic AI system that explicitly encodes the knowledge of domain experts would help less-experienced researchers come to better conclusions. Presenting analysis of datasets in clear, structured ways can help students learn to perform the same analysis. Finally, an automated system does not dismiss hypotheses due to personal bias, and can instead give every hypothesis equal treatment.

We created two discrete systems that work closely together to address these two problems. The Age Calculation Engine (ACE) stores background data and can calculate sample ages using any level of calculation sophistication and any set of background data the user desires. Calvin (named for the always-arguing comic character) forms and ranks arguments about what processes have affected the dated samples, a critical step in determining the overall age of a landform. ACE and Calvin provide several contributions to software engineering, AI, and the larger scientific community:

• ACE is an incredibly flexible system, able to store and present types of data determined at runtime in a seamless, consistent way

• The calculations performed by ACE can be determined by the user at runtime by visually assembling discrete components

• Calvin's rule base and ACE's data repository compose an explicit representation of the knowledge of two dozen experts in landform dating

• Calvin incorporates a rich system of confidence that captures the reasoning of real scientists in a useful way

• Finally, they are both real tools that are in daily use by real scientists

In the following section, we discuss the general problem of cosmogenic isotope dating, highlighting its challenges and the approach that experts take to solving it. Next, we describe how we used principles of software engineering to make ACE as flexible as possible. Then we show how Calvin uses argumentation, a symbolic AI technique, to automate reasoning about dated samples. Finally, we discuss our results.

2 Cosmogenic Isotope Dating

The first step in a new isotope dating project is to collect as many samples as possible from a landform. At least five samples is best [11]; five to ten samples is about the norm. Experts would prefer to collect far more samples, but often only a handful of suitable boulders are available. While collecting samples, the expert also makes qualitative field observations that are often crucial for interpreting initial dating results.

Once he has gathered a set of samples in the field, the expert dates each sample. This dating method is based on *in-situ* accumulation of rare nuclides in rocks exposed to cosmic radiation [14]. Because the production rates of these nuclides are known, their concentrations can be used to calculate how long these rocks have been exposed.

Production rates of cosmogenic nuclides depend on the local cosmic-ray intensity. Cosmic ray intensity is a itself a function of geomagnetic pole position, atmospheric compositions, and other variables, all of which are themselves complex functions over time. Prior to our work, the geoscientist would numerically integrate these various functions in Microsoft Excel to find the long-term production and average out short-term variations. The quality of this rate depends on the quality calibration and the quality of the data sets estimating various other geological variables over time. All of these variables mean that experts in isotope dating must collate and work with enormous amounts of data simply to date individual samples at the state of the art. Then, because not all experts use the same parameters for estimating cosmic ray intensity and production, it is also difficult to compare ages determined by different groups.

Once the expert has determined an exposure age for each individual sample, his work is still far from finished. The exposure age of each sample takes the form of a value with error bars, and the expert's next step is to derive an absolute landform age from the group of individual sample exposure times. For most landforms, the surface exposure times of boulders on the surface are true measure of the age of the landform. However, the different formation and evolution processes of different landforms complicate the expert's task of determining an overall age for a landform.

Instead, initial sample ages are usually spread over a wide range and the researcher must construct an explanation for the spread in apparent ages, usually a geologic process acting on the samples over time. Once he has found a process that explains the majority of the data (through the use of contradictory and often controversial heuristics), he uses further calculations and educated guesswork to remove its effects from the sample set and arrive at a single age for the landform. In real landforms, more than one process may have been at work, but experts generally focus on isolating the one that most affected the ages of the samples.

Isotope dating experts face two distinct but related problems in trying to determine a single age of a landform. First, they must date each individual sample. The background data in use (e.g. sea level and pole position estimates for the last several thousand years) is significant and varies between groups. This makes it quite difficult to place results, even from the same location, on the same time scale. Determining a sample's age involves a complex numeric integration with a large number of variables, and more variables are added to this calculation as the state of the art advances.

The second major problem in dating a landform is to determine its overall age from a set of samples. Here, experts we spoke to varied wildly in the level of sophistication they used in their analysis—one expert told the interviewer "it's always the oldest sample," while others spoke at great length about how to determine the most representative age. Knowledge about how to perform this analysis is largely not taught incourses; instead, students are expected to pick it up during graduate work by observing experts. This makes student education slow and difficult, as well as leading to publication of results that experts told us candidly were "obviously wrong."

We chose to address these two problems with two distinct systems that work closely together. For calculating the ages of individual samples, as well as storing sample data and collating background data, we designed and implemented ACE, a workflow-based design environment for cosmogenic nuclide dating [1]. To reason about the most likely landform age from a set of dated samples and store knowledge about how that reasoning is performed, we created Calvin, a symbolic argumentation system [12].

3 ACE: Design and Architecture

The Age Calculation Engine—ACE—is a design environment for developing and evaluating cosmogenic nuclide dating techniques. It is designed to meet the needs of geoscientists working on problems surrounding cosmogenic nuclide dating and, ultimately, to provide Calvin with dated sets of samples to reason over.

All information processed by ACE is stored in a repository. The Sample Browser provides the primary user interface for ACE, allowing users to sort, search and filter samples based on their attributes. A screenshot of ACE's sample browser is shown in Figure 2. In this screenshot, the sample browser has been asked to display attributes related to the age of samples (View: Ages), to only show samples with calculated ages (Filter: Dated Samples) and to sort the samples by experiment and then by age. The user could have further refined the display by entering a search term. Typing "26" as a query would further filter the results to only display samples TI2 and TI3, for instance.

From this browser, geoscientists can create experiments, which specify all of the parameters needed to date samples, as well as which collections of background data to use via the "Make Experiment..." button. The user can also ask for the samples to be dated ("Date Samples...") and then sent to Calvin for analysis ("Analyze Ages...").

The ACE workflow engine is used to apply experiments to undated samples, thereby dating them. It is also used to calibrate experiments to provide them with the "production rate" of a particular nuclide. Calibration is performed with respect to a calibration set, which contains samples that have been dated using other methods.

This process leads to a "production rate" that can then be used by dating workflows to determine the age of uncalibrated samples based on the amount of that same nuclide they contain. Workflows are simply groups of components that have been arranged in a particular way; a single component can be connected to multiple input and output components. This allows workflows to branch and loop based on conditional logic, as well as doing basic serial processing on a sample. For simplicity, the only thing passed between components is a set of samples; each component performs its calculation on the set of samples it receives and then passes the samples to subsequent components.

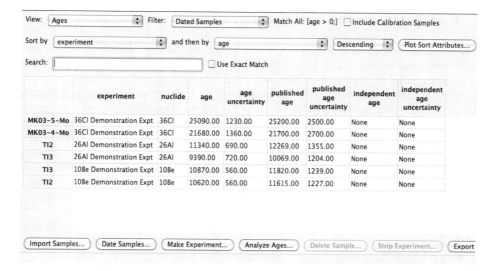

View: Ages	Filter: Dated Samples	Match All: [age > 0;] ☐ Include Calibration Samples

Sort by experiment and then by age | Descending | Plot Sort Attributes...

Search: [   ] ☐ Use Exact Match

	experiment	nuclide	age	age uncertainty	published age	published age uncertainty	independent age	independent age uncertainty
MK03-5-Mo	36Cl Demonstration Expt	36Cl	25090.00	1230.00	25200.00	2500.00	None	None
MK03-4-Mo	36Cl Demonstration Expt	36Cl	21680.00	1360.00	21700.00	2700.00	None	None
TI2	26Al Demonstration Expt	26Al	11340.00	690.00	12269.00	1355.00	None	None
TI3	26Al Demonstration Expt	26Al	9390.00	720.00	10069.00	1204.00	None	None
TI3	10Be Demonstration Expt	10Be	10870.00	560.00	11820.00	1239.00	None	None
TI2	10Be Demonstration Expt	10Be	10620.00	560.00	11615.00	1227.00	None	None

(Import Samples...) (Date Samples...) (Make Experiment...) (Analyze Ages...) (Delete Sample...) (Strip Experiment...) (Export)

Fig. 2. A screenshot of the ACE sample browser

In designing ACE, our key goals were flexibility and extensibility. The former was needed because geoscientists work with heterogeneous data types, and the latter was needed to allow these scientists to extend and expand the system without external support. Flexibility manifests in many ways throughout the system.

• Scientists can create multiple repositories and easily switch between them. Data is stored in a human-readable format. This approach allows scientists to make copies of their data, easily place it under version control, edit files by hand and gives them a sense of control over their data. Our geoscientist collaborators were adamant that they wanted to know where their data was stored, and this solution best meets that need.

• ACE allows data of all types to be imported into its repositories: samples, calibration sets, and data collections. Data collections of any type can be imported: the template editor provides users with the ability to specify the structure of data sets.

• Workflow structures can be further customized for individual experiments. Workflows consist of two types of entities: components and placeholders. A placeholder essentially acts as a template for a component which can be specified as part of the experiment specification. For instance, there are multiple sea-level datasets that geoscientists may use when determining if a particular sample was ever submerged. When an experiment is created, a scientist selects specific values for all of the placeholders contained in its underlying workflow. If he wants to understand the impact that different types of sea-level data have on the ages produced by the experiment's workflow, for instance, he can instantiate the experiment multiple times, selecting a different sea-level component each time.

ACE provides extensibility in a number of ways. Components can be added at any time and incorporated into new workflows. The factor editor allows users to define new types of placeholders that can then be incorporated into workflows. The template editor allows new data types to be defined and then incorporated into ACE in the form of data collections. Finally, the nuclide editor allows new nuclides to be defined that then allow new types of samples to be imported and analyzed.

4 Calvin: Design and Architecture

Calvin begins where ACE leaves off, with a set of individually dated samples. It analyzes groups of these samples to determine what process affected the whole landform. Our selection of an appropriate framework for solving this problem rested primarily on data we gathered during extensive interviews. From these interviews, we arrived at an argumentation framework as the best one for Calvin. This selection led to a need to represent both expert knowledge and expert sources and comparison of confidence.

We interviewed about two dozen experts in isotope dating, amassing around forty hours of formal interviews and a similar length of informal interviews. Transcripts of formal interviews are in [12]. Experts in isotope dating consistently use the method of multiple simultaneous hypotheses [4]. Then they form arguments for and against every hypothesis, judging their relative and absolute strength to arrive at a solution.

In our interviews, we learned that experts reason with contradictory heuristics:

Geologist: The thing about inheritance is, it's usually thought about as quantized, not incremental...

Interviewer: So it shouldn't be a spread of ages

Geologist: Yeah, however, you can convince me you would see a continuum. That is, not only do experts disagree with each other, they sometimes disagree with *themselves*. Human experts are able to sort out these conflicting impulses to believe or disbelieve a conclusion on the basis of specific evidence or additional facts:

Interviewer: So you explain the spread in ages with field observations?

Geologist: Well, but why did you sample those in the first place? You chose these because you thought they would give the age of the landform and you were wrong so why should I believe your follow-up [...] The ages that are obviously wrong in line with processes you are sure are active would give higher credibility so for example if there are lots of samples that are too young but you also observe that the landform is very active, [...] if you see ages that are consistent with that, you know that are too young, then you can be pretty sure. Finally, experts themselves know that they reason in the form of arguments:

Interviewer: So we're trying to understand what it is that you do **Geologist:** Well, what we do is we argue with each other.

Symbolic argumentation is a natural framework both to accurately reflect the structure of reasoning revealed in these interviews. It encodes domain knowledge directly in the form of rules and can present the reasoning behind its conclusions, making it an excellent teaching tool. It also elegantly captures the concept of reasoning with contradiction and problems of weighing confidence in competing arguments.

4.1 Reasoning Process

Only a few, known processes affect most landforms. Because the possible processes are known, experts do not generally need to form novel hypotheses to find an explanation for their data. Therefore, Calvin gives every hypothesis from the list of 'usual suspects' equal consideration, as recommended in [4] and by experts during interviews.

Most of Calvin's work revolves around generating arguments for each hypothesis in its list of candidate explanations. This process involves finding the applicable information in its knowledge base, unifying that knowledge with the data from ACE, and using that unification to construct a collection of arguments about the conclusion.

Calvin considers candidate hypotheses one at a time. Arguments for and against each hypothesis are built using backwards chaining. First, the engine finds all the rules in its knowledge base that apply to this hypothesis—i.e., those that refer to the same conclusion. Unification is applied to each of these rules, resulting in either a new conclusion to consider or a comparison to input data. Calvin builds the most complete possible set of arguments from its knowledge base for and against each hypothesis.

Every rule in Calvin contains both a conclusion and a template for evidence that will support that conclusion. The primary portion of a rule is an implication of the form $\mathbf{A} \Rightarrow \mathbf{C}$, where $\mathbf{A}$ may be either a single literal or the conjunction (or disjunction) of several literals, and $\mathbf{C}$ is the conclusion that $\mathbf{A}$ supports. Calvin uses its rules to form an argument (not a proof) for each element in $\mathbf{A}$. From arguments in favor of $\mathbf{A}$, Calvin creates an argument for $\mathbf{C}$. The representation of the argument contains both the rule and the arguments for the antecedents. However stronger arguments against the conclusion may be found, and Calvin's belief in it overturned. This is the main distinction between an argumentation system and a classical first-order logic system.

Calvin's rules contain several additional elements that serve important functions: a quality rating, a guard, and a confidence template. The quality rating and confidence template are used to judge the relative and absolute strengths of arguments; these are discussed in Section 4.2. Guards prevent the engine from building arguments using rules that are not applicable to the current case. For example, Calvin knows that snow cover is more likely if sample age is inversely correlated with elevation. This rule only makes sense for sample sets with large enough elevation ranges to have variable snowfall. Otherwise, random differences in the data might be interpreted as a meaningful correlation. The guard on this rule tells the engine to ignore the rule unless this precondition holds. Other argumentation systems typically do not require an explicit guard mechanism because they instead defeat rules explicitly [6], [9].

The antecedents in a rule are templates for the evidence that will satisfy that rule and therefore argue for the rule's conclusion. These patterns define both what evidence is needed to satisfy the rule and where that evidence can be located: that is, whether to build an argument for a new conclusion or refer to the data input by the user. Calvin has four types of evidence: observations, calculations, simulations (which are more complex calculations), and arguments. Calvin also forms confidence for weighing final arguments differently for different types of evidence (see Section 4.2).

The arguments for a conclusion $\mathbf{C}$ are a collection of trees constructed by Calvin's engine by unifying rules with evidence. Alternatively, each argument can be viewed as a tuple of the conclusion and support for the argument, as in the Logic of Argumentation of [8]. The root of each tree in the collection is a rule whose conclusion is $\mathbf{C}$, such as the rule $\mathbf{A} \Rightarrow \mathbf{C}$. Each child of this root is one of the literals in $\mathbf{A}$ unified with evidence. This evidence may be either additional collections of argument trees or a reference to the input data. Calvin's backwards-chaining engine generally makes no distinction between negative and positive evidence. This is not a valid method in classical logic, where the knowledge that $\mathbf{A} \Rightarrow \mathbf{C}$ certainly does not imply that $\overline{A} \Rightarrow \overline{C}$. However, Calvin's reasoning mimics that of experts, who are not necessarily logical. Experts not only apply rules in this negative fashion, they regard it as a sufficiently defensible practice that they discuss it in published reasoning. For example, [7] states that, since there is no visual evidence of erosion, erosion is unlikely.

4.2 Weighing Arguments

Some arguments carry greater weight than others, but precise comparisons between arguments are not always easy to perform. For example, some arguments for exhumation on a hypothetical moraine might be:

1. This moraine has a flat crest, which is a visual sign of matrix erosion. Matrix erosion causes exhumation.
2. This landform is a moraine, and moraines usually have a matrix, which is soft and erodes quickly. Matrix erosion causes exhumation.
3. This landform has samples as old as 50ky, and various processes often disturb the surface and cause exhumation over such a long time period.

Clearly (1) and (2) are similar arguments, sharing the same root rule. Calvin would derive these arguments as a single tree with two branches. However (1) is a stronger argument for exhumation because it draws on empirical observations rather than general knowledge about moraines. This issue is often handled in argumentation systems by referring to the *specificity* of arguments, with more-specific arguments carrying more weight [5]. However, (3) seems to contradict this choice of weighting: although it refers to information that is specific to this landform, it seems weaker than (1). Furthermore, the relationship between (2) and (3) is surprisingly difficult to quantify. How, then, are we—or Calvin—to judge the relative and absolute strengths of these three arguments in a way that preserves the intuitive relationships between them?

The central principal of Calvin's confidence system is that not only can specific *evidence* be trivial or critical, but the *knowledge* used to connect the evidence to the conclusion is also of variable quality. Defining confidence with two dimensions clarifies why one argument is better than another: (1) uses high-quality evidence and high-quality knowledge; (2) uses high-quality knowledge but moderate-quality evidence; and (3) uses high-quality evidence but low-quality knowledge. Separating the sources of confidence greatly enhances our understanding of the strengths of these three arguments. To instantiate this, Calvin represents confidence as a two-dimensional vector. One element of the vector is determined by the rules used to form the argument, and the other is determined by how closely the observed situation matched those rules.

As part of our knowledge engineering process, we asked experts about the strength of their belief in their heuristics to determine the appropriate qualitative validity to assign to each rule. When Calvin unifies evidence with a rule, it creates a confidence vector for the rule's conclusion from the closeness of the current situation to the rule's threshold(s) (closer to thresholds gives less confidence) and the validity assigned to the rule. Calvin's engine uses this confidence vector to find an overall confidence in chains of arguments and in sets of argument trees.

To judge the strengths of the arguments it generates, Calvin manipulates confidence values in two distinct ways. The first operates along a single chain of reasoning: snow cover is more likely in cold areas; this area is cold because it is at high elevation. It makes sense to choose the validity of the least-valid rule for the overall conclusion, so that the chain is only as strong as its weakest link. Applicability is 'created' by the direct use of observed evidence. In this case, how high the sampled area is compared to the rule's threshold determines the applicability. A few rules lower or raise the applicability of knowledge passed through them to handle cases where an `observation` is not specific to the knowledge being applied, as in argument (2).

The second and more-complicated use of confidence occurs when a number of different chains of reasoning are all applied to the same conclusion (because an argument is a *collection* of trees), e.g.: (a) erosion is more likely because the landform is old; (b) erosion is less likely because there is no visible sign of it. Note that a chain of reasoning supporting the conclusion might have higher validity but lower applicability than a chain of reasoning refuting the conclusion. There are often several independent chains of reasoning both supporting and refuting the conclusion, each with its own confidence level. Calvin, like many existing argumentation systems [10], assigns confidence in two stages, first locally up a single chain of reasoning and then globally across many chains of reasoning arguing about the same conclusion.

To determine its overall confidence in a conclusion, Calvin first aggregates groups of lower-validity confidences in into higher-validity confidences. Then, if the highest-validity confidences for and against the conclusion are at least two levels apart, the highest-validity confidence is returned intact as the overall confidence: it is sufficiently strong to completely override the weaker rebutting evidence. This difference implies a huge difference in overall strength—it is the difference between a logical tautology and a general rule of thumb. In contrast, a single level of difference in validity is less drastic, for example the difference between the preceding statement and a statement that 'snow cover is plausible in cold areas.' The resulting confidence in other situations is illustrated in Table 1. Calvin reduces its overall confidence in a conclusion according to how close two competing confidences are. Table 1 shows the possible ranks of confidence reduction and when they apply.

Table 1. Reduction Operations in Confidence Combination

Reduction Operation	Occurs When	
	Validity >, AND	**Validity =, AND**
Do Nothing	Applicability >>	
Applicability-	Applicability >=	Applicability >>
Applicability- -		'Against' Applicability >
Validity- -	Applicability <	
Validity-, Applicability-		'For' Applicability >
Validity-, Applicability-		Applicability =

4.3 Presenting Conclusions

Once Calvin has finished building arguments, it needs to present its reasoning and conclusions to the user, who makes the final decision about what arguments are most convincing. We strongly believe that information should be presented visually whenever possible, and worked toward that end. Calvin presents its results first as a summary screen showing all of the arguments it has produced and their overall confidence values. These are positioned on the screen and marked with colors based on their individual strength. The user can view the individual arguments for a conclusion by selecting it on the summary screen. A similar screen is presented for every conclusion about which Calvin generated a set of arguments. The user navigates between these screens by double-clicking on arguments in the summary screen or by selecting them from the left-hand navigation panel. Finally, whenever possible, Calvin shows its reasoning using graphs. Figure 3 shows some screenshots of Calvin's user interface.

5   Results

ACE has met all of its design goals: it provides a flexible and extensible design environment for cosmogenic nuclide dating techniques. During its design and implementation, our collaborators rigorously checked its calculations for accuracy. They (and their wider research community) have been actively using the software for more than a year without the need for our help in maintaining or debugging it. A review of posts on the ACE website reveal that aspects of ACE's flexibility and extensibility are being used to extend the system as geoscientists add new tools for their own use.

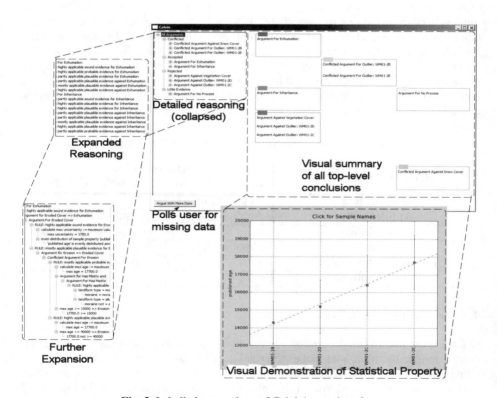

Fig. 3. Labelled screenshots of Calvin's user interface

To judge Calvin's success, we needed to compare its arguments to the arguments of domain experts. Experts typically publish some of their qualitative reasoning, including information about both rejected and accepted conclusions. We used these publications to assess Calvin's ability to reproduce expert human reasoning. Specifically, we compared Calvin's reasoning to the reasoning in eighteen randomly-selected papers discussing one or more isotope dating problems in detail. These publications provide a broad basis of comparison. To compare Calvin's output with this prose, we extracted every statement from these papers that made an assertion and distilled it to the conclusion being argued and the evidence presented for that conclusion. We then entered the data from the paper, ran Calvin, and compared its output to these argument summaries.

Calvin performed quite well at reproducing arguments published in isotope dating papers. For 62.7% of the arguments in published work, Calvin came to the same conclusion, supported by the same evidence, at about the same confidence level as the argument in the original paper (we found judging confidence levels from prose relatively difficult, and only divided these arguments into 'strong' and 'weak' categories). On a further 26.1% of these arguments, Calvin succeeded in two of these elements (recognizing the same evidence as important but to a different conclusion, coming to the same conclusion with different evidence or a vastly different confidence level) [12]. In a few cases, Calvin produced arguments that did not appear in the paper. In one such case, when examining [2], Calvin argued that the samples were exhumed because of a disagreement with ages determined for this landform via other methods. We consulted with a domain expert to judge Calvin's new argument:

I think I see both sides here. From the results, the fact that the ages are younger than the C14 data means that exhumation should be taken very seriously [...but] there is not much in the way of material that could bury them. However the peaks themselves are eroding...

Clearly choosing not to explicitly address exhumation in [2] was a major oversight! Although Calvin does not give the same mechanism for burial and exhumation, it has found a major gap in the reasoning published by these authors.

Calvin also produced arguments strikingly similar to the statements in some papers. These similarities were especially obvious when the authors expressed significant doubt about their own conclusions. For example, consider this passage from [3]:

"The ca. 56 ka age on the Jago lateral moraine appears to be a clear outlier that we attribute to inheritance. The age of the Okpilak ridge is uncertain; correlation with the Jago ridge supports the suggestion that the two older boulders from the Okpilak ridge contain inherited isotopes. Alternatively [...] the young age cluster on the Jago ridge records accelerated moraine degradation and consequent boulder exhumation [...] On the other hand, the stabilization age indicated by the [...] ca. 27 ka age is consistent with Hamilton's (1982) age constraints for deglaciation..."

Calvin finds it quite likely that the 56ka sample is an outlier and attributes the difference to inheritance. However it, too, grapples with explaining the age of the Okpalik ridge: inheritance is supported by correlation with the Jago moraine, the 25ka expected age, and the climate of the area. However, this implies that 2/3 of the samples from that ridge contain significant inheritance, leading to a conflicted overall argument for inheritance. Calvin also finds significant support for exhumation on both moraines, coming to the same uncertain conclusion as the authors.

6 Conclusion

Calvin and ACE are fully implemented and deployed software systems for experts in cosmogenic isotope dating. They have been downloaded from our website, http://ace.hwr.arizona.edu/, 178 times. ACE pushes the bounds of software flexibility, contributing new ideas about software design and data presentation. Although real experts are using it, no input has been needed from the original designers since its release. Building Calvin required us to solve a complex problem: how to determine and compare confidence. Our solution of a two-element vector to represent confidence and the associated system for weighing rebutting arguments appears to be novel. This system, while complex in its implementation, elegantly captures expert reasoning.

In designing both ACE and Calvin, we allowed the needs and desires, as well as the current processes, of existing experts in the field to guide our decisions. Because experts requested different or more sophisticated calculations, and above all more flexibility, every time we spoke with them about their desires for ACE, it is built to be as flexible a system as we could possibly make it. When we discussed groups of samples, experts presented their reasoning as arguments, replete with vague assertions and contradictions. Therefore, we designed and implemented Calvin as an argumentation system to generate arguments as close as possible to those presented by experts.

While our initial results are extremely promising, we look forward to examining the successes and shortcomings of our solutions in a more rigorous fashion. We would like to conduct a formal user study with scientists who have been using ACE for long enough to become 'expert' in using it. Calvin's performance will be more rigorously assessed using automatic annotation to extract arguments from published work [13].

ACE and Calvin are intended as general solutions for problems of data organization and analysis in any scientific field, not just cosmogenic isotope dating. To that end, we are now in the process of expanding both solutions to the similar (but hardly identical) problem of accurately dating layers in ice cores.

References

1. Anderson, K., Bradley, L., Zreda, M., Rassbach, L., Zweck, C., Sheehan, E.: ACE: A Design Environment for Cosmogenic Dating Techniques. In: 1st International Conference on Advanced Engineering Computing and Applications in Sciences, Tahiti (2007)
2. Ballantyne, C.K., Stone, J.O., Fifield, L.K.: Cosmogenic Cl-36 dating of postglacial landsliding at The Storr, Isle of Skye, Scotland. The Holocene 8(3), 347–351 (1998)
3. Briner, J.P., Kaufman, D.S., Manley, W.F., Finkel, R.C., Caffee, M.W.: Cosmogenic exposure dating of late Pleistocene moraine stabilization in Alaska. GSA Bulletin 117(7/8), 1108–1120 (2005)
4. Chamberlain, T.C.: The method of multiple working hypotheses. Science 148, 754–759 (1965)
5. Elvang-Gøransson, M., Krause, P., Fox, J.: Acceptability of Arguments as "Logical Uncertainty". In: European Conference on Symbolic and Quantitative Approaches to Reasoning and Uncertainty, Berlin (1993)

6. Farley, A.M.: Qualitative Argumentation. In: 11th International Workshop on Qualitative Reasoning, Cortona, Italy (1997)
7. Jackson Jr., L.E., Phillips, F.M., Shimamura, K., Little, E.C.: Cosmogenic 36Cl dating of the Foothills erratics train, Alberta, Canada. Geology 25(3), 195–198 (1997)
8. Krause, P., Ambler, S., Elvang-Gøransson, M., Fox, J.: A Logic of Argumentation for Reasoning Under Uncertainty. Computational Intelligence 11, 113–131 (1995)
9. Morge, M., Mancarella, P.: The Hedgehog and the Fox: An Argumentation-Based Decision Support System. In: Rahwan, I., Parsons, S., Reed, C. (eds.) ArgMAS 2007. LNCS (LNAI), vol. 4946, pp. 114–131. Springer, Heidelberg (2008)
10. Prakken, H.: A study of accrual of arguments, with applications to evidential reasoning. In: 10th International Conference on Artificial Intelligence and Law, New York, pp. 85–94 (2005)
11. Putkonen, J., Swanson, T.: Accuracy of cosmogenic ages for moraines. Quaternary Research 59, 255–261 (2003)
12. Rassbach, L.C.: Producing Expert Arguments about Geological History. Ph.D Thesis, Department of Computer Science, University of Colorado (2009)
13. White, E.: Pattern-Based Recovery of Argumentation from Scientific Text. Ph.D Thesis, Department of Computer Science, University of Colorado (2009)
14. Zreda, M., Phillips, F.: Cosmogenic nuclide buildup in surficial materials. In: Quaternary Geochronology: Methods and Applications, pp. 61–76 (2000)

Spatial Variable Importance Assessment for Yield Prediction in Precision Agriculture

Georg Ruß[1] and Alexander Brenning[2]

[1] Otto-von-Guericke-Universität Magdeburg, Germany
[2] University of Waterloo, Canada

Abstract. *Precision Agriculture* applies state-of-the-art GPS technology in connection with site-specific, sensor-based crop management. It can also be described as a data-driven approach to agriculture, which is strongly connected with a number of data mining problems. One of those is also an inherently important task in agriculture: yield prediction. Given a yield prediction model, which of the predictor variables are the important ones?

In the past, a number of approaches have been proposed towards this problem. For yield prediction, a broad variety of regression models for non-spatial data can be adapted for spatial data using a novel spatial cross-validation technique. Since this procedure is at the core of variable importance assessment, it will be briefly introduced here. Given this spatial yield prediction model, a novel approach towards assessing a variable's importance will be presented. It essentially consists of picking each of the predictor variables, one at a time, permutating its values in the test set and observing the deviation of the model's RMSE. This article uses two real-world data sets from precision agriculture and evaluates the above procedure.

Keywords: Precision Agriculture, Spatial Data Mining, Regression, Spatial Cross-Validation, Variable Importance.

1 Introduction

Data-driven technology has become part of our everyday lives, while data-driven management techniques have become necessary and common in industry and services. Improvements in efficiency can be made in almost any part of businesses. This is especially true for agriculture, due to the modernization and better affordability of state-of-the-art GPS technology. Agricultural companies nowadays harvest not only crops but also a growing amount of data. Site-specific crop management (SSM) therefore heavily depends on knowledge discovery from large amounts of site-specific, possibly noisy geodata. This led to the term *precision agriculture* (PA) being coined. PA is an agricultural concept based on the assumption of in-field heterogeneity. The abovementioned GPS, as well as ground-based, aerial or satellite sensors and image acquisition in connection with geographic information systems (GIS) allow to assess and understand variations. These data are nowadays routinely collected and available to farm operators. It can be expected that a large amount of information is contained, yet hidden, in these agricultural field data. This is usually information about the soil and crop properties enabling a

P.R. Cohen, N.M. Adams, and M.R. Berthold (Eds.): IDA 2010, LNCS 6065, pp. 184–195, 2010.
© Springer-Verlag Berlin Heidelberg 2010

higher operational efficiency – appropriate data processing techniques should therefore be applied to find this information. This is a rather common problem for which the term *data mining* has been coined. Data mining techniques aim at finding those patterns in the data that are both valuable and interesting for crop management. In PA, it must additionally be taken into account that the data are spatial: each data record has a specific location on the field and is accompanied by natural neighboring data points. Therefore, it must not be considered independent of its neighbors.

Yield prediction is a specific agricultural problem commonly occurring. As early as possible, a farmer would like to know how much yield he is about to expect. The ability to predict yield used to rely on farmers' long-term knowledge of particular fields, crops and climate conditions. However, this knowledge is assumed to be available in the data collected during normal farming operations throughout the season(s). A multitude of sensor data are nowadays collected, measuring a field's heterogeneity. These data are fine-scale, often highly correlated and carry spatial information which must not be neglected. Furthermore, it is of interest to know which of these sensor data are the most relevant for a yield prediction setup. Given novel sensors, we would like to assess whether they contribute novel information or whether this information is not already contained in more traditional data sources.

The problem of yield prediction can be treated as a problem of data mining and, specifically, regression. However, it should be noted that a regression problem on spatial data must be treated differently from regression on non-spatial data, as described in [7]. This article will serve as a continuation of [19]: in the previous article, the spatial data were treated with regression models which do not take the spatial relationships into account. This lead to serious underestimation of the true prediction error, which is shown in [20] where we compared the results on non-spatial data with those obtained on spatial data. This article builds on the previously established suitable spatial cross-validation framework (summarised in Section 3.1) and presents an approach to assess the importance of certain variables in the abovementioned precision agriculture data sets.

1.1   Research Target

The main research target of this work is to build upon yield prediction approaches to establish a novel approach towards assessing a variable's importance. The regression work presented in [19,23] will be used as a baseline for this work. The spatial regression model with spatial cross-validation has recently been described in [20] (a short summary is given below) and will be used as a core of the proposed variable importance assessment. Our approach will be described in detail and results from its application on two precision agriculture data sets will be detailed below.

1.2   Article Structure

This article will start with a brief introduction into the area of precision agriculture and a more detailed description of the available data in Section 2. This will be followed by an outline of the key techniques, a short summary of our novel spatial sampling technique described previously in [20], as well as our proposed approach towards variable importance assessment in Section 3. The results obtained from the modeling phase will be presented in Section 4. The article will be completed with a short conclusion in Section 5, which will also point out further lines of research.

2   Data Description

This section will present a summary on the available data sets.

The data available in this work were collected during the growing season of 2007 on two fields north of Köthen, Germany. The data for the two fields, called *F440* and *F611*, respectively, were interpolated using kriging [24] to a grid with a resolution of 10 by 10 meters. Each grid cell represents a record with all available information. The fields grew winter wheat. Nitrogen fertilizer (N) was applied three times during the growing season. Overall, for each field there are six input attributes – accompanied by the respective current year's yield (2007) as the target attribute. These available attributes

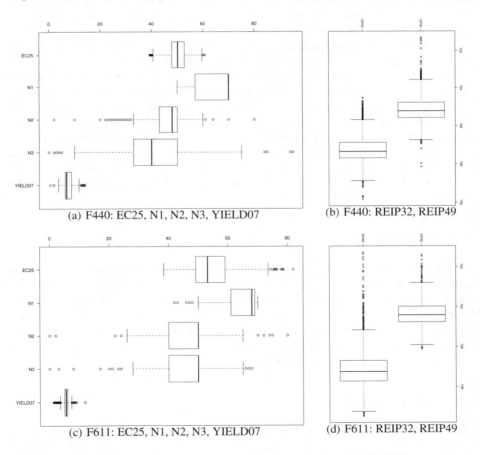

(a) F440: EC25, N1, N2, N3, YIELD07   (b) F440: REIP32, REIP49

(c) F611: EC25, N1, N2, N3, YIELD07   (d) F611: REIP32, REIP49

Fig. 1. Statistical Summary for the two available data sets (F440, F611)

Table 1. Statistical summary of data sets, see also Figure 1

	F440				F611			
	min	mean	median	max	min	mean	median	max
EC25	39.47	50.13	50.22	60.69	38.41	54.44	53.17	81.98
N1	50.00	63.57	70.00	70.00	42.00	65.09	68.00	70.00
N2	2.00	47.60	48.00	80.00	0.00	47.89	50.00	80.00
N3	0.00	37.98	40.00	95.00	0.00	45.61	50.00	68.00
REIP32	721.33	725.11	725.19	728.14	721.41	724.37	724.41	726.09
REIP49	724.50	727.20	727.34	729.82	721.30	727.12	727.23	729.41
YIELD07	0.49	7.37	6.89	13.92	1.32	5.42	5.51	11.88

will be described in the following. In total, for the F440 field there are 6446 records, for F611 there are 4970 records. Descriptive statistics are displayed in Table 1. For further information on the available data attributes we refer to [19].

The response variable YIELD07 (wheat yield) is measured in metric tons per hectare ($\frac{t}{ha}$). The soil's apparent electrical conductivity EC25 is measured by non-invasive geophysical instruments and represents a number of physical soil properties. The *red edge inflection point* (REIP32, REIP49) values are obtained through image processing of high-resolution imagery of the field. The plants' chlorophyll content can be measured by calculating the REIP value and allows to deduce the plants' state of nutrition and thus the previous crop growth. The 32 and 49 numbers in the indicators refer to the growing stage of winter wheat. The amount of fertilizer applied to each subfield can be measured, resulting in three attributes N1, N2, N3. N1 on the F440 field had only four levels from {50,57,60,70}.

3   Spatial Data Mining

Spatial autocorrelation is the correlation among values of a single variable attributable to the proximity of those values in geographic space, introducing a deviation from the independent observations assumption of classical statistics. Spatial autocorrelation can be assessed using the semivariogram, and its presence is often known beforehand because of the nature of the data at hand [9].

In previous articles using the above data, such as [21,19], the main focus was on finding a suitable regression model to predict the current year's yield sufficiently well. However, it should be noted that the used regression models, such as neural networks [21,22] or support vector regression [19], among others, generally assume statistical independence of the data records. However, with the given geolocated data records at hand, this is clearly not the case, due to (natural) spatial autocorrelation (cp. [7]). Therefore, the spatial relationships between data records have to be taken into account.

3.1   Spatial vs. Non-spatial Data Treatment

To account for these spatial relationships, a novel and model-independent spatial cross-validation technique has been presented in [20] and is summarised below. It has partly been adapted from existing approaches [4,5] towards the context of crop yield prediction and spatial regression more generally.

The approach consists of subdividing the agriculture site into spatially contiguous regions. This may be performed by overlaying the site with a regular grid. However, there are drawbacks with this approach: due to the fields being different, the grid would have to be manually adapted to each field being processed. Furthermore, agriculture fields are rarely of regular shape, hence at the field borders the grid cells are likely to be irregular as well, leading to further necessary processing. A third issue is to which of the surrounding grid cells a data record on the cell borders should be assigned. To overcome these issues, a clustering-based approach has been developed. This simple, yet effective method employs k-means clustering on the data records' coordinates (longitude, latitude) to partition the site into k contiguous parts of roughly equal size. This is depicted for the F440 site in Figure 2.

Fig. 2. k-means clustering on F440, $k = 10$

Having partitioned the field into k subfields, cross-validation at the level of spatial partitions may be carried out in order to assess the predictive performance of different regression models in the spatial domain. The only difference is that the subdivision of the whole data set into training and test subsets has to be done according to the spatial clusters determined in the previous step. This avoids the issue of having the same or similar samples in training and test sets, which non-spatial techniques mostly neglect. In a non-spatial setup, this leads to model overfitting and an underestimation of the prediction error (compare [4,6] for similar observations in a classification context). With the above procedure, the estimated prediction error is much less influenced by model overfitting. Therefore, the prediction error of the spatial procedure is usually much higher than the one in a non-spatial setup. This result could be confirmed in [20] using tree-based regression techniques as well as a support vector machine.

3.2 Regression Techniques and Error Estimation

In previous work ([19,21]), numerous regression modeling techniques have been compared on similar data sets. It was determined that among those models which represent non-linear relationships between variables, SVR has constantly shown favorable RMSE values. It has furthermore recently been shown to work rather successfully in spatial classification tasks, albeit without spatial cross-validation, as in [17]. Resampling-based estimation methods (such as cross-validation and the bootstrap) for dependent data in general have been investigated recently in the context of time series data [8] and paired data [6].

In this work, SVR will be compared against standard linear regression modeling and tree-based models, all of those in the aforementioned spatial cross-validation setup. Experiments are conducted in R [18]. It is assumed that the reader is mostly familiar with the regression techniques below. Therefore, the techniques used are described in short. References to further details are given, where appropriate.

Support Vector Regression. Support Vector Machines (SVMs) are a supervised learning method discovered by [1]. They were originally described for the use in classification, but can also be applied to regression tasks, where optimization of a cost function is achieved. The model produced by support vector regression depends only on a subset of the training data – which are essentially the support vectors. Further details can be found in [19]. In the current experiments, the *svm* implementation from the *e1071* R package has been used. We set a radial kernel and cost=50. These settings were determined empirically by best.svm.

Regression Trees. Regression trees have seen some usage in agriculture [10,12,16]. Essentially, they are a special case of decision trees where the outcome (in the tree leaves) is a continuous function instead of a discrete classification. The *rpart* R package has been used, with the settings for rpart.control of minsplit=30 and the complexity parameter cp=0.001, pruning and maxdepth were left at the defaults. These settings were determined experimentally.

Bootstrap Aggregating. Bootstrap aggregating (or bagging) [2] is generally described as a method for generating multiple versions of a predictor and using these for obtaining an aggregate predictor. In the regression case, the prediction outcomes are averaged. Multiple versions of the predictor are constructed by taking bootstrap samples of the learning set and using these as new learning sets. Bagging is generally considered useful in regression setups where small changes in the training data set can cause large perturbations in the predicted target variables. The bagging implementation in the R *ipred* package has been used here. We set nbagg=250, while leaving the parameters in rpart.control at their defaults.

Random Forests. According to [3], random forests are a combination of tree predictors such that each tree depends on the values of a random vector sampled independently and with the same distribution for all trees in the forest. Random forests are

basically a variant of bagging where regression trees are used as the internal predictor. In addition to resampling the observations, it also resamples the variables,
which prevents overfitting, especially in high-dimensional problems. The *random-
Forest* R package has been used. The setting for `ntree` was kept at the default of
500 trees to grow.

Linear Regression. Linear regression is the most widely used regression technique in
an agricultural context. It is therefore used as a benchmark model for accuracy
assessment. We use the implementation of ordinary-least-squares linear regression
lm from the *stats* package.

The performance of the models will be determined using the root mean squared error
(RMSE). The RMSE is based on the difference between an observed target value y_a and
the model prediction y.

3.3 Variable Importance

The interdependencies between variables in the data sets rule out standard feature selection approaches such as *forward selection* [14] or *backward elimination* [11]. A relatively new and intuitive computational approach for assessing variable importance is
based on measuring the increase in prediction error associated with permuting a predictor variable [26]. We adapt this approach to spatial prediction problems by assessing
RMSE increase on spatial cross-validation partitions rather than non-spatial test sets.

Given any model fitted on a cross-validation training sample, we choose one variable
at a time and permute its values randomly in the test set. The remaining variables are left
unchanged. We quantify the increase in RMSE caused by the permutation. No specific
model is needed, each of the regression models is suitable for assessing the variable
importance in this way. To obtain a sufficient number of replications, the permutation is
repeated 200 times for each variable. The permutation is embedded in a 10-fold leave-
one-out cross-validation setup, after having partitioned the agriculture sites into $k = 10$
sub-parts. The partitioning is rather stable due to the characteristics of the used clustering technique, therefore the k-means procedure is repeated only 10 times. The setting
of parameter $k = 10$ was determined empirically and is currently under investigation.

4 Results

The main research target of this article is to assess the importance of variables in a
spatial cross-validation setup. The results for the two available data sets described in
Section 2 are presented below.

4.1 Results for F440

The overall RMSE of different models for the F440 field can be seen in Figure 3(a). *lm*
returns the highest RMSE at 1.2 dt/ha, *rf* the lowest at around 1 dt/ha. This range has
to be kept in mind when considering the RMSE increase after variable permutation.

The relative order of the variable importance for the tree-based models *bagging*, *rf*
and *rt* is quite similar, which is due to the underlying tree construction. In each case,

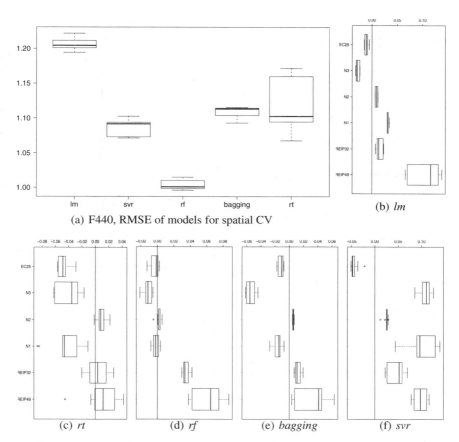

(a) F440, RMSE of models for spatial CV

(b) *lm*

(c) *rt*   (d) *rf*   (e) *bagging*   (f) *svr*

Fig. 3. F440: 3(a) shows each model's RMSE for a spatial cross-validation setup with 10 repetitions, 10 clusters; remaining figures show the increase in RMSE after permuting the respective variable (200 permutations): 3(b) *lm*, 3(c) *rt*, 3(d) *rf*, 3(e) *bagging*, 3(f) *svr*; the predictors are EC25, N3, N2, N1, REIP32, REIP49 (top to bottom)

the best predictor is the REIP49 variable with an increase of 0.06 at an average model RMSE of 1.0 (rf). This was expected, since the REIP49 value is closest to harvest and represents the amount of biomass on the field. For *bagging* and *rf*, the remaining variables increase the RMSE much less when permuted. For *rf*, the second most important predictor is the REIP32 variable – this is also the expected behaviour since the application of N2 and N3 tries to equalize the vegetation growth.

The remaining variables, especially the fertilizer dressings, are rather insignificant in the tree-based models. Since the N1 variable has only four different values in F440, it is clear that it will be rarely built into the trees since these are usually biased towards variables with a high number of values. Similarly, this also holds true for N2, N3: these have 45 and 50 different levels, whereas REIP32 and REIP49 have 367 and 397 different levels, respectively. Nevertheless, EC25 has 851 different levels and still has close to no importance for yield prediction. Another reason for the insignificance of the variables

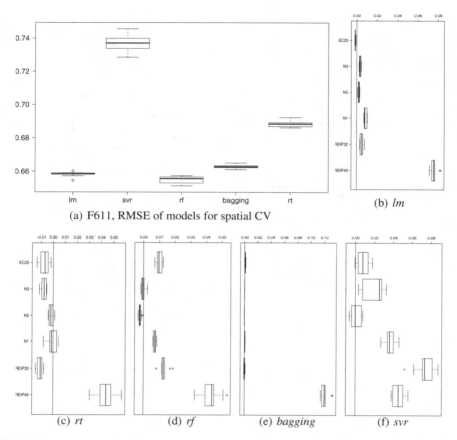

Fig. 4. F611: 4(a) shows each model's RMSE for a spatial cross-validation setup with 10 repetitions, 10 clusters; remaining figures show the increase in RMSE after permuting the respective variable (200 permutations): 4(b) *lm*, 4(c) *rt*, 4(d) *rf*, 4(e) *bagging*, 4(f) *svr*; the predictors are EC25, N3, N2, N1, REIP32, REIP49 (top to bottom)

with a low number of distinct levels is that it is much more likely that the variable's value in the test set is the same before and after the permutation.

Different results can be reported for *svr*. While the EC25 variable is still insignificant, most importance is given to N1, N3 and REIP49. This different ordering is likely to be due to *svr* measuring smooth non-linear variable importance with interaction, while tree-based models measure non-linear variable importance with higher-order interactions and discontinuities.

4.2   Results for F611

The overall RMSE for each of the models is quite different from the F440 site. *lm* returns an RMSE of 0.66 dt/ha and is very close to being the best model. *rf* and *bagging* seem are rather close around 0.66 dt/ha, while *rt* and *svr* are rather far from this mark at 0.69 and 0.73 dt/ha. This might hint to linear interactions between the variables. The rather bad performance of *svr* might as well be attributed to simple linear interactions.

The results for the variable importance are similar to the ones on the F440 site. Except for the *svr* model, the REIP49 value is by far the most important predictor. It influences the *lm* model's RMSE by 0.08 dt/ha at an average RMSE of 0.66 dt/ha. Similarly, the *bagging* model's RMSE is raised by 0.12 dt/ha at an average RMSE of roughly 0.66 dt/ha. There may yet be non-linear, high-order interactions, seen in the *svr*, where REIP32 is the most important variable, followed by REIP49 and N1. However, since the *svr*'s overall level of RMSE is higher at 0.74 dt/ha and the RMSE increase of the *REIP* values is around 0.07 and 0.04 dt/ha, this result should be taken with care.

4.3 Remarks

Assessing the importance of individual variables in multiple-variable models is difficult since the importance of any particular variable is influenced by other, correlated or inter-acting, variable in the data set. In our data sets, due to agricultural management decisions, the N2 and N3 variable are determined partly based on the REIP32 and REIP49 values and are therefore not fully independent of those. Therefore, e.g. if one of REIP32,REIP49 has been included in the model, the remaining variable N2,N3 is less likely to be chosen. If the other variable is included nevertheless, it is likely to have a smaller influence on the prediction than if included without the presence of the other variable.

5   Conclusions and Future Work

This article focused on a central data analysis task: regression. A procedure for measuring spatial variable importance has been developed and tested using two real-world data sets. This was achieved by adopting a variable importance approach and combining it with a clustering-based spatial cross-validation approach developed earlier [20]. The resulting spatial variable importance assessment was tested using two precision agri-culture data sets. The key question which of the available data attributes is informative regarding yield prediction was answered.

Based on practical experiences, the hypothesis that the vegetation indicators REIP49 and REIP32 should be most important for yield prediction could be confirmed. Although the different modeling techniques are partly biased (as explained), it is highly likely that the N1 and N3 dressings have a significant impact on yield, whereas the EC25 and N2 variables are rather unimportant. It can also be confirmed that the results of variable importance are quite similar for two different fields, growing the same crop in the same season and in the same climatic region.

The developed procedure may be applied to further areas where similar spatial data need to be analysed, such as land cover classification [5], landslide susceptibility mod-eling [4], species habitat analysis [13,15].

5.1   Future Work

Despite having improved and validated the yield prediction task, the data sets carry fur-ther information. From a theoretical point of view, our spatial cross-validation setup is a spatially constrained case of a standard cross-validation setup. Therefore, it would be interesting to see whether the spatial case converges towards the non-spatial case when the number of clusters is raised. Furthermore, additional predictor variables should be considered in future yield prediction setups.

Conditional permutation-based variable importance measures as proposed by [25] provide a framework for investigating the importance of variables conditional on other variables, which provides additional insights when interactions are present, in the context of the F440/F611 data sets, e.g. between N2/N3 and REIP32/REIP49, as noted above.

Acknowledgements

The F440 and F611 data sets were obtained from Martin Schneider and Peter Wagner, Professur für Landwirtschaftliche Betriebslehre, Martin-Luther-Universität Halle-Wittenberg, Germany.

References

1. Boser, B.E., Guyon, I.M., Vapnik, V.N.: A training algorithm for optimal margin classifiers. In: Proceedings of the 5th Annual ACM Workshop on Computational Learning Theory, pp. 144–152. ACM Press, New York (1992)
2. Breiman, L.: Bagging predictors. Technical report, Department of Statistics, Univ. of California, Berkeley (1994)
3. Breiman, L.: Random forests. Machine Learning, 45(1):5–32 (2001)
4. Brenning, A.: Spatial prediction models for landslide hazards: review, comparison and evaluation. Natural Hazards and Earth System Science 5(6), 853–862 (2005)
5. Brenning, A., Itzerott, S.: Comparing classifiers for crop identification based on multitemporal landsat tm/etm data. In: Proceedings of the 2nd workshop of the EARSeL Special Interest Group Remote Sensing of Land Use and Land Cover, September 2006, pp. 64–71 (2006)
6. Brenning, A., Lausen, B.: Estimating error rates in the classification of paired organs. Statistics in Medicine 27(22), 4515–4531 (2008)
7. Brenning, A., Piotraschke, H., Leithold, P.: Geostatistical analysis of on-farm trials in precision agriculture. In: Ortiz, J.M., Emery, X. (eds.) GEOSTATS 2008, Proceedings of the Eighth International Geostatistics Congress, December 12, vol. 2, pp. 1131–1136 (2008)
8. Bühlmann, P.: Bootstraps for time series. Statistical Science 17, 52–72 (2002)
9. Cressie, N.A.C.: Statistics for Spatial Data. Wiley, New York (1993)
10. Crone, S.F., Lessmann, S., Pietsch, S.: Forecasting with computational intelligence - an evaluation of support vector regression and artificial neural networks for time series prediction. In: International Joint Conference on Neural Networks, IJCNN 2006, pp. 3159–3166 (2006)
11. Dash, M., Liu, H.: Feature selection for classification. Intelligent Data Analysis 1, 131–156 (1997)
12. Huang, C., Yang, L., Wylie, B., Homer, C.: A strategy for estimating tree canopy density using landsat 7 etm+ and high resolution images over large areas. In: Proceedings of the Third International Conference on Geospatial Information in Agriculture and Forestry (2001)
13. Knudby, A., Brenning, A., LeDrew, E.: New approaches to modelling fish-habitat relationships. Ecological Modelling 221, 503–511 (2010)
14. Langley, P.: Selection of relevant features in machine learning. In: Proceedings of the AAAI Fall symposium on relevance, pp. 140–144. AAAI Press, Menlo Park (1994)

15. Leathwick, J.R., Elith, J., Francis, M.P., Hastie, T., Taylor, P.: Variation in demersal fish species richness in the oceans surrounding new zealand: an analysis using boosted regression trees. Marine Ecology Progress 321, 267–281 (2006)
16. Lobell, D.B., Ortiz-Monasterio, J.I., Asner, G.P., Naylor, R.L., Falcon, W.P.: Combining field surveys, remote sensing, and regression trees to understand yield variations in an irrigated wheat landscape. Agronomy Journal 97, 241–249 (2005)
17. Pozdnoukhov, A., Foresti, L., Kanevski, M.: Data-driven topo-climatic mapping with machine learning methods. Natural Hazards 50(3), 497–518 (2009)
18. R Development Core Team. R: A Language and Environment for Statistical Computing. R Foundation for Statistical Computing, Vienna, Austria (2009), ISBN 3-900051-07-0
19. Ruß, G.: Data mining of agricultural yield data: A comparison of regression models. In: Perner, P. (ed.) Advances in Data Mining. Applications and Theoretical Aspects. LNCS, vol. 5633, pp. 24–37. Springer, Heidelberg (2009)
20. Ruß, G., Brenning, A.: Data mining in precision agriculture: Management of spatial information. In: Proceedings of IPMU 2010. Springer, Heidelberg (submitted for review 2010)
21. Ruß, G., Kruse, R., Schneider, M., Wagner, P.: Estimation of neural network parameters for wheat yield prediction. In: Bramer, M. (ed.) Proceedings of AI in Theory and Practice II, IFIP 2008, July 2008, vol. 276, pp. 109–118. Springer, Heidelberg (2008)
22. Ruß, G., Kruse, R., Schneider, M., Wagner, P.: Optimizing wheat yield prediction using different topologies of neural networks. In: Verdegay, J., Ojeda-Aciego, M., Magdalena, L. (eds.) Proceedings of IPMU 2008, June 2008, pp. 576–582. University of Málaga (2008)
23. Ruß, G., Kruse, R., Wagner, P., Schneider, M.: Data mining with neural networks for wheat yield prediction. In: Perner, P. (ed.) ICDM 2008. LNCS (LNAI), vol. 5077, pp. 47–56. Springer, Heidelberg (2008)
24. Stein, M.L.: Interpolation of Spatial Data: Some Theory for Kriging, June 1999. Springer Series in Statistics. Springer, Heidelberg (1999)
25. Strobl, C., Boulesteix, A.-L., Kneib, T., Augustin, T., Zeileis, A.: Conditional variable importance for random forests. BMC Bioinformatics 9(1), 307 (2008)
26. Strobl, C., Boulesteix, A.-L., Zeileis, A., Hothorn, T.: Bias in random forest variable importance measures: Illustrations, sources and a solution. BMC Bioinformatics 8(1), 25 (2007)

Selecting the Links in BisoNets Generated from Document Collections

Marc Segond and Christian Borgelt

European Center for Soft Computing
Calle Gonzalo Gutiérrez Quirós s/n, E-33600 Mieres (Asturias), Spain
{marc.segond,christian.borgelt}@softcomputing.es

Abstract. According to Koestler, the notion of a *bisociation* denotes
a connection between pieces of information from habitually separated
domains or categories. In this paper, we consider a methodology to find
such bisociations using a network representation of knowledge, which is
called a *BisoNet*, because it promises to contain bisociations. In a first
step, we consider how to create BisoNets from several textual databases
taken from different domains using simple text-mining techniques. To
achieve this, we introduce a procedure to link nodes of a BisoNet and
to endow such links with weights, which is based on a new measure for
comparing text frequency vectors. In a second step, we try to rediscover
known bisociations, which were originally found by a human domain
expert, namely indirect relations between migraine and magnesium as
they are hidden in medical research articles published before 1987. We
observe that these bisociations are easily rediscovered by simply following the strongest links. Future work includes extending our methods to
non-textual data, improving the similarity measure, and applying more
sophisticated graph mining methods.

1 Introduction

The concept of association is at the heart of many of today's powerful ICT
technologies such as information retrieval and data mining. These technologies
typically employ "association by similarity or co-occurrence" in order to discover
new information that is relevant to the evidence already known to a user.

However, domains that are characterized by the need to develop innovative
solutions require a form of creative information discovery from increasingly complex, heterogeneous and geographically distributed information sources. These
domains, including design and engineering (drugs, materials, processes, devices),
areas involving art (fashion and entertainment), and scientific discovery disciplines, require a different ICT paradigm that can help users to uncover, select,
re-shuffle, and combine diverse contents to synthesize new features and properties leading to creative solutions. People working in these areas employ creative thinking to connect seemingly unrelated information, for example, by using
metaphors or analogical reasoning. These modes of thinking allow the mixing
of conceptual categories and contexts, which are normally separated. The functional basis for these modes is a mechanism called *bisociation* (see [1]).

P.R. Cohen, N.M. Adams, and M.R. Berthold (Eds.): IDA 2010, LNCS 6065, pp. 196–207, 2010.

According to Arthur Koestler, who coined this term, *bisociation* means to join unrelated, and often even conflicting, information in a new way. It means being "double minded" or able to think on more than one plane of thought simultaneously. Similarly, Frank Barron [2] says that the ability to tolerate chaos or seemingly opposite information is characteristic of creative individuals.

Several famous scientific discoveries are good examples of bisociations, for instance Isaac Newton's theory of gravitation and James C. Maxwell's theory of electromagnetic waves. Before Newton, a clear distinction was made between *sub-lunar* (below the moon) and *super-lunar physics* (above the moon), since it was commonly believed that these two spheres where governed by entirely different sets of physical laws. Newton's insight that the trajectories of planets and comets can be interpreted in the same way as the course of a falling body joined these habitually separated domains. Maxwell, by realizing that light is an electromagnetic wave, joined the domains of optics and electromagnetism, which, at his time, were also treated as unrelated areas of physical phenomena.

Although the concept of bisociation is frequently discussed in cognitive science, psychology and related areas (see, for example, [1,2,3]), there does not seem to exist a serious attempt at trying to formalize and computerize this concept. In terms of ICT implementations, much more widely researched areas include association rule learning (for instance, [4]), analogical reasoning (for example, [5,6]), metaphoric reasoning (for example, [7]), and related areas such as case-based reasoning (for instance, [8]) and hybrid approaches (for example, [9]).

In order to fill this gap in current research efforts, the BISON project[1] was created. This project focuses on a knowledge representation approach with the help of networks of named entities, in which bisociations may be revealed by link discovery and graph mining methods, but also by computer-aided interactive navigation. In this paper we report first results obtained in this project.

The rest of this paper is structured as follows: in Section 2 we provide a definition of the core notion of a *bisociation*, which guides our considerations. Based on this definition, we justify why a network representation—a so-called *BisoNet*—is a proper basis for computer-aided bisociation discovery. Methods for generating BisoNets from heterogeneous data sources are discussed in Section 3, including procedures for selecting the named entities that form its nodes and principles for linking them based on the information extracted from the data sources. In particular, we present a new measure for the strength of a link between concepts that are derived from textual data. Such link weights are important in order to assess the strength of indirect connections like bisociations.

Afterwards, in Section 5 we report results on a benchmark data set (consisting of titles and abstracts of medical research articles), in which a human domain expert already discovered hidden bisociations. By showing that with our system we can create a plausible BisoNet from this data source, in which we can rediscover these bisociations, we provide evidence that the computer-aided search for bisociations is a highly promising technology.

Finally, in Section 6 we draw conclusions from our discussion.

---

[1] See http://www.bisonet.eu/ for more information on this EU FP7 funded project.

2   Bisociation and BisoNets

Since the core notion of our efforts is *bisociation*, we start by trying to provide a sufficiently clear definition, which can guide us in our attempts to create a system able to support a user in finding bisociations. A first definition within the BISON project[2] characterizes *bisociation* as follows:

> A *bisociation* is a link L that connects two domains D_1 and D_2 that are unconnected given a specific context or view V by which the domains are defined. The link L is defined by a connection between two concepts c_1 and c_2 of the respective domains.

Although the focus on a connection between two habitually (that is, in the context a user is working in) separated domains is understandable, this definition seems somewhat too narrow. Linking two concepts from the same domain, which are unconnected within the domain, but become connected by employing indirect relations that pass through another domain, may just as well be seen as bisociations. The principle should rather be that the connection is not fully contained in one domain (which would merely be an association), but needs access to a separate domain. Taking this into account, we generalize the definition:

> A *bisociation* is a link L between two concepts c_1 and c_2, which are unconnected given a specific context or view V. The concepts c_1 and c_2 may be unconnected, because they reside in different domains D_1 and D_2 (which are seen as unrelated in the view V), or because they reside in the same domain D_1, in which they are unconnected, and their relation is revealed only through a *bridging concept* c_3 residing in some other domain D_2 (which is not considered in the view V).

In both of these characterizations we define domains formally as sets of concepts. Note that a *bridging concept* c_3 is usually also required if the two concepts c_1 and c_2 reside in different domains, since direct connections between them, even if they cross the border between two domains, can be expected to be known and thus will not be interesting or relevant for a user.

Starting from the above characterization of *bisociation*, a network representation, called a *BisoNet*, of the available knowledge suggests itself: each concept (or, more generally, any named entity) gives rise to a node. Concepts that are associated (according to the classical paradigm of similarity or co-occurrence) are connected by an edge. Bisociations are then indirect connections (technically paths) between concepts, which cross the border between two domains.

Note that this fits both forms of bisociations outlined above. If the concepts c_1 and c_2 reside in different domains, the boundary between these two domains necessarily has to be crossed. If they reside in the same domain, one first has to leave this domain and then come back in order to find a bisociation.

---

[2] See http://www.inf.uni-konstanz.de/bisonwiki/index.php5, which, however, is not publicly accessible at this time.

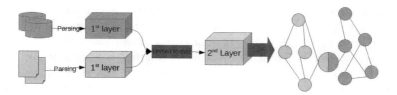

Fig. 1. Illustration of the structure of the BisoNet generator

3   BisoNet Generation

A system for generating BisoNets requires three ingredients: (1) A component
to access the original, usually heterogeneous data sources. In order to cope
with different data formats, we suggest, in Section 3.1, a two-layer architecture. (2) A method for choosing the named entities that are to form the nodes
of the BisoNet. Here we rely on standard keyword extraction techniques, as discussed in Section 3.2. (3) A procedure for linking the nodes of a BisoNet and for
endowing them with weights that indicate the association strength. For this we
suggest, in Section 4, a new association measure for keywords.

3.1   Data Access and Pre-processing

As explained above, a BisoNet is a network that promises to contain bisociations.
In order to generate such networks, we first have to consider two things: we must
be able to read different and heterogeneous data sources, and we have to be able
to merge the information derived from them in one BisoNet. Data sources can be
databases (relational or of any other type), text collections, raw text, or any data
that provide information about a domain. Due to the wide variety of formats
a data source can have, the choice we made here is not to provide an interface
of maximal flexibility that can be made to read any data source type, but to
structure our creation framework into two separate steps.

   In the first step, we directly accesses the data source and therefore a parser
has to be newly developed for or at least adapted to the specific format of the
data source. The second step is actual the BisoNet generation part. It takes its
information from the first step, always in the same format, and therefore can
generate a BisoNet from any data source, as far as it is parsed and exported in
the form provided by the first step process (see Figure 1 for a sketch).

   The way data should be provided to the second layer is fairly simple, because
in this paper we confine our considerations to textual data. As a consequence,
the second layer creates nodes from data that are passed as records containing
textual fields. These textual fields can contain, for now, either words or authors
names. This procedure and data format is well adapted to textual databases or
text collections, but is meant to evolve in future development in order to be
able to take other types of data sources into account. However, since most of the
data sources that we have used so far were textual data sources, this protocol

seems simple and efficient. Future extensions could consist in including raw data fields (for example, to handle images), and will then require an adaptation of the second layer to be able to create nodes from other objects than textual data.

The second layer builds a BisoNet by extracting keywords using standard text mining techniques such as stop word removal and stemming (see [10]). The extracted keywords are weighted by their TFIDF (Text Frequency - Inverse Document Frequency) value (see [11]), thus allowing us to apply a (user-defined) threshold in order to filter the most important keywords, as will be detailed in Section 3.2. Links between nodes are created according to the presence of co-occurrences of the corresponding keywords in the same documents, and are weighted using a similarity measure adapted to the specific requirements of our case, which will be presented in Section 4. In the case that author lists are provided with each text string, extracted keywords are also linked to the related authors. These links are weighted according to the number of times a keyword occurs in a given author's work.

3.2   Creating Nodes

In our BisoNets nodes represent concepts. As we only talk about textual databases, we made the choice to characterize concepts by keywords that are extracted from the textual records taken from the data sources. In the second layer of our framework, each textual record j is processed with a stop word removal algorithm. Then the text frequency values are computed for each remaining term i as follows: $\text{tf}_{i,j} = \frac{n_{i,j}}{\sum_k n_{k,j}}$, where $n_{i,j}$ is the number of occurrences of the considered term in textual record j and $\sum_k n_{k,j}$ is the sum of number of occurrences of all terms in textual record j.

Naturally, this procedure of keyword extraction is limited in its power to capture the contents of the text fields. The reason is that we are ignoring synonyms (which should be handled by one node rather than two or more), hyper- and hyponyms, pronouns (which may refer to a relevant keyword and thus may have to be counted for the occurrence of this keyword) etc. However, such linguistic properties are very difficult to take into account and need sophisticated tools (like thesauri etc.). Since such advanced text mining is not the main goal of our work (which rather focuses on BisoNet creation), keeping the processing simple seemed a feasible option. Nevertheless, advanced implementations may require such advanced processing, because ignoring, for example, synonyms and pronouns can distorts the statistics underlying, for instance, the term frequency value: ignoring pronouns that refer to a keyword, or not merging two synonyms makes the term frequency lower than it should actually be.

After all records have been processed, the inverse document frequency of each keyword i is computed the following way: $\text{idf}_i = \log \frac{|D|}{|\{d \in D | t_i \in d\}|}$, where $|D|$ is the total number of records in the database and $|\{d \in D \mid t_i \in d\}|$ is the number of records in which the term t_i appears.

Each node is then weighted with its corresponding average TFIDF value: $\text{tfidf}_i = \frac{1}{|D|} \sum_{j=1}^{|D|} \text{tf}_{i,j} \cdot \text{idf}_i$.

This TFIDF approach is a very well known approach in text mining that is easy to implement and makes one able to easily apply a threshold, thus selecting only the most important nodes (keywords). A node then contains, as an attribute, a list of the term frequency values of its associated term in the different documents of the collection. This allows us to compute similarity measures presented in Section 4 in order to create links.

According to the definition of a bisociation presented in Section 2, two concepts have to be linked by other concepts that are not in their proper domain (so-called *bridging concepts*). This leads us to introduce the notion of domains, into which the nodes are grouped, so that we can determine when borders between domains are crossed. In order to be able to classify nodes according to their membership in different domains, it is important that they keep, also as an attribute, the domains the data sources belong to, from which they have been extracted. Since the same keyword can occur in several data sources, taken from different domains, one has to be able (for example, for graph mining and link discovery purposes) to know whether a certain keyword has to be considered from a certain domain's point of view. The nodes therefore keep this information as vector of domains their associated keyword belongs to.

This can be interesting, for example, to mine or navigate the BisoNet, keeping in mind that a user may be looking for ideas related to a certain keyword belonging to a domain A. The results of a search for bisociations might also belong to domain A, because it is the domain of interest of the user. However, these results should be reached following paths using keywords from other domains, that is to say bisociations. This procedure provides related keywords of interest for the user, as they belong to its research domain, but they might be also original and new connections as they are the result of a bisociation process.

4 Linking Nodes: Different Metrics

As explained in Section 3.2, nodes are associated with a keyword and a set of documents in which this keyword occurs with a certain term frequency. Practically, this is represented using a vector of real values containing, for each document, the term frequency of the node's keyword. In order to determine whether a link should be created between two nodes or not, and if there is to be a link, to assign it a weight, we have to use a similarity measure to compare two nodes (that is to say: the two vectors of term frequency values).

Links in our BisoNets are weighted using similarity measures shown below. This approach allows us to use several different kinds of graph mining algorithms, such as simply thresholding the values to select a subset of the edges, or more complex ones, like calculating, for example, shortest paths.

4.1 Cosine and Tanimoto Measures

One basic metric that directly suggests itself is an adaptation of the Jaccard index (see [12]): $J(A, B) = \frac{|A \cap B|}{|A \cup B|}$.

Here $|A \cap B|$ represents the number of elements at the same index that both have a positive value in the two vectors and $|A \cup B|$ the total number of elements in the two vectors.

It can also be interpreted as a probability, namely the probability that both elements are positive, given that at least one is positive (contain a given term i, i.e., $\text{tf}_i > 0$).

Cosine similarity is a measure of similarity between two vectors of n dimensions by finding the angle between them. Given two vectors of attributes, A and B, the cosine similarity, $\cos(\theta)$, is represented using a dot product and magnitude as $\cos(\theta) = \frac{A \cdot B}{\|A\|\|B\|}$, where, in the case of text matching, the attribute vectors A and B are usually the tf-idf vectors of the documents.

This cosine similarity metric may be extended such that it yields the Jaccard index in the case of binary attributes. This is the Tanimoto coefficient $T(A, B)$, represented as $T(A, B) = \frac{A \cdot B}{\|A\|^2 + \|B\|^2 - A \cdot B}$.

These measures allow us to compare two nodes according to the number of similar elements they contain, but do not take into account the importance of the text frequency values.

4.2 The Bison Measure

In the Jaccard measure, as applied above, we would consider only whether a term frequency is zero or positive and thus neglect the actual value (if it is positive). However, considering two elements at the same index i in two vectors, one way of taking their values into account would be to use their absolute difference (that is, in our case, the absolute difference of the term frequency values for two terms, but the same document). With this approach, it is easy to compare two vectors (of term frequency values) by simply summing these values and dividing by the total number of values (or the total number of elements that are positive in at least one vector).

However, this procedure does not properly take into account that both values have to be strictly positive, because a vanishing term frequency value means that the two keywords do not co-occur in the corresponding document. In addition, we have to keep in mind that having two elements, both of which have a term frequency value of 0.2, should be less important than having two elements with a term frequency value of 0.9. In the first case, the keywords associated with the two nodes we are comparing appear only rarely in the considered document. On the other hand, in the latter case these keywords appear very frequently in this document, which means that they are strongly linked according to this document.

A possibility of taking the term frequency values itself (and not only their difference) into account is to use the product of the two term frequency values as a coefficient to the (absolute) difference between the term frequency values. This takes care of the fact that the two term frequency values have to be positive, and that the similarity value should be the greater, the larger the term frequency values are (and, of course, the smaller their absolute difference is). However, in our case, we also want to take into account that it is better to have two similar term frequency values of 0.35 (which means that the two keywords both appear rather infrequently in the document) than to have term frequency values of 0.3 and 0.7 (which means the first keywords appears rarely, while the other quite frequently).

In order to adapt the product to this consideration, we use the expression in Equation 1, in which k can be adjusted according to the importance one is willing to give to low term frequency values.

$$B(A, B) = (\text{tf}_i^A \cdot \text{tf}_i^B)^k \cdot (1 - |\text{tf}_i^A - \text{tf}_i^B|), \quad \text{tf}_i^A, \text{tf}_i^B \in [0, 1] \tag{1}$$

Still another thing that we have to take into account in our case is that the same difference between tf_i^A and tf_i^B can have a different impact depending on whether tf_i^A and tf_i^B are large or small. To tackle this issue, we combine Equation 1 with the use of the arctan function, and thus obtain the similarity measure shown in Equation 2, which we call the Bison measure. This form has the advantage that it takes into account that two term frequency values for the same index have to be positive, that the similarity should be the greater, the larger the term frequency values are, and that the same difference between tf_i^A and tf_i^B should have a different impact according to the values of tf_i^A and tf_i^B.

$$B(A, B) = (\text{tf}_i^A \cdot \text{tf}_i^B)^k \cdot \left(1 - \frac{|\arctan(\text{tf}_i^A) - \arctan(\text{tf}_i^B)|}{\arctan(1)}\right), \quad \text{tf}_i^A, \text{tf}_i^B \in [0, 1] \tag{2}$$

4.3   The Probabilistic Measure

Another way of measuring the similarity between two nodes is based on a probabilistic view. Considering two terms, it is possible to compute, for each document they appear into, the probability of randomly selecting this document by randomly choosing an occurrence of the considered term, all of which are seen as equally likely. This value is given by the law of conditional probabilities shown in Equation 3

$$P(d_i/t_j) = \frac{P(t_j/d_i) \cdot P(d_i)}{P(t_j)} \tag{3}$$
$$\text{with } P(t_j) = \sum_d P(t_j/d) \cdot P(d)$$

This leads us to represent a node by a vector of all the conditional probabilities of the documents they appear in instead of a vector of text frequencies.

Having this representation, we can compare two nodes using the similarity measure shown in Equation 4.

$$S(A, B) = \sqrt{\frac{1}{n} \cdot \sum_n (P(d_n/t_A) - P(d_n/t_B))^2} \tag{4}$$

We can add that $P(d_i/t_j)$ in Equation 3 is equivalent to the term frequency if $P(d_i)$ is constant, which is the case in most of the textual data sources. We can however use this $P(d_i)$ to give arbitrary weights to certain documents.

5   Benchmarks

Having shown how BisoNets can be built from textual data sources, we present benchmark applications in this section. The idea is to provide a proof of principle, that this approach of creating a BisoNet can help a user to discover bisociations.

In order to assess how effective the different similarity measures are, we count how many domain crossing links there are in the generated BisoNets, then we use different threshold values on the links in order to keep only the "strongest" edges according to the similarity measure used.

5.1   The Swanson Benchmark

Swanson's approach [13] to literature-based discovery of hidden relations between concepts A and C via intermediate B-terms is the following: if there is no known direct relation A-C, but there are published relations A-B and B-C one can hypothesize that there is a plausible, novel, yet unpublished indirect relation A-C. In this case the B-terms take the role of *bridging concepts*. In his paper [13], Swanson investigated plausible connections between migraine (A) and magnesium (C), based on the titles of papers published before 1987. He found eleven indirect relations (via bridging concepts B) suggesting that magnesium deficiency may be causing migraine.

We tried our approach on the Swansons data source which consists of 8000 paper titles, taken from the PubMed database, published before 1987 and talking about either migraine or magnesium, to see if it was possible to find again these relations between migraine and magnesium. In order to generate a BisoNet, we implemented a parser for text files containing the data from PubMed able to export them in the format understandable by the second layer of our framework. Then, this second layer performed the keywords extraction, using these keywords as nodes and linking these nodes in the way described in Section 3.

By ranking and filtering the edges we then produced BisoNets that contained the "strongest" edges and their associated nodes. The left graphic of Figure 2 shows how many domain crossing links that are kept using different threshold values on the edges. On this graphic, we can observe that the Bison measure is the one able to keep the most crossing-domain links even if only the very strongest edges are kept (threshold set to keep only the best 5% of the edges). These tests demonstrate that the Bison measure is very well suited for bisociation discovery, since with it the strongest links are the bisociative ones.

We can observe this also in Figure 3 where the difference between the Tanimoto and the Bison measure is graphically highlighted, showing that if we keep only the 5% best edges, the Tanimoto measure loses any relation between magnesium and migraine whereas the Bison measure manages to keep at least some.

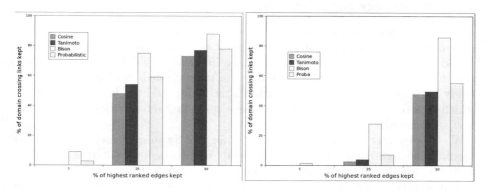

Fig. 2. Comparison between different similarity measures on the Swanson benchmark on the left and on the biology-music benchmark on the right

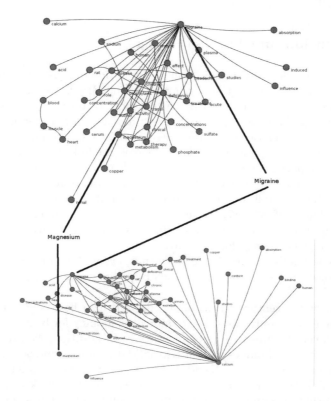

Fig. 3. Example of two BisoNets generated from the Swanson benchmark using the Bison similarity measure and the probabilistic similarity measure

5.2   The Biology and Music Benchmark

As we aim to discover bisociations, that is associations between concepts that appear unrelated from a certain, habitual point of view, an interesting benchmark would be to look for bisociations in data coming from very different domains. We therefore use here data from two databases: the PubMed database that has already been talked about in the Swanson benchmark, and the FreeDB[3] database which is a freely available music database providing music titles, music styles and artist names.

We use exactly the same procedure as for the Swanson benchmark, that is reading the databases, performing textual pre-processing on terms and then launching the BisoNet creation framework to obtain a BisoNet containing terms linked to each other using the similarity distances described in this article. We consider here as potential keywords every word and author in the articles of the PubMed database, and every word of song titles, authors and styles in the FreeDB database.

The right graphic of Figure 2 shows how many domain crossing links that are kept using different threshold values on the edges.

6   Conclusion and Further Work

In this article, we provided a definition of the notion of a bisociation, as understood by Koestler, which is the key notion of the BISON project. Building on this definition, we then defined the concept of a BisoNet, which is a network bringing together data sources from different domains, and therefore may help a user to discover bisociations. We presented a way we create nodes using simple text-mining techniques, and a procedure to generate links between nodes, which is based on comparing text frequency vectors using a new similarity measure.

We then tested our approach on benchmarks in order to rediscover bisociations between magnesium and migraine that have been discovered by Swanson using articles published before 1987. We see that bisociations between these two terms are easily discovered using the generated BisoNet, thus indicating that BisoNets are a promising technology for such investigations.

Using the second benchmark, we show that, even while mixing very different data sources, we are still able to produce BisoNets containing domain crossing links.

In summary, we venture to say that this work can be easily applied to any kind of textual data source in order to mine data looking for bisociations, thanks to the two layers architecture implementation. In addition, we are working on generalizing these techniques to non-textual data sources, introducing different types of attributes for the nodes, and therefore, other types of similarity measures in order to link the heterogeneous set of nodes. Further work also consists in performing other benchmarks and applying graph mining algorithms in order to confirm the quality of the so generated BisoNets.

---

[3] http://www.freedb.org/

Acknowledgments. The work presented here was supported by the European Commission under the 7th Framework Program FP7-ICT-2007-C FET-Open, contract no. BISON-211898.

References

1. Koestler, A.: The act of creation. London Hutchinson (1964)
2. Barron, F.: Putting creativity to work. In: The nature of creativity. Cambridge Univ. Press, Cambridge (1988)
3. Cormac, E.M.: A cognitive theory of metaphor. MIT Press, Cambridge (1985)
4. Agrawal, R., Imieliński, T., Swami, A.: Mining association rules between sets of items in large databases. In: Proceedings of the ACM SIGMOD internation conference on management of data, pp. 207–216 (1993)
5. Chalmers, D.J., French, R.M., Hofstadter, D.R.: High-level perception, representation and analogy: a critique of artificial intelligence methodology. Journal of Experimental and Theoretical Artificial Intelligence 4, 185–211 (1992)
6. Falkenhainer, B., Forbus, K.D., Gentner, D.: The structure mapping engine: algorithm and examples. Artificial Intelligence 41, 1–63 (1989)
7. Barnden, J.: An implemented system for metaphor-based reasoning - with special application to reasoning about agents. In: Nehaniv, C.L. (ed.) CMAA 1998. LNCS (LNAI), vol. 1562, pp. 143–153. Springer, Heidelberg (1999)
8. Aamodt, A., Plaza, E.: Case-based reasoning: foundational issues, methodological variations and system approaches. Artificial Intelligence Communications 7(1), 39–59 (1994)
9. Cardoso, A., Costa, E., Machado, P., Pereira, F., Gomes, P.: An architecture for hybrid creative reasoning. In: Soft Computing in Case Based Reasoning. Springer, Heidelberg (2000)
10. van Rijsbergen, C.J., Robertson, S.E., Porter, M.F.: New models in probabilistic information retrieval. In: British Library Research and Development Report, Number 5587. London British Library (1980)
11. Salton, G., Mc Gill, M.J.: Introduction to modern information retrieval. McGraw-Hill, New York (1983)
12. Jaccard, P.: Étude comparative de la distribution florale dans une portion des alpes et du jura. Bulletin de la Société Vaudoise des Sciences Naturelles 37, 547–579 (1901)
13. Don, R., Swanson, N.R., Smalheiser, V.I.T.: Ranking indirect connections in literature-based discovery: The role of medical subject headings. Journal of the American Society for Information Science and Technology (JASIST) 57(11) (September 2006)

Novelty Detection in Projected Spaces for Structural Health Monitoring

Janne Toivola, Miguel A. Prada, and Jaakko Hollmén

Aalto University School of Science and Technology,
Department of Information and Computer Science,
PO Box 15400, FI-00076 Aalto, Finland
{jannetoivola,miguel.prada,jaakko.hollmen}@tkk.fi

Abstract. The aim of Structural Health Monitoring (SHM) is to detect and identify damages in man-made structures such as bridges by monitoring features derived from vibration data. A usual approach is to deal with vibration measurements, obtained by acceleration sensors during the service life of the structure. In this case, only normal data from healthy operation are available, so damage detection becomes a novelty detection problem. However, when prior knowledge about the structure is limited, the set of candidate features that can be extracted from the set of sensors is large and dimensionality reduction of the input space can result in more precise and efficient novelty detectors. We assess the effect of linear, nonlinear, and random projection to low-dimensional spaces in novelty detection by means of probabilistic and nearest-neighbor methods. The methods are assessed with real-life data from a wooden bridge model, where structural damages are simulated with small added weights.

Keywords: novelty detection, dimensionality reduction, damage detection, structural health monitoring, sensor network.

1   Introduction

The monitoring process oriented to damage identification in civil, mechanical, and aerospace structures is known as Structural Health Monitoring (SHM) [8]. Current instrumentation technology makes it possible to continuously acquire and store vibration data from multiple parts of the structure. Consequently, signal processing and intelligent data analysis techniques are necessary to transform sensor data into information about the condition of the structure [8,21]. The usefulness of machine learning for SHM is addressed, e.g., in [22].

However, this is not a straightforward process, since SHM poses some distinctive challenges. Typically, it involves the analysis of the frequency domain of several signals with the aim to distinguish the effect of damages, with unknown characteristics, from the undamaged behavior. Additionally, current trends in SHM lead to use vibration data obtained from unknown excitation, input to a structure by ambient factors such as wind or traffic [6]. That way, the structure remains in its normal operating condition.

P.R. Cohen, N.M. Adams, and M.R. Berthold (Eds.): IDA 2010, LNCS 6065, pp. 208–219, 2010.
© Springer-Verlag Berlin Heidelberg 2010

The purpose of this work is to test the application of projection algorithms for damage detection in a setting where output acceleration measurements are collected by a sensor network. Our earlier work in [19] showed how the features explained in Section 2 can be used for "supervised" damage detection while considering a relatively small feature set. The feature sets were randomly selected subsets of the original large feature space and the selection process contributed to reduce dimensionality. Thus, it is expected that damage detection could also be possible with other suitable projections to lower dimensional spaces.

However, [19] used labeled data from damaged cases in the classifier training, which is prohibitively impractical in real world complex SHM applications. The prior knowledge about the structure and the possible damages must be assumed limited, in order to simulate realistic conditions in a complex SHM application. In this situation, where little is known about the damages that might appear in the structure and only information about the normal operation is available for training, the system should detect instances that do not fit in the model, i.e., the aim is novelty detection [22,4].

Under these assumptions, no criteria based on the physical model of the structure can be considered to select among potential features. Unlike in [22], we avoid performing supervised or manual selection of features, while still limiting the scope to transmissibility features. Therefore, the dimensionality of the input space becomes large and difficult to handle with data-based models.

Distances between randomly distributed data points in a high-dimensional feature space tend to be very similar and achieving a representative training set requires potentially an extremely large set of data. Also, some numerical issues arise in the implementation of the methods for high dimensions, as seen later in the experiments. The application of dimensionality reduction approaches [12] to transform data to simpler representations that preserve relevant information could then result in more accurate damage detectors. Apart from that advantage, improvement in the computational load of the monitoring process can be important if the ultimate aim is to achieve on-line detection.

In this work, three dimensionality reduction approaches: a flexible nonlinear technique, Curvilinear Component Analysis (CCA) [5]; the classical linear approach, Principal Component Analysis (PCA) [7]; and a computationally inexpensive[1] Random Projection (RP) [2] are assessed for novelty detection with density-based and distance-based methods.

In order to assess the performance of novelty detection, the test data set, unlike the training set, includes labeled normal and faulty instances. Four simple classification approaches are evaluated. Three of them are based on probabilistic models whereas the other one relies on a nearest-neighbor method. Interpretation of the results uses Receiver Operating Characteristic (ROC) curves and the area under the curve (AUC, aka. AUROC) [16,3].

The rest of the paper is organized as follows: Section 2 introduces the application field and the problem of feature extraction and selection in a sensor-network environment. Section 3 describes the three projection methods used in

---

[1] i.e., suitable for a wireless sensor network.

the paper and Sec. 4 explains the models for novelty detection. Section 5 describes the experiments and their results. Section 6 concludes the paper.

2   Features for Structural Health Monitoring

Damage detection in structural health monitoring is based on the principle that damages cause changes in the vibration response of a structure with respect to its normal behavior [21]. The measured vibration signals must be consequently processed with time- or frequency-based methods to extract features that are sensitive to damages. Researchers have proposed many damage-sensitive features, most of them in the frequency domain [13]. There are local and global approaches, general or specific to certain problems and they assume different levels of knowledge about the structure [21].

Some interesting features are those based on the concept of transmissibility [10,22], which describes how well vibration travels from one point of the structure to another and is therefore well-suited for sensor networks. These features are useful for detection of even nonlinear types of damage and can be used for damage localization, because the information they convey is local in nature [10]. Due to its differential nature, they are also less sensitive to the environmental variability of the measurements.

For that reason, the proposed features in this paper are, as in our previous one [19], (frequency specific) *transmissibility magnitudes*. They are defined as the magnitude of the ratio of acceleration amplitudes measured by two sensors, s_1 and s_2, at a specific frequency[2] f, during a time window i

$$T_i(s_1, s_2, f) = \left| \frac{X_{s_1}(f)}{X_{s_2}(f)} \right|. \tag{1}$$

The whole combination of pairs of sensors and frequency bins can easily give rise to a high-dimensional feature space, difficult to process by a novelty detection algorithm. In this work, we have 4541 features.

3   Dimensionality Reduction with PCA, CCA, and Random Projection

In this paper, three methods are considered to reduce the dimensionality of data: principal component analysis, curvilinear component analysis and random projection. They greatly differ both in the approach and computational cost.

Principal Component Analysis is a classical signal decomposition method used in signal processing and pattern recognition [7]. PCA decomposes the original measurement signal into components in a new, orthogonal coordinate system, which forms a basis. The important property of the basis is that its k leading orthogonal vectors are the ones that explain the most of the variance in original data. For that reason, PCA is useful for dimensionality reduction.

---

[2] More precisely, a *frequency bin* due to the discrete bins of the Discrete Fourier Transform used for computation.

Curvilinear Component Analysis is an adaptive algorithm for nonlinear dimensionality reduction, which minimizes a cost function based on inter-point distances in both input and output space [5]. The particular implementation used in this work is adapted to realistic noisy data [9]. Let D_{ij} be the Euclidean distance between vectors $\mathbf{x}_i$ and $\mathbf{x}_j$, in the d-dimensional input space, and Y_{ij} the corresponding distances between $\mathbf{y}_i$ and $\mathbf{y}_j$ in the k-dimensional output space. The function to minimize is

$$E = \sum_{ij} \begin{cases} (D_{ij} - Y_{ij})^2 F_\lambda(Y_{ij}) & \text{if } Y_{ij} > D_{ij} \quad \text{(Unfolding)} \\ (D_{ij}^2 - Y_{ij}^2)^2 F_\lambda(Y_{ij})/4D_{ij}^2 & \text{if } Y_{ij} <= D_{ij} \quad \text{(Projection)} \end{cases}, \quad (2)$$

where $F_\lambda(Y_{ij})$ is a monotonically decreasing function, exponential in this case. This technique also provides an interpolation-extrapolation method to project test data without the need of retraining the whole model.

Random Projection of data onto lower-dimensional space is an inexpensive method of linear dimensionality reduction that has, nevertheless, shown reasonable results, especially when applied to high-dimensional data sets for mappings to moderate numbers of dimensions [2]. It is justified by the Johnson-Lindenstrauss lemma, which states that a set of n points in a d-dimensional space can be embedded onto a randomly selected subspace whose dimensionality is logarithmic with respect to n, such that the pairwise distances change only by a small factor [1]. The implemented algorithm maps any d-dimensional vector $\mathbf{x}$ onto a k-dimensional vector $\mathbf{y}$, with $k << d$, by means of a sparse matrix $R_{k \times d}$, where r_{ij} is $\pm\sqrt{3}$ with probability $1/6$ each, or 0 with probability $2/3$, using the equation $\mathbf{y} = R\mathbf{x}$.

4   Novelty Detection in Projected Spaces

One cannot usually build a preliminary large-size structure just to try out all possible damages in advance. Thus, instead of having a conventional classification problem, we should deal with a *novelty detection* problem, i.e., try to detect data samples that are somehow different from the original set of data. This problem, which also appears in domains such as intrusion, fraud, or industrial fault detection, is also known as *anomaly detection* [4], *one-class classification*, or *data description* [17]: in order to detect damages (outliers) we need to be able to describe the normal (target) set of data well.

Since practically no samples from the outlier set are available, the decision boundary needs to be based on data from normal cases and some additional assumptions. Without the limiting assumptions, the optimal classifier would have too relaxed decision threshold and classify everything as "normal". However, finding the proper value of decision threshold is not considered a significant issue in this work, since ROC curves analyze the situation over all possible thresholds.

Many different novelty detection approaches have been proposed. A comprehensive review of recent research can be found in [4]. In this work, four novelty detection methods were assessed:

k-Nearest Neighbor (k-NN) method [7,17] compares the distance between a new data point x and its (kth) nearest neighbor $NN(x)$ in the training set with the distance between that neighbor $NN(x)$ and its nearest neighbor $NN(NN(x))$. Thus, the method assumes the relative scale between the features is appropriate.

Gaussian method [7] fits a single multivariate normal distribution to the training data and the area of low density ("tail" below some threshold) is assigned for outliers. For novelty detection, it is enough to compute the squared Mahalanobis distance with a full inverted covariance matrix to obtain results that are insensitive to scaling of dimensions.

Mixture of Gaussians (MoG) [15] consists of several normal component distributions. In our case, the component distributions were restricted to have diagonal covariance matrices to limit the number of free parameters. This corresponds to the naive-Bayes model used in [19], except this time the outlier data is unavailable and so the mixture components need to be fitted to the normal class by assigning weights through Expectation Maximization (EM).

Parzen density estimation [14] fits even more component distributions to the data space: one for each training vector. In this case, an equal and spherical covariance is assigned to each of the Gaussian kernels, i.e., all the dimensions of each component share the same length h. This single parameter is determined using a Maximum Likelihood solution [17].

5   Experiments and Results

In order to investigate the roles of the projection method, the dimensionality of the space, and the choice of novelty detection model in the accuracy of novelty detection, we performed empirical experiments where a series of methods were applied from raw data to decision (see Fig. 1).

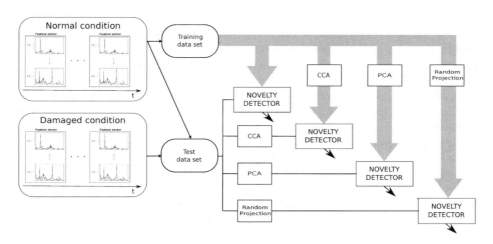

Fig. 1. General setup of the tests

PCA, CCA, and random projection were used to reduce the dimensionality of the original feature space to a previously fixed set of lower dimensionalities. All of them were implemented in Matlab and some functions included in SOM Toolbox [20] were used. Later, each of the four novelty detection methods were used to estimate a model from training data and provide the degree of novelty of the test data. The novelty detection phase was implemented by utilizing Data Description Toolbox (`dd_tools` [18]) for Matlab.

AUROC [16,3] was used as the performance measure to compare novelty detectors, because it integrates out the dependency on decision threshold, but closer analysis can still be conducted by inspecting the ROC curves to see what kind of trade-offs are made while varying the threshold.

5.1   Data Preprocessing

Data was measured from a wooden bridge structure in laboratory conditions. For that purpose, it was equipped with 15 acceleration sensors placed as depicted in Fig. 2. This setting was previously used in [11] and [19]. The bridge was subject to vibration produced with an electrodynamic shaker that simulated random ambient excitation. Small masses were attached to the structure during certain measurements in order to simulate damages, since they change the vibration profile locally. Unlike in [22], the location of the sensors was not optimized according to the known locations of the damages: sensors formed a regular lattice and some of the damages laid outside of it.

The sampling frequency was 256 Hz and the resulting data set consisted of 2509 blocks of 32 seconds each. The candidate features were the (frequency specific) transmissibility magnitudes below 120 Hz, with a frequency resolution of 0.5 Hz. These features were obtained after a 512-point Fast Fourier Transform (FFT) was used for the frequency analysis of signals.

Although there are 105 possible pairs of sensors (s_1, s_2), only pairs of adjacent sensors were considered. This is justified by the concept of nearest-neighbor coupling [10], which assumes that in the case where a single excitation is applied anywhere except at or near a boundary condition degree-of-freedom, transmissibility between two certain sensors s_1 and s_2 is only sensitive to the changes in

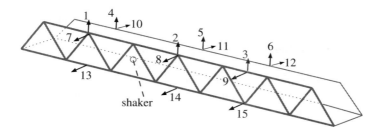

Fig. 2. Wooden bridge structure and placement of the sensors

stiffness or damping between them. Thus, there are 19 pairs of sensors and the final feature space, composed of all the transmissibility magnitudes at all pairs, has 4541 features. Consecutive transmissibility values were averaged to avoid aberrant values, so that only two final values were computed for each block and frequency bin, producing the 4541 feature values every 16 seconds.

75% of the normal instances in the data set were randomly selected for training, whereas the rest, along with all the faulty samples, were used for testing.

5.2   Projections

For a more convenient comparison, the target dimensionalities for the three projection algorithms were the same and covered different orders of magnitude: $\{2, 3, 4, 5, 8, 10, 16, 20, 32, 50, 100, 200, 500\}$. The random selection of the training samples and, therefore, the projection and classifier training was repeated 10 times for each combination to examine the statistics of the performance.

5.3   Novelty Detection Results

The main results of the paper are presented in four figures (Figures 3, 4, 5, and 6). In each of the figures, a different novelty detector was evaluated against the 13 projected training sets, which have been obtained with the three projection methods under evaluation (PCA, CCA, random projection). As a reference, also the performance for the original 4541-dimensional feature space is shown.

As shown in Figure 3, the best performance for the nearest-neighbor[3] novelty detector was achieved with data projected by PCA to the range of about 20 dimensions. Interestingly, there seems to be a decrease in the performance when either increasing or decreasing the number of features with respect to this optimum. The best results for the CCA-based projection were obtained when the number of features was 200 or over. Random projection reached the same level of performance than PCA for high dimensionalities, but the performance decreased rapidly with less than 50 projected features.

Figure 4 illustrates the use of a single Gaussian distribution as the density estimate in different projected spaces. CCA-based projection had the best performance reaching the one for the unprojected case at the dimensionalities above 100, unlike all the other projection methods. Similar results were achieved with Gaussian mixture models (Fig. 5), except that the specific implementation of the EM algorithm did not work for input dimensionalities of above 100: thus the worst-case AUROC values of 0.5 for high dimensional projection spaces[4].

Figure 6 depicts the performance of non-parametric Parzen density estimator. Again, CCA provided the best results, but PCA and RP catched up at 100 dimensions. At the highest dimensionalities, the implementation failed completely due to numerical issues.

---

[3] $k = 1$ was determined by leave-one-out density estimation [18].

[4] The worst-case value was set manually after observing the program fail.

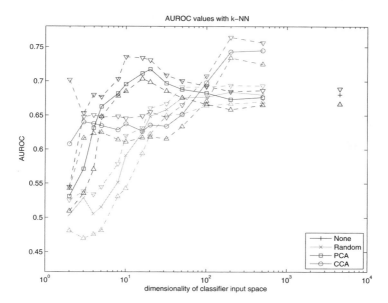

Fig. 3. The evolution of AUROC values with NN classifiers: horizontal axis shows dimensionality of the classifier input and the vertical axis reflects the diagnostic accuracy. Solid lines mark the medians of the AUROC values and dashed lines demonstrate the variance. The single case on the right is the result for unprojected data.

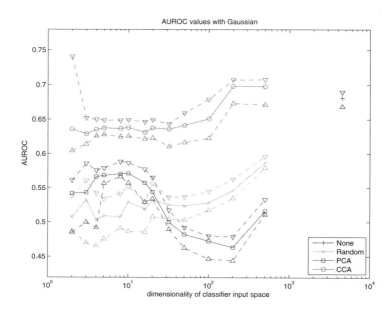

Fig. 4. Evolution of AUROC values with Gaussian classifiers (as in Fig. 3)

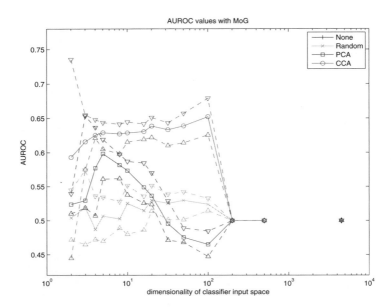

Fig. 5. Evolution of AUROC values with MoG classifiers (as in Fig. 3)

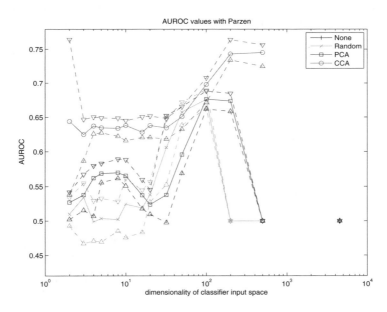

Fig. 6. Evolution of AUROC with Parzen density estimate classifiers (as in Fig. 3)

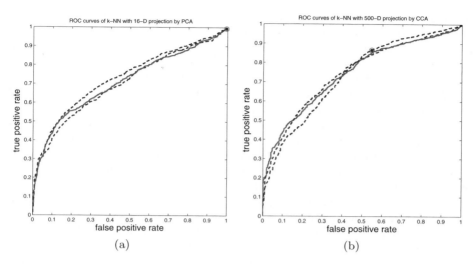

Fig. 7. ROC curves with lowest, median, and highest AUROC value produced by nearest neighbor method at (a) 16-dimensional projected space by PCA and (b) 500-dimensional projected space by CCA

The best median AUROC was 0.7450 and it was achieved with a 500-dim. CCA projection and a classifier based on Parzen density estimation, but the implementation started to suffer from numerical problems. The nearest neighbor classifier achieved similar performance with median AUROC of 0.7448, without suffering from numerical instability. Another close competitor was the 16-dimensional PCA, where the nearest neighbor method was able to reach a median AUROC of 0.7112. The corresponding ROC curves for the last two cases are shown in Figure 7 (a) and (b).

6   Summary and Conclusions

We have investigated three different projection methods in the dimensionality reduction of measurement data in a structural health monitoring application, where the data comes from a sensor network environment and has very large dimensionality. Novelty detection was performed in a density-based framework using non-parametric density estimation with Parzen windows, Mixture of Gaussians models, and single multivariate Gaussian distributions. It was also performed in a distance-based framework, using nearest neighbors. The accuracy of the novelty detectors was tested with labeled data in several projected spaces.

The experiments show that, in general, CCA is the best projection method for the novelty detectors assessed in this work. This agrees with the expected results, since the method should be more powerful due to its nonlinear nature. However, PCA was able to compete at lower dimensionalities (16 − 20) with a nearest neighbor classifier. The poor results with higher dimensionalities might be related to the aspect that the monitored features are supposed to be constants and large part of the variance is caused by noise.

It seems that, as expected, random projection preserves the structure of data well only for high output dimensionalities. In the experiments, there was a deterioration of performance for dimensions lower than 50. In general, the nearest neighbors method was the one that provided better results in a larger span of dimensionalities for all the projections.

Decisions derived from these conclusions must take into account the aims and requirements of the specific problem. For instance, if the damage detection must be carried out in a resource-constrained environment, we must keep in mind that CCA is the most computationally expensive method of projection, especially when the desired output dimensionality increases.

At least two directions for future research can be considered: searching for better feature extraction and better models for novelty detection (e.g. including temporal dynamics). On the feature extraction side, the applicability of transmissibility features needs to be investigated further. For example, the amount of noise and placement of the damage are assumed to have a large impact on the quality of the features and limit the damage detection performance.

Acknowledgments

The current work has been conducted in the project "Intelligent Structural Health Monitoring System (ISMO)", funded by Aalto University and its Multidisciplinary Institute in Digitalisation and Energy (MIDE).

References

1. Achlioptas, D.: Database-friendly random projections: Johnson-Lindenstrauss with binary coins. Journal of Computer and System Sciences 66(4), 671–687 (2003)
2. Bingham, E., Mannila, H.: Random projection in dimensionality reduction: applications to image and text data. In: Knowledge Discovery and Data Mining (KDD 2001), pp. 245–250 (2001)
3. Bradley, A.P.: The use of the area under the ROC curve in the evaluation of machine learning algorithms. Pattern Recognition 30(7), 1145–1159 (1997)
4. Chandola, V., Banerjee, A., Kumar, V.: Anomaly detection – a survey. ACM Computing Surveys 41(3), 15:1–15:44 (2009)
5. Demartines, P., Hérault, J.: Curvilinear component analysis: a self organizing neural network for non linear mapping of data sets. IEEE Transactions on Neural Networks 8, 148–154 (1997)
6. Deraemaeker, A., Reynders, E., Roeck, G.D., Kullaa, J.: Vibration-based structural health monitoring using output-only measurements under changing environment. Mechanical Systems and Signal Processing 22(1), 34–56 (2008)
7. Duda, R.O., Hart, P.E., Stork, D.G.: Pattern Classification, 2nd edn. John Wiley & Sons, Chichester (2001)
8. Farrar, C.R., Worden, K.: An introduction to structural health monitoring. Philosophical Transactions of the Royal Society A 365, 303–315 (2007)

9. Hérault, J., Jausions-Picaud, C., Guérin-Dugué, A.: Curvilinear Component Analysis for High-Dimensional Data Representation: I. Theoretical Aspects and Practical Use in the Presence of Noise. In: Mira, J. (ed.) IWANN 1999. LNCS, vol. 1607, pp. 625–634. Springer, Heidelberg (1999)
10. Johnson, T.J., Adams, D.E.: Transmissibility as a differential indicator of structural damage. Journal of Vibration and Acoustics 124(4), 634–641 (2002)
11. Kullaa, J.: Elimination of environmental influences from damage-sensitive features in a structural health monitoring system. In: Balageas, D.L. (ed.) Proceedings of the First European Workshop on Structural Health Monitoring 2002, Onera, pp. 742–749. DEStech Publications Inc. (2002)
12. Lee, J.A., Verleysen, M.: Nonlinear Dimensionality Reduction. In: Information Science and Statistics. Springer, Heidelberg (2007)
13. Montalvão, D., Maia, N.M.M., Ribeiro, A.M.R.: A Review of Vibration-based Structural Health Monitoring with Special Emphasis on Composite Materials. The Shock and Vibration Digest 38(4), 295–324 (2006)
14. Parzen, E.: On estimation of a probability density function and mode. The Annals of Mathematical Statistics 33(3), 1065–1076 (1962)
15. Redner, R., Walker, H.: Mixture densities, maximum likelihood and the EM algorithm. SIAM Review 26(2), 195–234 (1984)
16. Swets, J.A.: Measuring the accuracy of diagnostic systems. Science 240(4857), 1285–1293 (1988)
17. Tax, D.M.J.: One-class classification; Concept-learning in the absence of counter-examples. Ph.D. thesis, Delft University of Technology (June 2001)
18. Tax, D.: DDtools, Data Description Toolbox for Matlab, version 1.7.3 (December 2009)
19. Toivola, J., Hollmén, J.: Feature extraction and selection from vibration measurements for structural health monitoring. In: Adams, N.M., Robardet, C., Siebes, A., Boulicaut, J.-F. (eds.) IDA 2009. LNCS, vol. 5772, pp. 213–224. Springer, Heidelberg (2009)
20. Vesanto, J., Alhoniemi, E., Himberg, J., Kiviluoto, K., Parviainen, J.: Self-organizing map for data mining in MATLAB: The SOM toolbox. Simulation News Europe 9(25), 54 (1999)
21. Worden, K., Farrar, C.R., Manson, G., Park, G.: The fundamental axioms of structural health monitoring. Proceedings of the Royal Society A: Mathematical, Physical and Engineering Science 463(2082), 1639–1664 (2007)
22. Worden, K., Manson, G.: The application of machine learning to structural health monitoring. Philosophical Transactions of the Royal Society A: Mathematical, Physical and Engineering Sciences 365(1851), 515–537 (2007)

A Framework for Path-Oriented Network Simplification

Hannu Toivonen, Sébastien Mahler, and Fang Zhou

Department of Computer Science and
Helsinki Institute for Information Technology HIIT,
PO Box 68, FI-00014 University of Helsinki, Finland
firstname.lastname@cs.helsinki.fi

Abstract. We propose a generic framework and methods for simplification of large networks. The methods can be used to improve the understandability of a given network, to complement user-centric analysis methods, or as a pre-processing step for computationally more complex methods. The approach is path-oriented: edges are pruned while keeping the original quality of best paths between all pairs of nodes (but not necessarily all best paths). The framework is applicable to different kinds of graphs (for instance flow networks and random graphs) and connections can be measured in different ways (for instance by the shortest path, maximum flow, or maximum probability). It has relative neighborhood graphs, spanning trees, and certain Pathfinder graphs as its special cases. We give four algorithmic variants and report on experiments with 60 real biological networks. The simplification methods are part of ongoing projects for intelligent analysis of networked information.

1 Introduction

In many fields, information is naturally represented as networks of interlinked people, genes, computers, web pages, concepts, or other objects. Networks or graphs are a simple yet powerful formalism, but for finding or extracting the most relevant parts of large networks, intelligent data analysis can be useful.

As an example, consider biological networks and their analysis. Public biological databases are interlinked and form a huge graph of biological concepts. Intelligent query mechanisms allow users to extract smaller subgraphs, maximally relevant to user-specified query nodes [1,2]. In research efforts such as Bison [3], heterogeneous information repositories are merged to large networks which are then analyzed and explored with intelligent methods.

In this paper, we propose a generic framework and methods for simplification of large, weighted networks. The proposed methods can be used to improve the understandability of a given graph, to complement user-centric analysis methods, or as a pre-processing step for computationally more complex methods.

A property of primary interest in many applications is the strength of an (indirect) connection between some given nodes. Such measures are crucial, for example, in link prediction. The proposed framework builds on the assumption

P.R. Cohen, N.M. Adams, and M.R. Berthold (Eds.): IDA 2010, LNCS 6065, pp. 220–231, 2010.

that connections between nodes are measured using the best path between them and then removes edges while *keeping the original quality of connection for all pairs of nodes.*

The elegance of the proposed solution is in its wide genericity. It is applicable to different kinds of graphs (for example, flow networks and random graphs) and connectivity can be measured in different ways (for example, by the shortest path, maximum flow, or maximum probability). The proposed framework has both relative neighborhood graphs and spanning trees as its special cases.

On the other hand, the assumption that the connection between nodes is measured with the best path between them is quite strong. This assumption allows, however, a clear specification of the result without reference to an algorithm that computes it. Since the proposed methods are computationally efficient, they may be a practical compromise also in applications where more complex measures of connectivity would otherwise be preferred. We will address this in the experimental section.

The remainder of this article is organized as follows. We first formalize the problem of path-oriented network simplification in Section 2. In Section 3 we present a range of algorithms to prune redundant edges. We briefly review related work in Section 4. We present and discuss experimental results in Section 5 and finally draw some conclusions in Section 6.

2   Path-Oriented Edge and Graph Redundancy

Our goal is to simplify a given weighted graph $G = (V, E)$ by removing redundant edges. In this section we define the necessary notations and concepts, we give a simple theorem that allows efficient pruning, and we give some examples.

2.1   Definitions

We assume a weighted graph $G = (V, E)$ is given. In the following, we assume G is undirected, but the definitions and methods can be easily generalized for directed graphs. An *edge* $e \in E$ is a pair $e = \{u, v\}$ of nodes in V. Each edge has a *weight* $w(e) \in \mathbb{R}$. A *path* P is a set of edges $P = \{\{u_1, u_2\}, \{u_2, u_3\}, \dots, \{u_{k-1}, u_k\}\} \subset E$. We use the notation $u_1 \overset{P}{\leadsto} u_k$ to say that P is a path between u_1 and u_k, or, equivalently, to say that u_1 and u_k are the endvertices of P.

In order to allow different definitions of redundancy, we parameterize our problem and methods with a *path quality function* $q : \{P \mid P \text{ is a path in } G\} \to \mathbb{R}$. Without loss of generality, we assume that larger values of q indicate higher quality; this assumption can be easily reversed if necessary.

A natural and simple way to measure relatedness between two nodes u and v in a weighted graph is to consider the quality of the best path between them. This *best path quality* Q is thus defined as $Q(u, v; E) = \max_{P \subset E : u \overset{P}{\leadsto} v} q(P)$. If u and v are not connected, $Q(u, v; E) = -\infty$.

In this paper, we will study the problem of pruning a graph without affecting the best path quality for *any* pair of nodes. We say that an edge $e \in E$ is *redundant* if and only if

$$Q(u, v; E) = Q(u, v; E \setminus \{e\}) \quad \text{for all } \{u, v\} \in V, \tag{1}$$

in other words, if the best path quality Q does not depend on edge e for *any* nodes u, v in G.

Figure 1 illustrates the idea in a small graph. Here edges have lengths, and the length of an edge or a path corresponds to the length of the edge or path in the drawing of Figure 1 (i.e., path length is not defined by the number of edges in it). Now, while there is a direct edge $e = \{u, v\}$ between nodes u and v, there exists a shorter path between them. Since edge e does actually not belong to the shortest path between any pair of nodes in the graph, pruning it has no effect on any shortest path.

Fig. 1. Edge e is redundant

A *non-redundant graph* is a graph that contains no redundant edges. We define a *completely pruned graph* as a non-redundant graph that maintains the best path quality of the original graph for all its node pairs. Formally: given a graph $G = (V, E)$, a completely pruned graph $H = (V, F)$ is one where $F \subseteq E$, and $Q(u, v; E) = Q(u, v; F)$ for all $u, v \in V$, and H is non-redundant.

A couple of notes about pruning redundant edges that are in order, especially for the case in which node weights and path qualities may have ties: First, the trivial approach of taking the union of the best paths between all pairs of nodes does then not necessarily lead to a completely pruned graph, since ties might be solved differently for different pairs of nodes; second, a given graph may not have a unique completely pruned subgraph.

2.2 Monotone Path Quality Functions

Many path quality measures q are monotone in the sense that replacing a segment of a path by a better one with respect to q never decrease the quality of the whole path. Formally, let R and S be two paths with identical endvertices. Function q is *monotone* if for any path P containing R as a subpath, i.e., $P \supset R$, we have

$$q(R) \leq q(S) \Rightarrow q(P) \leq q(P \setminus R \cup S). \tag{2}$$

Monotonicity is a natural property for many path quality functions but not for all. Consider, for instance, average edge weight. A path consisting of edges with weights $10, 2, 1, 2, 10$ has a smaller average weight (5) than an alternative path with weights $10, 1, 10$ (average weight 7), even though the average of $2, 1, 2$ is larger than 1.

Monotonicity of path quality allows efficient pruning, as shown by the following theorem. We omit the proof for brevity.

Theorem 1. *Let $G = (V, E)$ be a graph and $e \in E$ an edge with endvertices w_1 and w_2, in other words $w_1 \overset{\{e\}}{\leadsto} w_2$. Edge e is redundant if and only if there* *exists another path* $S \subset E : w_1 \overset{S}{\rightsquigarrow} w_2, e \notin S$, *between the endvertices such that* $q(S) \geq q(e)$.

Theorem 1 says that redundancy of an edge (such as e in Figure 1) with respect to *all* pairs of nodes is equivalent to its redundancy with respect to its own endvertices. This means that edge redundancy can be evaluated efficiently by just checking if there is a path between the endvertices (u and v) which is at least as good as the direct edge. Redundancy with respect to all other pairs of nodes follows.

The following corollary is a special case of Theorem 1 for paths of length two.

Corollary 1. *Let* $G = (V, E)$ *be a graph and* $e = \{u, v\}$ *an edge in* E. *Edge* e *is redundant if there exists a path* $S = \{\{u, w\}, \{w, v\}\}$ *such that* $q(S) \geq q(e)$.

Corollary 1 gives an even faster way of identifying some redundant edges: for each edge e, find the shared neighbors w of the endvertices u, v and check if the path from u via w to v is at least as good as edge e itself. Obviously, this test cannot be used to infer *non*-redundancy of edges.

In Section 3 we will present algorithms that use Theorem 1 and Corollary 1 to solve the pruning problem with different trade-offs between completeness of pruning and time complexity.

Next, however, we give examples of different path quality functions q one could use in specific graph contexts.

2.3   Example Instances of the Framework

Flow networks are graphs where edge weights define their capacities. The maximum capacity $c(P)$ of a path is limited by each of its edges: $c(P) = \min_{\{u,v\} \in P} w(\{u, v\})$. The use of c as path quality function would guarantee that the amount of flow that the best path has is always conserved. The global property of network flow is much more commonly used; we will return to this in the experimental section.

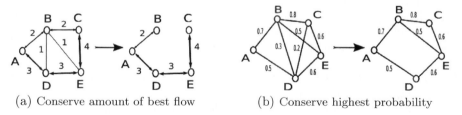

(a) Conserve amount of best flow   (b) Conserve highest probability

Fig. 2. Simplification of different types of graphs

Using the path capacity c above as path quality function actually has the property that completely pruned graphs are *spanning trees* that maximize the smallest edge weight in the tree (Figure 2a). Arbitrary spanning trees could be obtained by simply defining $q(P) = 1$, in other words, q indicates that the endpoints of path P are connected.

As a more complex example, assume that the weight $w(e) \in]0, 1]$ of an edge is the probability that the connection exists, and that edges are mutually independent. Such graphs are called *probabilistic* or *Bernoulli random graphs*. The best path is the one that most likely exists; the probability of a path P is simply the probability that all of its edges co-exist: $q(P) = \prod_{\{u,v\}\in P} w(\{u, v\})$. Figure 2b illustrates network simplification with this path quality function.

Shortest paths are commonly looked for in networks where edge weights correspond to distances between nodes. This is an example of a setting where the path quality—in this case path length—should be minimized rather than maximized. It is easy to change the definitions of this paper. Alternatively, one can transform the weights $w(e)$ to $w'(e) = e^{-w(e)}$ and use the same multiplicative q that was defined above for probabilistic networks.

A *relative neighborhood graph* discards those edges whose endvertices have a shared neighbor that is closer to both endvertices than the endvertices are to each other. Again, edge and path qualities are measured by distances, so we need to minimize $q(P) = \max_{\{u,v\}\in P} w(\{u, v\})$. An alternative is to transform $w'(e) = 1/w(e)$ and use the path quality function q defined above for flow networks. In either case, paths of at most two edges should be considered (cf. Corollary 1).

3   Algorithms

3.1   Variations

The four algorithmic variants we next present result from two axes of variation: (A) whether to use Theorem 1 or Corollary 1 to search and identify redundancies, and (B) whether to perform iterative search or static search.

Strategies to identify redundancy. Based on Theorem 1, the *global best path search* determines the redundancy of an edge by finding and evaluating the best path connecting its endpoints (and not including the edge itself). By the theorem, global best path search guarantees correct identification of redundancy.

Triangle search, in turn, takes advantage of Corollary 1 and identifies non-redundancy by only checking paths consisting of two edges. In other words, triangle search is based on 3-cliques search. Triangle search misses some redundant edges but is faster than global best path search.

Iterative versus static pruning. The *iterative* variant works dynamically: changes to the graph take effect immediately and may affect the redundancy of other edges. Iterative pruning results in a completely pruned graph. The result is not unique but depends on the order in which edges are processed.

The *static* variant, in turn, determines the redundancy of all edges in a single batch, based on the original graph only. Then, all redundant edges are removed.

There is another important difference between the static and iterative variants. If the static method would be applied directly based on the definition (1), pruning would be too aggressive. In the case of ties, too many edges would be removed, affecting some best path qualities, possibly even leading to disconnected components. Therefore an edge is removed only when the quality of the best path is strictly *higher* than the quality of the edge. This guarantees that all best path qualities are maintained. Static pruning thus prunes less edges than the iterative variant, and does not necessarily produce a non-redundant graph. The static method is faster, however, and its result is unique.

3.2   Outlines of Algorithms

Of the four algorithmic variants that we present, the *Iterative-Global* variant is the most complete and the only one guaranteed to produce a completely pruned graph. It is outlined as Algorithm 1. It first converts a multigraph (with parallel edges) into a simple one (Line 2). Then it finds, for each edge, the best possible alternative path P (Line 4). If it is at least as good as the edge, then the edge is pruned as redundant (Line 6).

Algorithm 1. Iterative-Global Algorithm

Input: A weighted graph $G(V, E)$, a path quality function q
Output: Subgraph $H \subset G$
 1: $F \leftarrow E$
 2: If F contains parallel edges, prune all but the best one.
 3: **for** each $e = \{u_i, u_j\} \in F$ **do**
 4:     Find path $P = \{\{u_i, u_{i+1}\}, \ldots, \{u_{j-1}, u_j\}\} \subset F \setminus \{e\}$ that maximizes $q(P)$
 5:     **if** $q(e) \leq q(P)$ **then**
 6:         $F \leftarrow F \setminus \{e\}$
 7: Return $H = (V, F)$

A straightforward implementation of the multigraph processing takes $O(|E|^2)$ time (Line 2). On Line 4, we use Dijkstra's algorithm with a complexity of $O((|E| + |V|) \log |V|)$ to find the best path. This is done for all $|E|$ edges. The computational complexity of the whole Iterative-Global method without any optimizations is then $O(|E|(|E| + |V|) \log |V|)$.

The *Iterative-Triangle* algorithm is very similar to the Iterative-Global one. The only difference is that on Line 4 of Algorithm 1 the best path search is replaced by the triangle search:

   4: Find path $P = \{\{u_i, u_k\}, \{u_k, u_j\}\} \subset F \setminus \{e\}$ that maximizes $q(P)$.

The computational cost of a triangle search for a single edge is $O(|V|)$. The total time complexity of Iterative-Triangle is thus $O(|E|^2 + |E||V|)$.

The *Static-Global* method, outlined in Algorithm 2, differs from Iterative-Global in two respects. First, all best paths are computed in a single batch in the set E of original edges (Lines 3–4). Second, the path quality check on Line 6 requires proper inequivalence.

Our implementation computes all-pairs shortest paths in time $O(|V|(|E| + |V|) \log |V|)$. The total time complexity is thus $O(|E|^2 + |V|(|E| + |V|) \log |V|)$. This could be improved slightly by using Johnson's algorithm [4].

Algorithm 2. Static-Global Algorithm

Input: A weighted graph $G(V, E)$, a path quality function q
Output: Subgraph $H \subset G$
1: $F \leftarrow E$
2: If F contains parallel edges, prune all but the best one.
3: **for** each $e = \{u_i, u_j\} \in F$ **do**
4:     Find path $P = \{\{u_i, u_{i+1}\}, \ldots, \{u_{j-1}, u_j\}\} \subset E \setminus \{e\}$ that maximizes $q(P)$
5: **for** each $e = \{u_i, u_j\} \in F$ **do**
6:     **if** $q(e) < q(P)$ **then**
7:         $F \leftarrow F \setminus \{e\}$
8: Return $H = (V, F)$

The *Static-Triangle* variant is again very similar to the global one, and the difference is again only to replace best path search on Line 4 of Algorithm 2 with the triangle search:

4: Find path $P = \{\{u_i, u_k\}, \{u_k, u_j\}\} \subset E \setminus \{e\}$ that maximizes $q(P)$.

The *Static-Triangle* variant is the fastest and the least complete of the four variants. Its worst-case computational complexity is identical to *Iterative-Triangle*. However, as pruning takes place during the process, the complexity is typically lower.

4   Related Work

Literature on network simplification and subgraph extraction is next. Here, we review some main approaches and their representatives.

Simplification of flow networks aims at removing edges while not affecting network flow for any node pair. This implies that the problem setting is more conservative than the one studied here. The methods proposed in [5,6] are based solely on the topology of the graph, not the weights. Generalization of those methods to other kinds of graphs is a topic for possible further work.

Pathfinder networks [7,8] are in many aspects similar to our pruned graphs and the global algorithm variants. The formulation is parameterized by r, to define Minkowski distance measure for pairs of nodes, and by q, a maximum path length considered (in other words, triangle search corresponds to $q = 2$ and global search to $q = |N| - 1$). Pathfinder networks then keep edges for which no better path exists with respect to r and q. While originally proposed for psychological research, Pathfinder networks are now gaining popularity in visualization of very large co-citation networks.

Neighborhood graphs originate from computational geometry. Given a set of points in some space, the task is to link proximal points by edges. When exactly to link two points varies between methods. A popular instance is Relative Neighborhood Graph [9], where an edge connects $u, v \in V$ if and only if $d(u, v) \leq max(d(u, z), d(z, v))$. See Veltkamp [10] for an overview of geometric graphs. The idea of relative neighborhood graphs can be applied to regular graphs—the distance between two nodes is the weight of the edge connecting them, or infinite if none exists. This is a special case of the framework proposed here.

Minimum spanning tree extraction is an old problem with specific solutions [11,12]. The model proposed in this paper can be used to find spanning trees, among others, but not necessarily minimal ones.

5 Experiments

To assess the methods proposed in the previous sections, we conducted experiments with various real graphs from the biomedical domain. With the experiments we aim to find initial answers to the following questions. How many edges are removed? How do the removed edges affect more complex measures of relatedness? What are the removed edges like semantically? How efficient and scalable are the methods?

5.1 Experimental Setup

Our data source is the Biomine database [1] which integrates information from twelve major biomedical databases. In the Biomine graph, nodes are biological entities such as genes, proteins, and biological processes. Edges correspond to known or predicted relations between entities, and have weights between 0 and 1.

For the tests, we picked 60 pairs of genes, such that each pair was related to the same phenotype according to Köhler et al. [13]. For each pair, the Biomine search engine[1] was then used to obtain a 500 node subgraph that contains the neighborhoods of the two given nodes. (Pairs whose neighborhoods were not connected were discarded.) For scalability tests, we additionally obtained a series of graphs for each pair, with sizes increasing from 500 to 3000 nodes.

We experimented with two classes of graphs, flow graphs and probabilistic ones, to get a perspective on the performance of the methods in different settings. In both cases, we directly used the weights provided by Biomine as the capacities or probabilities, respectively.

The algorithms were implemented in Java. Best paths were computed using a separate tool kindly provided by Lauri Eronen. All tests were run on standard PCs with $x86\_64$ architecture with Intel Core 2 Duo a 3.16GHz, running Linux.

5.2 Results

5.2.1 How Many Edges Are Removed?

We first evaluate the effectiveness of the methods in terms of the number of edges removed. Given a transformation of a graph $G = (V, E)$ to $H = (V, F)$, we measure the relative size reduction $s = (|E| - |F|)/|E|$.

---

[1] biomine.cs.helsinki.fi

The results obtained for flow graphs are shown in Figure 3a. The Iterative-Global variant is the most effective, pruning even more than 30% of edges on average. Static-Global follows, pruning approximately 25%. The two Triangle variants have roughly equal performance, both pruning slightly less than 20%. Figure 3b shows the results obtained for probabilistic graphs. The fraction of edges removed by Global variants is around 9%, and for Triangle variants around 7%.

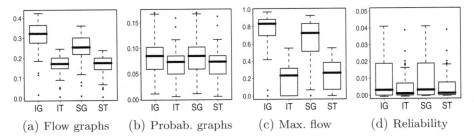

(a) Flow graphs   (b) Probab. graphs   (c) Max. flow   (d) Reliability

Fig. 3. (a) and (b): Fraction of edges removed by each of the four algorithmic variants. (c) and (d): Fraction of more complex measures lost in simplification. Each boxplot shows the distribution of results over 60 test graphs. IG=Iterative-Global, IT=Iterative-Triangle, SG=Static-Global, ST=Static-Triangle.

In absolute numbers, flow graphs lost approximately 120 to 240 edges out of 740 original ones. Probabilistic graphs lost approximately 50 to 60 edges. The results indicate that a relatively large number of edges can be removed without affecting the best path connectivity between *any* pair of nodes.

5.2.2   What Are the Effects on More Complex Connectivity Measures?

In order to get a better understanding of the characteristics of the proposed methods, we next evaluate their effect on some other measures.

Effect on maximum flow. For flow networks, a natural measure of connectivity between two given nodes is the maximum total flow from one node to the other, using all possible paths. In each of the graphs in our experiments, we also measured the maximum flow between the two nodes originally used to obtain the graph, computed with the Edmonds-Karp algorithm [14].

Figure 3c shows how much the maximum flow was reduced by each of the four algorithmic variants; $f = ((\text{MaxFlow}(G) - \text{MaxFlow}(H))/\text{MaxFlow}(G)$. Iterative-Global loses approximate 80% of the flow capacity, closely followed by Static-Global. The Triangle variants only lose about 30% on average. (Iterative-Triangle seems to have lost slightly less flow capacity than Static-Triangle, but this difference is due to handling edges in random order.)

Effect on graph reliability. In a probabilistic graph, the two-terminal network reliability (ttnr) is a natural measure of global connectivity between two given nodes [1]. The reliability can be estimated with a Monte Carlo approach: generate a large number of realizations of the probabilistic graph, and count the relative frequency of graphs containing a path between the two given nodes. In our experiments, we used 10 million Monte Carlo realizations in the evaluation of each graph to minimize estimation error.

Figure 3d shows the relative loss of reliability, $r = (\mathrm{ttnr}(G) - \mathrm{ttnr}(H))/\mathrm{ttnr}(G)$. All relative losses of Global variants are below 4%, and on average below 0.5%. Relative losses of Triangle variants are even less. In other words, edge pruning based on the best path quality had almost no effect on the more global network reliability.

5.2.3   What Are the Removed Edges Like Semantically?

An interesting issue is what the pruned edges are like. In Biomine, certain types of edges can be considered elementary; they connect entities that strongly belong together in biology. These include genes and the proteins they code for, homologous genes (in other words, the genes are essentially the same but in different organisms), and synonyms. An expert user most likely would not like any of these links to be pruned. On the other hand, since these relations are so elementary, other nodes need (and should) be connected to only one of them; the other connections could be considered semantically irrelevant.

With this idea, we designed the following experiment. We defined the edge types *codes for, is homologous to, subsumes,* and *has synonym* as "important." Then, we computed the number of those edges, adjacent to an important edge, that are "semantically irrelevant." For the sake of completeness, we also counted the number of "other edges" that are neither important nor adjacent to any important edge.

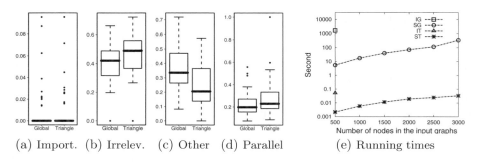

(a) Import. (b) Irrelev. (c) Other (d) Parallel   (e) Running times

Fig. 4. (a)–(d): Shares of different semantic categories among all removed edges (static methods in probabilistic graphs; note different vertical scales). (e): Mean running times (in logarithmic scale) of 60 runs as functions of the size of the input flow network.

An analysis of the edges removed by the simplification method in probabilistic graphs shows that practically none of the removed edges were important (Figure 4a), 32–56% were irrelevant (b), and 12–48% were "other edges" (c), in other words those on which our crude semantic classification could not decide, and 15–33% were parallel ones (d). Looking at each of the semantic categories, we observe that about 22–30% of semantically irrelevant edges were pruned, and 2–7% of other edges (results not shown). Even though the last percentage seems low, the category is by far the largest and, as stated above, stands for 12–48% of all removed edges. The results indicate that in our application the simplification method could considerably complement and extend expert-based or semantic methods, while not violating their principles.

5.2.4   How Efficient and Scalable Are the Methods?

Finally, we compare running times of the four variants. For this purpose, we used differently sized variants from 500 to 3000 nodes for each of the 60 graphs.

The mean running times for flow graphs are given in Figure 4e (results are similar for probabilistic graphs). Static-Triangle always needed less than 0.1 second to complete, even for a graph consisting of 3000 nodes. (The other variants were considerably slower. However, this comparison is not fully fair and should be considered at most indicative: Since the best path computation was implemented by an external tool, the global versions and especially the iterative versions suffered from the unnecessary cost of repetitive passing of graph files and starting new processes.)

6   Conclusion

We have addressed the problem of network simplification. The viewpoint is path-oriented: In the simplified network, and for any pair of its nodes, the best path qualities have been maintained. The framework is applicable to a large variation of network types and path qualities, some of which we illustrated with examples. Example instances include relative neighborhood graphs, spanning trees, and certain Pathfinder graphs.

Based on properties of monotone path quality functions, we gave four algorithmic variants of varying computational complexity that simplify a given network with varying degrees of completeness. Experiments performed on 60 real biological networks illustrate the potential of this approach. A rough semantic analysis of the simplification indicates that in our experimental setting, practically no semantically important edges were removed. Instead, the proposed method could complement semantics-based simplification by identifying additional redundant edges.

The simplification methods are part of larger on-going, system-oriented projects (Bison[2] and Biomine[3]) aimed at intelligent analysis of networked information. One of the next steps is validation of the simplification methods in user studies. For future work, an interesting topic is further generalization of the framework to more greedy network compression where some loss of best path qualities could be traded against removal of more edges.

---

[2] www.bisonet.eu

[3] biomine.cs.helsinki.fi

Acknowledgements. We would like to thank Lauri Eronen, Kimmo Kulovesi, Laura Langohr, Petteri Hintsanen, and Courtney Schirf for their help. This work has been supported by the Algorithmic Data Analysis (Algodan) Centre of Excellence of the Academy of Finland and by the European Commission under the 7th Framework Programme FP7-ICT-2007-C FET-Open, contract no. BISON-211898.

References

1. Sevon, P., Eronen, L., Hintsanen, P., Kulovesi, K., Toivonen, H.: Link discovery in graphs derived from biologican databases. In: Leser, U., Naumann, F., Eckmann, B. (eds.) DILS 2006, Part I. LNCS (LNBI), vol. 4705, pp. 35–49. Springer, Heidelberg (2006)
2. Hintsanen, P., Toivonen, H.: Finding reliable subgraphs from large probabilistic graphs. Data Mining and Knowledge Discovery 17, 3–23 (2008)
3. Berthold, M.R., Dill, F., Kötter, T., Thiel, K.: Supporting creativity: Towards associative discovery of new insights. In: Washio, T., Suzuki, E., Ting, K.M., Inokuchi, A. (eds.) PAKDD 2008. LNCS (LNAI), vol. 5012, pp. 14–25. Springer, Heidelberg (2008)
4. Johnson, D.B.: Efficient algorithms for shortest paths in sparse networks. Journal of the ACM 24(1), 1–13 (1977)
5. Biedl, T.C., Brejova, B., Vinar, T.: Simplifying flow networks. In: Nielsen, M., Rovan, B. (eds.) MFCS 2000. LNCS, vol. 1893, pp. 192–201. Springer, Heidelberg (2000)
6. Misiolek, E., Chen, D.Z.: Two flow network simplification algorithms. Information Processing Letters 97, 197–202 (2006)
7. Schvaneveldt, R., Durso, F., Dearholt, D.: Network structures in proximity data. In: The Psychology of Learning and Motivation: Advances in Research and Theory, vol. 24, pp. 249–284. Academic Press, New York
8. Quirin, A., Cordon, O., Santamaria, J., Vargas-Quesada, B., Moya-Anegon, F.: A new variant of the pathfinder algorithm to generate large visual science maps in cubic time. Information Processing and Management 44, 1611–1623 (2008)
9. Toussaint, G.T.: The relative neighbourhood graph of a finite planar set. Pattern Recognition 12(4), 261–268 (1980)
10. Veltkamp, R.C.: The gamma-neighborhood graph. Computational Geometry 1, 227–246 (1991)
11. Kruskal, J.B.: On the shortest spanning subtree of a graph and the traveling salesman problem. Proceedings of the American Mathematical Society 7, 48–50 (1956)
12. Osipov, V., Sanders, P., Singler, J.: The filter-kruskal minimum spanning tree algorithm. In: Finocchi, I., Hershberger, J. (eds.) ALENEX, pp. 52–61. SIAM, Philadelphia (2009)
13. Köhler, S., Bauer, S., Horn, D., Robinson, P.: Walking the interactome for prioritization of candidate disease genes. American Journal of Human Genetics 82(4), 949–958 (2008)
14. Edmonds, J., Karp, R.M.: Theoretical improvements in algorithmic efficiency for network flow problems. Journal of the Association for Computing Machinery 19(2), 248–264 (1972)

A Data-Driven Paradigm to Understand Multimodal Communication in Human-Human and Human-Robot Interaction

Chen Yu, Thomas G. Smith, Shohei Hidaka, Matthias Scheutz, and Linda B. Smith

Psychological and Brain Sciencs and Cognitive Science Program,
1101 East 10th Street, Indiana University, Bloomington, IN, 47405
{chenyu,thgsmith,shhidaka,mscheutz,smith4}@indiana.edu

Abstract. Data-driven knowledge discovery is becoming a new trend in various scientific fields. In light of this, the goal of the present paper is to introduce a novel framework to study one interesting topic in cognitive and behavioral studies -- multimodal communication between human-human and human-robot interaction. We present an overall solution from data capture, through data coding and validation, to data analysis and visualization. In data collection, we have developed a multimodal sensing system to gather fine-grained video, audio and human body movement data. In data analysis, we propose a hybrid solution based on visual data mining and information-theoretic measures. We suggest that this data-driven paradigm will lead not only to breakthroughs in understanding multimodal communication, but will also serve as a successful case study to demonstrate the promise of data-intensive discovery which can be applied in various research topics in cognitive and behavioral studies.

Keywords: Scientific Discovery, Cognitive and Behavioral Studies, Human-Human Interaction, Human-Robot Interaction, Information Visualization, Data mining.

1 Introduction

With advances in computing and sensing technologies, the dominant methodology of science has been changing over recent years. Bell et al. [1] predicted that the first three paradigms in science – empirical, theoretical and computational simulation – have successfully carried us to where we are and will continue to make incremental progress, but meanwhile dramatic breakthroughs will be achieved by the next fourth paradigm of science – data-intensive science, which will help bring about a profound transformation of scientific research (see also [2]). In brief, a vast volume of scientific data captured by new instruments in various labs is likely to be substantially publically accessible for the purposes of continued and deeper data analysis. This analysis will result in the development of many new theories from such data mining efforts. Indeed, data-driven discovery has already happened in various research fields, such as earth sciences, medical sciences, biology and physics, to name a few. However, cognitive and behavioral studies still mostly rely on traditional experimental paradigms

P.R. Cohen, N.M. Adams, and M.R. Berthold (Eds.): IDA 2010, LNCS 6065, pp. 232–244, 2010.

(reviewed below). The goal of the present paper is to introduce a contemporary framework to study one interesting topic in behavioral studies -- multimodal communication in human-human and human-robot interaction. We present an overall solution from data capture, through data coding and validation, to data analysis and visualization. We suggest that this data-driven paradigm will not only lead to breakthroughs in understanding multimodal communication but also more generally serve as a successful case study to demonstrate the promise of this data-intensive approach which can be applied in many other research topics in cognitive and behavioral studies.

Everyday human collaborative behavior (from maintaining a conversation to jointly solving a physical problem) seems so effortless that we often notice it only when it goes awry. One common cognitive explanation of how we (typically) manage to work so well together is called "mind-reading" [3]. The idea is that we form models of and make inferences about the internal states of others; for example, along the lines of "He is pointing at the object, so he must want me to pick it up." Accordingly, previous empirical methods on human-human communication are rather limited. For example, survey-based methods have been widely used to study human social interaction. This kind of measure relies on participants to recall and self-report their experiences, and although these reports may be predictive and diagnostic, they need not be objectively correct, and thus are at best an imperfect indication of what makes for "good" versus "not good" social interactions. Another popular approach is based on video coding in which human researchers code and interpret video data of human-human everyday interaction based on the prior notions about what is worth counting. But this rather subjective method may confirm what we already know but overlook important aspects of social interactions *that we do not yet know* – the ultimate goal of scientific discovery.

It is not at all clear that mind-reading theories about the states of others – and inferences from such internal representations – can explain the real-time smooth fluidity of such collaborative behaviors as everyday conversation or joint action. The real-time dynamics of the behaviors of collaborating social partners involve micro-level behaviors, such as rapid shifts of eye movements, head turns, and hand gestures, and how the partners co-organize in an interaction. These behaviors seem to be composed of coordinated adjustments that happen on time scales of fractions of seconds and that are highly sensitive to the task context and to changing circumstances. Previous survey and video-coding approaches don't have access to such fine-grained behavioral data, to say nothing of interpreting such micro-level behaviors. An understanding of micro-level real-time behaviors, however, has potential applications to building effective teams that can solve problems effectively, to building better social environments to facilitate human-human communication, to helping people that have various communication problems (e.g. autism), to building artificial agents (intelligent robots, etc.) that work seamlessly with people through human-like communication, and to building social training contexts for people to learn better (classroom interaction between teachers and students). Indeed, a fundamental problem in understanding both natural and artificial intelligent systems is the coordination of joint activity between social partners.

In both human-human communication and human-robot interaction, there is growing interest in micro-analytic studies of just what happens – in real time – as individual agents interact. Within this new trend, an understanding of human collaboration requires a level of analysis that concentrates on sensory-motor behaviors as a complex dynamic system in which the behaviors of social partners continually adjust to and influence each other. Although there is a growing consensus for the need for such an approach, there has been little progress. The limits to progress include issues concerning how to measure fine-grained behaviors in real-time interactions, and how to analyze, quantify, and model the results.

This paper presents a contemporary framework to study real-time multimodal communication between autonomous agents (humans or robots). In the following sections, we will introduce a set of novel solutions under this data-driven paradigm, including how to collect high-resolution behavioral data from multimodal interaction (Section 2), how to code and mange the whole dataset (Section 3), and how to analyze and visualize the data to discover new patterns and principles in both human-human and human-robot interaction (section 4). With this set of data capture, data coding and data analysis techniques, our framework allows us to study critical questions that cannot be asked before using traditional methods, to discover new knowledge that is unlikely to be acquired using traditional paradigms, and to demonstrate the power of this data-driven approach to cognitive and behavioral fields.

2   Data Collection – A Multimodal Sensing System

The first component in a complete data-driven paradigm is data acquisition. Toward this end, we have developed a multimodal sensing environment in which we ask two agents (humans or robots) to interact with each other with pre-defined communication tasks. We have successfully used this experimental setup to collect high-resolution data from three interaction scenarios (each with its own specific research goals): adult-adult interaction to capture the fundamental principles in human-human communication, child-parent interaction to study social environments of developing children, human-robot interaction to discover behavioral patterns that the robot should emulate in order to perform human-like interaction. For instance, we asked parents to teach children a set of novel object names, and we asked human participants to teach the robot those names as well. In some other experiments, we asked participants to learn from the robot who acted as a teacher by uttering those object names. For another example, in adult-adult interaction, an informed confederate was asked to behave in certain ways when he was interacting with his social partner. In all of the studies, multiple sensing systems are used to simultaneously record multimodal multi-streaming behavioral data from these two agents (be they humans or robots). As shown in Figure 1, the raw data collected from various sensing systems includes:

- **Video:** there are up to 6 video streams recorded simultaneously with a frequency of 30 frames per second, and the resolution of each frame is 720x480. Approximate 180,000 image frames were recorded in a 6-minute interaction.
- **Audio:** The speech of the participants is recorded at a frequency of 44.1kHz.
- **Body motion:** there are multiple position sensors in Polhemus motion tracking system, one on each participant's body part, e.g. the head or hands. Each sensor provided 6 dimensional (x,y,z, yaw, pitch, and roll) data points at a frequency of 120Hz. In a 6-minute interaction, we have collected 864,000 position data points from each participant.

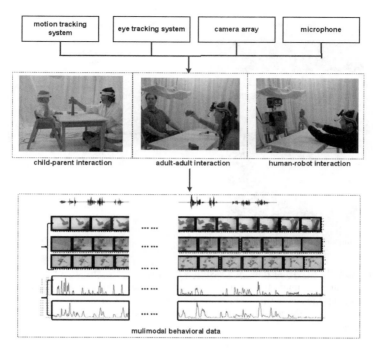

Fig. 1. A multimodal sensing system is developed to collect fine-grained behavioral data including motion tracking data, eye tracking data, video and audio data. We have successfully used this experimental paradigm to conduct studies of adult-adult interaction, child-parent interaction and human-robot interaction. In each study, we have collected multi-stream multimodal data for further data analysis and knowledge discovery.

- **Eye gaze:** an eye tracker records the course of a participant's eye movements over time at 60Hz.

These data are synchronized based on a central time-clock and therefore we can easily align them to analyze sequential patterns across data streams.

3 Coding of Multimodal Data

The next component in our data-driven paradigm is automatic data coding – deriving various time series from raw multimodal data.

Video Processing. The recording rate for each camera is 30 frames per second. The resolution of each image frame is 720x480 pixels. As shown in Figure 2, we analyze the image data in two ways: (1) At the pixel level, we use the saliency map model developed by Itti et al. [4] to measure which areas in an image are most salient based on motion, intensity, orientation and color cues. Itti's saliency map model applies bottom-up attention mechanisms to topographically encode for conspicuity (or "saliency") at every location in the visual input. (2) At the object level, the goal is to automatically extract visual information, such as the locations and sizes of objects,

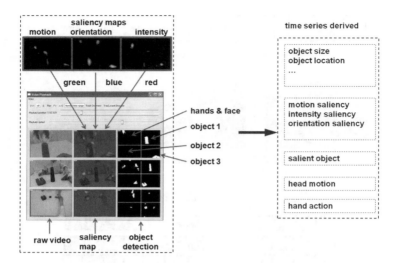

Fig. 2. An example of visual data processing with three raw video streams (the left column). We calculated saliency maps from each video stream (the middle column) and also extracted visual objects from the scene (the right column). Next, a set of time series are derived based on measures such as sizes and locations of each of those objects, visual saliency and also head and hand movements.

hands, and faces, from sensory data in each camera. These are based on computer vision techniques, and include several major steps. The combination of using pre-defined simple visual objects and utilizing start-of-the-art computer vision techniques results in high accuracy in visual data processing. The technical details can be found in [5].

Motion data Processing Six motion tracking sensors on participants' heads and hands recorded 6 DOF of their head and hand movements at the frequency of 240 Hz. Given the raw motion data {x, y, z, h, p, and r} from each sensor, the primary interest in the current work is the overall dynamics of body movements. We grouped the 6 DOF data vector into position {x, y, z} and orientation data {h, p, r}, and then we developed a motion detection program that computes the magnitudes of both position movements and orientation movements. We next cluster hand movement trajectories into several action prototypes (e.g. reaching, holding, and manipulating).

Speech processing We first segment the continuous speech stream into multiple spoken utterances based on speech silence. Next, we ask human coders to listen to the recording and transcribe the speech segments. From the transcriptions, we calculate the statistics of linguistic information, such the size of vocabulary, the average number of words per spoken utterance, the frequent frames in spoken utterances.

In addition to automatic coding, we realized that some information may be hard to extract automatically. For instance, whether a person is holding an object cannot be easily detected just based on the distances between hands and the visual objects captured from video cameras as one may put hands close to an object without holding it. In light of this, we have also developed a manual coding program to allow human coders to record those derived variables. In the future, we are interested in investigating a solution that can take advantage of both fast automatic coding and potentially more accurate human coding.

Overall, as a result of sensory data processing (shown in Figure 2), we derived more than 200 time series from various sensing systems and they capture different kinds of perception and action variables in multimodal social interaction, such as sizes and saliency of objects from different cameras, trajectories of head and hand movements, and the distances of objects to a participant. This data processing route has been used in different studies we've conducted using the multimodal sensing system.

4   Knowledge Discover and Data Mining

With huge amounts of multimodal data collected from various studies of human-human and human-robot studies, a critical component in data-intensive discovery is the ability to discover new patterns from such data. Now how can we discover what we do not know what we are looking for? Classic approaches to data-mining often require that one has some idea of what one is looking for. More specifically, advances in machine learning and data mining provide tools for the discovery of only pre-defined structures in complex heterogeneous time series (hidden Markov models, dynamic time warping, Markov random fields, to name a few, e.g. [6]). A relevant research field to knowledge discovery is information visualization with the goal to visually present data to highlight certain aspects of patterns and structures so that researchers can easily spot interesting patterns based on their visual perception systems. As shown in Figure 3, data mining and information visualization are traditionally treated as two irrelevant topics. Data mining algorithms rely on mathematical and statistical techniques to discover patterns while information visualization researchers are interested in finding novel techniques to visually present data in more informative ways. However, it is worth noting that these two topics share the same ultimate research goal – building tools and developing new techniques to allow users (e.g. researchers) to obtain a better understanding of massive data.

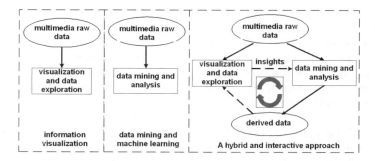

Fig. 3. Left: Information visualization techniques focus on developing informative ways to visualize data.   **Middle**: Data mining algorithms rely on mathematics and statistics to find complex patterns from data. **Right**: While data mining and information visualization are traditionally treated as two separate topics, they share the same research goal. In light of this, our hybrid and interactive approach builds the links between these two and by doing so forms a closed loop between visualization and data mining.

Discovering *new* knowledge requires the ability to detect unknown, surprising, novel, and unexpected patterns. For this purpose, we propose that the techniques developed in data mining and information visualization can be integrated to build a better pattern/knowledge discovery system. In the case of our multimodal data, a huge amount of information must be cut and summarized to be useful. But statistics and measures extracted from raw data may exclude embedded patterns or even be misleading. We need a mechanism to represent the overall statistics but still make fine-grained data accessible. Information visualization provides a unique opportunity to accomplish this task. Often, potential users of information visualization are not aware of the benefits of visualization techniques on data mining; or they use those techniques only as a *first* phase in the data analysis process. As shown in Figure 3 (right), we suggest a more interactive mode between data mining and information visualization. In our system, researchers can not only visualize raw data at the beginning but also visualize processed data and results. In this way, data mining and visualization can bootstrap each other – more informative visualization based on new results will lead to the discovery of more complicated patterns which in turn can be visualized again to lead to more findings. More importantly, researchers play a critical role in this human-in-the-loop knowledge discovery by applying data mining techniques on the data, examining visualization results and deciding what to focus on at the next round based on theoretical knowledge in one's mind. In this way, domain knowledge, computational power, and visualization tools can be integrated together to allow researchers to reduce the search space created by huge datasets, and quickly and effectively identify interesting patterns. In the following, we will briefly introduce visualization and information tools we developed and used in our data-driven research paradigm.

4.1 Visual Data Mining System

As we discussed earlier, most data mining algorithms can effectively search and discover only pre-determined patterns and those patterns need to fit a specific definition of statistical reliability. This limitation significantly constrains what can be achieved. A large amount of time must be invested in prototyping a number of pilot data analysis algorithms, many of which turn out to be dead ends. In light of this, we have developed a hybrid approach that allows us to use a small number of very promising data mining tools as a first pass, and then from these suggested interesting/unusual patterns, we perform more directed, more detailed and deeper analyses with human inspection -- adding domain-specific expertise as a part of data analysis, followed by more automatic data mining. This idea of interactive human-in-the-loop data mining is implemented by our information visualization system [7] which has 3 key components: (1) a smooth interface between visualization and data mining; (2) a flexible tool to explore and query temporal data derived from raw multimedia data; and (3) a seamless interface between raw multimedia data and derived time series and events. We have developed various ways to visualize both temporal correlations and statistics of multiple derived variables as well as conditional and high-order statistics. Our visualization tool allows us to explore, compare, and analyze multi-stream derived variables and simultaneously switch to access raw multimedia data. As shown in Figure 4, our visualization system follows the general principles of building scientific data visualization systems: "overview, zoom & filter, details-on-command" as

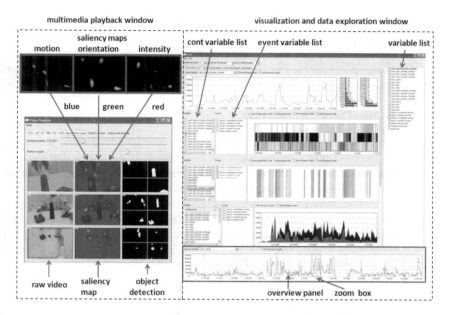

Fig. 4. There are two major display components in our visualization system: a multimedia playback window (left) and a visualization window (right). The multimedia playback window is a digital media player that allows us to access video and audio data and play back both raw and preprocessed data in various ways. The visualization window is the main tool that allows us to visually explore the derived data streams and discover new patterns.

proposed by [8]. We embody these principles in the case of multimedia visual data mining of social and behavioral data, which comprises two major display components as shown in Figure 4: a multimedia playback window and a visual data mining window. The multimedia playback window is a media player that allows us to access and process raw multimedia data, and plays them back in various ways. The visualization window is the main tool that allows us to manipulate and visually explore derived data streams to discover new patterns. More importantly, when we visually explore a dataset, these two display windows are coordinated to allow us to switch between synchronized raw data and derived data. We have developed various functions to visualize derived data streams individually or together to highlight different aspects of multimedia multivariate data (see [7] for details).

As an example to demonstrate the utilities of visual data mining, Figure 5 shows a set of eye movement data (e.g. where a person is looking at). Each stream in the figure corresponds to the same derived variable but collected from different participants. In this example, since all of the data streams are temporally aligned, we can easily compare those time series to spot interesting patterns. More specifically, there are at least two immediate outcomes from this visual exploration. First, we can discover those moments that all the participants behave similarly. This pattern can be spotted by examining multiple time series vertically. Moreover, we can visually examine the timing of their eye movement behaviors which usually cannot be captured by statistical analysis. Meanwhile, by examining those data streams horizontally, we can also easily find those individuals who are different with others (e.g. participant 3 in this example). Moreover, this explicit and informative visualization allows us to also discover *in what ways* those individuals are different. In the our example, participant 3 seems to always generate eye movements right before most of people do so – the pattern that can be easily detected through this visualization.

4.2 Information-Theoretic Measures

In multimodal communication, one agent's activities are embedded in, influenced by, and influence the momentary behaviors of the other social partner such that the whole human-human interaction can be viewed as two coupled complex systems. As the first steps to understand those two coupled complex systems, we use information-theoretic measures to measure information flows between various time series derived from the same agent and those time series derived from two agents. We will use the data from child-parent interaction as an example here. Given multi-streaming continuous time series extracted from child-parent interaction, we are interested in quantifying this multimodal inter-person information exchange at the bit level. Our data mining and pattern discovery process consists of two steps. We need to first convert a continuous time series into a discrete stream of system states so that we can form probabilistic distributions of the states of each variable over time. We can then apply information metrics (e.g. entropy and mutual information) to quantify the amount of information in bits.

The discretization technique we employed in the first step is based on Symbolic Aggregate Approximation (SAX) [8]. The goal here is to provide an efficient and accurate symbolic representation of time series which makes it easier to apply information theoretic measures. In brief, SAX first transforms the input time series data into Piecewise Aggregate Approximation (PAA) representation and then symbolizes the distribution space of PAA representation into a set of discrete symbols. Compared

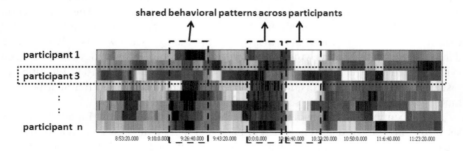

Fig. 5. Application of our visualization program to the problem of comparing the same derived variable collected from multiple participants. By visually exploring those multiple streams in parallel, researchers can easily detect the shared behavioral patterns across participants. Namely, most participants generate the same behaviors or perceive the same information at those moments. At those moments, they also demonstrate individual differences. Moreover, we can also easily identify individuals that are different with the whole group. For instance, participant 3 seems to be an outlier whose gaze data are quite different with other participants.

with other approaches, SAX allows lower-bounding distance measures to be defined on the symbolic space that are identical with the original data space. Thus, the information loss through this symbolization and its potential effects on subsequent data processing is minimal when we convert time series into this efficient symbolic representation.

With symbolic representations of various derived time series from multimodal human-human communication, we have applied and integrated various temporal data mining algorithms in our system. Here we will use *entropy rate* [9] as a simple example, which measures uncertainty in time series when the previous state of a series is given or the previous state of two series are given. In our case, the *entropy rate*, which measures the uncertainty in a distribution of the transitive probability from one state to another would be a suitable choice. Suppose that $I = \{i_1, i_2, \cdots, i_N\}$ is series of symbols, and the entropy rate of the series I is as follows.

$$H(I) = -\sum p\left(i_{n+1}, i_n^{(k)}\right) \log p\left(i_{n+1} \mid i_n^{(k)}\right)$$

where $p\left(i_{n+1} \mid i_n^{(k)}\right) = p\left(i_{n+1} \mid i_n, i_{n-1}, \cdots, i_{n-k+1}\right)$.

We next calculated the entropy rates of individual variables extracted from raw multimedia data. To capture temporal dynamics of each variable, instead of calculating the overall entropy over time, we defined a sliding window with the size of 2 seconds and applied this moving window to time series data so that a local entropy time series was computed. Figure 6 shows several individual entropy measures in parallel. The first two entropy time series H1 and H2 are from the child while H3 and H4 are from the parent. More specifically, H1 measures the entropy of the object held by the child's hands. H2 measures the entropy of the child's hands. H3 measures the entropy of the same object from the caregiver's view (captured by the caregiver's camera) and H4 measures the entropy of the parent's hands. By aligning these individual entropy measures side by side, we can immediately detect several patterns between these variables: 1) H1 and H2 are quite correlated; 2) Moreover, H2 is a precursor of H1 since the manipulation of the object causes the changes of the visual appearance of that object from the camera's view; 3) H3 and H4 are not correlated since the object is in the child's hands but not the parent's hands; and 4) H1 and H3 are not correlated since the object manipulated by the child is barely seen from the parent's view. Moreover, we can spot potentially important temporal events. For example, the red box in Figure 6 highlights such an event. In this example, the parent briefly took the object away from the child which causes the increase of the entropy on the parent's side (both the hands and the visual object) and as well as the decrease of the entropies on the child's side (the visual object is farther away; and the child's hand is not manipulating the object). From this example, we suggest that even simple information-theoretic measures, such as the entropy rate of a temporal variable, can lead to insightful results to quantify the dynamic communication between the two agents. We have developed various other measures such as mutual information and transfer entropy to quantify information flows not only in child-parent interaction and human-robot and adult-adult interaction.

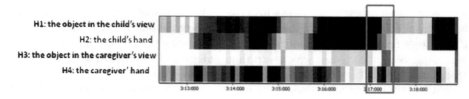

Fig. 6. An example of entropy rates from four time series – two from the child and two from the parent. From this example, we can see the moment with consequential information flows between those four variables and as well as which variable leads to changes of other variables.

4.3 Interactive Data Mining

We argue that a critical challenge of data-intensive discovery lies in not only pure amounts of data that need to be mined but also the huge search space of potentially interesting patterns created by the data. For example, in our dataset, one can treat each time series independently and by doing so, we just focus on patterns within a single time series. However, if we truly view multimodal communication between two agents as two complex systems, we need to analyze correlations embedded in a subset of two, three or more time series which leads to combinational exploration.

A solution for this challenge in particular and for intelligent data analysis of scientific discovery more generally clearly relies on advanced data mining algorithms to process huge amounts of data and extract potentially interesting patterns. But more importantly, we suggest that the exploratory nature of scientific discovery also requires an interactive platform allowing scientists to be in the loop of data mining, examine the current results generated and then guide data mining algorithms toward the right directions, which significantly enhances both effectiveness and efficiency of knowledge discovery. Thus, this human-guided computation can seamlessly integrate human expertise and statistical pattern discovery power.

Toward this end, our data mining system supports various procedures that allow us to examine both raw and derived data, and gain insights and hypotheses about interesting patterns embedded in the data. All this is accomplished by human observer's visual system. In order to quantify and extend these observations, researchers need to develop and use data mining algorithms to extract and measure the patterns detected in visual exploration. We notice that different researchers may have different preferences of programming languages and may prefer to use certain software packages. To increase the flexibility to be compatible with data mining, our system allows users to use any programming language to obtain new results. Thus, data researchers can implement new data mining algorithms using their own analysis tools (from Matlab, to R and to C/C++) and as far as they write the results into text files (e.g. CSV form) with pre-defined formats, our system monitors user's workspace in real time and will automatically load new derived variables into the variable list so that we can immediately visually examine these new results. In this way, our visualization system supports a close and flexible coupling between visual exploration and data mining. The insights gleaned from visualization can be used to guide further data mining. Meanwhile, the results from the next round of data mining can be visualized which allows us to obtain new insights and develop more hypotheses with the data. Overall, our data analysis system is "open-minded" by not adding any constraints, assumptions or simplification on raw and derived data, but instead allows us to guide the direction and systematically explore the data through informative visualization, which is truly the power of visual data mining.

5 Conclusions

Human-human and human-robot multimodal communication can be viewed as two coupled complex systems interacting with each other through perception and action. Inspired by this conceptualization, we invented and implemented a novel data-intensive paradigm that allows us to investigate micro-level behaviors, such as head turns and gaze shifts, generated by autonomous agents (humans or robots). To achieve this goal, our paradigm includes a multimodal sensing system to collect fine-grained sensory data, automatic coding programs to extract temporal variables from raw multimedia data, a visual data mining system to visualize multi-streaming data, a set of quantitative measures (e.g. information theoretic measures) to calculate information exchanges between variables and states derived from two agents, and an interactive framework that allows us to integrate information visualization and data mining. We have implemented each of these components and have begun to use this new paradigm to discover new knowledge in both human-human communication [5] and human-robot interaction [10]. We argue that data-intensive discovery approaches have great potentials to lead to lots of breakthroughs in cognitive and behavioral studies in the near future.

Acknowledgement

This research is supported by NSF BCS 0924248 and AFOSR FA9550-09-1-0665. We would like to thank Amanda Favata and Damian Flicker for data collection, and Yiwen Zhong for contributing to software development of the information visualization program.

References

1. Bell, G., Hey, T., Szalay, A.: Computer science. Beyond the data deluge. Science 323, 1297–1298 (2009)
2. Cohen, P.R., Adams, N.: Intelligent Data Analysis in the Twenty First Century. In: Proceedings of the Intelligent Data Analysis Conference, Lyon, France (2009)
3. Baron-Cohen, S.: Mindblindness: an essay on autism and theory of mind. MIT Press/Bradford Books (1995)
4. Itti, L., Koch, C., Niebur, E.: A Model of Saliency-Based Visual Attention for Rapid Scene Analysis. IEEE Transactions on Pattern Analysis and Machine Intelligence 20(11), 1254–1259 (1998)

5. Yu, C., Smith, L.B., Shen, H., Pereira, A.F., Smith, T.G.: Active Information Selection: Visual Attention Through the Hands. IEEE Transactions on Autonomous Mental Development 2, 141–151 (2009)
6. Oates, T., Cohen, P.R.: Searching for Structure in Multiple Streams of Data. In: Proceedings of the Thirteenth International Conference on Machine Learning, pp. 346–354 (1996)
7. Yu, C., Zhong, Y., Smith, T., Park, I., Huang, W.: Visual Data Mining of Multimedia Data for Social and Behavioral Studies. Information Visualization 8, 56–70 (2009)
8. Lin, J., Keogh, E., Li, W., Lonardi, S.: Experiencing SAX: A Novel Symbolic Representation of Time Series. Data Mining and Knowledge Discovery Journal, 107–144 (2007)
9. Kantz, H., Schreiber, T.: Nonlinear Time Series Analysis. Cambridge University Press, Cambridge (1997)
10. Yu, C., Scheutz, M., Schermerhorn, P.: Investigating Multimodal Real-Time Patterns of Joint Attention in an HRI Word Learning Task. In: 5th ACM/IEEE International Conference on Human-Robot Interaction (2010)

Using CAPTCHAs to Index Cultural Artifacts

Qiang Zhu and Eamonn Keogh

Dept. of Computer Science & Engineering
University of California, Riverside
Riverside, CA 92521
{qzhu,eamonn}@cs.ucr.edu

Abstract. Rock art, human-made markings on stone, is an important cultural artifact and the earliest expression of abstract thinking. While there are tens of millions of photographs of rock art in existence, there have been no large-scale attempts to organize, classify or cluster them. This omission is not due to a lack of interest, but reflects the extraordinary difficultly of extracting useful data from an incredibly heterogeneous and noisy dataset. As we shall show, rock art is likely to resist efforts of automatic extraction from images for a long time. In this work we show that we can use CAPTCHAs, puzzles designed to tell humans and computers apart, to segment and index rock art. Unlike other CAPT-CHAs which operate on inherently discrete data and expect discrete responses, our method considers inherently real-valued data and expects real-valued responses. This creates a challenge which we have overcome by using a recently introduced distance measure. We demonstrate our system is capable of acting as a secure CAPTCHA, while producing data that allows for indexing the rock art.

Keywords: CAPTCHA, Image Processing, Cultural Artifacts, Rock Art.

1 Introduction

Rock art is the archaeological term for human-made markings on stone, including petroglyphs, *carvings* into stone surfaces and pictographs, *paintings* on stone. Fig. 1 illustrates some examples of each, which hint at the astonishing variability of rock art in terms of complexity and appearance.

Petroglyphs and pictographs are perhaps the earliest expressions of abstract thinking. Studies of rock art have implications beyond anthropology and history. For example, a recent study postulates the existence of a now-extinct Australian bat species based on extraordinarily detailed pictographs known to be at least 17,500 years old [13].

Fig. 1. A selection rock art hints at their incredible variability, complexity and beauty

P.R. Cohen, N.M. Adams, and M.R. Berthold (Eds.): IDA 2010, LNCS 6065, pp. 245–257, 2010.
© Springer-Verlag Berlin Heidelberg 2010

Petroglyphs have been used in studies of climate change; the changing inventories of species in the Dampier Archipelago from the Pleistocene to the early Holocene period have been reconstructed partly by petroglyph evidence [4]. However, in spite of these successes, progress in petroglyph research has been frustratingly slow. A decade ago, Walt et al. summed up the state of petroglyph research by noting, *Complete-site and cross-site research thus remains impossible, incomplete, or impressionistic*" [15]. Surprisingly, there has been little change in the intervening decade. We believe that this is due *only* to the difficultly of extracting the petroglyphs from raw images. More concretely, we claim that given the extracted "outline" data, indexing, classification and clustering of rock art would be relatively easy. Since this is *the* fundamental assumption in our work, let us immediately demonstrate it. In Fig. 2 we have clustered eight rock art images, for which we have (human extracted) "skeleton" data, in the form of a binary bitmap.

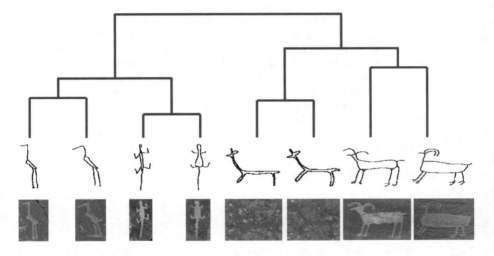

Fig. 2. A clustering of eight petroglyphs using the GHT measure proposed in [16]

This result hints at the fact that if we could only extract the skeletonized data, a wealth of opportunities for anthropological data mining would open up. However, as we shall demonstrate, in the vast majority of cases, the extraction of meaningful data from photographs of rock art is likely to be beyond the capabilities of image segmentation algorithms for a long time. With this in mind, we proposed to extract useful information from unconstrained images of rock art by turning the problem into a CAPTCHA [1]. CAPTCHAs ("Completely Automated Public Turing test to tell Computers and Humans Apart") are tests given by a machine to ensure that a response is generated by a human, not a computer. The most familiar instantiation of them is a sequence of distorted letters that the user must reproduce. Fig. 3 shows two examples.

Fig. 3. Two examples of CAPTCHAs. In order to solve the CAPTCHA, and get access to the next webpage (in this case, offering a free email account) the user must type in 28iVW and jw62K respectively.

These CAPTCHAs operate on inherently discrete data (*text*, albeit distorted) and expect discrete responses (keystrokes); we can therefore use equality tests to decide if the test was passed, i.e. equals('*28iVW* ','28iVW ')?

In contrast, our method considers inherently real-valued data (photographs of rock art) and expects real-valued responses (mouse movements). We cannot expect to test for equality. This creates a significant challenge which we have overcome by using a recently introduced distance measure [16] to test if a tracing of a petroglyph is close enough to a real pattern to indicate human intelligence.

2 Background and Related Work

2.1 Background on Rock Art

The earliest petroglyphs have traditionally been associated with the appearance of modern humans in Europe such as the famous example from the Lascaux Cave, France, and an early one from the Chauvet Cave, France which dates back to as early as 30,000 years ago [14]. Recent work has shown that the idea of expressing abstract motifs appears much earlier, 77,000 years ago in South Africa [8]. Given this long history, this art is one of the most valuable sources of humanity that has persisted to the present time.

Beyond their value as an aesthetic expression, petroglyphs provide a rich source of information for researchers. Repeated motifs can be identified and traced through time and space, which in turn may shed light on the dynamic histories of human populations, patterns of their migrations and interactions, and even continuities to present indigenous societies. However, the nature of petroglyphs poses an extremely difficult challenge. As in the case of any other artifacts of history, damages to petroglyphs are permanent and irreversible. In addition, unlike other artifacts that can be preserved and protected within the confines of a controlled environment in a museum, petroglyphs are mostly left in their natural settings, exposed to elements of nature that will erode them inevitably with time. There is an urgent need to identify petroglyphs and to archive them for humanity.

An understanding of *similarity* must be at the heart of any effort to analyze petroglyphs and other cultural artifacts. For example, an image of a horseman incised on a fossilized ostrich eggshell fragment was recently found among eolian deposits in the Gobi Desert, Mongolia [11]. An obvious thing to do with such an image in order to place it in a cultural context is to ask if a *similar* image exists among the many petroglyphs in the region. In Section 4.2 we show that we can support such queries.

2.2 Background on Image Processing

Another fundamental assumption in this work is that there is no automatic segmentation algorithm that can robustly segment rock art. To demonstrate this, we conducted a simple experiment on what is probably one of the most amiable images imaginable, the famous petroglyphs of Alta, Norway.

We took one image of a reindeer as shown in Fig. 4.*left*, and tried segmenting it with six different methods: the Sobel method, Prewitt method, Roberts method, Laplacian of Gaussian method, Zero-cross method and Canny method. In each case we spent fifteen minutes adjusting the parameters to achieve the best (subjectively) feature extraction. The best result, using the Prewitt method, is shown in Fig. 4.*right*.

 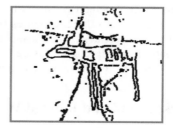

Fig. 4. *left*) Reindeer rock art from Norway, dating to 4200 to 500 BC. The rock carvings have been retouched in bright red by researchers, making them extremely high contrast. *right*) a segmentation of the image using the Prewitt method, carefully tuned.

Note that while our efforts have paid off in that we have captured much of the animal in question, we are missing a large section of the rump. What is worse, we have many spurious lines corresponding to cracks in the rock. Of course, it is possible that a more sophisticated algorithm could be tuned to do a better job; however, this tuned version is unlikely to generalize to other petroglyphs. Furthermore, it is worth restating that this example is among the highest contrast, cleanest examples of rock art.

2.3 Background on Human Computation

The last five years has seen a flurry of research on *Human Computation*, much of it leveraging off the pioneering work of Luis von Ahn [2]. The essence of human computation is to have computers do as much work as possible to solve a given problem, but to outsource certain critical steps to humans. These steps are ones which are difficult for computers, but simple for humans. One of the most famous examples is the *Google Image Labeler*, which is a program that allows the user to label random images to help improve the quality of Google's image search results. Like many such efforts, human time is donated for free, because the task is embedded in a fun game; hence the recently coined term, Games with a Purpose, or GWAP [3].

2.4 Distance Measures for Line Drawings

As noted in Section 2.1, an effective and robust similarity measure is crucial to mining petroglyphs and, as we shall see, in testing to see if a "skeleton" drawing submitted to a CAPTCHA can be attributed to human intelligence. After soliciting feedback and advice from various researchers in the data mining and image processing community, and testing dozens of possible measures, we proposed a distance measured based on the *Generalized Hough Transform* (GHT) [16]. The utility of this measure can be *subjectively* judged in Fig. 2 and *objectively* measured by classifying hand drawn symbols (Farsi digits, icons, etc.) that are "petroglyph-like" [16].

The GHT is a useful method to *detect* arbitrary two-dimensional shapes [5][12], in which shapes are constituted of *edge points* (simply the dark pixels in the binary representation of shapes). The goal of GHT is to find the *best fit* between a query shape Q and a candidate shape C. That is, if we place Q onto C (with only translation in the plane allowed), the number of matched edge points should be the maximal.

For clarity and simplicity, here we give a toy example to illustrate how it works. Fig. 5.*left* shows a query shape Q and candidate shapes C_1 and C_2. A *best fit* between Q and C_1 is also shown on the right of Fig. 5, and we can consider that Q is found in C_1 at this particular alignment.

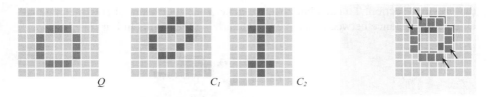

Fig. 5. *left*) Toy examples of a query Q and candidate matches C_1 and C_2. Each cell is a pixel, and the dark colors denote edge points of shapes. *right*) The GHT aligns Q and C_1 by maximizing matched edge points between them.

The GHT can effectively detect shapes, but it does not explicitly encode a distance measure. To find a numeric evaluation of it, we defined the *minimal unmatched edge points (MUE)* of Q, which is simply the number of edge points in Q minus maximal matched points. In our example, with the similar shape C_1, its value is $12 - 8 = 4$ (reflected by the four arrows in Fig. 5.*right*). If we had compared Q to C_2, the *MUE* would equal 6, meaning Q is less similar to C_2 than C_1.

We also considered several slight variations of *MUE* to enable higher-level data mining algorithms, and we will use one of them, the *clustering distance* variant [16], in all experiments in this paper.

3 CAPTCHA-ROCK

3.1 A Simple Image-Based Stickman CAPTCHA

While the goal of this research is to introduce a method that will allow us to capture data from real photographs of petroglyphs, for ease of exposition we will begin discussing the problem as if our only intention were to produce an image-based CAPTCHA with artificial data.

It is simple to write a program to produce random instances of a "stick figure"; Fig. 6 shows four examples.

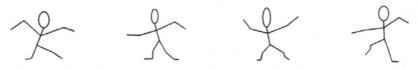

Fig. 6. Four examples of a parameterized Stickman

To ensure each stickman is unique (with very high probability), we have parameterized the code. The following features are parameterized:

- The head size and aspect ratio
- The length of the humerus, forearm, femur, tibia and foot
- The angles of knees, elbows, ankle and torso (these may be asymmetric)

There are other elements of a human stick figure that we could represent and parameterize, but this simple model is sufficient for our purposes.

For reasons that we will see shortly, it is useful to ask what the average distance is between two randomly created figures under the GHT-distance measure discussed in the previous section. To calculate this, we generated 1,000 pairs of stickmen and calculated the distance between each pair, summarizing the results in Fig. 7.

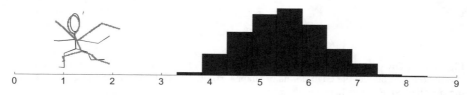

Fig. 7. *left*) A pair of randomly generated stickmen. *right*) The distribution of GHT distances between 1,000 pairs of randomly generated stickmen.

If we instead produce random stickmen, and ask humans to *trace* their outline on the screen with the mouse pointer (as in Fig. 8.*left*), we might expect the distances between the generated and traced outlines to be generally smaller.

To verify this, we generated 20 stickmen and asked volunteers to trace them. How well a person can trace the stickmen depends on their dexterity, input device, screen size, etc. Given these variations, we asked three volunteers to trace each stickman on their own machines. Fig. 8.*right* shows the distribution of these distances.

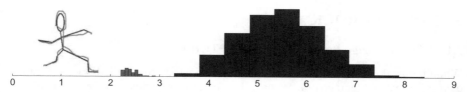

Fig. 8. *left*) A randomly generated stickman in black and a human tracing of it in red. *right*) The distribution of GHT distances between randomly generated stickmen and human tracings of them are shown with a finer bucket size (in red), because there is less data. The distribution of GHT distances between two randomly generated stickmen is shown for context (in blue).

It is easy to see that we could use these results to create a simple stickman CAPTCHA. We could produce a stickman, and ask the user to trace it. If a human traces the stickman, we can be near certain that the distance to the template will be less than 3 (from Fig. 8). For simplicity here we assume that the attacker has the code to produce the stickmen, and simply sends a random stickman as his guess. If that is so, his guess will almost certainly be greater than 3 (from Fig. 7/Fig. 8) and we can reject his attempt. Of course the attacker could use an image processing algorithm to produce a "customized guess", and we could counter by imbedding the stickman in field of distracters and distortions, however, a better idea is to find "stickmen" in rock art, the subject of the next section.

3.2   A CAPTCHA-ROCK System Helping Extract Data from Petroglyphs

Motivated by our experiences with the *stickmen* CAPTCHA, we can now ask: is it possible to design a CAPTCHA system which provides high security (serves as a CAPTCHA) while collecting useful information about rock art (serves as a Human Computation tool)? The reCAPTCHA [2] proposed by Luis von Ahn is the ideal paradigm to follow. In this system, which is designed to transcribe degraded text from scanned books and newspapers, each test gives the user two words to recognize, one of which is a "control word", whose answer is *known*, and the other one is an *unknown* word. If the user can correctly type the "control word", the reCAPTCHA assumes that the inputs come from a human and the answer for the "unknown word" is correct (or at least plausible). Once an "unknown word" receives enough "votes" from a same answer, it can become a "control word". This system has already transcribed several hundred million words, which OCR systems failed to parse.

We can use the same idea to build our CAPTCHA-ROCK system. An example is shown in Fig. 9, in which the user is asked to trace both petroglyphs correctly to pass the CAPTCHA.

Fig. 9. A CAPTCHA-ROCK consists of two rock art images: one control image and one unknown image. Note that users do not know which one is which.

There are still three extra problems/questions we must solve to make this work:

- How should we build the initial "control image" set?

To frustrate robots that break challenges by simple random guesses, the set of control words in reCAPTCHA contains more than 100,000 items. Do we also need such a large "control image" set? We believe that the answer is no. We can frustrate an attacker that attempts to simply memorize the entire control image set (with solution tracings) by performing simple scale and translation operations to images. This means that even if the attacker's algorithm correctly detects *which* image is the control image (perhaps by color), the relative location of the petroglyph within the image may have changed just enough so that even if the attacker sends the right trace, it will be in the wrong location.

As we shall show in the next section, our initial experiments show that even for a control set containing only 143 images, by using these simple scale and translation operations, CAPTCHA-ROCK has a pass rate of 0.020% to attackers, even after the attacker has been given a careful tracing for each image in the control set.

- Is one trace per image enough?

Assume two histograms in Fig. 8 have an overlap. To assure the low pass rate for robots, we have to set a smaller threshold. In this case a false negative occurs: some legitimate attempts by humans would be denied.

Our solution is to store multiple traces for one image. When a tentative solution is submitted by a user, we compare it to all traces and pass it if there is at *least* one distance below the threshold. Although human traces for the same image vary, by comparing to more than one "interpretation", the possibility of finding a close enough match increases. Note that this will not affect the pass rate for robot significantly. If a random trace is far from one trace, it is also far from other traces of the same image.

Based on our experiments which will be presented in Section 4.1, three traces per image improve the human pass rate, without helping the attackers.

- When can we promote an "unknown image" to a "control image"?

Once we have recorded three traces for an "unknown image", we promote it into the control set. Note that as a control image, the CAPTCHA-ROCK system will obtain more traces for the image. What should we do with these additional traces? We could ignore them, we could add them to the original three traces, or we could temporarily merge the new offering with the other three, expunging the one that has the furthest average distance from the others. We leave these considerations for future work.

4   Experimental Results

4.1   Quantitative Evaluation of CAPTCHA-ROCK System

We have designed all experiments such that they are not only reproducible, but *easily* reproducible. To this end, we have built a webpage [17] which contains all datasets and code used in this work. In this section, we intend to show that:

- Our CAPTCHA-ROCK is very easy for humans to solve (high pass rate) and hard for robots (low pass rate).
- Storing multiple traces for each image helps increase the pass rate for humans, while not affecting the pass rate for robots significantly.
- A small "control image" set is sufficient, at least to bootstrap the system.

We randomly chose 143 images from our rock art image database, and had four volunteers draw traces for each image. The volunteers worked completely independely of each other. We call this initial trace dataset *Trace_ini*.

For reasons we will see shortly, we performed two rounds of rescaling and 2-dimensional translation to each trace in *Trace_ini*. In the first round, we rescaled each trace image to 10%~50% of its original size, and translated it in 2 dimensions by plus/minus 0~3 times of the size in the X and Y axis independently. We call this new dataset *Trace_robot*. In the second round, every 4 traces of the same image in *Trace_ini* were performed by a same rescale and transition, and this dataset is called *Trace_human*.

As we assume that there is no automatic algorithm for extracting rock art data, we need to come up with an attack model. We make the pessimistic assumption that the attacker has our entire 143 image database, together with a human trace for each image. These seems to suggest that if the attacker simply submits a random tracing, he would have a one in 143 chance of passing the test, but recall that the images have been rescaled/translated in the plane. Such distortion means that even if the attacker happens to send the correct trace, it will probably not line up with the stored template, and will fail the test due to the penalty to the distance of centers of mass.

We first tested the system with one randomly chosen (of four possibilities) trace from *Trace_human* for the "control image". To model the attacks from robots, each time we picked one trace from *Trace_robot* (but not those from the same person of the challenge trace). There were thus 3×143 tries for each challenge. As the human input, we picked the other three traces of the "control image" in *Trace_human*.

Using a threshold of seven, only 41 of 245,388 robot tests could pass, a pass rate of 0.014%; whereas 1,632 of 1,716 human tests passed, a pass rate of 94.99%.

Then we tested with three traces for each image. As noted in Section 3.2, each input from the user was compared to three traces of the "control image", and if its distance to one of them was below the threshold, the user passed the test. Each time we picked three traces of the same image from *Trace_human* as traces of the "control image". To model the attacks from robots, each time we picked one trace from the fourth person in *Trace_robot*. Thus, there were 143 tries for each challenge. As the human input we picked the remaining trace of the "control image" in *Trace_human*.

Using the same threshold of 7, only 22 of 81,796 robot tests could pass, a pass rate of 0.020%; while only 5 of 572 human tests could not pass, a pass rate of 99.13%.

Although our pass rate for robots is slightly larger than the generally accepted figure of 0.01% [6], note that all results are based on the initial control image set, with only 143 images. We expect the robot rate to decrease with more data, while the human rate should stay almost constant. Further recall that these results assume the pessimistic and unrealistic assumption that the attacker has traces for the entire database.

4.2 Supporting Similarity Search

The major goal of this work is to produce a dataset that will enable research by anthropologists. However, a minor goal is to produce a tool for non-specialists to query a database of petroglyphs. This tool could be used to support tourism [7], and to encourage an appreciation of indigenous people's cultural achievements.

We envision the following scenario: *A hiker on a trail spots a petroglyph, and wants to know if it is known, and if so, what anthropologists and/or tribal historians have said about it. She photographs the petroglyph on her iPhone, traces the outline, and submits the query...*

In order for this query to return the correct answer, our system must have several invariances. Some are trivial, as we are operating on a binary representation of the data, color and contrast invariance is automatically achieved[1]. However, as shown in Fig. 10, there need to be at least somewhat invariant in size, angle of view, etc.

Fig. 10. *Left*) A petroglyph from Utah that has been indexed in our database. *Right*) An image of the same petroglyph found on Flickr.com. Could this image be used as a query to retrieve the anthropologist's annotated version in our database?

To test the feasibility of this scenario we obtained several examples of images of petroglyphs that we know are in our database (referred to the "control image" set in Section 4.1), but which were taken on a different day, by a different person, with a different camera etc. To normalize our expectations we also obtained photographs of petroglyphs that are known *not* to be in our database.

We had volunteers trace these petroglyph images. Note that in each case, these volunteers had not seen the data in the database, and were not familiar with our project.

Recall from the previous section that each petroglyph in our data collection had been traced by four independent volunteers. This means that for each petroglyph we had four models we could use to index it. We could also choose to have only one model for each petroglyph instead, by either averaging all four, or choosing the most typical one. However, here we kept all four models, both for simplicity, and because (as we shall see) it is instructive.

Our small dataset in this preliminary experiment does not warrant calculating precision/recall or similar statistics. Instead, we show typical results, and archive *all* results at [17]. Fig. 11 shows an example of a query using a (different photograph of) petroglyph that is in our database. The results are quite promising. Note that the query was taken from an image that was not as tightly cropped, and the user issuing the query (rightly or wrongly) traced a hook-like appendage on the left leg of the figure. Furthermore, note that among the four tracings in the database there is significant disagreement. For example, one individual did not trace the head as a circle. In spite of this, query-by-content is clearly successful in this example, as the first four matches are correct (the maximum possible).

In Fig. 12, we see two more queries for which the relevant petroglyph (traced from a different photograph) is known to be in the database. For the "wheel" the 1st, 2nd and 4th matches are correct, and the two others are at least plausible. For the bighorn sheep petroglyph, the first four matches are correct (the maximum possible), and the 5th match is also plausible.

---

[1] For faint petroglyphs changing the contrast/color balance can enhance the petroglyphs visibility[9][10].

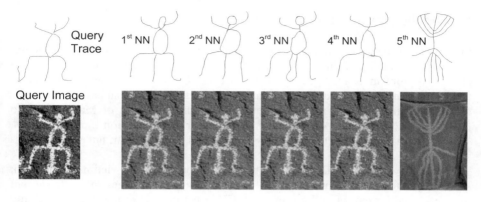

Fig. 11. *left*) A query petroglyph that happens to be in our database and its tracing. *right*) The five nearest neighbors to the query; the first four all refer to the same image, the correct target.

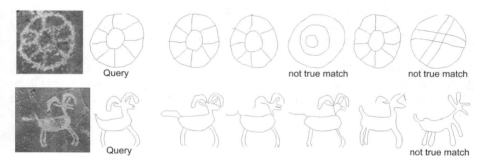

Fig. 12. An abstract (*top*) and animal petroglyph (*bottom*) which had been traced and issued as queries to our database. The list of the five nearest neighbors to each are shown left to right.

Finally, we consider the more difficult case, queries for which we know the relevant petroglyph is *not* in the database. Here the judgment of quality is subjective. Note also that we might expect to do better and better at this case as the database grows larger and larger. In Fig. 13 we show two queries and their best matches. In both cases the returned answers are reasonable.

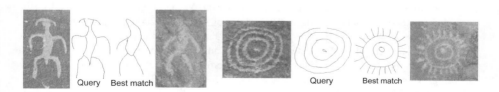

Fig. 13. *left*) An anthromorph is used as a query, and it retrieves another stylized human figure with similar limbs *right*) A petroglyph of concentric circles retrieves a "sunburst".

5   Conclusions and Future Work

In this work, we consider the problem of digitizing large collections of rock art to enable the data mining of this neglected cultural resource. We have framed the feature extraction problem as a CAPTCHA, the first CAPTCHA we are aware of to produce and expect *real-valued* data. There are many private individuals that have on the order of hundreds of thousand of rock art images (i.e. the collection of Mark and Billo [10]), and Flicker.com appears to have on the order of one million rock art images. We believe that we could process all this data in less than one year, under realistic assumptions.

We note several limitations of our work. We could become victims of our own success, given that there are *only* tens of millions of rock images in existence, but there is a need for tens of millions of CAPTCHAs per day. So even if we capture only a small fraction of the CAPTCHA market, we may run out of rock art images. We believe that we may be able to bypass this issue by generating synthetic rock art images, in a spirit similar to the stickmen shown in Section 3.1. In addition, a significant fraction of petroglyphs images may not be amenable to our system; our CAPTCHA is not usable by blind users; and our system may be difficult to use on small screens such as iPhones. All these issues are the subject of ongoing research.

Acknowledgements. This work was funded by NSF 0803410 and NSF 0808770. Field work for this project was funded by a National Geographic Society/Waitt Grant. We would like to thank the many donors of datasets, particularly Dr. Robert Mark and Evelyn Billo of www.rupestrian.com.

References

[1]   von Ahn, L., Blum, M., Hopper, N., Langford, J.: CAPTCHA: Using Hard AI Problems for Security. In: Advances in Cryptology. LNCS, pp. 294–311. Springer, Heidelberg

[2]   von Ahn, L., Maurer, B., McMillen, C., Abraham, D., Blum, M.: reCAPTCHA: Human-Based Character Recognition via Web Security Measures. Science, 1465–1468 (2008)

[3]   von Ahn, L.: Games with a purpose. Computer 39(6), 92–94 (2006)

[4]   Aseyev, I.V.: Horseman Image on an Ostrich Eggshell Fragment. Archaeology Ethnology & Anthropology of Eurasia 34/2, 96–99 (2008)

[5]   Ballard, D.H.: Generalizing the Hough Transform to Detect Arbitrary Shapes. Pattern Recognition 13, 111–122 (1981)

[6]   Chellapilla, K., Larson, K., Simard, P., Czerwinski, M.: Designing Human Friendly Human Interaction Proofs (HIPs). In: Proceedings of ACM CHI 2005, pp. 711–720 (2005)

[7]   Dickinson, E.A. (under review): Evoking the Sacred: Commercial Appropriations of Nature in "The Petroglyphs". Western Journal of Communication

[8]   Henshilwood, C.S., et al.: Emergence of Modern Human Behavior: Middle Stone Age Engravings from South Africa. Science 295, 1278–1280 (2002)

[9]   Landon, G.V., Seales, W.B.: Petroglyph Digitization: Enabling Cultural Heritage Scholarship. Machine Vision and Applications 17(6), 361–371 (2006)

[10] Mark, R.K., Billo, E.: Application of Digital Image Enhancement in Rock Art Recording. American Indian Rock Art V 28, 121–128 (2002)

[11] McDonald, J.J., Veth, P.M.: Pilbara and Western Desert Rock Art: Style Graphics in Arid Landscapes. In: Proceedings of the XXII Valcamonica Symposium, pp. 327–334 (2007)

[12] Merlin, P.M., Farber, D.J.: A Parallel Mechanism for Detecting Curves in Pictures. IEEE Trans. Comput. C24, 96–98 (1975)

[13] Pettigrew, J., Nugent, M., McPhee, A., Wallman, J.: An Unexpected, Stripe-faced Flying Fox in Ice Age Rock Art of Australia's Kimberley. Journal of Antiquity (2008)

[14] Valladas, H., Clottes, J., Geneste, J.-M., Garcia, M., Arnold, M., Cachier, H., Tisnérat-Laborde, N.: Palaeolithic Paintings: Evolution of Prehistoric Cave Art. Nature 413, 479 (2001)

[15] Walt, H., David, B., Brayer, J., Musello, C.: The Rock Art Database Project

[16] Zhu, Q., Wang, X., Keogh, E., Lee, S.H.: Augmenting the Generalized Hough Transform to Enable the Mining of Petroglyphs. In: KDD 2009, pp. 1057–1066 (2009)

[17] Zhu, Q.: CAPTCHA Rock Webpage (2010),
http://www.cs.ucr.edu/~qzhu/CAPTCHA_Rock.html

Author Index

Adams, Niall M.   1
Alexander, Zachary   18
Anderson, Ken   171

Berthold, Michael R.   1
Blockeel, Hendrik   91
Borgelt, Christian   196
Bosma, Carlos   91
Bradley, Elizabeth   18
Bradley, Liz   171
Brenning, Alexander   184

Calders, Toon   91
Cartwright, Hugh M.   137
Cellier, Peggy   30
Charnois, Thierry   30
Cohen, Paul R.   1
Crémilleux, Bruno   30

Dedeo, Simon   8
Diwan, Amer   18

Earle, Paul   42

Farmer, Doyne   8
Flack, Jessica C.   8
Foregger, David   159

Galenkamp, Hessel   91
Gama, João   114
Georgiopoulos, Michael   159
Getoor, Lise   6
Gonçalves, Nicolau   147
Gruchalla, Kenny   42
Guy, Michelle   42

Hassan, Rosline   54
Hidaka, Shohei   232
Hollmén, Jaakko   208
Horvath, Scott   42

Ismail, Waidah   54

Johansson, Ulf   67

Keogh, Eamonn   245
Klawonn, Frank   79
Knobbe, Arno   91
Koenders, Eddy   91
Kok, Joost   91
Koopman, Arne   91
Krakauer, David C.   8

Lewis, Rory A.   103
Löfström, Tuve   67

Mahler, Sébastien   220
Manuel, Julie   159
Marwah, Manish   125
Mederos, Boris   159
Mytkowicz, Todd   18

Obladen, Bas   91
Oliveira, Márcia   114
Ostrum, Chris   42

Patnaik, Debprakash   125
Plantevit, Marc   30
Prada, Miguel A.   208
Priest, Alexander C.   137

Rajasekharan, Jayaprakash   147
Ramakrishnan, Naren   125
Ramirez-Padron, Ruben   159
Rassbach, Laura   171
Rockmore, Daniel   8
Ruß, Georg   184

Scharfenberger, Ulrike   147
Scheutz, Matthias   232
Segond, Marc   196
Sharma, Ratnesh K.   125
Shmueli, Doron   103
Smith, Linda B.   232
Smith, Thomas G.   232
Sönströd, Cecilia   67
Swift, Stephen   54

Toivola, Janne   208
Toivonen, Hannu   220

Vigário, Ricardo   147

White, Andrew M.   103
Williamson, Alexander J.   137
Wüstefeld, Torsten   79

Yu, Chen   232

Zender, Lars   79
Zhou, Fang   220
Zhu, Qiang   245
Zreda, Marek   171
Zweck, Chris   171

Printing: Mercedes-Druck, Berlin
Binding: Stein+Lehmann, Berlin